# Humble
## HERO

### Ellen G. White

# Pacific Press®
## Publishing Association

Nampa, Idaho | Oshawa, Ontario, Canada
www.pacificpress.com

Cover design by Doug Church
Cover illustration by Eric Joyner
Inside design by Aaron Troia

Copyright © 2009 by
the Ellen G. White® Estate, Inc.
Printed in the United States of America
All rights reserved

Additional copies of this book are available by
calling toll-free 1-800-765-6955 or
online at www.adventistbookcenter.com

ISBN 978-0-8163-2337-1

September 2016

# Contents

# Foreword

*Humble Hero* is the story of a daring rescue. It tells how one selfless Person—Jesus Christ—risked everything to come here to earth and win back this renegade planet. He could not do so from the safety and comforts of heaven where, as God, He was revered. He must leave all of that behind and be born into this world as a baby, in a family that struggled for a living. For the most part, throughout His life the world did not welcome Him or even understand Him. People opposed Him, plotted to kill Him, eventually beat Him, spit on Him, and crucified Him, but they could not alienate Him or turn Him from His purpose. He died a conqueror, and He rose again to complete His rescue of all who would come to God through Him. There is no greater story in the history of the world or even of the universe.

This volume is an adaptation of *From Heaven With Love,* a 1984 condensed edition of Ellen G. White's classic volume, *The Desire of Ages.* The condensed volume included all the chapters of the original, using only Mrs. White's own words but shortening the account.

The current adaptation goes a step beyond this, using some words, expressions, and sentence constructions more familiar to twenty-first-century readers. Occasionally, it restores a sentence or clause deleted in the original condensation. Most of the Bible quotations are taken from the New King James Version, which closely resembles the King James Version that Mrs. White commonly used. It is hoped that readers who are new to Mrs. White's writings will enjoy this adaptation and that it will encourage them to read the original editions of her works.

*Humble Hero* presents the inspiring, life-changing story of Jesus Christ as the One who can satisfy the deep longings of every heart. It is not the book's purpose, however, to provide a harmony of the Gospels or to arrange the important events and wonderful lessons of Christ's life in a strictly chronological order. Its purpose is to present the love of God as revealed in His Son, to show the divine beauty of the life of Christ.

In the following pages, the author opens to the reader great riches from the life of Jesus. Fresh insights flash from many familiar passages of Scripture. The book presents Jesus Christ as the Fullness of the Godhead, the infinitely merciful Savior, the sinner's Substitute, the Sun of Righteousness, the faithful High Priest, humanity's compelling Example, the Healer of all human maladies and diseases, the tender, compassionate Friend, the Prince of Peace, the Coming King, the focus and fulfillment of the desires and hopes of all the ages.

There are five powerful volumes in the Conflict of the Ages series. This book was condensed and adapted from the third of the five. That many more readers may be drawn to God through these books and their presentation of Bible themes is the hope and prayer of

# Christ Before Coming to Earth

From the days of eternity the Lord Jesus Christ was One with the Father; He was the image of God, the expression of His glory. To show this glory, to reveal the light of God's love, Jesus came to our sin-darkened earth. Isaiah prophesied of Him, "They shall call His name Immanuel, . . . God with us." Matthew 1:23; cf. Isaiah 7:14.

Jesus was "the Word of God"— God's thought made audible. God gave this revelation not just for His earthborn children. Our little world is the lesson book of the universe. Both the redeemed and the unfallen beings will find their true knowledge and their joy in the cross of Christ. They will see that the glory shining in the face of Jesus is the glory of self-sacrificing love. They will see that for earth and heaven, the law of life is the law of self-renouncing love. The love that "does not seek its own" has its source in the heart of God and is shown in Jesus, the meek and lowly One.

In the beginning, Christ laid the foundations of the earth. His hand hung the worlds in space and fashioned the flowers of the field. He filled the earth with beauty and the air with song. See Psalms 65:6; 95:5. He wrote the message of the Father's love on everything.

Now sin has marred God's perfect work, yet that handwriting remains. Except for the selfish human heart, nothing lives just for itself. Every tree and shrub and leaf pours forth oxygen, without which neither people nor animals could live; and people and animals, in turn, support the life of tree and shrub and leaf. The ocean receives streams from every land, but it takes only to give back. The mists rising from it fall in showers to water the earth, so that plants may grow and bud. The angels of glory find their joy in giving. They bring light from above, moving upon the human spirit to bring the lost into fellowship with Christ.

But turning from all lesser examples, we see God in Jesus. We find that it is the glory of God to *give*. "I do not seek My own glory," said Christ, but the glory of Him who sent Me. John 8:50; 7:18. Christ received from God, but He took to give. Through the Son, the Father's life flows out to all. Through the Son, it returns in joyous service, a tide of love, to the great Source of all. In this way, through Christ the circle of blessing is complete.

## In Heaven This Law Was Broken!

Sin began in self-seeking. Lucifer, the covering cherub, wanted to be first in heaven. He tried to draw heavenly beings away from their Creator and win honor to himself. Putting his own evil characteristics on the Creator, he led angels to doubt the word of God and distrust His goodness. Satan led them to look on Him as severe and unforgiving. In this way, he deceived angels. In the same way, he deceived the human race, and the night of misery settled down on the world.

The earth was dark through misunderstanding of God. To bring the world back to God, Satan's deceptive power must be broken. God could not do this by force. He wants only the service of love, and love cannot be won by force or authority. Only love awakens love. To know God is to love Him. We must see His character in contrast to Satan's. Only one Being could do this work. Only He who knew the height and depth of God's love could make it known.

The plan for our redemption was not formulated after the fall of Adam. It was a revelation of "the mystery that was kept secret for long ages." Romans 16:25, NRSV. It was an unfolding of the principles that have been the foundation of God's throne from eternity. God foresaw sin's existence and made provision to meet the terrible emergency. He pledged to give His only-begotten Son, "that whoever believes in Him should not perish but have everlasting life." John 3:16.

Lucifer had said, "I will exalt my throne above the stars of God; . . . I will be like the Most High." But Christ, "though he was in the form of God, . . . emptied himself, taking the form of a slave, being born in human like-

ness." Isaiah 14:13, 14; Philippians 2:6, 7, NRSV.

## A Voluntary Sacrifice

Jesus could have kept the glory of heaven. But He chose to step down from the throne of the universe in order to bring life to the dying.

Nearly two thousand years ago, a voice was heard in heaven,

"A body You have prepared for Me. . . .
'Behold, I have come—
In the volume of the book
　it is written of Me—
To do Your will, O God.' "
　　　　　　　　　Hebrews 10:5–7

Christ was about to visit our world, to become flesh and blood. If He had appeared with the glory that was His before the world was created, we could not have endured the light of His presence. In order that we could behold it and not be destroyed, He shrouded His glory and veiled His divinity with humanity.

Types and symbols had foreshadowed this great purpose. The burning bush, in which Christ appeared to Moses, revealed God. This lowly shrub, that seemed to have no attractions, enshrined the Infinite. God shrouded His glory so that Moses could look on it and live. Similarly, in the pillar of cloud by day and the pillar of fire by night, God's glory was veiled so that finite human beings could look at it. So Christ was to come "in the likeness of men." He was the incarnate God, but His glory was veiled so that He could draw near to sorrowful, tempted men and women.

Through Israel's long wandering in the desert, the sanctuary was with them as the symbol of God's presence. See Exodus 25:8. Likewise, Christ pitched His tent by the side of our tents so that He could make us familiar with His divine character and life. "The Word became flesh and dwelt among us, and we beheld His glory, the glory as of the only begotten from the Father, full of grace and truth." John 1:14.

Since Jesus came to live with us, every son and daughter of Adam may understand that our Creator is the Friend of sinners. In every divine attraction in the Savior's life on earth, we see "God with us."

Satan represents God's law of love as a law of selfishness. He declares that it is impossible for us to obey its requirements. He blames the Creator for the fall of our first parents, leading people to look upon God as the author of sin, suffering, and death. Jesus was to unmask this deception. As one of us, He was to give an example of obedience. For this, He took upon Himself our nature and passed through our experiences. "In all things He had to be made like His brethren." Hebrews 2:17. If we had to bear anything that Jesus did not endure, then on this point Satan would claim that the power of God was not enough for us. Therefore, Jesus was "in all points tempted as we are." Hebrews 4:15. He endured every trial that we may face. And He exercised no power in His own behalf that is not freely offered to us. As a human being, He met temptation and overcame it in the strength that God gave Him. He made plain

the character of God's law, and His life testifies that it is possible for us also to obey the law of God.

By His humanity, Christ touched humanity; by His divinity, He takes hold of the throne of God. As Son of man, He gave us an example of obedience; as Son of God, He gives us power to obey. To us He says, "All authority has been given to Me in heaven and on earth." Matthew 28:18. "God with us" is the guarantee of our deliverance from sin, the assurance of power to obey the law of heaven.

Christ revealed a character that is the opposite of Satan's. "Being found in human form, He humbled Himself and became obedient to the point of death—even death on a cross." Philippians 2:8, NRSV. Christ took the form of a servant and offered the sacrifice, with Himself as the Priest and Himself as the Victim. "He was bruised for our iniquities; the chastisement for our peace was upon Him." Isaiah 53:5.

### Treated As We Deserve

Christ was treated as we deserve, that we might be treated as He deserves. He was condemned for our sins, in which He had no share, that we might be justified by His righteousness, in which we had no share. He suffered the death that was ours, that we might receive the life that was His. "By His stripes we are healed." Isaiah 53:5.

Satan determined to bring eternal separation between God and man; but in taking our nature, the Savior united Himself to humanity by a tie that will never be broken. "God so loved the world that He gave His only begotten Son." John 3:16. He gave Him, not only to die as our Sacrifice; He gave Him to become one of the human family, to keep His human nature forever.

"Unto *us* a Child is born, unto *us* a Son is given; and the government will be upon His shoulder." God has adopted human nature in the person of His Son and has carried it to the highest heaven. The "Son of man" shall be called, "Wonderful, Counselor, Mighty God, Everlasting Father, Prince of Peace." Isaiah 9:6, italics added. He who is "holy, harmless, undefiled, separate from sinners," is not ashamed to call us His brothers and sisters. Hebrews 7:26; 2:11. Heaven is enshrined in humanity, and humanity is enclosed in the embrace of Infinite Love.

God's lifting up of His redeemed people will be an eternal testimony to His mercy. "In the ages to come," He will "show the exceeding riches of His grace in His kindness toward us in Christ Jesus" in order that "the manifold wisdom of God" may be made known to "the principalities and the powers in the heavenly places." Ephesians 2:7; 3:10.

Through Christ's work, the government of God stands justified. The All-powerful One is revealed as the God of love. Christ has refuted Satan's charges and unmasked his character. Sin can never again enter the universe. Through eternal ages all are secure from apostasy. By love's self-sacrifice, Jesus has linked earth and heaven to the Creator in an unbreakable union.

Where sin increased, God's grace increased much more. The earth, the very field Satan claims as his, will be honored above all other worlds in the universe. Here, where the King of glory lived and suffered and died, here the dwelling place of God will be with humanity, and "God Himself will be with them and be their God." Revelation 21:3. Through endless ages the redeemed will praise Him for His unspeakable gift—Immanuel, "God with us."

# The People Who Should Have Welcomed Him

For more than a thousand years, the Jewish people had waited for the Savior's coming. And yet, when He came, they did not know Him. They did not see any beauty in Him that was attractive to them. See Isaiah 53:2. "He came to His own, and His own did not receive Him." John 1:11.

God had chosen Israel to preserve the symbols and prophecies that pointed to the Savior, to be like wells of salvation to the world. The Hebrew people were to reveal God among the nations. In the call of Abraham, the Lord had said, "In you all the families of the earth shall be blessed." Genesis 12:3. The Lord declared through Isaiah, "My house shall be called a house of prayer for all nations." Isaiah 56:7.

But Israel set their hopes on worldly greatness and followed the ways of the heathen. They did not change when God sent them warning by His prophets. They did not change when they suffered the punishment of heathen conquest and occupation. Every reformation was followed by deeper apostasy.

If Israel had been true to God, He would have made them "high above all nations which He has made, in praise, in name, and in honor." "The peoples who will hear all these statutes" will say, "Surely this great nation is a wise and understanding people." Deuteronomy 26:19; 4:6.

But because they were unfaithful, God could work out His plans only through trouble and affliction. They were brought to Babylon and scattered through the lands of the heathen. While they mourned for the holy temple that was destroyed, they spread a knowledge of God among the nations. Heathen systems of sacrifice were a perversion of the system God had appointed; from the Hebrews many learned the meaning of the sacrifices as God had planned them and in faith grasped the promise of a Redeemer.

Many exiles lost their lives because they refused to disregard the Sabbath and observe heathen festivals. As idol worshipers were stirred up to crush out the truth, the Lord brought His servants face to face with kings and rulers so that they and their people could receive light. The greatest monarchs were led to proclaim that the God whom their Hebrew captives worshiped was supreme.

During the centuries that followed the captivity in Babylon, the Israelites were cured of worshiping images, and they became convinced that their prosperity depended on obedience to the law of God. But for many of the people, the motive was selfish. They served God as the way to attain national greatness. They did not become the light of the world but shut themselves away in order to escape temptation. God had restricted their association with idol worshipers to prevent them from adopting heathen practices. But they had misinterpreted this teaching. They used it to build up a wall between Israel and other nations. The Jews were actually jealous that the Lord might show mercy to the Gentiles!

### How They Perverted the Sanctuary Service

After their return from Babylon, all over the country the Jews built synagogues where priests and scribes expounded the law. Schools claimed to teach the principles of righteousness. But during the captivity, many of the people had received heathen ideas, and they brought these ideas into their religious service.

Christ Himself had instituted the ritual service. It was a symbol of Him, full of vitality and spiritual beauty. But the Jews lost the spiritual life from their ceremonies and trusted the sacrifices and ordinances themselves instead of Him to whom they pointed. To replace what they had lost, the priests and rabbis made many requirements of their own. The more rigid they grew, the less they showed the love of God.

Those who tried to observe the exacting and burdensome requirements of the rabbis could find no rest from a troubled conscience. In this way, Satan worked to discourage the people, to lower their ideas of God's character, and to bring the faith of Israel into contempt. He hoped to establish his claim that no one could obey God's requirements. Even Israel, he declared, did not keep the law.

### Expecting a False Messiah

The Jews had no true concept of the Messiah's mission. They did not seek to be redeemed from sin but to be delivered from the Romans. They looked for the Messiah to exalt Israel to rulership over the world. This prepared the way for them to reject the Savior.

When Christ was born, the nation was restless under the rule of foreign masters and was racked with internal strife. The Romans appointed and removed the high priest, and evil men often secured the office by bribery and even murder. So the priesthood became more and more corrupt. The people were under merciless demands, and the Romans also taxed them heavily. Widespread discontent, greed, violence, distrust, and spiritual apathy were eating out the heart of the nation. In their darkness and oppression, the people longed for One who would restore the kingdom to Israel. They had studied the prophecies, but without spiritual insight. They interpreted prophecy in harmony with their selfish desires.

# Man's Sin and the "Fullness of the Time"

When Adam and Eve in Eden first heard the promise of the Savior's coming, they expected it to be fulfilled very soon. They welcomed their first-born son, hoping he might be the Deliverer. But those who first received the promise died without seeing it fulfilled. The promise was repeated through patriarchs and prophets, keeping alive the hope of His appearing, yet He did not come. The prophecy of Daniel revealed the time of His advent, but not all interpreted the message correctly. Century after century passed. Occupying nations oppressed Israel, and many were ready to exclaim, "The days are prolonged, and every vision fails." Ezekiel 12:22.

But like the stars that cross the sky in their appointed path, God's plans know no haste and no delay. In heaven's council, the hour for the coming of Christ had been set. When the great clock of time pointed to that hour, Jesus was born in Bethlehem.

"When the fullness of the time had come, God sent forth His Son." Galatians 4:4. The world was ripe for the coming of the Deliverer. The nations were united under one government. One language was widely spoken. From all lands the Jews who had been scattered gathered to Jerusalem for the annual feasts. As these returned to their homes in foreign lands, they could spread the news throughout the world about the Messiah's coming.

The heathen systems were losing their hold on the people. People longed for a religion that could satisfy the heart. Those looking for light were craving for a knowledge of the living God, for some assurance of life beyond the grave.

## Many Longed for a Deliverer

The Jews' faith had grown dim, and hope had nearly ceased to brighten the future. To the masses of people, death was a fearful mystery; beyond it was uncertainty and gloom. In "the region and shadow of death," mourners sat unconsoled. With longing they looked for the coming of the Deliverer, when the mystery of the future would be revealed.

Outside of the Jewish nation, there were some who were looking for truth, and to them God gave the Spirit of Inspiration. Their words of prophecy had kindled hope in the hearts of thousands in the Gentile world.

For hundreds of years, the Scriptures had been available in the Greek language, then widely spoken throughout the Roman Empire. The Jews were scattered everywhere, and to some extent, the Gentiles shared their expectation of the Messiah's coming. Among those whom the Jews called heathen were men who had a better understanding of the Scripture prophecies concerning the Messiah than the teachers in Israel had.

Some who hoped for His coming as a Deliverer from sin tried to study into the mystery of the Hebrew system. But the Jews were determined to maintain the separation between themselves and other nations, and they were unwilling to share the knowledge they had about the symbolic service. The true Interpreter, the One whom all these symbols represented, must come and explain their significance. God must teach humanity in the language of humanity. Christ must come to speak words they could clearly understand and to separate truth from the chaff that had made it powerless.

Among the Jews were some firm believers who preserved a knowledge of God. They strengthened their faith by remembering the assurance given through Moses, "The Lord your God will raise up for you a Prophet like me from your brethren. Him you shall hear in all things, whatever He says to you." Acts 3:22. They read how the Lord would anoint One "to preach good tidings to the poor," "to heal the brokenhearted, to proclaim liberty to the captives," and to declare "the acceptable year of the Lord." Isaiah 61:1, 2. He would establish "justice in the earth," and the isles would "wait for His law." Isaiah 42:4. Gentiles would come to His light, and kings to the brightness of His rising. See Isaiah 60:3.

The dying words of Jacob filled them with hope: "The scepter shall not depart from Judah, nor a lawgiver from between his feet, until Shiloh comes." Genesis 49:10. The fading power of Israel testified that the Messiah's coming was near. Many people expected a mighty prince who would establish his kingdom in Israel and come as a deliverer to the nations.

## How Satan Almost Succeeded

"The fullness of the time" had come. Humanity, degraded through ages of sin, called for the coming of the Redeemer. Satan had been working to make the gulf between earth and heaven deep and impassable. He had made people bold in sin. He intended to wear out the patience of God so that He would abandon the world to Satan's control.

Satan's battle for supremacy seemed almost entirely successful. It is true that in every generation, even among the heathen, there were those through whom Christ was working to uplift the people from sin. But these reformers were hated. Many suffered a violent death. The dark shadow Satan cast over the world grew deeper and deeper.

Satan's great triumph was in perverting the faith of Israel. The heathen had lost a knowledge of God and had become more and more corrupt. And so had Israel. The principle that we can save ourselves by our own works lay at the foundation of every heathen religion. It had now become the principle of the Jewish religion.

The Jews robbed the world by a counterfeit of the gospel. They had refused to surrender themselves to God for the salvation of the world, and they became agents of Satan for its destruction. The people whom God had called to be the pillar and ground of the truth were doing the work Satan wanted them to do, living in a way that misrepresented God's character and caused the world to look on Him as a tyrant. Priests in the temple lost the meaning of the service they performed. They were like actors in a play. Laws and ceremonies that God Himself had established were made the means of blinding the mind and hardening the heart. God could do no more for humanity through these channels.

### God Pities the Lost World

All the agencies for corrupting human hearts had been put in operation. The Son of God looked on the world with compassion and saw how men and women had become victims of satanic cruelty. Bewildered and deceived, they were moving on in a gloomy march toward death in which there is no hope of life, toward night after which comes no morning.

The bodies of human beings had become the habitat of demons. Supernatural beings worked people's senses, nerves, passions, and organs in indulging the most shameful lust. The stamp of demons was imprinted on human faces. What a spectacle for the world's Redeemer to behold!

Sin had become a science, and vice a part of religion. Rebellion and hostility were violent against heaven. The unfallen worlds had expected to see God sweep away the inhabitants of earth. And if He had done this, Satan was ready to carry out his plan to gain the allegiance of heavenly beings. He had claimed that the principles of God's government make forgiveness impossible. If the world had been destroyed, he would have blamed God and spread his rebellion to the worlds above.

But instead of destroying the world, God sent His Son to save it. He provided a way for its recovery. "When the fullness of the time" had come, God poured on the world a flood of healing grace that would never be obstructed or withdrawn till the plan of salvation would be fulfilled. Jesus came to restore in us the image of our Maker, to expel the demons that had controlled the will, to lift us up from the dust, and to reshape the marred character into the likeness of His divine character.

# Born in a Stable[*]

The King of glory bent low to take humanity. He hid His glory and shunned all outward display. Jesus did not want any earthly attraction to call people to His side. Only the beauty of heavenly truth must draw those who would follow Him. He wanted them to accept Him because of what the Word of God said about Him.

The angels watched to see how the people of God would receive His Son, clothed in the form of humanity. The angels came to the land where the light of prophecy had shone. They came unseen to Jerusalem and to the ministers of God's house.

Already an angel had announced the nearness of Christ's coming to Zacharias the priest as he ministered before the altar. Already John the Baptist, the forerunner of Jesus, was born, and news of his birth and the meaning of his mission had spread far and wide. Yet Jerusalem was not preparing to welcome her Redeemer. God had called the Jewish nation to communicate to the world that Christ was to be born of David's line, yet they did not know that His coming was near.

In the temple, the morning and evening sacrifices pointed to the Lamb of God, yet even here no one was preparing to receive Him. Priests and teachers recited their meaningless prayers and performed the rites of worship, but they were not prepared for the Messiah's appearing. The same indifference spread throughout the land of Israel. Hearts that were selfish and focused on worldly things were untouched by the joy that thrilled all heaven. Only a few were longing to see the Unseen.

Angels went with Joseph and Mary as they traveled from Nazareth to the City of David. The decree of Rome to register the peoples of her vast territory had extended to the hills of Galilee. Caesar Augustus became God's agent to bring the mother of Jesus to Bethlehem. She was of David's line, and the Son of David must be born in David's city. "Out of you [Bethlehem]," said the prophet, "shall come forth . . . the One to be ruler in Israel, whose goings forth [are] from of old, from everlasting." Micah 5:2.

But in the city of this royal line, Joseph and Mary were unrecognized, unhonored. Weary and homeless, they walked the narrow street to the east-

---

* This chapter is based on Luke 2:1–20.

# BORN IN A STABLE

ern edge of town in a fruitless search for a resting place for the night. There was no room at the crowded inn. At last they found refuge in a crude building where animals were kept, and here the Redeemer of the world was born.

The news filled heaven with rejoicing. Holy beings from the world of light were drawn to earth. Above the hills of Bethlehem a crowd of angels waited for the signal to declare the glad news to the world. The leaders in Israel could have shared the joy of announcing the birth of Jesus, but they were passed by. The bright rays from the throne of God will shine on those who seek light and accept it gladly. See Isaiah 44:3; Psalm 112:4.

**Only the Shepherds Cared**

In the very fields where the boy David had led his flock, shepherds keeping watch by night talked together of the promised Savior and prayed for His coming. And "an angel of the Lord stood before them. . . . Then the angel said to them, 'Do not be afraid, for behold, I bring you good tidings of great joy which will be to all people. For there is born to you this day in the city of David a Savior, who is Christ the Lord.' "

When they heard these words, dreams of glory filled the minds of the listening shepherds. The Deliverer has come! They associated power, exaltation, and triumph with His coming. But the angel prepared them to recognize their Savior in poverty and humiliation: "You will find a Babe wrapped in swaddling cloths, lying in a manger."

The heavenly messenger had qui-

eted their fears. He had told them how to find Jesus. He had given them time to become accustomed to the divine radiance. Then the whole plain lit up with the bright shining of the angels of God. Earth was hushed, and heaven stooped to listen to the song—

"Glory to God in the highest,
And on earth peace, good will toward men!"

Oh that today the human family could recognize that song! The song the angels sang will grow louder to the close of time and echo to the ends of the earth.

As the angels disappeared, the shadows of night once more fell on the hills of Bethlehem. But the brightest picture human eyes ever saw remained in the memory of the shepherds. They "said to one another, 'Let us now go to Bethlehem and see this thing that has come to pass, which the Lord has made known to us.' And they came with haste and found Mary and Joseph, and the Babe lying in a manger."

They left with great joy and told everyone they met the things they had seen and heard. "And all those who heard it marveled at those things which were told them by the shepherds."

Heaven and earth are no wider apart today than when shepherds listened to the angels' song. Angels from the courts above will accompany those in the common occupations of life who respond to God's leading.

In the story of Bethlehem is hidden "the depth of the riches both of the wisdom and knowledge of God." Romans 11:33. We are amazed at the

Savior's sacrifice in exchanging the throne of heaven for the manger. Human pride stands rebuked in His presence.

Yet this was only the beginning of His condescension! It would have been an almost infinite humiliation for the Son of God to take human nature even when Adam stood in innocence in Eden. But Jesus accepted humanity when the race had been weakened by four thousand years of sin. Like every child of Adam, He accepted the results of heredity. We can see what these results were in the history of His earthly ancestors. He came with just such a heredity to share our temptations and give us the example of a sinless life.

Satan hated Christ. He hated the One who pledged Himself to redeem sinners. Yet into the world where Satan claimed the right to rule, God permitted His Son to come as a helpless baby, subject to the weakness of humanity, to meet life's dangers just like everyone else, to fight the battle as every child of humanity must fight it—at the risk of failure and eternal loss.

The heart of the human father looks into the face of his little child and trembles at the thought of life's dangers. He longs to shield him from temptation and conflict. To meet a bitterer conflict and more fearful risk, God gave His only Son.

"In this is love." Wonder, O heavens! and be astonished, O earth!

# Joseph and Mary Dedicate Jesus[*]

About forty days after the birth of Christ, Joseph and Mary took Him to Jerusalem to present Him to the Lord and to offer a sacrifice. As our Substitute, Christ must fulfill the law in every point. He had already been circumcised as a pledge of His obedience to the law.

As an offering for the mother, the law required a lamb for a burnt offering and a pigeon or a turtledove for a sin offering. These offerings must be without blemish, for they represented Christ. He was the "lamb without blemish and without spot." 1 Peter 1:19. He was an example of what God intended humanity to be through obedience to His laws.

The dedication of the firstborn had its origin in earliest times. God had promised to give the Firstborn of heaven to save the sinner. Every household was to acknowledge this gift by consecrating the firstborn son. He was to be devoted to the priesthood, as a representative of Christ among us.

What meaning, then, was attached to Christ's dedication at the temple! But the priest did not see beyond the outward appearances. Day after day he conducted the ceremony of pre-senting the infants, giving little attention to parents or children unless he saw some indication of wealth or high position. Joseph and Mary were poor, and the priest saw only a Galilean man and woman, dressed in the humblest garments.

The priest took the Child in his arms and held Him up before the altar. After handing Him back to His mother, he inscribed the name "Jesus" on the roll. As the Baby lay in his arms, little did the priest think that he was enrolling the name of the Majesty of heaven, the King of glory, the One who was the Foundation of the Jewish system.

This Baby was the One who declared Himself to Moses as the I AM, He who in the pillar of cloud and of fire had been Israel's Guide. He was the Desire of all nations, the Root and Offspring of David, the Bright and Morning Star. Revelation 22:16. That helpless Baby was the hope of fallen humanity. He was to pay the ransom for the sins of the whole world.

Although the priest did not see or feel anything unusual, this occasion did not pass without some recognition of Christ. "There was a man in Jerusalem

---

[*] This chapter is based on Luke 2:21–38.

whose name was Simeon, . . . and the Holy Spirit was upon him. And it had been revealed to him by the Holy Spirit that he would not see death before he had seen the Lord's Christ."

## Venerable Simeon Recognized Jesus

As Simeon entered the temple, he was deeply impressed that the Infant being presented to the Lord was the One he had longed to see. To the astonished priest, he looked like a man filled with holy awe. He took the Child in his arms, while a joy he had never before felt entered his being. As he lifted the infant Savior toward heaven, he said,

"Lord, now You are letting Your servant
    depart in peace,
According to Your word;
For my eyes have seen Your salvation
Which You have prepared before the
    face of all peoples,
A light to bring revelation to the
    Gentiles,
And the glory of Your people Israel."

While Joseph and Mary stood by, amazed at Simeon's words, he said to Mary, "Behold, this Child is destined for the fall and rising of many in Israel, and for a sign which will be spoken against (yes, a sword will pierce through your own soul also), that the thoughts of many hearts may be revealed."

Anna, a prophetess, also came in and confirmed Simeon's testimony. Her face lighted up with glory, and she poured out her heartfelt thanks that she had been permitted to behold Christ the Lord.

These humble worshipers had studied the prophecies. But though the rulers and priests also had the precious prophecies, they were not walking in the way of the Lord, and their eyes were not open to see the Light of life.

Things are still this way. All heaven focuses its attention on events that religious leaders do not recognize. People acknowledge Christ in history, but they are no more ready today to receive Christ in the poor and suffering who plead for relief, in the righteous cause that involves poverty and scorn, than they were two thousand years ago.

As Mary looked at the Child in her arms and remembered the words the shepherds had spoken, she was full of bright hope. Simeon's words called to her mind the prophetic message of Isaiah:

The people who walked in darkness
Have seen a great light;
Those who dwelt in the land of the
    shadow of death,
Upon them a light has shined. . . .
For unto us a Child is born,
Unto us a Son is given;
And the government will be upon His
    shoulder.
And His name will be called
Wonderful, Counselor, Mighty God,
Everlasting Father, Prince of Peace.
                    Isaiah 9:2–6

## The Anguish Christ's Mother Must Know

Yet Mary did not understand Christ's mission. Simeon had prophesied of Him as a light to illuminate the Gentiles, and the angels had announced the Savior's birth as tidings of joy to all peoples. God wanted everyone to see in Him the Redeemer of the world. But many years must pass before even the mother of Jesus would understand.

Mary did not see the baptism of suffering needed to bring about the Messiah's reign on David's throne. In Simeon's words to Mary, "A sword will pierce through your own soul also," God in tender mercy gave the mother of Jesus a hint of the anguish that she had already begun to bear for His sake.

"Behold," Simeon had said, "this Child is destined for the fall and rising of many in Israel." Whoever would rise again must first fall. We must fall upon the Rock and be broken before Christ can lift us up. Self must be dethroned. The Jews would not accept the honor that comes through humiliation. This is the reason they would not receive their Redeemer.

"That the thoughts of many hearts may be revealed." The hearts of all, from the Creator to the prince of darkness, are revealed in the light of the Savior's life. Satan has represented God as selfish. But the gift of Christ testifies that while God's hatred of sin is as strong as death, His love for the sinner is stronger than death. Having set out to redeem us, God will not withhold anything necessary for completing His work. Having collected the riches of the universe, He gives them all into the hands of Christ and says, Use these gifts to convince the human race that there is no love greater than Mine. They will find their greatest happiness in loving Me.

## How Everyone Will Judge Himself

At the cross of Calvary, love and selfishness stood face to face. Christ had lived only to comfort and bless, and by putting Him to death, Satan showed his hatred against God. The real purpose of his rebellion was to dethrone God and to destroy Jesus, through whom God was showing His love.

The life and death of Christ also reveal the thoughts of men and women. Jesus' life called everyone to self-surrender and to fellowship in suffering. All who were listening to the Holy Spirit were drawn to Him. Those who worshiped self belonged to Satan's kingdom. In their attitude toward Christ, all would show on which side they stood. In this way, everyone passes judgment on himself.

In the day of final judgment, the Cross will be presented, and every mind will understand its real significance. Sinners will stand condemned before the vision of Calvary with its mysterious Victim. All will see what their choice has been. Every question in the controversy will have been made plain. God will stand clear of blame for the existence or continuance of evil. It will be proven that there was no defect in God's government, no cause for dissatisfaction. Both the loyal and the rebellious will declare,

"Just and true are Your ways,
O King of the saints! . . .
Your judgments have been manifested."
Revelation 15:3, 4

# "We Have Seen His Star"*

Now after Jesus was born in Bethlehem of Judea in the days of Herod the king, behold, wise men from the East came to Jerusalem, saying, 'Where is He who has been born King of the Jews? For we have seen His star in the East and have come to worship Him.' "

The wise men from the East belonged to a class that represented wealth and learning. Among these were upright men who studied the indications of God in nature and were honored for their integrity and wisdom. The wise men who came to Jesus were such men.

As they studied the starry heavens, these devout, educated men saw the glory of the Creator. Seeking clearer knowledge, they turned to the Hebrew Scriptures. There were prophetic writings in their own land that predicted the coming of a divine teacher. Balaam's prophecies had been handed down by tradition from century to century. But in the Old Testament, the wise men learned with joy that the Savior's coming was near. The whole world was to be filled with a knowledge of the glory of the Lord.

The wise men had seen a mysterious light in the heavens that night when the glory of God flooded the hills of Bethlehem. A glowing star appeared and lingered in the sky, an event that stirred keen interest. That star was a group of shining angels, but the wise men did not know this. Yet they were impressed that the star held special importance to them.

Could this strange star have been sent as a sign of the Promised One? See Numbers 24:17. The wise men had welcomed the light of truth that Heaven had sent. Now it was shining on them in brighter rays. God instructed them through dreams to go in search of the newborn Prince.

The Eastern country was rich in precious things, and the wise men did not set out empty-handed. They brought the most costly gifts in the land as an offering to Him in whom all the families of the earth would be blessed.

## A Journey by Night

They had to travel by night in order to keep the star in view, but at every pause for rest the travelers searched the prophecies. The conviction deepened that God was guiding

---

* This chapter is based on Matthew 2.

them. The journey, though long, was a happy one.

They had reached the land of Israel and had Jerusalem in sight, when suddenly the star rested above the temple. Eagerly they hurried onward, confidently expecting the Messiah's birth to be the joyful subject on every tongue. But to their amazement, they found that their questions called forth no joy but rather surprise and fear, even mingled with contempt.

The priests boasted of their religion and piety while they denounced the Greeks and Romans as sinners. The wise men were not idol worshipers, and in the sight of God, they stood far higher than His professed followers, yet the Jews looked on them as heathen. Their eager questions touched no chord of sympathy.

### Herod's Jealousy Awakened

The wise men's strange errand created an excitement among the people of Jerusalem that reached to the palace of King Herod. The crafty Edomite was troubled at the suggestion of a possible rival. Being of foreign blood, he was hated by the people. His only security was to stay in Rome's favor. But this new Prince had a higher claim—He was born to the kingdom.

Herod suspected the priests of plotting with the strangers to stir up a rebellion and unseat him. He was determined to thwart the scheme by outsmarting them. He called in the priests and questioned them regarding the place of the Messiah's birth.

This inquiry from one who was not rightfully king, and made at the re-

quest of strangers, stung the pride of the Jewish teachers. They turned to the rolls of prophecy with indifference, and this enraged the jealous tyrant. He thought they were trying to conceal their knowledge. With an authority they dared not disregard, he commanded them to make a close search and to tell him the birthplace of their expected King. "So they said to him, 'In Bethlehem of Judea, for thus it is written by the prophet:

"But you Bethlehem, in the land of Judah,
Are not the least among the rulers of Judah;
For out of you shall come a Ruler,
Who will shepherd My people Israel." ' "

Herod now invited the wise men to a private interview. Anger and fear were raging in his heart, but he put on a calm exterior and claimed to welcome with joy the birth of Christ. He urged his visitors, "Search diligently for the young Child, and when you have found Him, bring back word to me, that I may come and worship Him also."

The priests were not as ignorant as they pretended. The report of the angels' visit to the shepherds had come to Jerusalem, but the rabbis had treated it as unworthy of notice. They themselves might have been ready to lead the visitors to Jesus' birthplace, but instead, the wise men came to call their attention to the birth of the Messiah.

If accepted, the reports that the shepherds and the wise men brought would disprove the priests' claim to be the spokesmen of the truth of God. These proud, educated teachers would not stoop to be instructed by heathen people. It could not be, they said, that God had passed them by, to communicate with ignorant shepherds or pagan Gentiles. They would not even go to Bethlehem to see whether these things were true. And they led the people to consider the interest in Jesus as merely fanatical excitement. This is when the priests and rabbis began to reject Christ. Their pride and stubbornness grew into a settled hatred of the Savior.

As the shadows of night fell, the wise men left Jerusalem alone. But to their great joy, they saw the star again and were directed to Bethlehem. Disappointed by the careless attitude of the Jewish leaders, they left Jerusalem less confident than when they had entered it.

### No Royal Guard

At Bethlehem they found no royal guard to protect the newborn King. None of the world's honored men were there. Jesus was cradled in a manger, with His parents as His only guardians. Could this be the One who would "raise up the tribes of Jacob," be "a light to the Gentiles," and "salvation to the ends of the earth"? Isaiah 49:6.

"When they had come into the house, they saw the young Child with Mary His mother, and fell down and worshiped Him." Then they poured out their gifts—"gold, frankincense, and myrrh." What a faith they had!

The wise men had not seen through Herod's plot, and they prepared to return to Jerusalem to tell him of their success. But in a dream they received a message to have no further communication with him. Avoiding Jerusalem, they set out for their own country by another route.

Joseph also received a dream warning Him to escape to Egypt with Mary and the Child. Joseph obeyed without delay, leaving at night for greater security.

The wise men's inquiries in Jerusalem, the resulting interest among the people, and even Herod's jealousy drew the attention of the priests and rabbis and directed minds to the prophecies concerning the Messiah and the great event that had taken place.

Determined to shut out the divine light from the world, Satan used his evil skills to their maximum to destroy the Savior. But He who never slumbers nor sleeps provided a refuge for Mary and the Child Jesus in a heathen land. And through the gifts of the wise men from a heathen country, the Lord supplied the funds for the journey to Egypt and for their stay in a land of strangers.

### Herod's Terrible Massacre

In Jerusalem, Herod waited impatiently for the wise men to return. As time passed and they did not appear, he became suspicious. Had the rabbis seen through his plot, and had the wise men purposely avoided him? The thought made him furious. Through force he would make an example of this Child-King.

Herod sent soldiers to Bethlehem with orders to put to death all the children two years old and under. The quiet homes of the City of David witnessed scenes that had been opened to the prophet six hundred years before:

"A voice was heard in Ramah,
Lamentation, weeping, and great mourning,
Rachel weeping for her children,
Refusing to be comforted, because they are no more."

The Jews had brought this disaster on themselves by rejecting the Holy Spirit, their only Shield. They had searched for prophecies that they could interpret to exalt themselves and show how God despised other nations. It was their proud boast that the Messiah was to come as a king and trample down the heathen in His anger. In this way, they stirred up the hatred of their rulers. Through their misrepresentation of Christ's mission, Satan had intended to bring about the Savior's destruction, but instead it returned on their own heads.

Soon after the slaughter of the children, Herod died a fearful death.

Joseph was still in Egypt, and now an angel told him to return to Israel. Thinking of Jesus as the Heir to David's throne, Joseph wanted to make his home in Bethlehem. But when he learned that Archelaus had been made king in Judea in place of his father, he feared that the son might carry out the father's evil intentions.

God directed Joseph to a place of safety, Nazareth, his former home. For nearly thirty years, Jesus lived here, "that it might be fulfilled which was spoken by the prophets, 'He shall be called a Nazarene.'" Galilee had a much larger mixture of foreign inhabitants than Judea, so there was less interest in matters relating especially to the Jews.

This was the Savior's reception when He came to earth. God could not entrust His beloved Son to human beings, even while carrying forward His work for their salvation! He commissioned angels to accompany Jesus and protect Him until He could accomplish His mission and die by the hands of those whom He came to save.

# The Child Jesus<sup>*</sup>

Jesus spent His childhood and youth in a little mountain village. He bypassed the wealthy homes and the famous places of learning to make His home in despised Nazareth.

"The Child grew and became strong in spirit, filled with wisdom; and the grace of God was upon Him." In the sunlight of His Father's face, Jesus "increased in wisdom and stature, and in favor with God and men." Luke 2:52. His mind was active and penetrating, with a thoughtfulness and wisdom beyond His years. His powers of mind and body developed gradually, in keeping with the laws of childhood.

As a child, Jesus showed a loveliness of attitude, a patience that nothing could disturb, and a truthfulness that would never sacrifice integrity. In principle He was firm as a rock, but His life revealed the grace of unselfish courtesy.

Jesus' mother watched His powers unfold, and she worked to encourage that bright, receptive mind. Through the Holy Spirit she received wisdom to cooperate with Heaven in the development of this Child who could claim only God as His Father.

In the days of Christ, religious instruction for the young had become formal. To a great degree, tradition had replaced the Scriptures. The mind was crowded with material that the higher school of the courts above would not recognize. Students found no quiet hours to spend with God, to hear His voice speaking to the heart. They turned away from the Source of wisdom. What people considered a "superior" education was the greatest hindrance to real development of the youth. Their minds became cramped and narrow.

The Child Jesus did not receive instruction in the synagogue schools. From His mother and the scrolls of the prophets, He learned of heavenly things. As He grew into youth, He did not seek the schools of the rabbis. He did not need the education obtained from such sources. His thorough acquaintance with the Scriptures shows how diligently He studied God's Word when He was young.

## Nature Supplemented the Bible

The great library of God's created works was spread out before Him. He had made all things, and now He studied the lessons His own hand had writ-

---

* This chapter is based on Luke 2:39, 40.

ten in earth and sea and sky. He gathered much scientific knowledge from nature—from plants, animals, and man. The parables by which He loved to teach lessons of truth show how He gathered spiritual teaching from nature and the surroundings of His daily life.

As Jesus was trying to understand the reason of things, heavenly beings helped Him. From the first dawning of intelligence, He was constantly growing in spiritual grace and knowledge of truth.

Every child may gain knowledge as Jesus did. As we try to become acquainted with our heavenly Father, angels will draw near, our minds will be strengthened, our characters elevated and refined. We will become more like our Savior. And as we gaze at the beautiful and grand things in nature, our hearts are drawn to God. The spirit is awed, the soul invigorated by coming in contact with the Infinite through His works. Communion with God through prayer develops mental and moral power.

While Jesus was a child, He thought and spoke as a child, but no trace of sin marred the image of God in Him. But He was not exempt from temptation. The people of Nazareth were well known for their wickedness. See John 1:46. Jesus had to be constantly on guard in order to preserve His purity. He was subject to all the conflicts we have to meet so that He could be an example to us in childhood, youth, and manhood.

From His earliest years, heavenly angels guarded Jesus, yet His life was one long struggle against the powers of darkness. The prince of darkness tried every possible way to ensnare Jesus with temptation.

Jesus was familiar with poverty, self-denial, and need. This experience was a protection for Him. He had no idle time to open the way for corrupting friendships. Nothing—not gain or pleasure, applause or criticism—could get Him to consent to a wrong act. Christ, the only sinless One who ever inhabited the earth, lived among the wicked inhabitants of Nazareth for nearly thirty years. This fact is a rebuke to those who think they are dependent on place, fortune, or prosperity to live a blameless life.

## As a Carpenter, Christ Honored Work

Jesus had been the Commander of heaven, and angels had delighted to obey His word. Now He was a willing servant, a loving, obedient son. With His own hands, He worked in the carpenter's shop with Joseph. He did not use divine power to ease His burdens or lighten His work.

Jesus used His physical powers carefully in order to stay healthy, so that He could do the best work.

He was not willing to be deficient, even in handling tools. He was perfect as a workman, just as He was perfect in character. By example He taught us to do our work with exactness and thoroughness and that labor is honorable. God gave us work as a blessing, and only the diligent worker finds the true glory and joy of life. God's approval rests on children and youth who take their part in the duties of the home, sharing the burdens of father and mother.

Jesus was an earnest and constant worker. He expected much, so He attempted much. He said, "I must work the works of Him who sent Me while it is day; the night is coming when no one can work." John 9:4. Jesus did not avoid care and responsibility, as many do who claim to be His followers. Because they seek to escape this discipline, many are weak, inefficient, spineless, and almost useless when difficulties come. We are to develop the positive attitude and strength of character that Christ revealed, through the same discipline He endured. The grace He received is for us.

Our Savior shared the condition of the poor. Those who have a true understanding of His life will never feel that the rich should be honored above the worthy poor.

## A Cheerful Singer

Jesus often expressed the gladness of His heart by singing psalms and heavenly songs. Often the people of Nazareth heard His voice raised in praise and song. As his companions complained of being tired, the sweet melody from His lips cheered them.

Through those secluded years at Nazareth, His life flowed out in streams of sympathy and tenderness. Old people, the sorrowing, the sin-burdened, children at play, little creatures of the groves, the patient work animals—all were happier for His presence. He whose word upheld the worlds would stoop to relieve a wounded bird. There was nothing unworthy of His notice, nothing to which He refused to minister.

So He grew in wisdom and stature, in favor with God and man. He showed Himself able to sympathize with everyone. An atmosphere of hope and courage surrounded Him, making Him a blessing in every home. Often on the Sabbath day He was called on to read the lesson from the prophets, and the hearts of the hearers thrilled as new light shone out from the sacred text.

Yet during all the years at Nazareth, He made no show of miraculous power. He assumed no titles. His quiet and simple life teaches an important lesson: the freer the life of a child is from artificial excitement, and the more in harmony with nature, the more favorable it is for physical and mental vigor and spiritual strength.

Jesus is our Example. In His home life He is the Pattern for all children and youth. The Savior stooped to accept poverty, so that He could teach how closely we in humble places in life may walk with God. His work began in dedicating to God the lowly trade of the craftsmen who work for their daily bread.

He was doing God's service just as much when laboring at the carpenter's bench as when working miracles for the multitude. Every youth who follows Christ's example of faithfulness and obedience in His lowly home may also claim these words spoken by the Father: "Behold! My Servant whom I uphold, my Elect One in whom My soul delights!" Isaiah 42:1.

# The Passover Visit*

Among the Jews, the twelfth year was the dividing line between childhood and youth. In keeping with this custom, Jesus made the Passover visit to Jerusalem with Joseph and Mary when He reached the required age.

The journey from Galilee took several days, and travelers united in large groups for companionship and protection. The women and old men rode on oxen or donkeys over the steep, rocky roads. The stronger men and youth traveled on foot. The whole land was bright with flowers and glad with the song of birds. Along the way, fathers and mothers repeated to their children the wonders that God had done for His people in ages past, and brightened their journey with song and music.

Passover observance began with the birth of the Hebrew nation. On the last night of their slavery in Egypt, God directed the Hebrews to gather their families in their own homes. Having sprinkled the doorposts with the blood of the lamb they had slaughtered, they were to eat the lamb, roasted, with unleavened bread and bitter herbs. "It is the Lord's Passover." Exodus 12:11. At midnight all the firstborn of the Egyptians were killed. Then the Hebrews

went out from Egypt as an independent nation. From generation to generation, they were to repeat the story of this wonderful deliverance.

After the Passover came the seven-day feast of unleavened bread. All the ceremonies of the feast were symbols of the work of Christ. The slain lamb, the unleavened bread, the sheaf of first fruits, represented the Savior. But with most of the people in the days of Christ, this feast had become no more than formalism. But how significant it was to the Son of God!

For the first time, the Child Jesus looked on the temple. He saw the white-robed priests performing their solemn ministry and the bleeding victim on the altar of sacrifice. He witnessed the impressive rites of the Passover service. Day by day, He saw their meaning more clearly. Every act seemed involved with His own life. New impulses were awakening within Him. Silent and absorbed, He seemed to be studying out a great problem. The mystery of His mission was opening to the Savior.

Completely focused on contemplating these scenes, Jesus lingered in the temple courts when the Passover

---

* This chapter is based on Luke 2:41–51.

services ended. When the worshipers left Jerusalem, He was left behind.

In this visit, Jesus' parents wanted to bring Him into contact with the great teachers in Israel. They hoped He might be impressed by the learning of the rabbis and would pay more attention to their requirements. But in the temple, Jesus had been taught by God. What He had received, He began at once to share.

An apartment connected with the temple had been made into a sacred school. Here the Child Jesus came, seating Himself at the feet of the learned rabbis. As One seeking for wisdom, He questioned these teachers regarding the prophecies and about events then taking place that pointed to the coming of the Messiah.

His questions suggested deep truths that had been hidden for a long time but were vital to salvation. While showing how the wisdom of the wise men was narrow and superficial, every question placed truth in a new light. The rabbis spoke of the wonderful exaltation that the Messiah's coming would bring to the Jews, but Jesus presented the prophecy of Isaiah and asked the meaning of those Scriptures that point to the suffering and death of the Lamb of God. See Isaiah 53.

The doctors turned on Him with questions and were amazed at His answers. With the humility of a child, He gave the words of Scripture a depth of meaning that the wise men had not imagined. The lines of truth He pointed out, had they been followed, would have worked a reformation in the religion of the day; and when Jesus began His ministry, many would have been prepared to receive Him.

In this thoughtful Galilean Boy, the rabbis recognized great promise. They wanted to have charge of His education. A mind so original, they thought, must be brought under their molding.

The words of Jesus moved their hearts as they had never before been moved by words from human lips. God was seeking to give light to those leaders. If Jesus had seemed to be trying to teach them, they would have refused to listen. But they told themselves that they were teaching Him—or at least testing His knowledge of the Scriptures. Jesus' youthful modesty and grace disarmed their prejudices. Their minds opened to the Word of God, and the Holy Spirit spoke to their hearts.

They could see that prophecy did not sustain their expectation of the Messiah, but they would not admit that they had misunderstood the Scriptures they claimed to teach.

**His Parents Become Worried**

Meanwhile, in leaving Jerusalem, Joseph and Mary had lost sight of Jesus. The pleasure of traveling with friends absorbed their attention, and they did not notice His absence until night came. Then they missed the helpful hand of their Child. Supposing Him to be with their group, they had not been worried. But now their fears arose. Shuddering, they remembered how Herod had tried to destroy Him in His infancy. Dark dread filled their hearts.

Returning to Jerusalem, they launched their search. The next day, in the temple, a familiar voice caught their attention. They could not mistake it—so serious and earnest, yet so full of melody. In the school of the rabbis, they found Jesus.

When He was with them again, His mother said in words that implied reproof, "Son, why have You done this to us? Look, Your father and I have sought You anxiously."

"Why did you seek Me?" answered Jesus. "Did you not know that I must be about My Father's business?" When they did not seem to understand, He pointed upward. On His face was a light. Divinity was flashing through humanity. They had listened to what was passing between Him and the rabbis and were astonished at His questions and answers.

Jesus was occupied in the work He had come into the world to do, but Joseph and Mary had neglected theirs. God had shown them high honor in committing His Son to them. But for an entire day, they had lost sight of Him, and when their anxiety was relieved, they had not condemned themselves but had blamed Him.

It was natural for Jesus' parents to look on Him as their own Child. His life in many respects was like that of other children, and it was difficult to realize that He was the Son of God. The gentle reproof that His words conveyed was designed to impress them with the sacredness of their trust.

In His answer to His mother, Jesus showed for the first time that He understood His relationship to God. Mary did not understand His words, but she knew He had disclaimed being Joseph's Son and had declared His Sonship to God.

Jesus returned home from Jerusalem with His earthly parents and helped them in their life of labor. For eighteen more years, He acknowledged the tie that bound Him to the home at Nazareth. He performed the duties of a son, a brother, a friend, and a citizen.

Jesus wanted to return from Jerusalem in quietness, with those who knew the secret of His life. By the Passover service, God was trying to remind His people of His wonderful work in delivering them from Egypt. In this work, He wanted them to see a promise of deliverance from sin. The blood of Christ was to save them. God wanted to lead them to prayerful study regarding Christ's mission. But as the crowds left Jerusalem, the excitement of travel and social interaction often absorbed their attention, and they forgot the service they had witnessed. The Savior was not attracted to their fellowship.

### Jesus Helps His Mother

Returning from Jerusalem, Jesus hoped to direct Joseph and Mary to the prophecies about the suffering Savior. On Calvary, He tried to lighten His mother's grief; He was thinking of her now. Mary was to witness His last agony, and Jesus wanted her to understand His mission so that she could endure when the sword would pierce through her soul. How much better she could have accepted the anguish of His death if she had understood the Scriptures to which He was now trying to turn her thoughts!

By one day's neglect, Joseph and Mary lost the Savior, but it cost them three days of anxious search to find Him. It is this way with us as well. By idle talk, evilspeaking, or neglect of prayer, in one day we may lose the Savior's presence, and it may take many days to find Him and regain the peace we have lost.

We should be careful not to forget Jesus and drift along unaware that He is not with us. Absorbed in worldly things, we separate ourselves from Him and from the heavenly angels. These holy beings cannot remain where people don't want the Savior's presence and don't notice His absence.

Many attend religious services and are refreshed by the Word of God, but by neglecting to meditate and pray, they lose the blessing. By separating themselves from Jesus, they have shut away the light of His presence.

It would be good for us to spend a thoughtful hour each day in thinking about the life of Christ. We should take it point by point and let the imagination grasp each scene, especially the closing ones. If we do, our confidence in Him will be more constant, our love will be awakened, and we will be filled with His spirit. Beholding the beauty of His character, we will be "transformed into the same image from glory to glory." 2 Corinthians 3:18.

# Christ's Problems
## as a Child

Under synagogue teachers, Jewish youth were instructed in the countless regulations that orthodox Israelites were expected to observe. But these things did not interest Jesus. From childhood He acted independently of rabbinical laws. He constantly studied the Scriptures, and the words, "Thus says the Lord," were always on His lips.

He saw that people were departing from the Word of God and insisting on rites that had no value. They found no peace in their faithless services. They did not know the freedom of spirit that comes by serving God fully. Though Jesus could not approve of mingling human requirements with divine instructions, He did not attack the teachings or practices of the highly educated teachers. When criticized for His own simple habits, He presented the Word of God to justify His conduct.

Jesus tried to please those with whom He came in contact. Because He was so gentle and unobtrusive, the scribes and elders supposed that they could easily influence Him by their teaching. But He asked for their authority in Scripture. He would listen to every word that proceeds from the mouth of God, but He could not obey human inventions. Jesus seemed to know the Scriptures from beginning

to end, and He presented them in their true meaning. The rabbis claimed it was their responsibility to explain the Scriptures and His place to accept their interpretation.

They knew that no authority for their traditions could be found in Scripture. Yet they were angry because Jesus did not obey their commands. Failing to convince Him, they went to Joseph and Mary and presented His noncompliance to them. This brought Him rebuke and censure.

At a very early age, Jesus began to act for Himself in character formation. Not even love for His parents could turn Him from obedience to God's Word. But the influence of the rabbis made His life bitter. He had to learn the hard lesson of silence and patient endurance.

His brothers, as the sons of Joseph were called, sided with the rabbis. They valued human instruction more highly than the Word of God, and they condemned Jesus' strict obedience to God's law as stubbornness. Yet the knowledge He showed in answering the rabbis surprised them, and they could not help but see that He was an instructor to them. They recognized that His education was of a higher type than their own, but they did not realize that He had access to a source of knowledge about which they were ignorant.

## How Jesus Respected All People Alike

Christ found religion fenced in by high walls of seclusion, as if it were too sacred a matter for everyday life. Jesus overthrew these walls. Instead of secluding Himself in a hermit's cave in order to show His heavenly character, He set to work earnestly for humanity. He taught that religion is not meant only for set times and places. This was a rebuke to the Pharisees. It showed that their self-absorbed devotion to personal interest was far from true godliness. This made them angry, so they tried to make Him conform to their regulations.

Jesus had little money to give, but He often denied Himself food in order to relieve those who were more needy than He. When His brothers spoke harshly to poor, degraded people, Jesus spoke words of encouragement to them. To those in need He would give a cup of cold water and quietly place His own meal in their hands.

All this displeased His brothers. They were older, and they felt that He should have to obey their commands. They accused Him of thinking that He was superior to them and setting Himself above the teachers, priests, and rulers. They often tried to intimidate Him, but He went right on, making the Scriptures His guide.

## Jesus' Problems With His Family

Jesus' brothers were jealous of Him and showed determined unbelief and contempt. They could not understand His conduct. His life presented great contradictions. He was the divine Son of God and yet a helpless child. As Creator, the earth was His possession, yet poverty marked His life experience. He did not run after worldly greatness, and in even the lowliest position He was content. This angered His brothers. They could not account for His constant peace under trial and hardship.

Jesus' brothers misunderstood Him because He was not like them. In looking to others, they had turned away from God, and they did not have His power in their lives. The forms of religion they observed could not transform the character. Jesus' example was a continual irritation to them. He hated sin and could not witness a wrong act without pain that was impossible to disguise. Because the life of Jesus condemned evil, people opposed Him; they commented with a sneer on His unselfishness and integrity. His patience and kindness they called cowardice.

Of the bitterness that falls on the human race, there was no part that Christ did not taste. Some made unkind remarks about Him because of His birth. Even in childhood He had to meet scornful looks and evil whisperings. If He had responded by an impatient word or look or even one wrong act, He would have failed at being a perfect example. If so, He would have failed to carry out the plan for our redemption. If He had even admitted that there could be an excuse for sin, Satan would have triumphed, and the world would have been lost. Often He was called a coward for refusing to

CHRIST'S PROBLEMS AS A CHILD

join with His brothers in some forbidden act, but His answer was, It is written, "The fear of the Lord, that is wisdom, and to depart from evil is understanding." Job 28:28.

Some people felt at peace in His presence, but many avoided Him, feeling rebuked by His stainless life. Young companions enjoyed His presence, but they were impatient with His determination to do right, and they pronounced Him narrow and strict. Jesus answered. It is written, "How can young people keep their way pure? By guarding it according to your word. . . . I treasure your word in my heart, so that I may not sin against you." Psalm 119:9, 11, NRSV.

Often He was asked, "Why are You bent on being so different from us all?" He replied. It is written, "Blessed are those who keep his testimonies, who . . . do no iniquity; they walk in His ways." Psalm 119:2, 3.

When questioned why He did not join in the amusements of the young people of Nazareth, He said. It is written, "I will delight myself in Your statutes; I will not forget Your word." Psalm 119:16.

Jesus did not contend for His rights. He did not retaliate when people treated Him roughly, but He bore insult patiently. Again and again He was asked, "Why do You submit to such hateful treatment, even from Your brothers?" He said. It is written,

> My son, do not forget my law,
> But let your heart keep my commands; . . .
> Let not mercy and truth forsake you:
> Bind them around your neck,
> Write them on the tablet of your heart,
> And so find favor and high esteem
> In the sight of God and man.
> Proverbs 3:1-4

## Why He Had to Be Different

Jesus' course of action was a mystery to His parents. He seemed to be Someone set apart. He found His hours of happiness when He was alone with nature and with God. Early morning often found Him in some secluded place, meditating, searching the Scriptures, or in prayer. From these quiet hours He would return home to take up His duties again.

Mary believed that the Holy Child born to her was the Messiah, yet she dared not express her faith. Throughout His life she shared in His sufferings. With sorrow she witnessed the trials that came on Him in His childhood and youth. When she stood up for what she knew to be right in His conduct, she herself was brought into difficulty. She considered the home relationships and the mother's watchcare over her children to be vital in the formation of character. The sons and daughters of Joseph knew this, and by appealing to her anxiety, they tried to correct the practices of Jesus according to their standard.

Mary often reasoned strongly with Jesus, urging Him to conform to the rules of the rabbis. But not even she could persuade Him to change His habits of thinking on the works of God and trying to ease suffering. When the priests and teachers sought her aid in controlling Jesus, she was greatly troubled; but peace came to her heart as

He presented Scripture upholding His practices.

At times she wavered between Jesus and His brothers, who did not believe that He was the One sent by God, but she had abundant evidence that He had a divine character. His life was like yeast working amid the elements of society. Undefiled, He walked among the thoughtless, the rude, the uncourteous, amid unjust tax collectors, reckless spenders, unrighteous Samaritans, heathen soldiers, rough peasants, and the mixed multitude. He spoke a word of sympathy as He saw people weary yet forced to carry heavy burdens. He repeated to them lessons He had learned from nature about the love and goodness of God.

He taught all to see themselves as blessed with precious talents. By His own example, He taught that we are to cherish every moment of time as a treasure and to use it for holy purposes. He passed by no human being as worthless but tried to inspire hope in the most rough and unpromising, assuring them that they could develop such a character as would make it clear to everyone that they were the children of God. Often He met those who had no power to break from Sa-

tan's trap. To such people, discouraged, sick, tempted, and fallen, Jesus would speak words of tenderest pity.

Others He met were fighting a hand-to-hand battle with the enemy of souls. These He encouraged to keep on, for angels of God were on their side and would give them victory. Those whom He helped were convinced that here was Someone in whom they could trust with perfect confidence.

Jesus was interested in every phase of suffering, and to every sufferer He brought relief. His kind words were like a soothing ointment. No one could say that He had worked a miracle, but virtue—the healing power of love—went out from Him. So in an unobtrusive way, He worked for people, starting in His very childhood.

Yet through childhood, youth, and manhood, Jesus walked alone. There was no one like Him in such purity and faithfulness. See Isaiah 63:3. He knew that unless there was a decided change in the principles and purposes of the human race, all would be lost. Filled with intense commitment, He carried out the plan for His life that He Himself would be the Light of all humanity.

# The Voice in the Wilderness *

Christ's forerunner came from among the faithful in Israel. Zacharias, an aged priest, and his wife Elizabeth were "both righteous before God," and in their quiet lives the light of faith shone out like a star amid the darkness. This godly pair was given the promise of a son who would "go before the face of the Lord to prepare His ways."

Zacharias had gone to Jerusalem to minister for one week in the temple. As he stood before the golden altar in the Holy Place of the sanctuary, suddenly he became aware of an angel of the Lord "standing on the right side of the altar." For years he had prayed for the coming of the Redeemer. Now these prayers were about to be answered.

The angel greeted him with the joyful assurance: " 'Do not be afraid, Zacharias, for your prayer is heard; and your wife Elizabeth will bear you a son, and you shall call his name John. . . . He will be great in the sight of the Lord, and shall drink neither wine nor strong drink. He will also be filled with the Holy Spirit. . . . He will also go before Him in the spirit and power of Elijah, "to turn the hearts of the fathers to the children," and the disobe-

dient to the wisdom of the just, to make ready a people prepared for the Lord.' And Zacharias said to the angel, 'How shall I know this? For I am an old man, and my wife is well advanced in years.' "

For a moment the aged priest forgot that what God promises, He is able to perform. What a contrast between his unbelief and the faith of Mary! Her answer to the angel's announcement was, "Behold the maidservant of the Lord! Let it be to me according to your word." Luke 1:38.

The birth of a son to Zacharias, like the birth of Abraham's child and Mary's, was to teach a great truth: in every believing soul, God's power will do what human power cannot. Through faith the child of promise was given. Similarly, through faith spiritual life is born, and God enables us to do the works of righteousness.

Five hundred years before, the angel Gabriel had revealed to Daniel the prophetic period that would reach to the coming of Christ. Zacharias knew that the end of this period was near, and this encouraged him to pray for the Messiah's coming. Now, the very

---

* This chapter is based on Luke 1:5–23, 57–80; 3:1–18; Matthew 3:1–12; Mark 1:1–8.

same angel through whom God had given the prophecy had come to announce its fulfillment.

## Zacharias Doubted

Zacharias had expressed doubt about the angel's words. Now he was not to speak again until they were fulfilled. "Behold, you will be mute and not able to speak until the day these things take place, because you did not believe my words which will be fulfilled in their own time." It was the duty of the priest in this service to pray for pardon of sins and for the coming of the Messiah. But when Zacharias attempted to do this, he could not speak a word. As he came out from the Holy Place, his face was shining with the glory of God, and the people "perceived that he had seen a vision in the temple." Zacharias "remained speechless," but he communicated to them what he had seen and heard.

Soon after the birth of the promised child, the father's speech was restored. "And all these sayings were discussed throughout all the hill country of Judea. And all those who heard them kept them in their hearts, saying, 'What kind of child will this be?' " All this called attention to the Messiah's coming.

The Holy Spirit rested on Zacharias, and he prophesied about the mission of his son:

"You, child, will be called the prophet of the Highest;
For you will go before the face of the Lord to prepare His ways,
To give knowledge of salvation to His people

By the remission of their sins."

"So the child grew and became strong in spirit, and was in the deserts till the day of his manifestation to Israel." God had called the son of Zacharias to the greatest work ever committed to human beings. And the Spirit of God would be with him if he obeyed the angel's instruction.

John was to bring the light of God to the people. He must impress them with their need of God's righteousness. Such a messenger must be holy, a temple for the Spirit of God to dwell in. He must have good physical health and mental and spiritual strength. For this reason, it would be necessary for him to control his appetites and passions.

In the time of John the Baptist, greed for riches and the love of luxury and display were everywhere. Sensual pleasures, feasting and drinking, were causing physical harm, numbing the spiritual perceptions, and lessening the awareness of sin. John was to stand as a reformer. By his self-denying life and plain dress, he was to rebuke the excesses of his time. This was the reason an angel from the throne of heaven gave the lesson about temperance to his parents.

Childhood and youth is the time to develop the power of self-control. Habits established in early years decide whether we will be victorious or defeated in the battle of life. Youth—the sowing time—determines the character of the harvest for this life and the life to come.

In preparing the way for Christ's first advent, John was a representative of those who prepare a people for our

Lord's second coming. The world is set in self-indulgence. Errors and myths are everywhere. All who would perfect holiness in the fear of God must learn temperance and self-control. See 2 Corinthians 7:1. They must keep the appetites and passions under the control of the higher powers of the mind. This self-discipline is essential if we are to develop that mental strength and spiritual insight that enable us to understand and practice the truths of God's Word.

### John's Unusual Education

In the natural order of things, the son of Zacharias would have been educated in the rabbinical schools. But since this would have unfitted him for his work, God called him to the desert, so that he could learn of nature and nature's God.

John found his home in the barren hills, wild ravines, and rocky caves. Here his surroundings helped him form habits of simplicity and self-denial. Here he could study the lessons of nature, of revelation, and of God's leading. From his childhood, his God-fearing parents had kept his mission before him, and he had accepted the holy trust. The solitude of the desert was a welcome escape from society in which unbelief and impurity had become almost universal. He avoided constant contact with sin in order not to lose the sense of its exceeding sinfulness.

But John did not spend his life in austere religious gloom or in selfish isolation. From time to time, he went out to mingle in society, always an interested observer of what was happening in the world. Illuminated by the divine Spirit, he studied human nature to understand how to reach people's hearts with the message of heaven. The burden of his mission was on him. By meditation and prayer, he set about to prepare himself for the life work before him.

Although he was in the wilderness, John was not exempt from temptation. Satan tried to overthrow him, but his spiritual perceptions were clear, and through the Holy Spirit he was able to detect and resist the tempter's approaches.

Like Moses in the mountains of Midian, John was shut in by God's presence. The gloomy and terrible aspect of nature in his wilderness home vividly pictured the condition of Israel. The vineyard of the Lord had become a desolate waste. But above, over the dark clouds, arched the rainbow of promise.

Alone in the silent night, John read God's promise to Abraham of descendants as numberless as the stars. The light of dawn told of Him who would be like "the light of the morning when the sun rises, a morning without clouds." 2 Samuel 23:4. And in the brightness of noonday, he saw the splendor when "The glory of the Lord shall be revealed, and all flesh shall see it together." Isaiah 40:5.

With awed yet elated spirit he searched in the prophetic scrolls for the revelations of the Messiah's coming. Shiloh was to appear before a king would cease to reign on David's throne. Now the time had come. A Roman ruler sat in the palace on Mount Zion. By the sure word of the Lord, the Christ was already born.

### Isaiah's Portrayals Studied

John studied Isaiah's grand portrayals

of the Messiah's glory day and night. See Isaiah 11:4; 32:2; 62:4. The glorious vision filled the heart of the lonely exile. He looked on the King in His beauty, and self was forgotten. He saw the majesty of holiness and felt himself to be inefficient and unworthy. He was ready to go forward as Heaven's messenger, unshaken by anything human, because he had looked upon the Divine. He could stand fearless in the presence of earthly monarchs, because he had bowed low before the King of kings.

John did not fully understand the nature of the Messiah's kingdom, but his hope centered on the coming of a King in righteousness and the establishment of Israel as a holy nation.

He saw his people self-satisfied and asleep in their sins. The message God had given him was to startle them from their dullness and apathy. Before the seed of the gospel could take root, the soil of the heart must be broken up. Before they would seek healing from Jesus, they must be awakened to their danger from the wounds of sin.

God does not send messengers to lull the unsanctified into fatal security. He lays heavy burdens on the conscience of the wrongdoer and pierces the soul with arrows of conviction. Ministering angels present the fearful judgments of God to deepen the sense of need. Then the hand that has humbled in the dust lifts up the repentant one.

### On the Edge of Revolution

When the ministry of John began, the nation was moving toward revolution. Archelaus had been removed as king, and Judea had been brought di-rectly under the control of Rome. The tyranny and extortion of the Roman governors and their efforts to introduce heathen symbols and customs kindled revolt, which had been quenched in the blood of thousands of Israel's bravest.

Amid the discord and strife, a voice spoke up in the wilderness, startling and stern yet full of hope: "Repent, for the kingdom of heaven is at hand!" With a new, strange power, it moved the people. Here was an announcement that the coming of Christ was right upon them. With the spirit and power of Elijah, John denounced the national corruption and rebuked the prevailing sins. His words were pointed and convincing. The nation was stirred. Crowds flocked to the wilderness.

John called the people to repentance. As a symbol of cleansing from sin, he baptized them in the waters of the Jordan. By doing so, he declared that those who claimed to be the chosen people of God were defiled by sin. Without purification of heart, they could have no part in the Messiah's kingdom.

Princes and rabbis, soldiers, tax collectors, and peasants came to hear the prophet. Many repented and received baptism in order to participate in the kingdom he announced.

Many scribes and Pharisees came confessing their sins and asking for baptism. They had led the people to hold a high opinion of their piety, but now the guilty secrets of their lives were unveiled. But John was impressed that many of these men had no real conviction of sin. They were following their own self-interest. As friends of the prophet, they hoped to find favor with the coming Prince. And by receiving baptism, they thought they would strengthen their influence with the people.

### John's Sharp Rebuke to Hypocrites

John met them with the scathing question, "Brood of vipers! Who warned you to flee from the wrath to come? Therefore bear fruits worthy of repentance." Because the Jews had separated themselves from God, they were suffering under His judgments. This was the cause of their bondage to a heathen nation. Because in times past the Lord had shown them great favor, they excused their sins. They deceived themselves into thinking that they were better than others and entitled to His blessings.

John declared to the teachers of Israel that their pride, selfishness, and cruelty showed them to be a deadly curse to the people. In view of the light they had received from God, they were even worse than the heathen. God was not dependent on them to fulfill His plans. He could call others to His service.

"Even now," said the prophet, "the ax is laid to the root of the trees. Therefore every tree which does not bear good fruit is cut down and thrown into the fire." If the fruit is worthless, the name cannot save the tree from destruction. John told the Jews plainly that if their life and character were not in harmony with God's law, they were not His people.

All who became citizens of Christ's kingdom, he said, would give evidence of faith and repentance. Their lives would exhibit kindness and devotion. They would minister to the needy, shield the defenseless, and be examples of virtue and compassion.

"I indeed baptize you with water unto repentance, but He who is coming after me is mightier than I, whose sandals I am not worthy to carry. He will baptize you with the Holy Spirit and fire." Isaiah had declared that the Lord would cleanse His people "by the spirit of judgment and by the spirit of burning." Isaiah 4:4.

The Spirit of God will consume sin in all who submit to His power. See Hebrews 12:29. But if any cling to sin, then the glory of God, which destroys sin, must destroy them. At the second advent of Christ, the wicked will be consumed "with the breath of His mouth" and destroyed "with the brightness of His coming." 2 Thessalonians 2:8. The glory of God that gives life to the righteous will destroy the wicked.

In the time of John the Baptist, Christ was about to appear as the Revealer of God's character. His very presence would make people aware of their sin. Only as they were willing to be cleansed from sin could they enter into fellowship with Him.

In this way, John the Baptist declared God's message to Israel. Many accepted it and sacrificed everything in order to obey. More than a few cherished the hope that he might be the Messiah. But as John saw the people turning to him, he took every opportunity to direct their faith to the One who was to come.

# The Baptism of Jesus*

The message of John the Baptist reached the poor people in the remote hill towns and the fishermen by the sea, and in these simple, earnest hearts, it found its greatest response. In Nazareth, it was told in the carpentry shop that had been Joseph's, and One recognized the call. His time had come. He said Goodbye to His mother and followed the crowds that were flocking to the Jordan.

Jesus and John the Baptist were cousins, yet they had had no direct acquaintance with each other. This was part of God's plan. No one would be able to say that they had conspired together to support each other's claims.

John knew about the events that had marked the birth of Jesus and also about the visit to Jerusalem in His boyhood and His sinless life. He believed Him to be the Messiah, but the fact that Jesus had remained in the shadows, giving no special evidence of His mission, gave John opportunity for doubt. The Baptist, however, waited in faith. God had revealed to him that the Messiah would seek baptism from him and that he would receive a sign of His divine character.

When Jesus came to be baptized, John recognized in Him a purity of character that no one had ever before seen in anyone. His very presence was awe-inspiring. This was in harmony with what had been revealed to John about the Messiah. Yet how could he, a sinner, baptize the Sinless One? Why should He who needed no repentance submit to a rite that was a confession of guilt that must be washed away?

As Jesus asked for baptism, John hesitated, saying, " 'I have need to be baptized by You, and are You coming to me?' But Jesus answered and said to him, 'Permit it to be so now, for thus it is fitting for us to fulfill all righteousness.' Then he allowed Him. . . . When He had been baptized, Jesus came up immediately from the water; and behold, the heavens were opened to Him, and He saw the Spirit of God descending like a dove and alighting upon Him."

### Sinless Christ Baptized

Jesus did not receive baptism as a confession of His own guilt. He identified Himself with sinners, taking the steps that we are to take and doing the

---

* This chapter is based on Matthew 3:13–17; Mark 1:9–11; Luke 3:21, 22.

work that we must do. His life of suffering and patient endurance after His baptism was also an example to us.

Coming up out of the water, Jesus bowed in prayer on the river bank. He was now entering the conflict of His life. Though He was the Prince of Peace, His coming must be like the unsheathing of a sword. The kingdom He had come to establish was the opposite of the one the Jews desired. They would see Him as the enemy and destroyer of Israel's rituals and system, condemn Him as a transgressor, and denounce Him as the devil. No one on earth had understood Him, and He must still walk alone. His mother and brothers did not comprehend His mission. Even His disciples did not understand Him.

As Someone united to us, He must bear our guilt and woe. The Sinless One must feel the shame of sin. The Peace-Lover must live with strife, the truth must abide with falsehood, and purity with depravity. Every sin, every conflict, every defiling lust was torture to His spirit.

He must walk the path alone. The redemption of the world must rest on Him who had accepted the weakness of humanity. He saw and felt it all, but His determination remained firm.

The Savior poured out His soul in prayer. He knew how sin had hardened the hearts of men and women, how difficult it would be for them to comprehend His mission and accept salvation. He pleaded with the Father for power to overcome their unbelief, to break the chains with which Satan had held them, and to conquer the destroyer.

Never before had angels heard such a prayer. The Father Himself would answer the request of His Son. The heavens opened, and a dovelike form of purest light descended on the Savior's head.

Few people at the Jordan except John recognized the heavenly vision. Yet the solemn sense of God's presence rested on the assembly. Christ's upturned face was glorified as they had never before seen any human face. From the open heavens, they heard a Voice: "This is My beloved Son, in whom I am well pleased."

### Endorsed by Heaven

God spoke these words to inspire faith in those who witnessed the scene and to strengthen the Savior for His mission. Even though the sins of a guilty world were laid on Christ, and regardless of the humiliation He accepted by taking our fallen nature on Himself, the Voice from heaven declared Him to be the Son of the Eternal.

John had been deeply moved. As the glory of God encircled Jesus and the Voice from heaven was heard, John knew that it was the world's Redeemer whom he had baptized. Stretching out his hand and pointing to Jesus, he called out, "Behold! The Lamb of God who takes away the sin of the world!" John 1:29.

None among the hearers, and not even John himself, grasped the significance of the words, "the Lamb of God." Many of the people of Israel regarded the sacrificial offerings much as the heathen looked on their sacrifices—gifts to calm the Deity's anger. God wanted to teach them that from His own love comes the gift that reconciles them to Himself.

The message spoken to Jesus, "This is My beloved Son, in whom I am well pleased," embraces humanity. With all our sins and weaknesses, God does not cast us aside as worthless. "He made us accepted in the Beloved." Ephesians 1:6. The glory that rested on Christ is God's pledge of His love for us. It tells us of the power of prayer—how the human voice may reach the ear of God and our requests find acceptance in the courts of heaven.

By sin, earth was cut off from heaven, but Jesus has connected it to the sphere of glory again. The light that fell on our Savior's head will fall on us as we pray for help to resist temptation. The Voice that spoke to Jesus says to every believing soul, This is My beloved child, in whom I am well pleased.

Our Redeemer has opened the way so that the most sinful, oppressed, and despised people may find access to the Father. All may have a home in the mansions that Jesus has gone to prepare.

# The Wilderness Temptation*

"Then Jesus was led up by the Spirit into the wilderness to be tempted by the devil. And when He had fasted forty days and forty nights, afterward He was hungry."

Jesus did not invite temptation. He went to the wilderness to be alone, to think about His mission. By fasting and prayer, He was to brace Himself for the bloodstained path He must travel. But Satan thought this was the best time to approach Him.

Mighty issues were at stake. Satan claimed the earth as his and presented himself as "the prince of this world." He declared that humanity had chosen him as their ruler and that through human beings he held dominion over the world. Christ had come to disprove Satan's claim. As the Son of man, Christ would stand loyal to God. This would show that Satan had not gained complete control of the human race and that his claim to the world was false. Anyone who wanted deliverance from his power would be set free.

Satan had known that he did not hold absolute control over the world. In humanity, there was a power that withstood his reign. See Genesis 3:15. In the sacrifices that Adam and his sons offered, he saw a symbol of communion between earth and heaven, and he set himself to intercept it. He misrepresented God and misinterpreted the rites that pointed to the Savior. He led people to fear God as one who delighted in their destruction. The sacrifices that should have revealed His love, they offered only to appease His wrath.

When God gave His written Word, Satan studied the prophecies. From generation to generation, he worked to blind the people so that they would reject Christ at His coming.

When Jesus was born, Satan knew that One had come to dispute his rulership. The Son of God had come to this earth as a man, and this filled him with alarm. His selfish heart could not understand such love. Since he had lost heaven, he was determined to cause others to share his fall. He would cause them to undervalue heavenly things and set their hearts on things of earth.

## Satan Determined to Win

From the time when the Commander of heaven was a baby in Bethlehem, the evil one continually attacked Him. In the councils of Satan with his

---

* This chapter is based on Matthew 4:1–11; Mark 1:12, 13; Luke 4:1–13.

angels, it was determined that He must be overcome.

The forces of evil followed Him closely to engage in warfare against Him and to overcome Him if possible.

At the Savior's baptism, Satan heard the voice of Jehovah testifying to Jesus' divinity. Now that Jesus had come "in the likeness of sinful flesh" (Romans 8:3), the Father Himself spoke. Before this, He had communicated with humanity *through* Christ; now He communicated with humanity *in* Christ. Now it was clear that the connection between God and mankind had been restored.

Satan saw that he must either conquer or be conquered. He rallied all the energies of apostasy against Christ.

Many look on this conflict between Christ and Satan as having no particular effect on their own life. But within every human heart, the conflict is repeated. The enticements Christ resisted were those we find so difficult to withstand. With the weight of the sins of the world on Him, Christ withstood the test on appetite, on the love of the world, and on a love of display that leads to presumption. These were the temptations that overcame Adam and Eve and that overcome us so easily.

Satan had pointed to Adam's sin as proof that no one could obey God's law. In our humanity, Christ was to succeed where Adam failed. But when Adam was attacked by the tempter, he had none of the effects of sin on him. He stood in the strength of perfect manhood, possessing full vigor of mind and body. Surrounded with the glories of Eden, he was in daily fellowship with heavenly beings.

It was not this way with Jesus when He entered the wilderness to cope with Satan. For four thousand years the race had been decreasing in physical strength, in mental power, and in moral worth; and Christ took on Himself the weaknesses of degenerated humanity. Only in this way could He rescue us from the lowest depths of our degradation.

## He Took All Humanity's Liabilities

Many claim that it was impossible for Christ to be overcome by temptation. If so, then He could not have been placed in Adam's position nor have gained the victory that Adam failed to gain. If in any sense we have a more trying conflict than Christ had, then He would not be able to help us. But our Savior took humanity, with all its liabilities. He took the nature of man, with the possibility of yielding to temptation. We have nothing to bear that He has not endured.

With Christ, as with Adam and Eve in Eden, appetite was the subject of the first great temptation. "And when He had fasted forty days and forty nights, afterward He was hungry. Now when the tempter came to Him, he said, 'If You are the Son of God, command that these stones become bread.' "

These first words betrayed the tempter's character. "If You are the Son of God." Here Satan introduced a hint of distrust. If Jesus would do what Satan suggested, He would be accepting the doubt. Satan had tried to plant the thought in Eve's mind that withholding such beautiful fruit contradicted God's love for them. Similarly, the tempter now tried to plant his own sentiments in Christ. "If You are the Son of God." In his voice was an expression of utter disbelief. Would God treat His own Son like this, leaving Him in the desert with wild beasts, without food, without companions, without comfort? He hinted at the idea that God never meant His Son to be in such a condition as this. "If You are the Son of God, show Your power. Command this stone to become bread."

### The Temptation to Doubt

The words from heaven, "This is My beloved Son," were still sounding in the ears of Satan. But he was determined to make Christ disbelieve this testimony. The Word of God was Christ's assurance of His divine mission; the Word declared His connection with heaven. Satan intended to make Him doubt that Word. If he could shake Christ's confidence in God, Satan knew that he could overcome Jesus. He hoped that under the force of despair and hunger, Christ would lose faith in His Father and work a miracle in His own behalf. If He had done this, the plan of salvation would have been broken.

Satan made the most of his supposed advantage. One of the most powerful of the angels, he said, had been banished from heaven. The appearance of Jesus indicated that He was that fallen angel, forsaken by God and deserted by everyone. A divine being would establish his claim by working a miracle: "If You are the Son of God, command this stone to become bread." Such an act of creative power, the tempter urged, would be conclusive evidence of Divinity. It would

bring the controversy to an end.

But the Son of God was not to prove His divinity to Satan. If Christ had followed the suggestion of the enemy, Satan would still have said, "Show me a sign that I may believe you to be the Son of God." And Christ was not to exercise divine power for His own benefit. He had come to bear trials as we must, giving us an example. His wonderful works were all for the good of others. Strengthened with the memory of the Voice from heaven, Jesus rested in His Father's love.

Jesus met Satan with Scripture. "It is written," He said. The weapon of His warfare was the Word of God. Satan demanded a miracle from Christ. But a firm reliance on a "Thus says the Lord" is greater than all miracles. It was a sign that could not be disputed. As long as Christ held to this position, the tempter could gain no advantage.

In the time of Christ's greatest weakness, Satan attacked Him with the fiercest temptations. This is how Satan has taken advantage of humanity's weakness. See Numbers 20:1–13; 1 Kings 19:1–14. When we are perplexed or afflicted by poverty or distress, Satan is there to tempt, to attack our weak points of character, to shake our confidence in God. Often the tempter comes as he came to Christ, pointing out our weakness to us. He hopes to discourage us and break our hold on God. But if we would reply to him as Jesus did, we would escape many a defeat.

Christ said to the tempter, "Man shall not live by bread alone, but by every word that proceeds from the mouth of God." In the wilderness more than fourteen hundred years before, God sent His people a constant supply of manna from heaven. This was to teach them that while they trusted in God and walked in His ways, He would not forsake them. By the word of God help had been given to the Hebrews, and by the same word it had been given to Jesus. He awaited God's time to bring relief. He would not obtain food by following Satan's suggestions. It is better to endure whatever may happen than to depart in any way from God's will.

Often the follower of Christ is brought to the point where it appears that obedience to some plain requirement of God will cut off his means of support. Satan would make him believe that he must sacrifice his honest convictions. But the only thing we can rely on is the Word of God. See Matthew 6:33. When we learn the power of His Word, we will not follow Satan's suggestions in order to get food or save our lives. We will obey God's command and trust His promise.

In the last great conflict with Satan, those who are loyal to God will see every earthly support cut off. Because they refuse to break His law, they will be forbidden to buy or sell. See Revelation 13:11–17. But God has promised the obedient one, "He will dwell on high; . . . bread will be given him, His water will be sure." Isaiah 33:16. When the earth will be wasted with famine, he will be fed. See Psalm 37:19

## Intemperance Corrupts Morals

In all ages, temptations appealing to the physical nature have been most successful in corrupting mankind. Through intemperance, Satan works to destroy the mental and moral powers. Thus it becomes impossible for people to appreciate things of eternal worth. Through sensual indulgence, Satan seeks to blot from the soul every trace of likeness to God.

Christ declares that before His second coming, the condition of the world will be like it was in the days before the Flood, and like it was in Sodom and Gomorrah. We should understand clearly the lesson of the Savior's fast. We can only estimate the evil of unrestrained indulgence when we see the inexpressible anguish Christ endured. Our only hope of eternal life is through bringing our appetites and passions into subjection to the will of God.

In our own strength, it is impossible to deny the urges of our fallen nature. But by passing over the ground we must travel, our Lord has prepared the way for us to overcome. He would not have us be intimidated and discouraged. "Be of good cheer," He says, "I have overcome the world." John 16:33.

Anyone who is struggling against the power of appetite should look to the Savior in the wilderness of temptation. See Him in His agony on the cross, as He exclaimed, "I thirst." His victory is ours.

"The ruler of this world is coming," said Jesus, "and he has nothing in Me." John 14:30. Nothing in Him responded to Satan's deceptive reasoning. He did not consent to sin. Not even by a thought did He yield to temptation. It may be this way with us as well. Christ's humanity was united with divinity; He was fitted for the conflict by the indwelling of the Holy Spirit. And He came to make us partakers of the divine nature. God reaches for the hand of faith in us to direct it to grasp firmly onto the divinity of Christ, so that we may reach perfection of character.

Christ has shown us how to accomplish this. By what means did Christ overcome Satan? By the Word of God. "It is written," He said. And every promise in God's Word is ours. See 2 Peter 1:4. When temptation strikes, look to the power of the Word. All its strength is yours. See Psalms 119:11; 17:4.

# The Victory*

Then the devil took Him up into the holy city, set Him on the pinnacle of the temple, and said to Him, 'If You are the Son of God, throw Yourself down. For it is written: "He shall give His angels charge concerning you," and, "In their hands they shall bear you up, lest you dash your foot against a stone." ' "

Satan still appeared as an angel of light, and he made it evident that he was acquainted with the Scriptures. Jesus had used the Word to sustain His faith, and the tempter now used it to make his deception seem acceptable. Satan urged the Savior to give still another evidence of His faith.

But again he prefaced the temptation with the hint of distrust: "If You are the Son of God." Christ was tempted to answer the "if," but He refused to do anything that would involve the slightest acceptance of the doubt.

The tempter thought to take advantage of Christ's humanity and urge Him to go beyond what God allowed. But while Satan can invite, he cannot compel to sin. He said, "Cast Yourself down," knowing that he could not cast Him down. Nor could Satan force Je-

sus to cast Himself down. Unless Christ consented to temptation, He could not be overcome.

The tempter can never force us to do evil. The will must consent, faith must let go its hold on Christ, before Satan can exercise his power on us. But every sinful desire we cherish is an open door that he can enter to tempt and destroy us. And every failure on our part gives him opportunity to throw contempt on Christ.

When Satan quoted the promise, "He shall give His angels charge concerning you," he omitted the words, "to keep you in all your ways," that is, in all the ways of God's choosing. Jesus refused to go outside the path of obedience. He would not force God to come to His rescue and so fail to give us an example of trust and submission.

Jesus declared to Satan, "It is written again, 'You shall not tempt the Lord your God.' " God had already testified that Jesus was His Son. To ask for proof now would be putting God's word to the test—tempting Him. We should not present our requests to God to *prove* whether He will fulfill His word, but *because* He

---

* This chapter is based on Matthew 4:5–11; Mark 1:12, 13; Luke 4:5–13.

will fulfill it; not to prove that He loves us, but because He loves us. See Hebrews 11:6. Presumption is Satan's counterfeit of faith. Faith claims God's promises and brings forth fruit in obedience. Presumption also claims the promises, but it uses them to excuse transgression. Faith would have led our first parents to trust the love of God and obey His commands. Presumption led them to disobey His law, believing that His great love would save them from the results of their sin. It is not faith that claims the favor of Heaven without complying with the conditions on which God grants His mercy.

### Venturing on Satan's Ground

If Satan can cause us to place ourselves unnecessarily in the way of temptation, he knows that victory is his. God will preserve everyone who walks in the path of obedience. But to leave that path is to step onto Satan's ground. The Savior has instructed us, "Watch and pray, lest you enter into temptation." Mark 14:38.

Often when we are placed in a difficult situation, we doubt that the Spirit of God has led us. But it was the Spirit's leading that brought Jesus into the wilderness. When God brings us into trials, He has a purpose to accomplish for our good. Jesus did not presume on God's promises by deliberately choosing to go into temptation. Neither did He give up to feelings of despair when temptation came upon Him. Nor should we. See 1 Corinthians 10:13; Psalm 50:14, 15.

Jesus was the Victor in the second temptation, and now Satan showed himself in his true character—as a mighty angel, though fallen. He proclaimed himself the leader of rebellion and the god of this world. Placing Jesus on a high mountain, he caused the kingdoms of the world to pass in panoramic view before Him. The sunlight lay on templed cities, marble palaces, fertile fields, and fruit-laden vineyards. The traces of evil were hidden. The eyes of Jesus gazed on a scene of incredible beauty and prosperity. Then He heard the tempter's voice: "All these things I will give You." "If You will worship before me, all will be Yours."

Ahead of Christ lay a life of sorrow, hardship, and conflict, and a shameful death. Christ could deliver Himself from the dreadful future by acknowledging Satan's supremacy. But to do this would be to yield the victory in the great controversy. If Satan succeeded now, it would be the triumph of rebellion.

### Christ Could Not Be Bought

When the tempter offered Christ the kingdom and glory of the world, he was proposing that Christ would rule subject to Satan. This was the same rulership on which the Jews had set their hopes. They desired the kingdom of this world. But Christ declared to the tempter, "Get behind Me, Satan! For it is written, 'You shall worship the Lord your God, and Him only you shall serve.' " Christ would not be bought. He had come to establish a kingdom of righteousness, and He would not abandon His plan.

Satan approaches people with the same temptation, and here he has better success than with Christ. He offers them the kingdom of this world on condition that they will sacrifice integrity, disregard conscience, indulge selfishness, and acknowledge his supremacy. Satan says, "Whatever may be true regarding eternal life, to make a success in this world, you must serve me. I can give you riches, pleasures, honor, and happiness. Do not be carried away with notions of honesty or self-sacrifice."

So most people agree to live for self, and Satan is satisfied. But he offers what is not his to give and what is soon to be taken away from him. In return, he tricks them out of their claim to the inheritance of the children of God.

### Satan Remains a Defeated Enemy

When Jesus dismissed him with such authority, Satan had proof that He was the Son of God. Divinity flashed through suffering humanity. Twisting with humiliation and rage, Satan was forced to withdraw from the presence of the world's Redeemer. Christ's victory was as complete as the failure of Adam had been.

So we may resist temptation and force Satan to leave us. Jesus gained the victory through submission and faith in God, and by the apostle He says to us, "Therefore submit to God. Resist the devil and he will flee from you. Draw near to God and He will draw near to you." James 4:7, 8. "The name of the Lord is a strong tower; the righteous run to it and are safe." Proverbs 18:10. Satan trembles before the weakest person who finds refuge in that mighty name.

After the enemy had left, Jesus fell exhausted, with the pale look of death on His face. Angels had watched their loved Commander as He had endured the test, greater than we will ever be called to endure. They now ministered to the Son of God as He lay like one dying. They strengthened Him with food and comforted Him with the assurance that all heaven triumphed in His victory. Warming to life again, His great heart went out in sympathy for mankind, and He went on His way to complete the work He had begun. He would not rest until the enemy was completely defeated and our fallen race redeemed.

We can never realize the cost of redemption until the redeemed stand with the Redeemer before the throne of God. Then, as the glories of the eternal home burst on our delighted senses, we will remember that Jesus left all this for us; that for us He took the risk of failure and eternal loss.

"Worthy is the Lamb who was slain
To receive power and riches and
    wisdom,
And strength and honor and glory and
    blessing!"

Revelation 5:12

# "We Have Found the Messiah"*

John the Baptist was now preaching at Bethabara, beyond Jordan, where people daily crowded the banks of the Jordan. John's preaching had taken a deep hold on the nation. He had not recognized the authority of the Sanhedrin by seeking their approval, yet interest in his work seemed to increase continually.

The Sanhedrin was made up of priests, rulers, and teachers. In the days of Jewish independence, the Sanhedrin was the supreme court of the nation. Though now reduced in power by the Roman governors, it still exercised a strong influence in civil as well as religious matters. The Sanhedrin could no longer afford to put off an investigation of John's work. Some recalled the angel's revelation to Zacharias in the temple that had pointed to his child as the Messiah's herald. The excitement concerning John's ministry now reminded the leaders of these things.

It had been a long time since Israel had had a prophet. John's demand for confession of sin seemed new and startling. Many leaders would not go to hear John for fear that they might be led to reveal the secrets of their lives. Yet his preaching was a direct announcement of the Messiah.

It was well known that the seventy weeks of Daniel's prophecy, covering the Messiah's arrival, were nearly ended, and all were eager to share in the national glory they expected would follow. The popular enthusiasm was so great that the Sanhedrin would soon be forced either to approve or to reject John's work. Already it was becoming a serious question how to maintain their power over the people. In hope of coming to some conclusion, they sent a delegation of priests and Levites to the Jordan to confer with the new teacher.

A large crowd was listening to John's words when the delegates approached. The haughty rabbis came with an air of authority designed to impress the people and gain the esteem of the prophet. With respect, almost fear, the crowd opened to let them pass. The great men, in their rich robes, in the pride of rank and power, stood before the prophet of the wilderness.

"Who are you?" they demanded.

Knowing what was in their thoughts, John answered, "I am not the Christ."

---

* This chapter is based on John 1:19–51.

"What then? Are you Elijah?"

"I am not."

"Are you the Prophet?"

"No."

"Who are you, that we may give an answer to those who sent us? What do you say about yourself?"

"I am 'the voice of one crying in the wilderness: " 'Make straight the way of the Lord,' " ' as the prophet Isaiah said."

Anciently, when a king traveled through his realm, men were sent ahead to level the steep places and fill up the hollows so that the king could travel safely. The prophet Isaiah used this custom to illustrate the work of the gospel. "Every valley shall be exalted, and every mountain and hill shall be made low." Isaiah 40:4. When the Spirit of God touches the heart, it brings human pride low. The person sees that worldly pleasure, position, and power are worthless. Then only humility and self-sacrificing love are exalted as having any value. This is the work of the gospel, of which John's message was a part.

The rabbis continued their questioning: "Why then do you baptize if you are not the Christ, nor Elijah, nor the Prophet?" The words "the Prophet" referred to Moses. When the Baptist began his ministry, many thought he might be Moses risen from the dead.

Many people also believed that before the Messiah came, Elijah would personally appear. John denied this expectation, but later Jesus said, referring to John, "And if you are willing to receive it, he is Elijah who is to come." Matthew 11:14. John came in the spirit and power of Elijah, to do a work like Elijah did. But the Jews did not receive his message. To them he was not Elijah.

## Many Today Fail to "See" Christ

Many of those gathered at the Jordan had been present at Jesus' baptism, but only a few among them were aware of the sign then given. During the preceding months of John's ministry, many had refused to obey the call to repentance. So when Heaven bore testimony to Jesus at His baptism, they did not perceive it. Eyes that had never turned in faith to Him did not behold the revelation of the glory of God. Ears that had never listened to His voice did not hear the words of witness. It is still this way now. Often Christ and ministering angels make their presence felt in the assemblies of the people, yet many do not know it. They detect nothing unusual. But to some the Savior's presence is revealed. They are comforted, encouraged, and blessed.

The deputies from Jerusalem had demanded of John, "Why then do you baptize?" and they were waiting for his answer. Suddenly, as his glance swept over the crowd, his face lighted up, and his whole being was stirred with deep emotion. With outstretched hands he cried, "I baptize with water, but there stands One among you whom you do not know. It is He who, coming after me, is preferred before me, whose sandal strap I am not worthy to loose."

The message was distinct and unmistakable, to be carried back to the Sanhedrin. The Messiah was among them! In amazement, priests and rulers gazed around them, but among the crowd they could not distinguish the One of whom John had spoken.

At the baptism of Jesus, John's mind was directed to the words of Isaiah, "He was led as a lamb to the slaughter." Isaiah 53:7. During the weeks that followed, John studied the prophecies and the sacrificial service with new interest. He saw that Christ's coming had a deeper significance than priests or people had recognized. When he saw Jesus among the crowd after He returned from the desert, he waited almost impatiently to hear the Savior declare His mission; but He spoke no word and gave no sign. Jesus did not respond to the Baptist's announcement of Him. He mingled with the disciples of John, taking no measures to call attention to Himself.

The next day John saw Jesus coming toward him. With the light of the glory of God resting on him, the prophet stretched out his hands, declaring, "Behold! The Lamb of God who takes away the sin of the world! This is He of whom I said, 'After me comes a Man who is preferred before me.' . . . I saw the Spirit descending from heaven like a dove, and He remained upon Him. . . . He who sent me to baptize with water said to me, . . . 'This is He who baptizes with the Holy Spirit.' And I have seen and testified that this is the Son of God."

### Christ's Appearance Was Ordinary

Was this the Christ? With awe and wonder the people looked on the One John had just declared to be the Son of God. John's words had deeply moved them. He had spoken in the name of God. They had listened to him day after day as he condemned their sins, and the conviction strengthened that God had sent him. But who was this One greater than John? Nothing in His dress and bearing represented any high rank. Apparently He was a simple person, dressed in the humble garments of the poor.

Some in the crowd had been at Christ's baptism and had heard the voice of God. But the Savior's appearance had changed greatly. At His baptism they had seen His face transformed in the light of heaven. Now He looked worn and gaunt. Only John had recognized Him.

But the people saw a face where divine compassion blended with conscious power. Every glance, every feature of His face, was marked with humility and expressive of matchless love. He impressed the onlookers with a sense of power that was hidden, yet could not be completely concealed. Was this the One for whom Israel had waited so long?

Jesus came in poverty and humiliation so that He could be our Example as well as our Redeemer. If He had appeared with kingly pomp, how could He have taught humility? Where would the lowly in life have found hope if Jesus had come to live as a king among us?

But to the crowd, it seemed impossible to find a connection between the One John had indicated and their high expectations. Many were disappointed and perplexed.

The words they so much wanted to hear—that Jesus would now restore the kingdom to Israel—He had not spoken. The priests and rabbis were ready to receive such a king. But One who intended to establish a kingdom of righteousness in their hearts, they would not accept.

## John Directs His Followers to Jesus

On the following day, while two disciples were near, John again saw Jesus. Again the face of the prophet lighted up as he called out, "Behold the Lamb of God!" The disciples did not fully understand. What did the name mean that John had given Him—"the Lamb of God"?

Leaving John, they went looking for Jesus. One of them was Andrew, the brother of Simon; the other was John the evangelist. These were Christ's first disciples. They followed Jesus—anxious to speak with Him, yet awed and silent, lost in the thought, *Is this the Messiah?*

Jesus knew that the two were following Him. They were the first fruits of His ministry, and joy came into the heart of the divine Teacher as these souls responded to His grace. Yet when He turned to them, He asked only, "What do you seek?"

They exclaimed, "Rabbi [Teacher], . . . where are You staying?" In a brief interview by the roadside, they could not receive what they longed for. They wanted to be alone with Jesus and hear His words.

"He said to them, 'Come and see.' They came and saw where He was staying, and remained with Him that day."

If John and Andrew had possessed the unbelieving spirit of the priests and rulers, they would not have been learners but critics, to judge His words.

But they had responded to the Holy Spirit's call in the preaching of John the Baptist, and now they recognized the heavenly Teacher. The words of Jesus were full of freshness and beauty to them. A divine illumination was shining on the Old Testament Scriptures. Truth stood out in new light.

The disciple John was a man of earnest and deep affection, eager yet thoughtful. He had begun to discern "the glory as of the only begotten of the Father, full of grace and truth." John 1:14.

Andrew set out to share the joy that filled his heart. Going in search of his brother Simon, he announced, "We have found the Messiah." Simon also had heard the preaching of John the Baptist, and he hurried to the Savior. Christ's eye read his character and life history. His impulsive nature, his loving, sympathetic heart, his ambition and self-confidence, his fall, his repentance, his labors, and his martyr death—the Savior read it all. He said, " 'You are Simon the son of Jonah. You shall be called Cephas' (which is translated, A Stone)."

"The following day Jesus . . . found Philip and said to him, 'Follow Me.' " Philip obeyed the command, and he also became a worker for Christ.

Philip called Nathanael, who had been among the crowd when the Baptist pointed to Jesus as the Lamb of God. As Nathanael looked at Jesus, he was disappointed. Could this man, carrying the marks of toil and poverty, be the Messiah? Yet the message of John had brought conviction to Nathanael's heart.

## Nathanael's Secret Prayers Are Heard

When Philip called him, Nathanael had gone alone to a quiet grove to meditate on the prophecies concerning the Messiah. He prayed that if the One John had announced was the Deliverer, God would help him to know this. The Holy Spirit gave him assurance that God had come to His people. Philip knew that his friend was searching the prophecies, and while Nathanael was praying under a fig tree, Philip discovered his refuge. They had often prayed together in this secluded spot, hidden by the foliage.

Philip's message, "We have found Him of whom Moses in the law, and also the prophets, wrote," seemed to Nathanael to be a direct answer to his prayer. But Philip added, "Jesus of Nazareth, the son of Joseph." Prejudice arose in Nathanael's heart, and he exclaimed, "Can anything good come out of Nazareth?"

Philip said, "Come and see." Jesus saw Nathanael coming to Him, and said of him, "Behold, an Israelite indeed, in whom is no guile!" In surprise, Nathanael exclaimed, "How do You know me?" Jesus answered, "Before Philip called you, when you were under the fig tree, I saw you."

It was enough. The divine Spirit that had brought assurance to Nathanael in his solitary prayer under the fig tree spoke to him in the words of Jesus. Nathanael had come to Christ with an honest desire for truth, and now his desire was met. He said, "Rabbi, You are the Son of God! You are the King of Israel!"

If Nathanael had trusted to the rabbis for guidance, he would never have found Jesus. It was by seeing and judging for himself that he became a disciple. So today, many trust to human authority. Like Nathanael, we need to study God's Word for ourselves and pray for the Holy Spirit's enlightenment. He who saw Nathanael under the fig tree will see us in the secret place of prayer. Angels are near to those who humbly seek for divine guidance.

The foundation of the Christian church began with the calling of John, Andrew, Simon, Philip, and Nathanael. John directed two of his disciples to Christ. Then one of these, Andrew, found his brother. Philip was then called, and he went in search of Nathanael. These examples teach the importance of making direct appeals to our family, friends, and neighbors. There are those who have never made a personal effort to bring even one soul to the Savior.

Many have gone down to ruin who might have been saved if their neighbors, ordinary men and women, had put forth personal effort for them. In the family, the neighborhood, the town where we live, there is work for us to do. As soon as someone is converted, a desire is born within him to tell others what a precious Friend he has found in Jesus.

## The Strongest Argument

Philip did not ask Nathanael to accept someone else's testimony, but to see Christ for himself. One of the most effective ways of winning souls to Jesus is by showing His character in our daily life. People may reject our logic or resist our appeals, but a life of love, totally without selfish motives, is an argument they cannot refute.

The Word of God, spoken by someone who has personally been sanctified through it, has a life-giving power that attracts those who hear it. When we have received the truth and loved it, we will make known what we ourselves have heard, seen, and experienced of the Word of Life. Testimony like this rings true to receptive hearts and leads to sanctification of character.

And those who try to give light to others will themselves be blessed. "He who waters will also be watered himself." Proverbs 11:25. In order to enter into Christ's joy—the joy of seeing people redeemed by His sacrifice—we must take part in His labors to redeem them.

Nathanael's first expression of faith was like music to the ears of Jesus. "Because I said to you, 'I saw you under the fig tree,' do you believe? You will see greater things than these." The Savior looked forward with joy to His work of preaching good news to the meek, binding up the brokenhearted, and proclaiming liberty to the captives of Satan. He added, "Most assuredly, I say to you, hereafter you shall see heaven open, and the angels of God ascending and descending upon the Son of Man."

Here Christ virtually says, "On the bank of the Jordan the heavens were opened, and the Spirit descended. But if you believe on Me, your faith will increase and grow stronger. You will see that the heavens are opened, never to be closed. I have opened them to you." The angels of God are ascending, carrying the prayers of the needy and distressed to the Father above, and descending, bringing hope, courage, and life to the children of earth.

Angels are constantly going from earth to heaven and from heaven to earth. Through Christ, by the ministry of His heavenly messengers, every blessing comes from God to us. In taking humanity on Himself, our Savior unites His interests with those of the fallen sons and daughters of Adam, while through His divinity He grasps the throne of God.

# Jesus Attends a Wedding*

At a household gathering in a little Galilean village, Jesus used His power to add joy to a wedding feast. In this way, He showed His sympathy with us and His desire to minister to our happiness. In the wilderness, He Himself had drunk the cup of sorrow, but He came from there to give us the cup of blessing.

There was to be a marriage at Cana. The bride and groom were relatives of Joseph and Mary, and Jesus and His disciples were invited.

Mary, His mother, had heard of the sign God gave at the Jordan, at His baptism. The news had brought to her mind once again the scenes that for many years she had hidden in her heart. Mary was deeply stirred by the mission of John the Baptist. Now his connection with Jesus kindled her hopes anew. She had treasured every evidence that Jesus was the Messiah, yet doubts and disappointments also came to her. She longed for the time when His glory would be revealed.

Death had separated Mary from Joseph, who had shared her knowledge of the mystery of Jesus' birth. Now there was no one with whom she could talk about her hopes and fears.

She thought deeply about the words of Simeon, "A sword will pierce through your own soul also." Luke 2:35. With an anxious heart, she waited for Jesus' return.

At the marriage feast, she met Him, and He was the same tender, dutiful Son. Yet He was not the same. His face showed traces of His conflict in the wilderness, and a new expression of dignity and power gave evidence of His heavenly mission. With Him was a group of young men who called Him Master. These companions told Mary what they had seen and heard at the baptism and elsewhere.

As the guests assembled, there was an atmosphere of suppressed excitement. As Mary saw the many glances directed toward Jesus, she longed to have Him prove that He was the Honored of God.

It was the custom for marriage festivities to continue several days. On this occasion, before the feast ended, the supply of wine ran out. As a relative, Mary had assisted in the feast, and she now said to Jesus, "They have no wine." These words were a suggestion that He could supply their need. But Jesus answered, "Woman, what

* This chapter is based on John 2:1–11.

does your concern have to do with Me? My hour has not yet come."

This form of addressing her expressed no coldness or discourtesy. In Oriental custom, it was used toward persons to whom one desired to show respect. Christ Himself had given the commandment, "Honor your father and your mother." Exodus 20:12. Both at the marriage feast and on the cross in His last act of tenderness toward His mother, the love He expressed in His tone, look, and manner interpreted His words.

At His visit to the temple when He was a boy, Christ had said to Mary, "Did you not know that I must be about My Father's business?" Luke 2:49. Now He repeated the lesson. There was danger that Mary would think that her relationship to Jesus gave her the right, in some degree, to direct Him in His mission. For thirty years He had been a loving, obedient Son, but now He must go about His Father's work. As Savior of the world, no earthly ties must hold Him from His mission. This lesson is also for us. No earthly attraction, no ties of human relationship, should turn our feet from the path in which God calls us to walk.

Mary could find salvation only through the Lamb of God. Her connection with Jesus did not give her a spiritual relationship to Him that was different from that of any other human being. The Savior's words make clear the distinction between His relation to her as the Son of man and as the Son of God. The family ties between them in no way placed her on an equality with Him.

"My hour has not yet come." As Christ walked among us, He was guided step by step by the Father's will. In saying to Mary that His hour had not yet come, He was replying to her unspoken thought—the expectation she cherished that He would reveal Himself as the Messiah and take the throne of Israel. But the time had not come. Jesus had accepted the normal condition of humanity not as a King but as "a Man of sorrows and acquainted with grief." Isaiah 53:3.

## Mary's Faith Is Rewarded

Though Mary did not have a right concept of Christ's mission, she trusted Him completely. To this faith He responded. Jesus performed His first miracle to honor her trust and to strengthen the faith of His disciples. From the prophecies the disciples understood without a doubt that Jesus was the Messiah, but they were bitterly disappointed by the unbelief, deep-seated prejudice, and hatred that the priests and rabbis displayed toward Jesus. The Savior's early miracles strengthened the disciples to stand against opposition.

Mary said to those serving at the tables, "Whatever He says to you, do it."

Beside the doorway stood six large stone water jars. Jesus told the servants to fill these with water. Then He said, "Draw some out now, and take it to the master of the feast." Instead of water, the jars yielded wine.

When he tasted the wine the servants brought, the ruler of the feast found it superior to any he had ever before drunk. Turning to the bridegroom, he said, "Every man at the beginning sets out the good wine, and when the guests have well drunk, then that which is inferior; but you have kept the good wine until now"!

The gifts the world offers may please the eye and fascinate the senses, but they prove unsatisfying. The "wine" turns to bitterness, the good times to gloom. What began with songs and mirth ends in weariness and disgust. But the gifts of Jesus are always fresh and new. The feast that He provides never fails to give satisfaction and joy. There can be no short supply. If you abide in Him, a rich gift today ensures that you will receive a richer gift tomorrow.

The gift of Christ to the marriage feast was a symbol. Human hands brought the water to fill the jars, but the word of Christ alone could give it life-giving power. The word of Christ provided ample supply for the feast. His grace is similarly abundant to blot out iniquity and to renew and sustain the spiritual life. The wine Christ provided for the feast, and which He gave the disciples as a symbol of His own blood, was the pure juice of the grape. Isaiah refers to this when he speaks of the new wine "in the cluster," and says, "Do not destroy it, for a blessing is in it." Isaiah 65:8.

In the Old Testament, Christ gave the warning, "Wine is a mocker, intoxicating drink arouses brawling, and whoever is led astray by it is not wise." Proverbs 20:1. He Himself provided no such beverage. Satan tempts men and women to indulge in things that will cloud their reason and numb their spiritual perceptions, but Christ teaches us to bring the lower nature into subjection. It was Christ who directed that John the Baptist should drink neither wine nor strong drink. He commanded similar abstinence for Samson's mother. And He pronounced a curse on anyone who would put the bottle to his neighbor's lips. See Habakkuk 2:15. Christ did not contradict His own teaching. The unfermented wine that He provided for the wedding guests was a wholesome and refreshing drink.

As the guests commented about the wine, some asked questions that drew from the servants an account of the miracle. When finally the assembled guests looked for Jesus, He had quietly slipped away.

Attention now turned to the disciples, giving them the opportunity to acknowledge their faith in Jesus. They told what they had seen and heard at the Jordan. News of the miracle spread and was carried to Jerusalem. With new interest the priests and elders searched the prophecies pointing to Christ's coming.

## Christ Broke Down Class Barriers

Jesus began His work by coming into close sympathy with humanity. While He showed the greatest reverence for the law of God, He rebuked the pretended piety of the Pharisees and tried to free the people from the senseless rules that bound them. He was attempting to break down the barriers that separated the different classes of society, so that He could bring them all together as children of one family.

Jesus denounced self-indulgence, yet He was social in His nature. He accepted the hospitality of all classes, visiting the homes of rich and poor, educated and ignorant, trying to raise their thoughts from ordinary life to things that are eternal. No shadow of foolish merriment marred His conduct, yet He found pleasure in scenes of innocent happiness. The Son of man did not find the joy of a Jewish marriage displeasing. By attending, Jesus honored marriage as a divine institution.

In both the Old and New Testaments, marriage represents the tender and sacred union that exists between Christ and His people. To the mind of Jesus, the wedding's gladness pointed to the rejoicing on that day when He will bring home His bride, the redeemed, to the Father's house. "As the bridegroom rejoices over the bride, so shall your God rejoice over you." "He will rejoice over you with gladness, . . . He will rejoice over you with singing. Isaiah 62:5; Zephaniah 3:17. John the apostle wrote, "I heard, as it were, the voice of a great multitude, . . . saying, . . . 'Let us be glad and rejoice and give Him glory, for the marriage of the Lamb has come, and His wife has made herself ready.' " Revelation 19:6, 7.

Jesus reached the hearts of the people by going among them as Someone who desired their good. He met them in the streets, in private houses, on boats, in synagogues, by the shores of the lake, and at the marriage feast. He showed interest in their everyday lives. His strong personal sympathy helped to win hearts. He prepared for His work among people in their daily life by praying alone in the mountains. From these sessions, He went out to relieve the sick and to break the chains from Satan's captives.

Jesus trained His disciples by personal contact and association. Sometimes sitting on the mountainside, sometimes beside the sea, or walking with them along the roads, He taught them the mysteries of God's kingdom. He did not sermonize. He did not command His disciples to do this or that, but said, "Follow Me." On His journeys, He took them with Him, so that they could see how He taught the people.

All who preach Christ's Word should follow His example. We should not take ourselves out of society, but meet all classes of people where they are. It is not only pulpit preaching that touches people's hearts with divine truth. Another place to work, every bit as promising, is in the home of the lowly, in the mansion of the great, and in gatherings for innocent social enjoyment.

We will not mingle with the world to unite with them in foolishness. We should never give approval to sin by our words or our deeds, our silence or our presence. Wherever we go, we are to carry Jesus with us. We should all become witnesses for Jesus. We should put social power, sanctified by the grace of Christ, to good use in winning souls. Let the world see that we want others to share our blessings and privileges, that religion does not make us unsympathetic or demanding. Everyone who has found Christ should minister as He did for the benefit of others.

We should never give the world the false impression that Christians are a gloomy, unhappy people. Christ's followers are not statues, but living men and women who are partakers of the divine nature. The light that shines on them they reflect on others in works that glow with the love of Christ.

# Christ Confronts Corruption in the Temple[*]

Now the Passover of the Jews was at hand, and Jesus went up to Jerusalem." Jesus had not yet announced His mission publicly, and He mingled unnoticed with the crowd. On these occasions, the Messiah's coming was often the theme of conversation. Jesus knew that their hope of national greatness would be disappointed, for it was based on a misinterpretation of Scripture. With deep earnestness, He explained the prophecies and tried to stir up the people to study God's Word more closely.

At Jerusalem during the Passover week, large numbers of people assembled from all parts of Palestine, and even from distant lands. The temple courts were filled with a great variety of people. Many were unable to bring with them the sacrifices they were to offer as representing the one great Sacrifice. For their convenience, animals were bought and sold in the outer court.

Every Jew was required to pay "a ransom for himself" each year, and the money collected helped to support the temple. See Exodus 30:12–16. Besides this, people brought large sums as freewill offerings to be deposited in the temple treasury. And all foreign coins had to be changed for a coin called the temple shekel, which was accepted for the service of the sanctuary. The money-changing gave opportunity for fraud and extortion. It had grown into a disgraceful business, which was a source of income to the priests.

The worshipers had been taught to believe that if they did not offer sacrifices, the blessing of God would not rest on their children or their lands. The dealers demanded exorbitant prices for the animals sold, and they shared their profits with the priests and rulers, who enriched themselves this way at the expense of the people.

## Financial Corruption at the Heart of God's Work

Sharp bargaining, the lowing of cattle, the bleating of sheep, the cooing of doves, mingled with the chinking of coin and angry disputing. The confusion was so great that the uproar drowned out the words directed to the Most High. The Jews rejoiced over their temple and regarded a word spoken in criticism of it as blasphemy, but

---

[*] *This chapter is based on John 2:12–22.*

the love of money had overruled their concerns for its honor. They had wandered far from the purpose of the service that God Himself had established. Wherever God reveals His presence, the place is holy. See Exodus 19:12, 13. God's temple grounds should have been regarded as sacred. But in their hurry to get rich, all this was forgotten.

The priests and rulers should have corrected the abuses of the temple court and given the people an example of integrity. Instead of watching out for their own profit, they should have been ready to help those who were not able to buy the required sacrifices. But greed had hardened their hearts.

Those who were in poverty and distress—the blind, the lame, the deaf—came to this feast. Some were brought on beds. Many were too poor to buy the humblest offering for the Lord or even to buy food to satisfy their own hunger. The statements of the priests greatly distressed them. The priests boasted of their holiness, but they had no sympathy or compassion. The poor, the sick, the dying, stirred no pity in their hearts.

As Jesus came into the temple, He saw the unfair transactions. He saw the distress of the poor, who thought that without shedding of blood there would be no forgiveness for their sins. He saw the sacred, outer court of His temple converted into a place of unholy business.

Something had to be done. The worshipers offered sacrifices without understanding that they represented the only perfect Sacrifice. And among them, unrecognized and unhonored, stood the One that all their service symbolized. He saw that the offerings were perverted and misunderstood. No link connected the priests and rulers to God. Christ's work was to establish an entirely different worship.

With a searching glance, Christ took in the scene before Him. With prophetic eye, He looked into future years, centuries, and ages. He saw how priests and rulers would forbid the gospel to be preached to the poor, how the love of God would be concealed from sinners, and people would put His grace up for sale. His face showed indignation, authority, and power. The people's attention was drawn to Him. The eyes of those engaged in their unholy business were riveted on His face. They felt that this Man read their inmost thoughts and discovered their hidden motives. Some tried to hide their faces.

The sound of selling and bargaining stopped. The silence became painful. It was as if the assembly were arraigned before God's court of justice. Looking at Christ, they saw divinity flash through humanity. The Majesty of heaven stood as the Judge will stand at the last day—not encircled with the glory that He will have then, but with the same power to read the soul. His eye took in every individual. His form seemed to rise above them in commanding dignity, and a divine light illuminated His countenance. His clear, ringing voice—the same that had proclaimed the law on Mount Sinai—echoed through the temple: "Take these things away! Do not make My Father's house a house of merchandise!"

Raising the whip of cords that He had gathered up on entering the temple grounds, Jesus ordered the bargainers to leave the temple. With a zeal and severity He had never before shown, He overthrew the tables of the money-changers. The coins fell, ringing sharply on the marble pavement. No one questioned His authority. None dared stop to gather up their ill-gotten gain. Jesus did not strike them with the whip of cords, but in His hand that simple scourge seemed like a flaming sword. Officers of the temple, priests, brokers, and cattle traders, with their sheep and oxen, rushed from the place with the one thought of escaping from the condemnation of His presence.

### The Temple Cleansed by the Presence of the Lord

Panic swept over the crowd, who felt the commanding presence of His divinity. Even the disciples trembled, awestruck by Jesus' words and manner, so unlike His usual behavior. They remembered that it was written about Him, "Zeal for Your house has eaten Me up." Psalm 69:9. Soon the courts of the temple were free from unholy commerce. Deep silence and solemnity settled on the scene of confusion. The presence of the Lord had made sacred the temple constructed in His honor.

In cleansing the temple, Jesus announced His mission as the Messiah and began His work. The temple was designed to be an object lesson for Israel and for the world. God intended that every created being should be a temple for the Creator to live in. Darkened and defiled by sin, human hearts no longer revealed the glory of the Divine One. But by the incarnation of the Son of God, God dwells in humanity, and through saving grace the heart becomes His temple again.

God planned that the temple at Jerusalem should be a continual witness to the high destiny open to every person. But the Jews did not yield themselves as holy temples for the Divine Spirit. The courts of the temple, filled with unholy trade, represented all too accurately the temple of the heart, defiled by sensual passion and unholy thoughts. In cleansing the temple, Jesus announced His mission to cleanse the heart from sin—the earthly desires, selfish lusts, and evil habits that corrupt the soul.

"The Lord, whom you seek,
Will suddenly come to His temple,
Even the Messenger of the covenant,
In whom you delight. . . .

"But who can endure the day of His
    coming?
And who can stand when He appears?
For He is like a refiner's fire. . . .
He will sit as a refiner and a purifier of
    silver;
He will purify the sons of Levi,
And purge them as gold and silver."
                    Malachi 3:1–3

"Do you not know that you are the temple of God and that the Spirit of God dwells in you? If anyone defiles the temple of God, God will destroy him. For the temple of God is holy, which temple you are." 1 Corinthians 3:16, 17.

No one by himself can cast out the evil agencies that have taken possession of the heart. Only Christ can cleanse the soul temple. But He will not force His way in. He says, "Behold, I stand at the door and knock. If anyone hears My voice and opens the door, I will come in to him." Revelation 3:20. His presence will cleanse and sanctify the soul so that it may be a holy temple to the Lord, "a dwelling place of God in the Spirit." Ephesians 2:22.

### A Preview of the Final Judgment

Overcome with terror, the priests and rulers had run from the temple court and from the searching look that read their hearts. In this scene, Christ saw a symbol of the dispersion of the whole Jewish nation for their wickedness and unrepentant rebellion.

Why did the priests run away? Why did they not stand their ground? The One who commanded them to go was a carpenter's son, a poor Galilean. Why did they not resist Him? Why did they leave their wrongly acquired profits and run at the command of One whose appearance was so humble?

Christ spoke with the authority of a king, and in His appearance and the tone of His voice, there was something that they had no power to resist. At His word of command, they realized their true position as hypocrites and robbers. When Divinity flashed through humanity, they felt as if they were standing before the throne of the eternal Judge, who had passed sentence on them for time and eternity. For a time, many believed Him to be the Messiah. The Holy Spirit flashed into their minds the words of the prophets concerning Christ. Would they yield to this conviction?

They would not repent. They knew they had been guilty of extortion. Because Christ knew their thoughts, they hated Him. His public rebuke was humiliating to their pride, and they were jealous of His growing influence with the people. They determined to challenge Him regarding the power by which He had driven them out.

Slowly and thoughtfully, but with hate in their hearts, they returned to the temple. What a change had taken place! When they ran, the poor remained behind, and these were now looking to Jesus, whose face expressed His love and sympathy.

The people pressed their way into Christ's presence with urgent appeals: "Master, bless me!" His ear heard every cry. All received attention. Everyone was healed of whatever disease he had.

As the priests and temple officials witnessed this great work, the sounds that fell on their ears were a revelation to them. The people were telling about the pain they had suffered, about disappointed hopes, painful days, and sleepless nights. When hope seemed dead, Christ had healed them. "The burden was so heavy," one said, "but I have found a Helper. He is the Christ of God, and I will devote my life to His service." Parents said to their children, "He has saved your life—lift up your voice and praise Him!" Hope and gladness filled the hearts of children and youth, fathers and mothers, friends and spectators. They were restored in both soul and body, and they returned home proclaiming the love of Jesus.

At Jesus' crucifixion, those who had been healed did not join in shouting, "Crucify Him, crucify Him." Their sympathies were with Jesus, for they had felt His wonderful power. They knew that He was their Savior. They listened to the apostles, and they became agents of God's mercy and instruments of His salvation.

The crowd that had run from the temple court slowly drifted back after a while, but their faces showed that they were uncertain and timid. They were convinced that Jesus fulfilled the prophecies concerning the Messiah. The sin of profaning the temple belonged mostly to the priests. Their decisions had turned the court into a marketplace. The people were comparatively innocent. But the priests and rulers considered Christ's mission as an upstart, and they questioned His right to interfere with what the authorities of the temple permitted. They were offended because He had interrupted their business, and they stifled the convictions of the Holy Spirit.

### The Beginning of the Final Rejection of Christ

The priests and rulers should have seen that Jesus was the Anointed of the Lord, for they held the sacred scrolls that described His mission. They knew that the cleansing of the temple showed more than human power. Much as they hated Jesus, they could not free themselves from the thought that He might be a prophet God had sent to restore the temple's sanctity. With a respect born of this fear, they went to Him and asked, "What sign do You show to us, since You do these things?"

Jesus had shown them a sign. In doing the work that the Messiah was to do, He had given convincing evidence of His character. Now He answered them by a parable, showing that He read their evil intent and saw where it would lead. "Destroy this temple, and in three days I will raise it up."

In these words, He referred not only to the destruction of the Jewish temple and worship, but to His own death—the destruction of the temple of His body. The Jews were already plotting to kill Him. As the priests and rulers returned to the temple, they had proposed to kill Jesus and so be rid of the troubler. Yet they took His words as applying only to the temple at Jerusalem, and they exclaimed indignantly, "It has taken forty-six years to build this temple, and will You raise it up in three days?" Now they felt that Jesus had justified their unbelief, and they were confirmed in rejecting Him.

Christ knew that His enemies would twist His words and turn them against Him. At His trial and on Calvary, they would fling these words at Him. But to explain them now would give His disciples a knowledge of His sufferings and bring on them sorrow that they were not yet able to bear. And an explanation would prematurely reveal to the Jews the result of their prejudice and unbelief. They had already entered on a path that they would steadily follow until He would be led as a lamb to the slaughter.

Christ knew that these words would be repeated. Spoken at the Passover, they would come to the ears of thousands who would then carry them to all parts of the world. After He had risen from the dead, their meaning would be plain. To many, they would be conclusive evidence of His divinity.

The Savior's words, "Destroy this temple, and in three days I will raise it up," had a deeper meaning than the hearers grasped. The temple services symbolized the sacrifice of the Son of God. The entire plan of sacrificial worship foreshadowed the Savior's death to redeem the world. The ritual system had no value apart from Him. When the Jews sealed their rejection of Christ by delivering Him to death, they rejected everything that gave significance to the temple and its services. Its sacredness had ended. It was doomed to destruction. From that day, sacrificial offerings were meaningless. In putting Christ to death, the Jews virtually destroyed their temple. When Christ was crucified, the inner veil of the temple was torn in two from top to bottom, signifying that the great final sacrifice had been made. The system of sacrificial offerings was forever at an end.

"In three days I will raise it up." From the opened tomb of Joseph, Jesus came out as a Conqueror. By His death and resurrection, He became the minister of the "true tabernacle which the Lord erected, and not man." Hebrews 8:2. Men had constructed the Jewish temple, but the sanctuary above was built by no human architect.

" ' "The Man whose name is the BRANCH! . . .
He shall build the temple of the Lord; . . .
He shall bear the glory,
And shall sit and rule on His throne;
So shall He be a priest on His throne." ' "

Zechariah 6:12, 13

The sacrificial service that had pointed to Christ came to an end, but the eyes of men and women were turned to the true sacrifice for the sins of the world. The earthly priesthood ceased, but we look to Jesus, the Minister of the new covenant. "The way into the holiest of all was not yet made manifest, while as the first tabernacle was yet standing. . . . But Christ being come an high priest of good things to come, by a greater and more perfect tabernacle, not made with hands, . . . by his own blood he entered in once into the holy place, having obtained eternal redemption for us." Hebrews 9:8–12, KJV.

"Therefore He is also able to save to the uttermost those who come to God through Him, since He ever lives to make intercession for them." Hebrews 7:25. Though the heavenly sanctuary and our great High Priest would be invisible to human sight, yet the disciples would experience no break in their fellowship and no reduction of power because of the Savior's absence. While Jesus ministers in the sanctuary above, by His Spirit He is still the Minister of the church on earth. His parting promise is fulfilled, "Lo, I am with you always, even to the end of the age." Matthew 28:20. His energizing presence is still with His church.

"We do not have a High Priest who cannot sympathize with our weaknesses, but was in all points tempted as we are, yet without sin. Let us therefore come boldly to the throne of grace, that we may obtain mercy and find grace to help in time of need." Hebrews 4:15, 16.

# Nicodemus Comes to Jesus at Night*

Nicodemus, a highly educated and honored member of the national council, had been stirred by the teaching of Jesus. Though rich and well-read, he had been strangely attracted by the humble Nazarene. The lessons from the Savior's lips had greatly impressed him, and he wanted to learn more.

Christ's use of His authority in cleansing the temple had ignited the hatred of the priests and rulers. They felt they should not tolerate such boldness from an obscure Galilean. But not all agreed about putting an end to His work. Some feared to oppose One whom the Spirit of God so evidently moved. They knew that the Jews were subjects of a heathen nation because they had stubbornly rejected God's reproofs. They feared that in plotting against Jesus the priests and rulers were following in the steps of their ancestors and would bring fresh disasters on the nation. Nicodemus shared these feelings. In the Sanhedrin, Nicodemus advised caution and moderation. He urged that if Jesus really carried authority from God, it would be dangerous to reject His warnings. The priests did not dare to ignore this counsel.

Nicodemus had anxiously studied the prophecies relating to the Messiah. The more he searched, the stronger was his conviction that Jesus was the One who was to come. He had been distressed by how the priests had profaned the temple. He witnessed Jesus driving out the buyers and the sellers. He saw the Savior healing the sick, and he saw their looks of joy and heard their words of praise. He could not doubt that Jesus of Nazareth was the One sent from God.

He greatly wanted to talk with Jesus, but he was unwilling to go to Him openly. If the Sanhedrin heard about this visit, they would scorn and denounce him. He decided to try for a secret meeting. By special inquiry, he learned where the Savior went for the night on the Mount of Olives. He waited until the city was hushed in sleep, and then he went looking for Jesus.

In Christ's presence, Nicodemus felt strangely timid, and he tried to conceal this. "Rabbi, we know that You are a teacher come from God; for no one can do these signs that You do unless God is with him." He chose his words to express and to invite confidence, but they really expressed unbelief. He

* This chapter is based on John 3:1–17.

did not acknowledge Jesus to be the Messiah, but only a teacher sent from God.

Jesus gazed at the speaker, as if reading his very soul. He saw before Him someone who was seeking after truth. Wanting to deepen the conviction already in His listener's mind, He came directly to the point, saying kindly, "Very truly, I tell you, no one can see the kingdom of God without being born from above." John 3:3, NRSV.

Nicodemus had come to enter into a discussion, but Jesus laid open the foundation principles of truth. He said, "You don't need to have your curiosity satisfied, but to have a new heart. You must receive a new life from above before you can appreciate heavenly things. Until this change takes place, discussing My authority or My mission with Me will result in no saving good."

Nicodemus had heard John the Baptist's preaching about repentance. Yet the heart-searching message of the Baptist had not brought him to conviction of sin. He was a strict Pharisee and prided himself on his good works. People thought highly of him for his acts of kindness, and he felt sure of God's favor. He was startled at the thought of a kingdom too pure for him to see in his present state.

The figure of the new birth was not completely new to Nicodemus. Converts from heathenism were often compared to children just born. So he must have understood that Christ's words were not literal. But as an Israelite, he felt that he needed no change. This is why he was surprised and irritated by the Savior's words. The pride of the Pharisee was struggling against the honest desire of the seeker after truth.

Surprised out of his self-composure, he answered in words full of irony, "How can a man be born when he is old?" Like many others, he revealed that nothing in the natural heart responds to spiritual things. Spiritual things are spiritually discerned.

Raising His hand with quiet dignity, the Savior applied the truth even more closely and with greater assurance: "Most assuredly, I say to you, unless one is born of water and the Spirit, he cannot enter the kingdom of God." Nicodemus knew that Christ was referring to water baptism and the renewing of the heart by the Spirit of God. He was convinced that he was in the presence of the One whom John the Baptist had foretold.

### The Mystery of the New Birth Explained

Jesus continued, "That which is born of the flesh is flesh, and that which is born of the Spirit is spirit." By nature the heart is evil. See Job 14:4. No human invention can find a remedy for the sinning soul. "The carnal mind is enmity against God." "Out of the heart proceed evil thoughts, murders, adulteries, fornications, thefts, false witness, blasphemies." Romans 8:7; Matthew 15:19. The fountain of the heart must be purified before the stream can become pure. Those who try to reach heaven by their own works in keeping the law are attempting the impossible. The Christian's life is not a modification of the old but a transformation of nature, a death to self and sin, and a new life altogether. This change can come about only by the Holy Spirit.

Nicodemus was still perplexed, and Jesus used the wind to illustrate His meaning. "The wind blows where it wishes, and you hear the sound of it, but cannot tell where it comes from and where it goes. So is everyone who is born of the Spirit."

We hear the wind rustling the leaves and flowers, yet it is invisible. So with the work of the Holy Spirit on the heart. A person may not be able to tell the exact time or place or trace the process of conversion, but this does not prove that he is unconverted. By an agency as unseen as the wind, Christ is constantly working on the heart. Little by little, the Spirit makes impressions that tend to draw the heart to Christ. These may come through reading the Scriptures or hearing the Word from the living preacher. Suddenly, as the Spirit comes with more direct appeal, the heart gladly surrenders to Jesus. Many call this "sudden conversion," but it is the result of long wooing by the Spirit of God—a patient, protracted process.

Wind produces effects that we can see and feel. So the work of the Spirit on the heart will reveal itself in every act of the person who has felt its saving power. The Spirit of God transforms the life. We put away sinful thoughts and renounce evil deeds. Love, humility, and peace take the place of anger, envy, and strife. Joy takes the place of sadness. When by faith we surrender to God, the power that no human eye can see creates a new being in the image of God. We may know the beginning of redemption here, through personal experience. Its results reach through eternal ages.

## Nicodemus Begins to See the Light

While Jesus was speaking, some gleams of truth penetrated the ruler's mind. Yet he did not fully understand the Savior's words. He said wonderingly, "How can these things be?"

"Are you the teacher of Israel, and do not know these things?" Jesus asked. Instead of feeling irritated over Jesus' plain words of truth, Nicodemus should have had a humble opinion of himself because of his spiritual ignorance. Yet Christ spoke with such solemn dignity and earnest love that Nicodemus was not offended.

But as Jesus explained that His mission was to establish a spiritual kingdom instead of a temporal one, Nicodemus was troubled. Jesus saw this and added, "If I have told you earthly things and you do not believe, how will you believe if I tell you heavenly things?" Not grasping the nature of Christ's work on earth, Nicodemus could not understand His work in heaven.

The Jews whom Jesus had driven from the temple were eager to maintain an appearance of holiness, but they neglected holiness of heart. While they insisted on the letter of the law, they were constantly violating its spirit. Their great need was for the change that Christ had been explaining to Nicodemus—a new moral birth, a cleansing from sin, and a renewing of holiness.

There was no excuse for Israel's blindness regarding the work of regeneration. David had prayed, "Create in me a clean heart, O God, and renew a steadfast spirit within me." Through Ezekiel God had promised, "I will give you a new heart and put a new spirit within you; I will take the heart of stone out of your flesh and give you a heart of flesh. I will put My Spirit within you and cause you to walk in My statutes." Psalm 51:10; Ezekiel 36:26, 27.

Nicodemus now began to comprehend the meaning of these scriptures. He saw that the most rigid outward obedience to just the letter of the law could entitle no one to enter the kingdom of heaven.

Nicodemus was being drawn to Christ. As the Savior explained the new birth to him, he longed for this change in himself. How could it take place? Jesus answered his unspoken question: "As Moses lifted up the serpent in the wilderness, even so must the Son of Man be lifted up, that whoever believes in Him should not perish but have eternal life."

The symbol of the uplifted serpent made the Savior's mission plain to Nicodemus. When the people of Israel were dying from the sting of the fiery serpents, God directed Moses to make a serpent of bronze and place it high in the middle of the congregation. All who would look at it would live. The serpent was a symbol of Christ. As the image made in the likeness of the destroying serpents was lifted up for their healing, so One made "in the likeness of sinful flesh" was to be their Redeemer. Romans 8:3. God wanted to lead the Israelites to the Savior. Whether to heal their wounds or pardon their

sins, they could do nothing for themselves but show their faith in the Gift of God. They were to look and live.

Those who had been bitten by the serpents might have demanded a scientific explanation of how looking would heal them. But no explanation was given. To refuse to look was to die. Nicodemus received the lesson and carried it with him. He searched the Scriptures in a new way, not for discussion but to receive life for the soul. He submitted to the leading of the Holy Spirit.

Thousands today need to learn the same truth Nicodemus learned from the uplifted serpent. "There is no other name under heaven given among men by which we must be saved." Acts 4:12. Through faith we receive the grace of God, but faith is not our Savior. It earns nothing. It is the hand by which we lay hold on Christ, who is the remedy for sin. We cannot even repent without the aid of the Spirit of God. The Scripture says of Christ, "Him God has exalted to His right hand to be Prince and Savior, to give repentance to Israel and forgiveness of sins." Acts 5:31. Repentance comes from Christ as truly as does pardon.

How, then, are we to be saved? "Behold! The Lamb of God who takes away the sin of the world!" John 1:29. The light shining from the cross reveals the love of God. His love is drawing us to Himself. If we do not resist this drawing, we will be led to the foot of the cross in repentance for the sins that have crucified the Savior. Then through faith the Spirit of God produces a new life in the soul. He brings the thoughts and desires into obedience to Christ. He creates the heart and the mind anew in the image of Jesus, who works in us to subdue all things to Himself. Then He writes the law of God in the mind and heart, and we can say with Christ, "I delight to do Your will, O my God." Psalm 40:8.

In the conversation with Nicodemus, Jesus unfolded the plan of salvation. In none of His later instruction did He explain so fully, step by step, the work necessary to be done in the hearts of all who wish to inherit the kingdom of heaven. At the very beginning of His ministry, He opened the truth to a member of the Sanhedrin, an appointed teacher of the people. But the leaders of Israel did not welcome the light. Nicodemus hid the truth in his heart, and for three years there was little apparent fruit.

But the words Jesus spoke at night on the lonely mountain were not lost. In the Sanhedrin council, Nicodemus repeatedly defeated plans to destroy Jesus. When at last He was lifted up on the cross, Nicodemus remembered, "As Moses lifted up the serpent in the wilderness, even so must the Son of Man be lifted up, that whoever believes in Him should not perish but have eternal life." The light from that secret meeting illuminated the cross of Calvary, and Nicodemus saw in Jesus the world's Redeemer.

After the Lord ascended, when persecution scattered the disciples, Nicodemus came forward boldly. He used his wealth to sustain the infant church that the Jews had expected to disappear at the death of Christ. In the time of danger, he who had been so cautious and questioning was firm as a rock, encouraging the faith of the disciples and furnishing funds to carry forward the work of the gospel. He became poor in this world's goods, but he never hesitated in the faith that had its beginning in that nighttime conference with Jesus.

Nicodemus told John the story of that interview, and John recorded it for the instruction of millions. The truths taught there are as important today as they were on that solemn night on the shadowy mountain, when the Jewish ruler came to learn the way of life from the lowly Teacher of Galilee.

# "He Must Increase, But I Must Decrease"*

If John the Baptist had announced himself as the Messiah and raised a revolt against Rome, priests and people would have flocked to support him. Satan stood ready to urge on him everything that appeals to the ambition of the world's conquerors. But he had firmly refused the splendid bribe. The attention fixed upon him he directed to Another.

Now he saw the tide of popularity turning away from himself to the Savior. Day by day the crowds around him lessened as the people flocked to hear Jesus. The number of Christ's disciples increased daily.

But the disciples of John looked with jealousy on Jesus' growing popularity. They stood ready to criticize His work, and it was not long before they found opportunity. A question arose between John's disciples and the Jews about whether baptism cleansed the person from sin. They argued that the baptism of Jesus differed essentially from John's. Soon they were disputing with Christ's disciples over what form of words was proper to use at baptism, and finally about their right to baptize at all. The disciples of John came to him with their complaints, saying, "Rabbi, He who was with you beyond the Jordan, to whom you have testified—behold, He is baptizing, and all are coming to Him!"

Satan used these words to bring temptation on John. If John had expressed disappointment at being surpassed, he would have sown seeds of strife, encouraged envy and jealousy, and seriously slowed the gospel's progress.

By nature John had the faults and weaknesses common to humanity, but the touch of divine love had transformed him. He lived in an atmosphere uncontaminated with selfishness and ambition. He revealed no sympathy with his disciples' dissatisfaction but showed how gladly he welcomed the One for whom he had prepared the way.

He said, "A man can receive nothing unless it has been given to him from heaven. You yourselves bear me witness, that I said, 'I am not the Christ,' but, 'I have been sent before Him.' He who has the bride is the bridegroom; but the friend of the bridegroom, who stands and hears him, rejoices greatly because of the bridegroom's voice." John represented himself as the friend who acted as

---

* This chapter is based on John 3:22–36.

a messenger between the engaged parties, preparing the way for the marriage. When the bridegroom had received his bride, the mission of the friend was completed. He rejoiced in the happiness of the couple whose union he had promoted. In the same way, it was John's joy to witness the success of the Savior's work. He said, "Therefore this joy of mine is fulfilled. He must increase, but I must decrease."

Looking in faith to the Redeemer, John had risen to the height of self-denial. He had been only a voice, a cry in the wilderness. Now with joy he accepted silence and obscurity, so that everyone might turn their eyes to the Light of life.

John's soul was emptied of self but was filled with the light of God. John said, "He who comes from above is above all. . . . For He whom God has sent speaks the words of God, for God does not give the Spirit by measure." Christ could say, "I do not seek My own will but the will of the Father who sent Me." John 5:30.

It is the same way with the followers of Christ. We can receive Heaven's light only as we are willing to be emptied of self and consent to bring every thought into captivity to the obedience of Christ. God gives the Holy Spirit beyond measure to all who do this.

The success of Christ's work, which the Baptist had received with joy, was reported also to the authorities at Jerusalem. The priests and rabbis had been jealous of John's influence as they saw the people leaving the synagogues and flocking to the wilderness. But here was One who had even greater power to attract the crowds. Those leaders in Israel were not willing to say with John, "He must increase, but I must decrease."

## Christ's Example of Avoiding Misunderstanding

Jesus knew that the storm was building that would sweep away one of the greatest prophets ever given to the world. Wanting to avoid all occasion for conflict, He quietly left for Galilee. We also, while remaining loyal to the truth, should try to avoid everything that may lead to misunderstanding. Whenever circumstances threaten to cause division, we should follow the example of Jesus and of John the Baptist.

God had called John to lead out as a reformer. But his work was not sufficient to lay the foundation of the Christian church. Another work had to be done, which his testimony could not accomplish. His disciples did not understand this. When they saw Christ coming in to take the work, they were jealous.

The same dangers still exist. God calls someone to do a certain work, and when he has carried it as far as he is qualified, the Lord brings in others to carry it further. But many feel that the success of the work depends on the first laborer. Jealousy comes in, and the work of God is marred. The one wrongly honored is tempted to cherish self-confidence. The people rely on the human instrument for guidance and are led away from God.

Happy are those who are willing for self to be humbled, who can say with John the Baptist, "He must increase, but I must decrease."

# Jesus and the Woman With Five Husbands*

On the way to Galilee, Jesus traveled through Samaria. It was noon when He reached Jacob's well. Tired from His journey, He sat down to rest while His disciples went to buy food.

Jews and Samaritans were bitter enemies. The rabbis said it was lawful to trade with Samaritans in case of necessity, but a Jew would not borrow from a Samaritan nor accept a kindness, not even a morsel of bread or a cup of water. In buying food, the disciples were acting in harmony with the customs of their nation. But it did not enter the thought even of Christ's disciples to ask a favor of the Samaritans.

As Jesus sat by the well, He was faint from hunger and thirst. The journey had been long, and the noonday sun beat down on Him. His thirst increased at the thought of the cool, refreshing water so near, but He had no rope nor water jar, and the well was deep.

A woman of Samaria approached, and seeming not to notice His presence, she filled her pitcher with water. As she turned to go, Jesus asked for a drink. No Oriental would withhold such a favor. Offering a drink to the thirsty traveler was a duty so sacred that Arabs would go out of their way to perform it.

The Savior was looking to find the key to the woman's heart, and with the tact that springs from divine love, He asked a favor. Trust awakens trust. The King of heaven came to this outcast woman, asking a service from her. He who made the ocean, who controls the waters of the deep, who opened the springs and channels of the earth, was dependent on a stranger's kindness for even a drink of water.

The woman saw that Jesus was a Jew. In her surprise, she forgot to grant His request, but tried to learn the reason for it. "How is it," she asked, "that You, being a Jew, ask a drink from me, a Samaritan woman?"

Jesus answered, "If you knew the gift of God, and who it is who says to you, 'Give Me a drink,' you would have asked Him, and He would have given you living water."

"Had you asked of Me, I would have given you a drink of the water of everlasting life."

## The Woman's Interest Is Awakened

The woman's light, bantering

---

* This chapter is based on John 4:1–42.

manner began to change. "Sir, You have nothing to draw with, and the well is deep. Where then do You get that living water? Are You greater than our father Jacob, who gave us the well, and drank from it himself?" She saw before her only a thirsty traveler. In her mind, she compared Him with Jacob. She was looking backward to the fathers, and forward to the Messiah's coming, while the Messiah Himself was beside her, and she did not know Him. How many thirsty souls today are close by the Living Fountain, yet looking far away for the Water of Life!

Solemnly, earnestly, Jesus said, "Whoever drinks of this water will thirst again, but whoever drinks of the water that I shall give him will never thirst. But the water that I shall give him will become in him a fountain of water springing up into everlasting life."

People everywhere are longing for something to fill the unsatisfied need of the soul. Only One can meet that lack—Christ, "the Desire of all nations." The divine grace that He gives is like living water, purifying and invigorating the whole being.

Jesus did not convey the idea that merely one drink of the water of life would be enough. All who taste the love of Christ will continually long for more, but they seek for nothing else. The riches, honors, and pleasures of the world do not attract them. The constant cry of their hearts is, "More of You." Our Redeemer is an inexhaustible fountain. We may drink, and drink again, and we will always find a fresh supply.

Jesus had stirred the woman's interest and awakened a desire for the gift He had mentioned. "Sir, give me this water, that I may not thirst, nor come here to draw."

## The Dark Secrets of Her Past

Jesus now abruptly turned the conversation. Before this woman could receive the gift He longed to give her, she must come to recognize her sin and her Savior. Jesus said to her, "Go, call your husband, and come here." She answered, "I have no husband." But the Savior continued, "You have well said, 'I have no husband,' for you have had five husbands, and the one whom you now have is not your husband; in that you spoke truly."

The woman trembled. A mysterious hand was turning the pages of her life history. Who was He, that He could read the secrets of her life? Thoughts of eternity came to her, and of the future judgment, when all that is now hidden will be revealed.

She tried to change the subject away from this unwelcome direction. "Sir, I perceive that You are a prophet." Then, hoping to silence conviction, she turned to points of religious controversy.

Patiently Jesus watched for the opportunity to bring the truth home to her heart again. "Our fathers worshiped on this mountain," she said, "and you Jews say that in Jerusalem is the place where one ought to worship." Just in sight was Mount Gerizim, a subject of dispute between Jews and Samaritans. For many generations, the Samaritans had intermingled with idol worshipers, whose religion gradually contaminated their own.

When the temple at Jerusalem was rebuilt in the days of Ezra, the Samaritans wanted to join the Jews in its construction. The Jews refused, and bitter feelings sprang up between the two peoples. The Samaritans built a rival temple on Mount Gerizim. But enemies destroyed their temple, and they seemed to be under a curse. Yet they would not acknowledge the temple at Jerusalem as the house of God nor admit that the religion of the Jews was superior.

In answer to the woman, Jesus said, "Believe Me, the hour is coming when you will neither on this mountain, nor in Jerusalem, worship the Father. You worship what you do not know; we know what we worship, for salvation is of the Jews." Now Jesus sought to break down the prejudice of this Samaritan against the Jews. God had entrusted great truths of redemption to the Jews, and the Messiah was to appear from among them.

Jesus wanted to lift the thoughts of His hearer above controversy. "The hour is coming, and now is, when the true worshipers will worship the Father in spirit and truth; for the Father is seeking such to worship Him. God is Spirit, and those who worship Him must worship in spirit and truth."

Not by seeking a holy mountain or a sacred temple are we brought into communion with heaven. In order to serve God rightly, we must be born of the divine Spirit. This will purify the heart and renew the mind, making us willingly obedient to all His requirements. This is true worship. It is the fruit of the Holy Spirit's working.

Wherever someone reaches out after God, there we may see the Spirit's working, and God will reveal Himself to that person.

As the woman talked with Jesus, she was impressed with His words. As Jesus had spread out her past life before her, she realized her soul's thirst, which the waters of the well of Sychar could never satisfy. Nothing before had so greatly awakened her to a higher need. Jesus read the secrets of her life, yet she felt that He was her Friend, pitying and loving her. While the purity of His presence condemned her sin, He had spoken no word to denounce her, but had told her of His grace that could renew her life. The question arose in her mind, *Could this be the long-looked-for Messiah?* She said to Him, " 'I know that Messiah is coming' (who is called Christ). 'When He comes, He will tell us all things.' " Jesus answered, "I who speak to you am He."

As the woman heard these words, faith sprang up in her heart. She accepted the wonderful announcement from the lips of the divine Teacher.

This woman was in a receptive state of mind. She was interested in the Scriptures, and the Holy Spirit had been preparing her to receive more light. Greater understanding on Old Testament prophecies was already flashing into her mind. The water of life that Christ gives to every thirsty soul had begun to spring up in her heart.

The plain statement that Christ made to this woman could not have been made to the self-righteous Jews. But what He had withheld from them, and what He later told the disciples to keep secret, He revealed to her. Jesus saw that she would make use of her knowledge in bringing others to share His grace.

When the disciples returned from their errand, they were surprised to find their Master speaking with the woman. He had not taken the refreshing drink He had asked for, and He did not stop to eat the food His disciples had brought. When the woman had gone, the disciples urged Him to eat. They saw Him silent, His face beaming with light, and they were afraid to interrupt, but they thought it was their duty to remind Him of His physical needs. Jesus recognized their loving interest and said, "I have food to eat of which you do not know."

The disciples wondered who could have brought Him food. He explained, "My food is to do the will of Him who sent Me, and to finish His work." To minister to someone hungering and thirsting for truth was more comforting and refreshing to Him than eating or drinking.

Our Redeemer hungers for the sympathy and love of those He has purchased with His blood. As the mother watches for a smile of recognition from her little child, which signals the dawning of intelligence, so does Christ watch for the expression of grateful love, which shows that spiritual life is begun in the heart.

The woman had been filled with joy as she listened to Christ's words. Leaving her waterpot, she returned to the city to carry the message to others. She forgot her errand to the well, she forgot the Savior's thirst, which she had intended to supply. With her heart overflowing with gladness, she hurried to share with others the light she had received.

"Come, see a Man who told me all things that I ever did," she said to the men of the city. "Could this be the Christ?" There was a new expression on her face, a change in her whole appearance. "They went out of the city and came to Him."

As Jesus still sat by the well, He looked over the fields of grain spread out before Him, their tender green touched by the golden sunlight. Pointing His disciples to the scene, He used it as a symbol: "Do you not say, 'There are still four months and then comes the harvest'? Behold, I say to you, lift up your eyes and look at the fields, for they are already white for harvest!" As He spoke, He looked on the groups coming to the well. Here was a harvest ready for the Reaper.

### The Cycle of Gospel Harvesting

"He who reaps receives wages, and gathers fruit for eternal life, that both he who sows and he who reaps may rejoice together. For in this the saying is true 'One sows and another reaps.' " Those who receive the gospel are to be His living instruments. One scatters the seed, another gathers the harvest, and both rejoice together in the results of their labor.

Jesus said to the disciples, "I sent you to reap that for which you have not labored; others have labored, and you have entered into their labors." The disciples were entering into other people's labors. An unseen agency had worked silently but effectively to produce the harvest. Christ was about to water the seed with His own blood.

His disciples were coworkers with Christ and with holy men of old. By the Spirit's outpouring at Pentecost, thousands were to be converted in a day. This was the result of Christ's sowing, the harvest of His work.

The Samaritans came and heard Jesus, and they believed. Crowding around Him at the well, they asked Him question after question, and eagerly they received His explanations of many things that had been obscure to them. Their perplexity began to clear away. Anxious to hear more, they invited Him to their city and begged Him to remain with them. For two days He stayed in Samaria, and many more believed.

Jesus performed no miracles among them, except to reveal the secrets of her life to the woman at the well. Yet many received Him. In their new joy, they said to the woman, "Now we believe, not because of what you said, for we have heard for ourselves and know that this is indeed the Christ, the Savior of the world."

### Christ Breaks Down Walls of Prejudice

Jesus had begun to break down the partition wall between Jew and Gentile and to preach salvation to the world. He mingled freely with the Samaritans and accepted this despised people's hospitality. He slept under their roofs, ate with them at their tables, taught in their streets, and treated them with the greatest kindness and courtesy.

In the temple at Jerusalem, a low wall separated the outer court from other portions of the sacred building. Inscriptions on this wall stated that only Jews were allowed to pass this boundary. If a Gentile had dared to enter the inner enclosure, he would have paid the penalty with his life. But Jesus, the Originator of the temple, brought to the Gentiles the salvation that the Jews rejected.

The disciples were amazed at Jesus' conduct. During the two days in Samaria, loyalty to Him kept their prejudices under control, but their hearts had not changed. They were slow to learn to give up their contempt and hatred to make room for pity and sympathy. But after the Lord ascended, His lessons came back to them with new meaning. They recalled the Savior's look, His words, the respect and tenderness of His attitude toward these despised strangers. When Peter went to preach in Samaria, he brought the same spirit into his work. When John was called to Ephesus and Smyrna, he remembered the experience at Shechem and the divine Teacher's own example.

Those who call themselves the Savior's followers may despise and shun the outcast, but no circumstance of birth or nationality, no condition of life, can turn away His love from anyone, no matter how sinful. We are to give the gospel invitation to everyone. At Jacob's well Jesus did not neglect the opportunity to speak to one woman, a stranger living in open sin.

Often He began His lessons with only a few people gathered around Him, but one by one the passersby paused to listen, until a crowd of people, in wonder and awe, heard the words of God through the heaven-sent Teacher. Sometimes only one person may hear the message from a worker for Christ today, but who can tell how far-reaching its influence will be?

The Samaritan woman proved to be a more effective missionary than Jesus' own disciples. Through her, a whole cityful of people came to hear the Savior. Every true disciple is born into the kingdom of God as a missionary. Whoever drinks of the living water becomes a fountain of life. The receiver becomes a giver. The grace of Christ in the heart is like a spring in the desert, refreshing all and making those who are ready to die eager to drink the water of life.

# "Unless You See Signs and Wonders"*

The Galileans who returned from the Passover brought back the report of Jesus' wonderful works. Many of the people were sad to see the abuses of the temple and the greed and arrogance of the priests. They hoped that this Man, who had evicted the rulers from the temple, might be the expected Deliverer. They had heard reports that the Prophet had declared Himself to be the Messiah.

The news of Christ's return to Cana soon spread throughout Galilee. In Capernaum, this drew the attention of a Jewish nobleman who was an officer in the king's service. The officer's son was suffering from a disease that seemed to be incurable. When the father heard of Jesus, he determined to ask Him for help. He hoped that a father's prayers might awaken the sympathy of the Great Physician.

When he reached Cana, he pressed his way through a crowd to the Savior's presence. His faith grew weak when he saw only a plainly dressed man, dusty and worn with travel. Yet he talked with Jesus anyway, told his errand, and urged the Savior to accompany him to his home.

Jesus knew that the father had made conditions in his own mind concerning his belief in Him. Unless his request was granted, he would not receive Jesus as the Messiah. While the officer waited in an agony of suspense, Jesus said, "Unless you people see signs and wonders, you will by no means believe."

The Savior contrasted the father's questioning unbelief with the simple faith of the Samaritans, who asked for no miracle or sign. His word had a convincing power that reached their hearts. Christ was pained that His own people failed to hear the voice of God speaking to them through His Son.

Yet the nobleman had a degree of faith, for he had come to ask for what seemed to him the most precious of all blessings. Jesus desired not only to heal the child but to lead the officer and his household to share in the blessings of salvation and to kindle a light in Capernaum. But the nobleman must realize his need before he would want the grace of Christ. Many Jews were interested in Jesus from selfish motives. They staked their faith on whether He would grant them some temporal favor, but they did not see

---

* This chapter is based on John 4:43–54.

their need of divine grace.

Like a flash of light, the Savior's words to the nobleman revealed to him his own heart. He saw that his motives were selfish. His wavering faith appeared in its true character. In deep distress he realized that his doubt might cost the life of his son. In an agony of pleading he begged, "Sir, come down before my child dies!" His faith took hold on Christ as did Jacob, when he cried out as he wrestled with the Angel, "I will not let You go unless You bless me!" Genesis 32:26.

Like Jacob, he succeeded. "Go your way; your son lives," Jesus said. The nobleman left the Savior's presence with a peace and joy he had never known before.

At the same hour, those who were watching beside the dying child at Capernaum saw a sudden, mysterious change. The feverish complexion gave way to the soft glow of returning health. Strength returned to the feeble, wasting form. No signs of his sickness lingered on the child. His burning flesh had become soft and moist, and he sank into a quiet sleep. The family were amazed and greatly cheered.

The officer could have reached Capernaum on the evening after his encounter with Jesus, but he did not hurry toward home. It was the next morning when he arrived in Capernaum. What a homecoming that was! When he had gone to find Jesus, his heart was heavy with sorrow. How different his feelings were now! As he traveled in the quiet of the early morning, all nature seemed to be praising God with him. While he was still some distance from home, servants came out to relieve the suspense they were sure he must feel. He showed no surprise at the news they brought, but asked what time it was when the child began to get better. They answered, "Yesterday at the seventh hour the fever left him." At the very moment when the father's faith grasped Jesus' assurance, "Your son lives," divine love touched the dying child.

The father hurried on to greet his son. He hugged him to his heart as one who had been restored from the dead, and he thanked God again and again for the wonderful healing.

Later, when the nobleman learned more of Christ, he and all his household became disciples. News of the miracle spread, and it prepared the way for Christ's personal ministry in Capernaum.

Like the anxious father, we often are led to seek Jesus by the desire for some earthly benefit, and our confidence in His love depends on whether He grants our request. The Savior longs to give a greater blessing than we ask, and He delays the answer so that He may show us the evil of our own hearts and our need of His grace. He wants us to turn away from the selfishness that leads us to seek Him.

The nobleman wanted to *see* the fulfillment of his prayer before he would believe, but he had to accept the word of Jesus that his request was heard and the blessing granted. We are to believe, not because we see or feel that God hears us. We are to trust His promises. When we have asked for His blessing, we should believe that we receive it and thank Him that we *have* received it. Then we are to go about our duties, knowing that we will experience the blessing when we need it most.

# Bethesda and the Sanhedrin*

Now there is in Jerusalem by the Sheep Gate a pool, which is called in Hebrew, Bethesda, having five porches. In these lay a great multitude of sick people, blind, lame, paralyzed."

At certain times the waters of this pool were agitated, and many people believed that this was supernatural and that whoever stepped in first would be healed of whatever disease he had. Hundreds of sufferers visited the place; but the crowd was so great when the water was troubled that they trampled underfoot men, women, and children weaker than themselves. Many who succeeded in reaching the pool died on its brink. People had put up shelters around the place. Some of the sick spent the night in these porches, creeping to the edge of the pool day after day, hoping for relief.

Jesus was again at Jerusalem. Walking alone, in apparent meditation and prayer, He came to the pool. Seeing the poor sufferers, He longed to exercise His healing power and make every one of them whole. But it was the Sabbath day, and He knew that such an act of healing would stir up the prejudice of the Jews so much that it would cut short His work.

The Savior, however, saw one case of supreme wretchedness, a man who had been a helpless cripple for thirty-eight years. People considered his disease as a judgment from God. Alone and friendless and feeling shut out from God's mercy, the suffering man had spent long years in misery. When it was expected that the waters would be troubled, those who pitied his helplessness would carry him to the porches. But at the crucial moment, he had no one to help him in. He had seen the rippling of the water, but he had never been able to get farther than the edge of the pool. His constant efforts and continual disappointment were quickly wearing away his strength.

The sick man was lying on his mat when a compassionate face bent over him. The hopeful words, "Do you want to be made well?" got his attention. He felt that in some way he was going to have help. But the glow of encouragement soon faded. He remembered how often he had tried to reach the pool. "Sir, I have no man to put me into the pool when the water is stirred up; but while I am coming, another steps down before me."

* This chapter is based on John 5.

Jesus did not ask this suffering man to exercise faith in Him. He simply said, "Rise, take up your bed and walk." But the man's faith took hold of that word. Every nerve and muscle in his crippled body thrilled with new life. He set his will to obey Christ, and his muscles responded. Springing to his feet, he discovered the he could move freely and easily.

## The Secret of Spiritual Healing

The man could have stopped to doubt and lost his one chance of healing. But he believed Christ's word, and in acting on it he received strength. Through the same faith we may receive spiritual healing. Sin has cut us off from the life of God and crippled us. By ourselves we are no more capable of living a holy life than the sick man was capable of walking. Many who realize their helplessness and long for spiritual life are trying in vain to obtain it. The Savior is bending over these discouraged, struggling ones, saying, "Do you want to be made well?"

Do not wait to feel whole. Believe His word, and put your will on the side of Christ. In acting on His word, you will receive strength. Whatever may be the evil that binds both soul and body, Christ is able to deliver. He will give life to the person that is "dead in trespasses." Ephesians 2:1.

The restored paralytic bent down to pick up his rug and blanket, and when he straightened up, he looked around for his Deliverer. But Jesus was lost in the crowd. As he hurried on his way with firm, free step, rejoicing in his newfound strength, he told

several of the Pharisees of his cure. He was surprised at the coldness with which they listened.

They interrupted him, asking why he was carrying his bed on the Lord's Day. In his joy, the man had forgotten it was the Sabbath. He answered boldly, "He who made me well said to me, 'Take up your bed and walk.' " They asked who had done this, but he could not tell. These rulers wanted direct proof so that they could condemn Jesus as a Sabbath breaker. He had not only broken the law in healing the sick man on the Sabbath, but had committed a serious evil by telling him to carry his bed away.

## Meaningless Requirements

The Jews had so perverted the law with meaningless requirements that they made it a yoke of slavery and made observing it an intolerable burden. A Jew was not allowed to kindle a fire nor even light a candle on the Sabbath. As a result, the people were dependent on the Gentiles for many services that their rulers told them they must not do for themselves. They thought salvation was restricted to the Jews, and that since others were already beyond hope, doing these forbidden things would not make matters worse for them. But God has given no commandments that cannot be obeyed by everyone.

In the temple, Jesus met the man who had been healed. He had come to bring a sin offering and also a thank offering for the great mercy he had received. Jesus made Himself known to him. The healed man was overjoyed to meet his Deliverer. Not knowing how they hated Jesus, he told the Pharisees that He was the One who had performed the cure. "For this reason the Jews persecuted Jesus, and sought to kill Him, because He had done these things on the Sabbath."

Jesus was brought before the Sanhedrin to answer the charge of Sabbath breaking. If the Jews had been an independent nation, such a charge would have served their purpose to put Him to death. But their accusations against Christ would have no weight in a Roman court. They hoped, however, to accomplish other goals. Christ was gaining an influence greater than their own, and many who were not interested in the rantings of the rabbis were attracted to His teaching. He spoke of God not as an avenging judge, but as a tender Father. By His words and works of mercy, He was breaking the oppressive power of human commandments and was presenting the love of God.

### People Gathering to Jesus

One of the earliest prophecies of Christ says,

"The scepter shall not depart from Judah,
Nor a lawgiver from between his feet,
Until Shiloh comes;
And to Him shall be the obedience of the people."

Genesis 49:10

The people were gathering to Christ. If the priests and rabbis had not gotten in the way, His teaching would have brought about such a reformation as this world has never witnessed. But these leaders determined to break down Jesus' influence. It would help if they could arraign Jesus before the Sanhedrin and have Him openly condemned. Whoever dared to speak against the rabbinical requirements was regarded as guilty of treason. On this ground the rabbis hoped to create suspicion of Christ as someone who was trying to overthrow established customs, in this way causing division among the people and preparing the way for the Romans to trample them down completely.

After Satan had failed to overcome Christ in the wilderness, he combined his forces to oppose Christ and hinder His work. He matured his plans to blind the minds of the Jewish people so that they would not recognize their Redeemer, filling their leaders with his own hatred against the Champion of truth. He would lead them to reject Christ and to make His life as bitter as possible, hoping to discourage Him in His mission.

Jesus had come to "magnify the law and make it honorable." Isaiah 42:21. He had come to free the Sabbath from those burdensome requirements that had made it a curse instead of a blessing. For this reason, He had chosen the Sabbath for the healing at Bethesda. He could have healed the sick man on any other day or simply have cured him without telling him to carry away his bed. But He selected the worst case and told the man to carry his bed through the city to call attention to the great work done for him. This would open the way for Him to denounce the Jews' restrictions regarding the Lord's Day and to declare their traditions not valid.

Jesus stated that the work of relieving the afflicted was in harmony with the Sabbath law. God's angels are always ministering to suffering humanity. "My Father has been working until now, and I have been working." All the days are God's, in which to carry out His plans for the human race. If the Jews' interpretation of the law was correct, then the One who instituted the Sabbath must bring a temporary close to His labor and stop the never-ending routine of the universe.

Should God forbid the sun to perform its function on the Sabbath? Must He command the brooks to pause in their watering of fields and forests? Must wheat and corn stop growing? Must trees and flowers put forth no bud nor blossom on the Sabbath?

God could not for a moment remove His hand, or mankind would faint and die. We also have work to perform on this day. The sick must be cared for and the wants of the needy be supplied. God's holy rest day was made for us. God does not want His creatures to suffer an hour's pain that can be relieved on the Sabbath.

The Sabbath law forbids secular labor on the rest day of the Lord. The work that earns our livelihood must stop. No labor for worldly pleasure or profit is lawful on that day. But as God ended His labor of creating and rested on the Sabbath, so we are to leave the occupations of daily life and devote those sacred hours to healthful rest, worship, and holy deeds. Christ's healing the sick honored the Sabbath.

But the Pharisees were still more upset. Jesus had not only broken the law, according to their understanding, but in calling God His Father, He had declared Himself equal with God. They accused Him of blasphemy. These opponents of Christ could only refer to their customs and traditions, and these seemed weak and stale when compared to the arguments Jesus had drawn from the Word of God and the unending round of nature. But the rabbis evaded the points He made and tried to stir up anger against Him because He claimed to be equal with God. If they had not feared the people, the priests and rabbis would have killed Jesus on the spot. But popular sentiment in His favor was strong. Many justified His healing of the lame man at Bethesda.

### Jesus Dependent on the Father's Power

Jesus rejected the charge of blasphemy. "My authority," He said, "is that I am the Son of God, One with Him in nature, will, and purpose. I cooperate with God."

"The Son can do nothing of Himself, but what He sees the Father do." The priests and rabbis were taking the Son of God to task for doing the very work He had been sent into the world to do. They felt self-sufficient and sensed no need of a higher wisdom. But the Son of God was surrendered to the Father's will and dependent on His power. Christ made no plans for Himself. Day by day the Father unfolded His plans. So should we depend on God, so that our lives may be the simple working out of His will.

The words of Christ teach that we should think of ourselves as inseparably bound to our Father in heaven.

Whatever our status in life, we are dependent on God. He has appointed us our work and has given us resources for that work. As long as we surrender the will to God and trust in His strength and wisdom, He will guide us in safe paths, to fulfill our appointed part in His plan. But those who depend on their own wisdom and power are separating themselves from God and fulfilling the purpose of the enemy of God and humanity.

The Sadducees believed that there would be no resurrection of the body, but Jesus told them that one of the greatest works of His Father is raising the dead, and that He Himself had power to do the same work. "As the Father raises the dead and gives life to them, even so the Son gives life to whom He will." "The hour is coming, and now is, when the dead will hear the voice of the Son of God; and those who hear will live." Christ declared that the power that gives life to the dead was among them, and they were to see it revealed. This same resurrection power gives life to the soul and sets us "free from the law of sin and death." Romans 8:2. Through faith we are kept from sin. Those who open their hearts to Christ become partakers of the mighty power that will bring their bodies out from the grave.

The humble Nazarene rose above humanity, threw off the appearance of sin and shame, and stood revealed, the Son of God, One with the Creator of the universe. His hearers were spellbound. No one ever spoke words like His or carried himself with such kingly majesty. His words were clear and plain, fully declaring His mission.

"The Father judges no one, but has committed all judgment to the Son. . . . The Father . . . has given Him authority to execute judgment also, because He is the Son of Man."

The priests and rulers set themselves up as judges to condemn Christ's work, but He declared Himself to be their Judge and the Judge of all the earth. Every blessing from God to the fallen race has come through Him. As soon as there was sin, there was a Savior. He who has given light to all, He who has followed us with tender pleading, seeking to win us from sin to holiness, is both our Advocate and Judge. He who has been seeking through all the ages to free the captives from the deceiver's grasp is the One who will pass judgment on every person.

Because He has tasted the last drops of human affliction and temptation and understands our frailties; because He has withstood the temptations of Satan and will deal justly and tenderly with those that His own blood has been poured out to save—because of this, God has appointed the Son of man to execute judgment.

But "God did not send His Son into the world to condemn the world, but that the world through Him might be saved." John 3:17. And Jesus declared to the Sanhedrin, "He who hears My word and believes in Him who sent Me has everlasting life, and shall not come into judgment, but has passed from death into life."

## Resurrection of Life

"The hour is coming all who are in the graves will hear His voice and come forth—those who have done good, to the resurrection of life, and those who have done evil, to the resurrection of condemnation."

The only light that can lighten the gloom of the grave was shining on Israel. But self-will is blind. Jesus had violated the traditions of the rabbis, and they refused to believe.

The time, the place, and the intensity of feeling that filled the assembly combined to make Jesus' words before the Sanhedrin even more impressive. The highest religious authorities of the nation were seeking the life of Him who declared Himself to be Israel's Restorer. The Lord of the Sabbath they called before the court to answer the charge of breaking the Sabbath. His judges looked on Him with astonishment and rage, but His words were unanswerable. He denied the right of priests and rabbis to interfere with His work. He refused to plead guilty to their charges or be taught by them.

Instead of apologizing, Jesus rebuked the rulers for their ignorance of the Scriptures. He declared that they had rejected the Word of God because they had rejected Him whom God had sent. "You search the Scriptures, for in them you think you have eternal life; and these are they which testify of Me."

The Old Testament Scriptures radiate with the glory of the Son of God. The entire divine system of Judaism was a compact prophecy of the gospel. Through the patriarchal line and the legal system, heaven's glorious light made plain the footsteps of the Redeemer. Every sacrifice showed Christ's death. In every cloud of incense, His righteousness ascended. In the awe-filled mystery of the Holy of Holies, His glory dwelt.

## The Council Fails to Intimidate Jesus

The Jews supposed that in their mere outward knowledge of the Scriptures they had eternal life. But having rejected Christ in His Word, they rejected Him in person. "You are not willing to come to Me," He said, "that you may have life."

The Jewish leaders had studied the teachings of the prophets, not with a sincere desire to know the truth, but with the purpose of finding evidence to support their ambitious hopes. When Christ came in a manner different from what they expected, they would not accept Him and tried to prove that He was a deceiver. The more directly the Savior spoke to them in His works of mercy, the more determined they were in resisting the light.

Jesus said, "I do not receive honor from men." It was not the Sanhedrin's approval He desired. He was clothed with the honor and authority of Heaven. If He had wanted it, angels would have come to worship Him. But for their own sake and for the sake of the nation whose leaders they were, He wanted the Jewish rulers to recognize His character.

"I have come in My Father's name, and you do not receive Me; if another comes in his own name, him you will receive." When others would come, pretending to have the character of Christ but seeking their own glory, they would be accepted. Why? Because those who seek their own glory appeal to the desire for self-exaltation in others. The Jews would receive the false teacher because he flattered their pride. But the teaching of Christ was spiritual and demanded the sacrifice of self; therefore, they would not accept it. To them His voice was the voice of a stranger.

Are there not many religious leaders in our day who are rejecting the Word of God in order to keep their own traditions?

"If you believed Moses, you would believe Me; for he wrote about Me. But if you do not believe his writings, how will you believe My words?" If they had listened to the divine Voice that spoke through their great leader, Moses, they would have recognized it in the teachings of Christ.

The priests and rabbis saw that there was no excuse for their opposition to Jesus, yet this did not quench their murderous hatred. Fear seized them as they saw the convincing power that accompanied His ministry, but they locked themselves in darkness.

They had failed to undermine the authority of Jesus or alienate the people, many of whom were convicted by His words. The rulers themselves felt deep condemnation, yet they were determined to take His life. They sent messengers to warn the people against Jesus as an impostor. They sent spies to report what He said and did. The precious Savior was now most surely standing under the shadow of the cross.

# The Imprisonment and Death of John*

John the Baptist had been first in announcing Christ's kingdom, and he was first also in suffering. From the free air of the wilderness, he was now shut in by the walls of a dungeon, a prisoner in the fortress of Herod Antipas. Herod himself had listened to the Baptist and trembled at the call to repentance. "Herod feared John, knowing that he was a just and holy man." John condemned his sinful relationship with Herodias, his brother's wife. For a time, Herod feebly tried to break the chain of lust that held him, but Herodias fastened him more firmly in her grasp and took revenge on the Baptist by persuading Herod to put him in prison.

The gloom and inaction of his prison life weighed heavily on John. As week after week passed, bringing no change, despondency and doubt crept over him. His disciples brought him news of Jesus' works and how the people were flocking to Him. But if this new Teacher was the Messiah, why did He do nothing to bring about John's release? This brought doubts to John's mind that otherwise would never have arisen. Satan rejoiced to see how

the words of these disciples bruised the soul of the Lord's messenger. How often the friends of a good man prove to be his most dangerous enemies!

John the Baptist expected Jesus to take the throne of David. As time passed and the Savior made no claim to kingly authority, John became perplexed. He had expected Jesus to pull down the high places of human pride and power. The Messiah would thoroughly clean out His threshing floor, gather the wheat into His barn, and burn up the chaff with unquenchable fire. See Isaiah 40; Matthew 3. Like Elijah, he looked for the Lord to reveal Himself as a God who would answer by fire.

The Baptist had stood as someone who spoke out fearlessly against wickedness, in high places and low. He had dared to face king Herod with the plain rebuke of sin. And now from his dungeon he watched for the Lion of the tribe of Judah to throw down the pride of the oppressor and to deliver the poor. But Jesus seemed satisfied with healing and teaching the people. He was eating at the tables of the tax collectors, while every day the Roman

---

* This chapter is based on Matthew 11:1–11; 14:1–11; Mark 6:17–28; Luke 7:19–28.

oppression rested more heavily on Israel, while King Herod and his illicit lover worked their will, and the cries of the poor and suffering went up to heaven.

## A Terrible Disappointment

All this seemed a mystery. The whisperings of demons tortured John's spirit, and the shadow of a terrible fear crept over him. Could it be that the long-hoped-for Deliverer had not yet appeared? John had been bitterly disappointed in the result of his mission. He had expected that the message from God would have the same effect as when the law was read in the days of Josiah and of Ezra (2 Chronicles 34; Nehemiah 8), that a deep work of repentance would follow. Had his whole life been sacrificed in vain? Had his work for his own disciples been fruitless? Had he been unfaithful in his mission, so that he was now cut off from labor? If the promised Deliverer had appeared and John had been found true to his calling, would not Jesus now overthrow the oppressor's power and set free the one who had announced His arrival?

But the Baptist did not surrender his faith in Christ. The Voice from heaven, the descending dove, the spotless purity of Jesus, the power of the Holy Spirit that had rested on John as he came into the Savior's presence, the testimony of the Scriptures—all testified that Jesus was the Promised One.

John determined to send a message to Jesus. He entrusted it to two of his disciples, hoping that an interview with the Savior would confirm their faith. And he longed for some word from Christ spoken directly for himself.

The two disciples came to Jesus with their message: "Are You the Coming One, or do we look for another?" The question was keenly bitter and disappointing to Jesus' human nature. If John, the faithful forerunner, failed to understand Christ's mission, what could He expect from the self-seeking multitude?

The Savior did not answer the disciples' question immediately. As they stood puzzled by His silence, the sick and afflicted were coming to be healed. The blind, the diseased, were eagerly pressing into the presence of Jesus. The voice of the mighty Healer penetrated the deaf ear. A word, a touch of His hand, opened the blind eyes. Jesus rebuked disease and banished fever. His voice reached the dying, and they arose in health and vigor. While He healed their diseases, the poor peasants and laborers who were shunned by the rabbis as unclean gathered close around Him, and He spoke to them the words of eternal life.

## Jesus Presents Evidence

So the day passed, with the disciples of John seeing and hearing everything. At last Jesus called them to Him and told them to go and tell John what they had witnessed, adding, "Blessed is he who is not offended because of Me." The evidence of His divinity was clear. His glory was evident in His condescension to our low condition.

The disciples carried the message, and it was enough. John remembered the prophecy concerning the Messiah:

"The Lord has anointed Me
To preach good tidings to the poor;
He has sent Me to heal the broken-
    hearted,
To proclaim liberty to the captives."
                                    Isaiah 61:1

The works of Christ declared Him to be the Messiah. Jesus was to do His work, not with the clash of weapons and the overturning of thrones and kingdoms, but through speaking to the hearts of men and women by a life of mercy and self-sacrifice.

The principle of the Baptist's own life was the principle of the Messiah's kingdom. But what was convincing evidence to him of Christ's divinity would be no evidence to the leaders in Israel. John saw that the Savior's mission could win only hatred and condemnation from them. He, the forerunner, was drinking of the cup that Christ Himself must drain to its dregs.

The Savior's gentle reproof was not lost on John. Understanding more clearly now the nature of Christ's mission, he yielded himself to God for life or for death, whatever might best serve the interests of the cause he loved.

The Savior's heart went out in sympathy to the faithful witness in Herod's dungeon. He would not leave the people to conclude that God had forsaken John or that his faith had failed in the day of trial. "What did you go out into the wilderness to see?" He said. "A reed shaken by the wind?"

Like tall reeds beside the Jordan, the rabbis who had stood as critics of the Baptist's mission were swayed this way and that by the winds of popular opinion. Yet for fear of the people, they dared not openly oppose his work. But God's messenger was of no such cowardly spirit. John had spoken with equal plainness to Pharisees, Sadducees, King Herod and his court, princes and soldiers, publicans and peasants. He was no trembling reed. In prison, he maintained the same loyalty to God. In his faithfulness to principle, he was firm as a rock.

### No Man Greater

Jesus continued, "What did you go out to see? A man clothed in soft garments? Indeed those who are gorgeously appareled and live in luxury are in kings' courts." Rich clothing and the luxuries of this life are not what God's servants may expect. The priests and rulers arrayed themselves in rich robes. They were more anxious to gain the admiration of others than to win the approval of God. They did not give their allegiance to God but to the kingdom of this world.

"But what did you go out to see?" asked Jesus. "A prophet? . . . This is he of whom it is written: 'Behold, I send My messenger before Your face, who will prepare Your way before You.' For I say to you, among those born of women there is not a greater prophet than John the Baptist." Yet, said Jesus, "He who is least in the kingdom of God is greater than he." In the announcement to Zacharias before the birth of John, the angel had declared, "He will be great in the sight of the Lord." Luke 1:15. In the estimation of Heaven, what constitutes greatness? Not what the world counts as greatness. It is moral worth that God values. Love and purity are the attributes He prizes most. John was great in the sight of the Lord when he refused to seek honor for himself but pointed everyone to Jesus as the Promised One. His unselfish joy in the ministry of Christ presents the highest kind of nobility ever revealed in humanity.

### More Than a Prophet

John was "more than a prophet." While prophets had seen Christ's advent from far off, John had the privilege of seeing Him and presenting Him to Israel as the One sent by God. The prophet John was the lesser light to be followed by a greater. No other light ever will shine so clearly on fallen men and women as the teaching and example of Jesus.

Aside from the joy that John found in his mission, his life had been one of sorrow. His was a lonely assignment. And he was not permitted to see the result of his own labors. It was not his privilege to be with Christ and behold the light that radiated through every word of Christ, shedding glory on the promises of prophecy.

Herod believed that John was a prophet of God and fully intended to set him free. But he feared Herodias. She knew that by direct measures she could never win Herod's consent to the death of John, so she resolved to accomplish her purpose by scheming. On the king's birthday he would have guests in for a celebration. There would be feasting and drunkenness. She might find a way then to influence Herod according to her will.

When the great day arrived, the king was feasting and drinking with his lords. Herodias sent her daughter into the banquet hall to dance for the guests. Salome was in the first flush of womanhood, and her sensuous beauty captivated the lordly revelers. It was a flattering compliment to Herod when this daughter of Israel's priests and princes danced for his guests.

The king was dazed with wine. Passion controlled him, and reason was dethroned. He saw only the pleasure-mad guests, the banquet, the wine, the flashing lights, and the girl dancing before him. In the recklessness of the moment, he wanted to make some display that would exalt him in the eyes of the great men of his realm. With an oath, he promised the daughter of Herodias whatever she might ask, even to half of his kingdom.

Salome hastened to her mother. What should she ask? The answer was ready—the head of John the Baptist. Salome shrank from presenting the request, but the determination of Herodias prevailed. The girl returned with the terrible demand: "I want you to give me at once the head of John the Baptist on a platter."

Herod was astonished and perplexed. He was horror-stricken at the thought of taking John's life. Yet he was unwilling to appear fickle or rash. He had made the oath in honor of his guests, and if one of them had offered a word against the fulfillment of his promise, he would gladly have spared the prophet. He gave them opportunity to speak in the prisoner's behalf. They knew John to be a servant of God. But though shocked at the girl's demand, they were too drunk to protest. No voice was raised to save the life of Heaven's messenger. These men of high positions carried great responsibilities, yet they had given themselves up to drunkenness. Their heads were turned by the giddy scene of music and dancing, and conscience lay sleeping. By their silence, they pronounced the sentence of death on the prophet of God, to satisfy the revenge of an immoral woman.

Herod reluctantly commanded the prophet's execution. Soon the head of John was brought in. Never more would that voice be heard calling for repentance. The revels of one night cost the life of one of the greatest of the prophets.

How often have the innocent been sacrificed through the intemperance of those who should have been guardians of justice! All who put the intoxicating drink to their lips make themselves responsible for all the injustice they may commit under its benumbing power. Those who have jurisdiction over the lives of others should be held guilty of a crime when they yield to intemperance. They need full command of their physical, mental, and moral powers in order to possess vigor of intellect and a high sense of justice.

Herodias gloated in her revenge and assured herself that Herod's conscience would no longer be troubled. But no happiness resulted. People came to abhor her name, while Herod was tormented by remorse. He was constantly trying to find relief from a guilty conscience. As he recalled John's self-denial, his solemn, earnest appeals, his sound judgment in counsel, and then remembered how he had come to his death, Herod could find no rest. In the affairs of state, receiving honors from others, he bore a smiling face while he concealed an anxious heart oppressed with fear. He was convinced that God had witnessed the drunken scene of the banqueting room, that He had seen Herodias's gloating and the insult she offered to the severed head of the one who had condemned her behavior.

When Herod heard of Christ's works, he thought God had raised John from the dead. He was in constant fear that John would avenge his death by condemning him and his house. Herod was reaping the result of sin—"a trembling heart, failing eyes, and anguish of soul. . . . In the morning you shall say, 'Oh, that it were evening!' And at evening . . . 'Oh, that it were morning!' because of the fear which terrifies your heart." Deuteronomy 28:65–67. No torture is worse than a guilty conscience that gives no rest day nor night.

### The Reason Christ Did Not Deliver John

Many minds question why John the Baptist was left to languish and die in prison. But this dark outcome can never shake our confidence in God when we remember that John was only a sharer in the sufferings of Christ. All who follow Christ will wear the crown of sacrifice. Satan will war against the principle of self-sacrifice wherever it appears.

Satan had been untiring in his efforts to draw the Baptist away from a life of unreserved surrender to God, but he had failed. In Jesus' temptation in the wilderness, Satan had been defeated. Now he determined to bring sorrow on Christ by striking John. The One whom he could not entice to sin, he would cause to suffer.

Jesus did not intervene to deliver His servant. He knew that John would bear the test. The Savior would gladly have come to brighten John's dungeon gloom with His own presence. But He must not imperil His own mission. For the sake of thousands who in later years must pass from prison to death, John was to drink the cup of martyrdom. As the followers of Jesus would languish in lonely cells or die by the sword, the rack, or the flames, apparently forsaken by God and man, what a comfort to their hearts would be the thought that John the Baptist had passed through a similar experience!

John was not forsaken. He had the companionship of heavenly angels, who opened to him the prophecies concerning Christ and the precious promises of Scripture. To John, as to those who came after him, the assurance was given, "Lo, I am with you always, even to the end of the age." Matthew 28:20.

God never leads His children otherwise than they would choose to be led if they could see the end from the beginning and discern the purpose they are fulfilling as coworkers with Him. Not Enoch, who was translated to heaven, not Elijah, who ascended in a chariot of fire, was greater or more honored than John the Baptist, who died alone in the dungeon. "To you it has been granted on behalf of Christ, not only to believe in Him, but also to suffer for His sake." Philippians 1:29. Of all the gifts that Heaven can bestow upon us, fellowship with Christ in His sufferings is the most weighty trust and the highest honor.

# How Daniel Identified Jesus as the Christ

The Messiah's coming had been announced first in Judea. On the hills of Bethlehem, the angels had proclaimed the birth of Jesus. The wise men had come to Jerusalem searching for Him.

If the leaders in Israel had received Christ, He would have honored them as His messengers to carry the gospel to the world. But Israel did not know the time of her visitation by God. The jealousy and distrust of the Jewish leaders had ripened into open hatred, and the hearts of the people were turned away from Jesus. The Sanhedrin was intent on putting Him to death, and so Jesus left Jerusalem and the people who had been instructed in the law and turned to another class to proclaim His message.

In every succeeding generation, the history of Christ's withdrawal from Judea has been repeated. When the Reformers preached the Word of God, they had no thought of separating from the established church. But the religious leaders would not tolerate the light, and those who carried it were forced to seek another class who were longing for truth. In our day, few professed followers of the Reformers are listening for the voice of God, ready to accept truth in whatever form it may come. Often those who follow in the steps of the Reformers are forced to turn away from churches they love in order to declare the plain Word of God. Many have to leave the church of their heritage in order to be obedient to God.

The people of Galilee represented a more promising field for the Savior's work. Less under the control of bigotry, their minds were more open to receiving truth. A much larger mixture of people of other nations lived there than in Judea.

As Jesus traveled through Galilee, teaching and healing, crowds came, many even from Judea. Enthusiasm ran so high that it was necessary to take precautions so that the Roman authorities would not start to fear an uprising. Hungering and thirsting hearts feasted on the grace of a merciful Savior.

## Prophet Daniel Foretold Christ's Ministry

The central theme of Christ's preaching was, "The time is fulfilled, and the kingdom of God is at hand. Repent, and believe the gospel." Mark 1:15. The gospel message that the Savior gave was based on the prophecies. The "time" which He declared fulfilled was the period made known to Daniel.

"Seventy weeks," the angel Gabriel said,

"are determined
For your people and for your holy city,
To finish the transgression,
To make an end of sins,
To make reconciliation for iniquity,
To bring in everlasting righteousness,
To seal up the vision and prophecy,
And to anoint the Most Holy."
                              Daniel 9:24

A day in prophecy stands for a year. See Ezekiel 4:6. The seventy weeks, or 490 days, represent 490 years.

The Bible gives a starting point for this period:

"Know therefore and understand,
That from the going forth of the
     command
To restore and build Jerusalem
Until Messiah the Prince,
There shall be seven weeks and sixty-
     two weeks,"

sixty-nine weeks, or 483 years. Daniel 9:25.

The command to restore and build Jerusalem, as completed by the decree of Artaxerxes Longimanus (see Ezra 6:14; 7:1, 9), went into effect in the autumn of 457 B.C. From this time, 483 years extend to the autumn of A.D. 27. According to the prophecy, this period would reach to the Messiah, the Anointed One. In A.D. 27, at His baptism, Jesus received the anointing of the Holy Spirit and began His ministry soon afterward. Then the message went out, "The time is fulfilled." Then, the angel said, "He shall confirm the covenant with many for one week [seven years]." KJV. For seven years after the Savior entered on His ministry, the gospel was to be preached especially to the Jews—for three and a half years by Christ Himself, and afterward by the apostles. "In the middle of the week He shall bring an end to sacrifice and offering." Daniel 9:27. In the spring of A.D. 31, Christ, the True Sacrifice, was offered on Calvary. Then the veil of the temple was torn in two, showing that the sacrificial service had lost its sacredness and significance. The time had come for the earthly sacrifice and offering to cease.

The one week—seven years—ended in A.D. 34. Then, by stoning Stephen, the Jews finally sealed their rejection of the gospel. Persecution scattered the disciples, who "went everywhere preaching the word." Acts 8:4. A little later, Saul the persecutor was converted and became Paul, the apostle to the Gentiles.

The angel had definitely pointed out the time of Christ's coming, His death, and the giving of the gospel to the Gentiles. It was the privilege of the Jews to understand these prophecies and to recognize their fulfillment in Jesus' mission. Referring to the prophecy given to Daniel concerning their time, Christ said, "Whoever reads, let him understand." Matthew 24:15. After His resurrection, He explained to the disciples in "all the Prophets" "the things concerning Himself." Luke 24:27. The Savior had spoken through the prophets and "testified beforehand the sufferings of Christ and the glories that would follow." 1 Peter 1:11.

It was Gabriel, the angel next in rank to the Son of God, who came with the divine message to Daniel. It was Gabriel whom Christ sent to open the future to John; and a blessing is pronounced on those who read and hear the words of the prophecy and keep the things written in it. See Revelation 1:3. God will bless the reverent, prayerful study of the prophetic Scriptures.

The message of Christ's first advent announced the kingdom of His grace. Likewise, the message of His second advent announces the kingdom of His glory. And the second message, like the first, is based on the prophecies. The Savior Himself has given signs of His coming, and He says, "Take heed to yourselves, lest your hearts be weighed down with carousing, drunkenness, and cares of this life, and that Day come on you unexpectedly." "Watch therefore, and pray always that you may be counted worthy to escape all these things that will come to pass, and to stand before the Son of Man." Luke 21:34, 36.

The Jews misinterpreted the Word of God and did not know the time of their visitation by God. They spent the years of Christ's ministry and that of His apostles in plotting to destroy the Lord's messengers. Earthly ambitions absorbed them. Similarly today, the kingdom of this world absorbs people's thoughts, and they don't notice the rapidly fulfilling prophecies and the signs of the swift-coming kingdom of God. While we are not to know the hour of our Lord's return, we may know when it is near. "Therefore let us not sleep, as others do, but let us watch and be sober." 1 Thessalonians 5:6.

# "Is Not This the Carpenter's Son?"*

One shadow intruded on the bright days of Christ's ministry in Galilee—the people of Nazareth rejected Him. "Is this not the carpenter's son?" they said. Matthew 13:55. During His youth, Jesus had worshiped among His friends and family in the synagogue at Nazareth. Since the beginning of His ministry, He had been away from them, but when He appeared again, their expectations rose to the highest pitch. Here were the familiar faces He had known from infancy. Here were His mother, His brothers and sisters, and all eyes turned toward Him as He entered the synagogue on the Sabbath and took His place among the worshipers.

In the regular service, the elder urged the people still to hope for the Coming One who would reign gloriously and banish all oppression. He tried to encourage his hearers by going over the evidence that the Messiah's coming was near. He emphasized the thought that He would lead armies to deliver Israel.

When a rabbi was present, he was expected to deliver the sermon, and any Israelite could give the reading from the prophets. On this Sabbath,

Jesus was asked to take part in the service. He "stood up to read. And He was handed the book of the prophet Isaiah." The scripture He read was understood as referring to the Messiah:

"The Spirit of the Lord is upon Me,
Because He has anointed Me to preach
    the gospel to the poor;
He has sent Me to heal the broken-
    hearted,
To preach deliverance to the captives
And recovery of sight to the blind,
To set at liberty those who are
    oppressed,
To preach the acceptable year of the
    Lord.

"Then He closed the book, and gave it back to the attendant and sat down. And the eyes of all who were in the synagogue were fixed on Him. . . . So all bore witness to Him, and marveled at the gracious words which proceeded out of His mouth."

Explaining the words He had read, Jesus spoke of the Messiah as One who would relieve the oppressed, heal the afflicted, restore sight to the blind, and reveal the light of truth. The wonderful meaning of His words thrilled

---

* This chapter is based on Luke 4:16–30.

the hearers with a power they had never felt before. The tide of divine influence broke every barrier down. As the Holy Spirit moved their hearts, they responded with fervent amens and praises to the Lord.

But when Jesus announced, "Today this Scripture is fulfilled in your hearing," they suddenly were called upon to think of the claims of Him who had been addressing them. He had represented them, children of Abraham, as being in bondage, prisoners to be delivered from the power of evil, in darkness, and needing the light of truth. This offended their pride. Jesus' work for them was to be entirely different from what they wanted. He might investigate their deeds too closely. They shrank from inspection by those clear, searching eyes.

"Who is this Jesus?" they questioned. He who had claimed the glory of the Messiah was the Son of a carpenter. They had seen Him toiling up and down the hills. They were acquainted with His brothers and sisters, and they knew His life and labors. They had seen Him develop from childhood to manhood. Although His life had been spotless, they would not believe that He was the Promised One. They opened the door to doubt, and their hearts became harder for having been briefly softened. With intense energy, Satan worked to fasten them in unbelief.

They had been stirred by the conviction that it was their Redeemer who addressed them. But Jesus now gave them evidence of His divinity by revealing their secret thoughts. "No prophet is accepted in his own country. But I tell you truly, many widows were in Israel in the days of Elijah, when the heaven was shut up three years and six months, and there was a great famine throughout all the land; but to none of them was Elijah sent except to Zarephath, in the region of Sidon, to a woman who was a widow. And many lepers were in Israel in the time of Elisha the prophet, and none of them was cleansed, except Naaman the Syrian."

The prophets whom God had chosen were not allowed to labor for a hardhearted, unbelieving people. In the days of Elijah, Israel had rejected the Lord's messengers, so God found a refuge for His servant in a heathen land, with a woman who did not belong to the chosen people. But this woman's heart was open to the greater light that God sent through His prophet.

In Elisha's time, the lepers of Israel were passed by for the same reason. But Naaman, a heathen nobleman, was ready to receive the gifts of God's grace. He was not only cleansed from leprosy but blessed with a knowledge of the true God. The heathen who choose the right as far as they can distinguish it are in a better condition than those who profess to serve God but disregard light and whose daily lives contradict their profession.

## Jesus Set Their Real Condition Before Them

The words of Jesus to His hearers struck at the root of their self-righteousness. Every word cut like a knife as He set their real condition before them. They now scorned the faith that Jesus had inspired in them at first. They would not admit that He who had come from poverty and lowliness was anything other than a common man. Their unbelief bred hatred. In anger, they shouted out against the Savior. Fierce national pride stirred within them, and a tumult of voices drowned out His words. He had offended their prejudices, and they were ready to commit murder.

The assembly broke up. Laying hands on Jesus, they rushed Him from the synagogue and out of the city. Eager for His destruction, they hurried Him to the top of a cliff, intending to throw Him down headfirst. Shouts filled the air. Some were throwing stones at Him, when suddenly He disappeared. Heavenly messengers were with Him in the midst of that maddened crowd, and they conducted Him to safety.

So, in all ages, the forces of evil array themselves against Christ's faithful followers. But armies of heaven surround all who love God, to deliver them. In eternity, we will know that messengers from God were with our every step from day to day.

Jesus could not give up on His hearers in the synagogue without one more call to repentance. Toward the close of His ministry in Galilee, He again visited the home of His childhood. The fame of His preaching and miracles had filled the land. None in Nazareth could now deny that He possessed more than human power. There were whole villages around them in which He had healed all the sick.

Again as they listened to His words, the Divine Spirit moved on the Nazarenes. But even now they would not admit that this Man, brought up among them, was greater than themselves. They still resented the fact that while He had claimed to be the Promised One, He had really denied them a place with Israel, for He had shown them to be less worthy of God's favor than a heathen man and woman. Though they questioned, "Where did this Man get this wisdom and these mighty works?" (Matthew 13:54), they would not receive Him as the Christ of God. Because of their unbelief, the Savior could not work many miracles among them, and reluctantly He left, never to return.

Unbelief, having once been cherished, continued to control the people of Nazareth, the Sanhedrin, and the nation. They rejected the Holy Spirit, and this resulted in the cross of Calvary, the destruction of their city, and the scattering of the nation.

Christ longed to open the precious treasures of truth to Israel! But they clung to their creed and useless ceremonies. They spent their money for chaff and husks when the bread of life was within their reach. Again and again, Christ quoted from the prophets and declared, "Today this scripture is fulfilled in your hearing." If they had honestly searched the Scriptures, bringing their theories to the test of God's Word, Jesus would not have needed to declare, "See! Your house is left to you desolate." Luke 13:35. They might have avoided the disaster that laid their proud city in ruins.

But the lessons of Christ demanded repentance. If they accepted His teachings, they must change their practices and surrender their cherished hopes.

They must go contrary to the opinions of the great thinkers and teachers of the time.

Spiritual pride filled the Jewish leaders. They loved the highest seats in the synagogue. The sound of their titles on the lips of others gratified them. As real devotion declined, they became more jealous for their traditions and ceremonies. Selfish prejudice darkened their minds, and they could not harmonize the power of Christ's convicting words with the humility of His life. His poverty seemed completely inconsistent with His claim to be the Messiah. Why was He so unassuming? If He was what He claimed to be, why was He satisfied to be without the force of arms? Without such force, how could the power and glory they had waited for so long bring the nations under the authority of the city of the Jews?

But it was not simply the absence of outward glory in His life that led the Jews to reject Jesus. He was the embodiment of purity, and they were impure. His sincerity revealed their insincerity and made them see iniquity in its hateful character. Such a light was unwelcome. They could have accepted the disappointment of their ambitious hopes better than Christ's reproof of their sins and the condemnation they felt even from the presence of His purity.

# The Call by the Sea*

Day was breaking over the Sea of Galilee. The disciples, tired after a night of fruitless labor, were still in their fishing boats on the lake. Jesus had come to spend a quiet hour by the waterside in the early morning. He hoped for a little rest from the crowds that followed Him day after day. But soon the people began to gather and press in close to Him on every side.

To escape the pressure, Jesus stepped into Peter's boat and told him to pull out a little from the shore. Here everyone could see and hear Him better, and from the boat He taught the crowds on the beach. He, the Honored One of heaven, was declaring the great things of His kingdom in the open air to the common people. The lake, the mountains, the spreading fields, the sunlight flooding the earth, all illustrated His lessons and impressed them on the mind. And no lesson fell fruitless. Every message came to someone as the word of eternal life.

The prophets had looked forward to scenes like this, and wrote:

"The land of Zebulun and the land of Naphtali,

The way of the sea, beyond the Jordan, Galilee of the Gentiles:
The people who sat in darkness saw a great light,
And upon those who sat in the region and shadow of death
Light has dawned."

Looking down the ages, Jesus saw His faithful ones in prison and courtroom, in temptation, loneliness, and affliction. In the words He spoke to those gathered around Him on the shores of the Sea of Galilee, He was also speaking to these others the words that would be a message of hope in trial, comfort in sorrow, and light in darkness. That Voice speaking from the fisherman's boat would be heard speaking peace to human hearts to the close of time.

When He finished His message, Jesus told Peter to launch out into the sea and let his net down for a catch. But Peter was discouraged. All night he had caught nothing. During the lonely hours, he had thought of John the Baptist languishing in his dungeon, of what might happen to Jesus and His followers, of the poor success of their mission to Judea, and of the

* This chapter is based on Matthew 4:15–22; Mark 1:16–20; Luke 5:1–11.

hatred of the priests and rabbis. As he watched by the empty nets, the future seemed dark with discouragement. "Master, we have toiled all night and caught nothing; nevertheless at Your word I will let down the net."

After working all night without success, it seemed hopeless to throw the net into the clear waters of the lake, but love for their Master moved the disciples to obey. Simon and his brother let down the net. When they tried to pull it in, there were so many fish that they had to call James and John to help them. When they got the catch on board, both boats were so heavily loaded that they were in danger of sinking.

## Unholiness Revealed

To Peter, this miracle was a greater revelation of divine power than any other he had ever witnessed. In Jesus, he saw One who held all nature under His control. Shame for his unbelief, gratitude for Christ's condescension, and above all, the sense of his uncleanness in the presence of infinite purity overwhelmed him. Peter fell at the Savior's feet, exclaiming, "Depart from me, for I am a sinful man, O Lord!"

The same presence of divine holiness had caused the prophet Daniel to fall like a dead man before the angel. See Daniel 10:8. Isaiah exclaimed, "Woe is me, for I am undone! Because I am a man of unclean lips, . . . for my eyes have seen the King, the Lord of hosts." Isaiah 6:5. It has been like this with all to whom God has granted a view of His greatness and majesty.

The Savior answered Peter, "Do not be afraid. From now on you will catch men." After Isaiah had seen God's holiness and his own unworthiness, he was entrusted with the divine message. After Peter had been led to renounce himself, he received the call to work for Christ.

The disciples had witnessed many of Christ's miracles and had listened to His teaching, but none of them had left their former employment completely. The imprisonment of John the Baptist had been a bitter disappointment to them. If this was the outcome of John's mission, they could have little hope for their Master, with the religious leaders united against Him. It was a relief to return to their fishing for a little while. But now Jesus called them to abandon their former life and unite their interests with His. Peter had accepted the call. On reaching shore, Jesus invited the three others, "Follow Me, and I will make you fishers of men." Immediately they left everything and followed Him.

## Sacrifice Rewarded

Before asking them to leave their fishing boats, Jesus had given them the assurance that God would supply their needs. He richly repaid them for the use of Peter's boat. He who is "rich to all who call upon Him," has said, "Give, and it will be given to you: good measure, pressed down, shaken together, and running over." Romans 10:12; Luke 6:38. This was the measure He had used in rewarding Peter's service. And every sacrifice made in His ministry will be repaid. See Ephesians 2:7; 3:20.

During that sad night on the lake,

separated from Christ, unbelief pressed hard upon the disciples. But Jesus' presence ignited their faith and brought joy and success. It is the same with us: apart from Christ our work is fruitless, and it is easy to distrust and complain. But when we labor under His direction, we rejoice in the evidence of His power. He inspires us with faith and hope. He whose word could gather the fish from the sea can also impress human hearts and draw them so that His servants may become "fishers of men."

Christ was abundantly able to qualify humble and unschooled men for the position for which He had chosen them. The Savior did not despise education. When it is controlled by the love of God, intellectual culture is a blessing. But the wise men of His time were so self-confident that they could not become colaborers with the Man of Nazareth. They scorned Christ's efforts to teach them. The first thing that all who want to become workers with God need to learn is the lesson of self-distrust. Then they are prepared to receive the character of Christ. This does not come through education in scientific schools.

### How True Servants Are Educated

Jesus chose unschooled fishermen because they had not been trained in the faulty customs of their time. They were men of natural ability, and they were humble and teachable. In the common walks of life, many people are patiently going about their daily work, unconscious that they possess powers that, if called into action, would raise them to equality with the world's most

honored leaders. They need the touch of a skillful hand to awaken those dormant abilities. This is the kind of men Jesus called to be His colaborers. When the disciples emerged from the Savior's training, they had become like Him in mind and character.

Education's highest work is to infuse that vitalizing energy that comes through the contact of mind with mind and heart with heart. Only life can create life. What a privilege, then, the disciples had for three years to be in daily contact with that divine life! John the disciple said, "Of His fullness we have all received, and grace for grace." John 1:16. The lives of these men, the characters they developed, and the mighty work God did through them are a testimony to what God will do for all who are teachable and obedient. There is no limit to the usefulness of those who will put self aside, make room for the working of the Holy Spirit on their hearts, and live a life completely consecrated to God. If we will accept the necessary discipline, God will teach us hour by hour. He takes people as they are and educates them for His service, if they will yield themselves to Him. The Spirit of God, received into the heart, will energize all its powers. The mind that we devote entirely to God develops harmoniously and receives strength to comprehend and fulfill His requirements. The weak character becomes strong and steady.

Constant devotion establishes so close a relationship between Jesus and His followers that Christians become like Him in mind and character. They will have clearer and broader views, their understanding will be sharper, their judgment better balanced. They are enabled to produce much fruit to the glory of God. Christians in humble life have obtained an education in the highest of all schools. They have sat at the feet of Him who spoke as "no man ever spoke."

# Busy and Happy Days at Capernaum*

In between His journeys here and there, Jesus stayed at Capernaum on the shores of the Sea of Galilee, and it came to be known as "His own city." Matthew 9:1. The shores of the lake and the hills that encircle it a little distance away were dotted with towns and villages. The lake was covered with fishing boats. Everywhere was the stir of busy, active life.

Capernaum was on the highway from Damascus to Jerusalem and Egypt and to the Mediterranean Sea, so people from many lands passed through it. Here Jesus could meet all nations and all ranks, and His lessons would be carried to other countries. This would stir investigation of the prophecies, direct attention to the Savior, and bring His mission before the world. Angels were preparing the way for His ministry, moving on people's hearts and drawing them to the Savior.

In Capernaum, the nobleman's son whom Christ had healed was a witness to His power. The court official and his household joyfully testified of their faith. When news spread that the Teacher Himself was among them, the whole city became excited. On the Sabbath, the people crowded the synagogue until great numbers had to turn away.

All who heard the Savior "were astonished at His teaching, for His word was with authority." "He taught them as one having authority, and not as the scribes." Luke 4:32; Matthew 7:29. The teaching of the scribes and elders was cold and formal. They claimed to explain the law, but no inspiration from God stirred their own hearts or the hearts of their hearers.

Jesus' work was to present the truth. His words shed a flood of light on the teachings of the prophets. Never before had His hearers seen such depth of meaning in the Word of God.

Jesus made truth beautiful by presenting it in the most direct and simple way. His language was pure, refined, and clear as a running stream. His voice was like music to those who had listened to the monotonous tones of the rabbis.

### No Doubts or Hesitancy

He spoke as one having authority. The rabbis spoke with doubt and hesitancy, as if Scripture might be inter-

* This chapter is based on Mark 1:21–38; Luke 4:31–44.

preted to mean one thing or exactly the opposite. But Jesus taught Scripture as having unquestionable authority. Whatever His subject, He presented it with power.

Yet He was earnest rather than forcible. He revealed God in every theme. Jesus worked to break the spell of shortsightedness that keeps people absorbed in earthly things. He showed the true value of the things of this life as subordinate to eternal interests, but He did not ignore their importance. He taught that a knowledge of divine truth prepares us to perform the duties of everyday life better. Conscious of His relationship to God, He still recognized His unity with every member of the human family.

He knew "how to speak a word in season to him who is weary." Isaiah 50:4. He had the tact to meet prejudiced minds and to surprise them with illustrations that got their attention. He took His illustrations from the things of daily life. These were simple, but they had a wonderful depth of meaning. The birds, the lilies, the seed, the shepherd, the sheep—with these objects Jesus illustrated immortal truth; and from that time on, when His hearers happened to see these things, they recalled His lessons.

Christ never flattered people or praised them for their clever inventions, but deep, unprejudiced thinkers received His teaching and found that it tested their wisdom. His words charmed the highly educated and always profited the uneducated. He made even the heathen understand that He had a message for them.

Even amid angry enemies, He was surrounded with an atmosphere of peace. The loveliness of His character, the love He expressed in look and tone, drew to Him all who were not hardened in unbelief. Those in difficulty felt that He was a faithful and tender Friend, and they wanted to know more of the truths He taught. They longed to have the comfort of His love with them continually.

Jesus watched the faces of His hearers. Faces that expressed interest gave Him satisfaction. As the arrows of truth pierced through the barriers of selfishness and brought about repentance and gratitude, the Savior was glad. When His eye recognized faces He had seen before, His own face lighted up with joy. When plainly spoken truth touched some cherished idol, He noticed the change of expression that revealed that the light was unwelcome. When He saw men and women refuse the message of peace, it pierced His heart to the very depths.

In the synagogue, Jesus was interrupted while speaking of His mission to set free the captives of Satan. A madman rushed from among the people, crying out, "Let us alone! What have we to do with You, Jesus of Nazareth? Did you come to destroy us? I know who You are—the Holy One of God!"

The scene was all confusion and alarm. The people's attention was diverted from Christ, and His words went unheard. But Jesus rebuked the demon, saying, " 'Be quiet, and come out of him!' And when the demon had thrown him in their midst, it came out of him and did not hurt him."

Satan had darkened the mind of

this poor sufferer, but in the Savior's presence, the man began to long for freedom from Satan's control. But the demon resisted. When the man tried to appeal to Jesus for help, the evil spirit put words in his mouth, and he cried out in an agony of fear.

The demon-possessed man partially understood that he was in the presence of One who could set him free. But when he tried to come within reach of that mighty hand, another's will held him, another's words found expression through him. The conflict between the power of Satan and his own desire for freedom was terrible.

The demon exerted all his power to keep control of his victim. It seemed that the tortured man would surely lose his life in the struggle with the enemy that had ruined his best years. But the Savior spoke with authority and set the captive free. The man stood before the amazed people, happy in the freedom of self-possession. Even the demon had testified to the divine power of the Savior. The eye that had so recently glared with insanity now beamed with intelligence and overflowed with grateful tears.

The people exclaimed, "What is this? What new doctrine is this? For with authority He commands even the unclean spirits, and they obey Him."

This man had been fascinated by the pleasures of sin and had thought to make life a grand carnival. He did not dream of becoming a terror to the world and a disgrace to his family. He thought he could spend his time in innocent folly. But intemperance and a failure to take life seriously perverted his nature, and Satan took absolute

control of him. When he would have sacrificed wealth and pleasure to regain control of his life, he had become helpless in the grasp of the evil one. Satan had taken possession of all his abilities. When the poor man was finally in his power, the demon became relentless in his cruelty. It is like this with everyone who yields to evil. The fascinating pleasure of the early days ends in despair or the madness of a ruined life.

The same evil spirit controlled the unbelieving Jews, but with them he took on an air of piety. Their condition was more hopeless than that of the demon-possessed man, for they felt no need of Christ and so were held firmly under Satan's power.

Christ's personal ministry on earth was the time of greatest activity for the forces of the kingdom of darkness. For ages Satan had been working to control the bodies and souls of men and women, to bring sin and suffering on them; then he had blamed all this misery on God. Jesus was revealing the character of God to them, breaking Satan's power and setting his captives free. Love and power from heaven were moving human hearts, and the prince of evil was angry. At every step he challenged the work of Christ.

## Satan Works Under Disguise

This is how it will be in the final conflict between righteousness and sin. While new life and power are descending on the disciples of Christ, a new life is energizing the agencies of Satan. With skill gained through centuries of conflict, the prince of evil works in disguise, clothed as an angel of light. Huge numbers are "giving heed to deceiving spirits and doctrines of demons." 1 Timothy 4:1.

The leaders and teachers of Israel were neglecting the only means by which they could have resisted evil spirits. It was by the Word of God that Christ overcame the wicked one. By their interpretation, the Jewish leaders made God's Word say things that God had never given. They argued over technicalities, and in doing so they denied essential truths. In this way, they robbed God's Word of its power, and evil spirits accomplished their will.

History is repeating. With the open Bible in front of them, many religious leaders of our time are destroying faith in it as the Word of God. They dissect the Word and set their own opinions above its plainest statements. This is why unbelief is growing rapidly and iniquity is everywhere.

Those who turn from the plain teaching of Scripture and the convicting power of God's Holy Spirit are inviting the control of demons. Criticism and speculation concerning the Bible have opened the way for spiritism to gain a foothold even in the professed churches of our Lord Jesus Christ. Side by side with the preaching of the gospel, lying spirits are at work. Many people tamper with these manifestations just from curiosity, but when they see evidence of more than human power, they are lured on until the mysterious power of a will stronger than their own controls them. The defenses of the soul are broken down. Secret sins or master passions may hold them captive as helpless as the demon-possessed man of Caper-

naum. Yet their condition is not hopeless.

They can overcome by the power of the Word. If we desire to know and to do God's will, His promises are ours: "You shall know the truth, and the truth shall make you free." "If anyone wants to do His will, he shall know concerning the doctrine, whether it is from God." John 8:32; 7:17. Through faith in these promises, every man and woman may be delivered from the snares of error and the control of sin.

### There Is Hope for Every Lost Person

None have fallen so low, none are so evil, that they cannot find deliverance in Christ. The demon-possessed man could speak only the words of Satan, yet Jesus heard his heart's unspoken appeal. No cry from someone in need will be ignored, even if it doesn't use just the right words. The Savior invites those who will consent to enter into covenant relation with the God of heaven, "Let him take hold of My strength, that he may make peace with Me; and he shall make peace with Me." Isaiah 27:5. Angels of God will fight for them with victorious power. "Can . . . the captives of a tyrant be rescued? . . . I will contend with those who contend with you, and I will save your children." Isaiah 49:24, 25, NRSV.

While the congregation in the synagogue were still spellbound, Jesus left for Peter's home for a little rest. But here also a shadow had fallen. Peter's mother-in-law lay sick, stricken with a "high fever." Jesus rebuked the disease, and the healed woman got up and provided refreshments for the Master and His disciples.

News of Christ's work spread rapidly throughout Capernaum. For fear of the rabbis, the people dared not come for healing on the Sabbath, but as soon as the sun had disappeared below the horizon, the inhabitants of the city hurried toward the humble home that sheltered Jesus. They brought the sick into the Savior's presence.

Hour after hour they came and went, for no one could know whether tomorrow would find the Healer still among them. Never before had Capernaum witnessed a day like this. The air was filled with the voice of triumph and shouts of deliverance. The Savior rejoiced in His power to restore the suffering ones to health and happiness.

It was far into the night when the crowds left and silence settled down on Simon's home. The long, exciting day was past, and Jesus needed rest. But while the city was still wrapped in slumber, "a long while before daylight, He went out and departed to a solitary place; and there He prayed."

Jesus often sent His disciples to visit their homes and rest, but He gently resisted their efforts to draw Him away from His labors. All day He worked, and at evening or in the early morning He went to the mountains to talk with His Father. Often He spent the entire night in prayer and meditation, returning at daybreak to His work among the people.

Early in the morning, Peter and his companions came to Jesus, saying that already the people were looking for Him. The authorities at Jerusalem were trying to find a way to murder Him; even His own townsfolk had attempted to take His life; but Capernaum had welcomed Him with enthusiasm, and this had raised the hopes of the disciples again. It might be that the supporters of the new kingdom might come from the liberty-loving Galileans. So it was with surprise that they heard Christ's words, "Let us go on to the neighboring towns, so that I may proclaim the message there also; for that is what I came out to do." Mark 1:38, NRSV. Jesus was not satisfied to attract attention to Himself as a wonder worker or healer. While the people were eager to believe that He had come as a king to establish an earthly reign, He wanted to turn their minds away from the earthly to the spiritual.

And the attention of the careless crowd jarred on His spirit. The homage the world gives to position, wealth, or talent was foreign to the Son of man. Jesus used none of the means that people employ to win the loyalty of others. Prophecy had said of Him, "He will not cry or lift up His voice, or make it heard in the street; . . . he will faithfully bring forth justice." Isaiah 42: 2, 3, NRSV.

The life of Jesus included no noisy arguments, no showy worship, no act to gain applause. Christ was hid in God, and God was revealed in the character of His Son.

The Sun of Righteousness did not burst on the world in splendor, to dazzle the senses with His glory. Quietly and gently the daylight dispels the darkness and wakes the world to life. So did the Sun of Righteousness arise, "with healing in His wings." Malachi 4:2.

# The First Leper to Be Cleansed by Christ*

Of all diseases known in the East, leprosy was most dreaded. Its incurable and contagious character and its horrible effect on its victims filled the bravest with fear. The Jews regarded it as a judgment for sin, calling it "the finger of God." It was looked upon as a symbol of sin.

Like someone already dead, the leper was shut out from any place that people occupied. Whatever he touched was unclean. The air was polluted by his breath. Anyone suspected of having the disease must present himself to the priests. If they declared him a leper, he was doomed to associate only with other lepers. The law was inflexible. Kings and rulers were not exempt.

The leper must bear the curse apart from friends and family. He was required to announce his calamity and sound the alarm, warning everyone to avoid his contaminating presence. The cry, "Unclean! Unclean!" coming in mournful tones from the lonely exile was a signal people heard with fear and revulsion.

News of Christ's work reached many of these sufferers, igniting a

gleam of hope. But since the days of Elisha, no one had ever seen a leper cleansed. There was one man, however, in whose heart faith began to spring up. Yet how could he present himself to the Healer? And would Christ heal him? Would He take notice of one who was suffering the judgment of God? Would He pronounce a curse on him?

The leper thought of all that people had told him about Jesus. Not one who had gone to Him for help had been turned away. The suffering man determined to find the Savior. Perhaps he could cross His path in some remote place along the mountain roads or as He was teaching outside the towns. This was his only hope.

The leper was guided to the Savior as He taught beside the lake. Standing far away, the leper caught a few words from the Savior's lips. He saw Him laying His hands on the sick, the lame, the blind, and the paralyzed, and those who had been dying of various illnesses rose up and praised God for their deliverance. Faith strengthened in his heart. He went closer, forgetting the restrictions laid on him and the fear

---

* This chapter is based on Matthew 8:2–4; 9:1–8, 32–34; Mark 1:40–45; 2:1–12; Luke 5:12–28.

everyone had for him. He thought only of the blessed hope of healing.

He was a repulsive spectacle, his decaying body horrible to look at. When people saw him, they fell back in terror, crowding one another in their eagerness to avoid any contact with him. Some tried to prevent him from approaching Jesus, but he neither saw nor heard them. He saw only the Son of God. Hurrying to Jesus, he threw himself at His feet with the cry, "Lord, if You are willing, You can make *me* clean." (Italics added.)

Jesus replied, "I am willing; be cleansed," and laid His hand on him.

Immediately a change came over the leper. His flesh became healthy, the nerves sensitive, the muscles firm. The rough, scaly surface on his skin disappeared, and a soft glow, like that of a healthy child's skin, took its place.

Christ urgently instructed the man about the necessity of silence and prompt action. Jesus said to him, "See that you say nothing to anyone; but go your way, show yourself to the priest, and offer for your cleansing those things which Moses commanded, as a testimony to them." If the priests knew the facts concerning the healing, their hatred of Christ might lead them to give a dishonest judgment. Jesus wanted the man to present himself at the temple before rumors of the healing had reached them. In this way, the restored leper could secure an impartial decision and be permitted to unite with his family and friends again.

The Savior also knew that if news of this leper's healing spread, other sufferers from this disease would crowd around Him, and the cry would be raised that the people would be contaminated. Many lepers would not use the gift of health as a blessing to themselves or others. And by drawing lepers around Him, Jesus would open the way for His enemies to accuse Him of breaking down the restrictions of the law. This would hinder His preaching.

A large crowd had seen the leper's healing and were eager to learn of the priests' decision. When the man returned to his friends, there was great excitement. The man made no effort to hide his cure. It would have been impossible to conceal anyway, but the leper told it widely, thinking that Jesus had laid this restriction on him only out of modesty. He did not understand that every such exhibit of power made the priests and elders more determined to destroy Jesus. The restored man rejoiced in the vigor of manhood and felt it impossible to hold back from giving glory to the Physician who had made him whole. But his act of spreading the matter far and wide caused the people to flock to Jesus in such great numbers that He was forced for a time to stop His work.

Every act of Christ's ministry had a far-reaching purpose. He tried in every way to reach the priests and teachers, who were steeped in prejudice and tradition. By sending the healed leper to the priests, He gave them a testimony designed to disarm their prejudices. The Pharisees had claimed that Christ was opposed to the law, but His instruction to the cleansed leper to present an offering according to the law disproved this charge. Christ gave evidence of His love for humanity, His respect for the law, and His power to deliver from sin and death.

The same priests who had condemned the leper to banishment certified his cure publicly. And the healed man, reinstated in society, was a living witness for his Benefactor. Joyfully he praised the name of Jesus. The priests received an opportunity to know the truth. During the Savior's life, His mission seemed to call forth little response of love from them, but after His ascension "a great many of the priests were obedient to the faith." Acts 6:7.

## How Christ Cleanses the Life From Sin

The work of Christ in cleansing the leper illustrates His work in cleansing the life from sin. The man who came to Jesus was "full of leprosy." The disciples tried to prevent their Master from touching him. But in laying His hand on the leper, Jesus received no defilement. His touch conveyed life-giving power.

It is the same with the leprosy of sin—deadly, impossible for human power to cleanse. "From the sole of the foot even to the head, there is no soundness in it, but wounds and bruises and putrefying sores." Isaiah 1:6. But Jesus has healing virtue. Whoever will fall at His feet, saying in faith, "Lord, if You are willing, You can make me clean," will hear the answer, "I am willing; be cleansed."

In some cases of healing, Jesus did not immediately grant the blessing. In the case of the leper, though, as soon as the sick man appealed for help, Jesus granted it. When we pray for earthly blessings, the answer may be delayed, or God may give us something other than what we ask for. But not so when we ask for deliverance from sin. It is His will to cleanse us, make us His children, and enable us to live a holy life. Christ "gave Himself for our sins, that He might deliver us from this present evil age, according to the will of our God and Father." Galatians 1:4. "If we ask anything according to his will, he hears us. And if we know that he hears us in whatever we ask, we know that we have obtained the requests made of him." 1 John 5:14, 15, NRSV.

In healing the paralyzed man at Capernaum, Christ again taught the same truth. He performed the miracle to show His power to forgive sins. Like the leper, this paralytic had lost all hope. His disease was the result of a life of sin, and remorse made his sufferings all the more bitter. He had appealed to the Pharisees and doctors, but they coldly pronounced him incurable and gave him up to the wrath of God.

Seeing no prospect of aid from anywhere, the paralyzed man had sunk into despair. Then he heard of Jesus. Friends encouraged him to believe that he too might be cured if he could be carried to Jesus.

## The Burden of Sin

It was not physical restoration he longed for as much as relief from the burden of sin. If he could receive the assurance of forgiveness and peace with Heaven, he would be content to die. The dying man had no time to lose. He begged his friends to carry him on his bed to Jesus, and this they gladly set out to do. But the crowd was so dense where the Savior was that it was impossible for the sick man and his friends even to come within hearing of His voice.

Jesus was teaching in the house of Peter with His disciples close around Him. And "there were Pharisees and teachers of the law sitting by, who had come out of every town of Galilee, Judea, and Jerusalem" as spies. The crowds swarmed around outside—the eager, the reverent, the curious, the unbelieving. "And the power of the Lord was present to heal." But the Pharisees and doctors did not detect the Spirit's presence. They felt no need, and the healing was not for them. "He has filled the hungry with good things, and the rich He has sent away empty." Luke 1:53.

The friends carrying the paralyzed man tried to push their way through the crowd, but they could not. Would the sick man have to give up all hope? At his suggestion, his friends carried him to the top of the house, broke up the roof, and let him down at the feet of Jesus.

The Savior saw the pleading eyes riveted on Him. He understood the case. While the paralytic was at home, Jesus had brought conviction to his conscience. When he repented of his sins, the life-giving mercies of the Savior had first blessed his longing heart. Jesus had watched the first glimmer of faith grow stronger with every effort to come into His presence.

Now, in words that fell like music on the sufferer's ear, the Savior said, "Son, your sins are forgiven you." The burden of despair rolled from the sick man's soul; the peace of forgiveness radiated from his face. His pain was gone, his whole being was transformed. The helpless paralytic was healed, the guilty sinner pardoned!

In simple faith he accepted the words of Jesus. He made no further request but lay in blissful silence. The people looked on with awe.

The rabbis remembered how the man had appealed to them for help, and they had refused him hope or sympathy, declaring that he was suffering the curse of God for his sins. They noticed the interest with which all were watching the scene, and they felt a terrible fear of losing their influence over the people. Looking into one another's faces, they read the same thought—something must be done to arrest the tide of feeling. Jesus had declared the sins of the paralyzed man forgiven. The Pharisees could present this as blasphemy, a sin worthy of death. "Why does this Man speak blasphemies like this? Who can forgive sins but God alone?"

Looking intently at them, Jesus said, " 'Why do you reason about these things in your hearts? Which is easier, to say to the paralytic, "Your sins are forgiven you," or to say, "Arise, take up your bed and walk"? But that you may know that the Son of Man has power on earth to forgive sins'— He said to the paralytic, 'I say to you, arise, take up your bed, and go your way to your house.' "

Then the man who had been carried to Jesus on a stretcher rose to his feet with the ease and strength of youth. Every organ of his body sprang into activity. The glow of health replaced the pale look of approaching death. "Immediately he arose, took up the bed, and went out in the presence of them all, so that all were amazed and glorified God, saying, 'We never saw anything like this!' "

Creative power restored health to that decaying body. The same Voice that spoke life to Adam created from the dust of the earth spoke life to the dying paralytic. And the same Power that gave life to the body had renewed the heart. Christ told the paralytic to arise and walk, "that you may know that the Son of Man has power on earth to forgive sins."

### Spiritual Healing Often Precedes Physical Healing

Thousands today suffering from physical disease, like the paralyzed man, long for the message, "Your sins are forgiven." Sin is the foundation of their sicknesses. The Healer of the soul alone can give vigor to the mind and health to the body.

Jesus still has the same life-giving power as He did when He healed the sick and spoke forgiveness to the sinner. He "forgives all your iniquities"; He "heals all your diseases." Psalm 103:3; see 1 John 3:8; John 1:4–10; 10:10; 1 Corinthians 15:45.

As the man who had been cured passed through the crowd carrying his burden as if it were light as a feather, the people stepped back to give him room. With a look of awe on their faces, they whispered softly among themselves, "We have seen strange things today!"

The Pharisees were speechless with amazement and overwhelmed with defeat. Confused and humiliated, they recognized but did not acknowledge the presence of a superior Being. From Peter's home, where they had seen the paralytic restored, they went away set in unbelief, determined to invent new schemes for silencing the Son of God.

In the home of the healed man, there was great rejoicing. His family gathered around with tears of joy, scarcely daring to believe their eyes. The flesh that had been shrunken and gray was now fresh and ruddy. He walked with a firm, free step. Joy and hope were written on his face. Purity and peace had taken the place of the marks of sin and suffering. This man and his family were ready to lay down their lives for Jesus. No doubt dimmed their faith in Him who had brought light into their darkened home.

# Matthew: From Tax Collector to Apostle*

Roman officials in Palestine were hated. The fact that a foreign power had imposed taxes was a continual irritation, a reminder to the Jews that they had lost their independence. And the tax collectors, the publicans, were not just instruments of Roman oppression, they were extortioners on their own account, enriching themselves at the expense of the people. A Jew who accepted this office was despised and classed with the worst of society.

Levi-Matthew, whom Jesus would call to His service, was just such a person—a tax collector. Matthew had listened to the Savior's teaching, and as the Spirit of God revealed his sinfulness, he longed to seek help from Christ; but knowing how the rabbis kept most other people away, he had no thought that this Great Teacher would notice him.

Sitting at his toll booth one day, Matthew saw Jesus approaching. He was astonished to hear Jesus say to him, "Follow Me."

Matthew "left all, rose up, and followed Him." There was no hesitation, no questioning, no thought of the profitable business he would be ex-

changing for poverty and hardship. It was enough for him to be with Jesus, to listen to His words, and unite with Him in His work.

It was the same way when Jesus called Peter and his companions to follow Him. Immediately they left their boats and nets. Some had friends who depended on them for support, but when they received the Savior's invitation, they did not ask, "How will I live and provide for my family?" When Jesus later asked them, "When I sent you without money bag, sack, and sandals, did you lack anything?" they could answer, "Nothing." Luke 22:35.

Matthew in his wealth and Andrew and Peter in their poverty faced the same test. At the moment of success, when the nets were filled with fish and the impulses of the old life were strongest, Jesus asked the disciples at the sea to leave everything for the gospel. Everyone is tested this way, to see which is stronger—the desire for temporary prosperity or for fellowship with Christ.

No one can succeed in the service of God unless his whole heart is in the work. No one who holds anything back can be the disciple of Christ, much less His colaborer. When men

---

* This chapter is based on Matthew 9:9–17; Mark 2:14–22; Luke 5:27–39.

and women appreciate the great salvation Jesus has provided, their lives will reflect the self-sacrifice of His life. Wherever He leads the way, they will follow.

The call of Matthew made many people angry. For Christ to choose a tax collector as one of His closest companions was an offense against religious, social, and national customs. By appealing to prejudice, the Pharisees hoped to turn popular feeling against Jesus. But Jesus' choice created widespread interest among the publicans. In the joy of his new discipleship, Matthew made a feast at his house and called together his relatives, friends, and former associates. Not only were tax collectors included, but many others who were shunned by their more scrupulous neighbors.

### External Distinctions Meant Nothing

The feast was given in honor of Jesus, and He did not hesitate to accept. He knew very well that it would give offense to the Pharisees and their followers and would also make the people question what He was doing. But no political concerns could influence His movements.

Jesus sat as an honored guest at the table of the publicans. By sympathy and social kindliness, He showed that He recognized the dignity of humanity, and people longed to become worthy of His confidence. His presence awakened new impulses and opened the possibility of a new life to these outcasts of society.

Many people were impressed who did not acknowledge the Savior until after His ascension. When three thousand were converted in a day, many of them had first heard the truth at the table of the tax collectors. To Matthew himself, the example of Jesus at the feast was a constant lesson. The despised publican became one of the most devoted evangelists, following in his Master's steps.

### Attempt to Alienate Disciples

The rabbis grasped the opportunity to accuse Jesus, but they chose to work through the disciples. By stirring up their prejudices, they hoped to alienate them from their Master. "Why does your Teacher eat with tax collectors and sinners?" they questioned.

Jesus did not wait for the disciples to answer. He replied Himself: "Those who are well have no need of a physician, but those who are sick. . . . I did not come to call the righteous, but sinners, to repentance." The Pharisees claimed to be spiritually whole and therefore to have no need of a physician, but they regarded the tax collectors and Gentiles as dying from diseases of the soul. Then was it not His work, as a Physician, to go to the very people that needed His help?

Jesus said to the rabbis, "Go and learn what this means: 'I desire mercy and not sacrifice.' " They claimed to expound the Word of God, but they were completely ignorant of its spirit.

The Pharisees were silenced for the time but were only the more determined in their hostility. They next tried to turn the disciples of John the Baptist against the Savior. These Pharisees had pointed with scorn to the Baptist's simple habits and coarse garments and had declared him a fanatic. They had tried to stir up the people against him. The Spirit of God had moved on the hearts of these scorners, convicting them of sin, but they had declared that John was devil-possessed.

Now when Jesus came mingling with the people, eating and drinking at their tables, they accused Him of being a glutton and a drunkard. They would not consider that Jesus was eating with sinners in order to bring the light of heaven to those who sat in darkness. They would not consider that every word dropped by the divine Teacher was living seed that would germinate and bear fruit to the glory of God. They had determined not to accept the light, and although they had opposed the mission of the Baptist, they were now ready to cultivate the friendship of his disciples, hoping to win their cooperation against Jesus. They claimed that Jesus was setting aside the ancient traditions, and they contrasted the austere piety of the Baptist with how Jesus feasted with publicans and sinners.

At this time the disciples of John were in great sorrow. With their beloved teacher in prison, they spent their days in mourning. And Jesus was making no effort to release John. He even appeared to discredit his teaching. If John had been sent by God, why did Jesus and His disciples follow a course so widely different?

The disciples of John thought there might be some basis for the Pharisees' charges. They observed many rules established by the rabbis. The Jews practiced fasting as an act of merit. The most rigid of them fasted two days every week. The Pharisees and John's disciples were fasting when the latter came to Jesus with the inquiry, "Why do we and the Pharisees fast often, but Your disciples do not fast?"

Tenderly Jesus answered. He did not try to correct their false concept of fasting, but only to set them right regarding His own mission. John the Baptist himself had said, "He who has the bride is the bridegroom; but the friend of the bridegroom, who stands and hears him, rejoices greatly because of the bridegroom's voice. Therefore this joy of mine is fulfilled." John 3:29. The disciples of John could not fail to remember these words of their teacher. Taking up the illustration, Jesus said, "Can you make the friends of the bridegroom fast while the bridegroom is with them?"

The Prince of heaven was among His people. God had given His greatest Gift to the world. Joy to the poor, for He had come to make them heirs of His kingdom. Joy to the rich, for He would teach them to secure eternal riches. Joy to the ignorant, for He would make them wise unto salvation. Joy to the educated, for He would open to them deeper mysteries than they had ever understood. This was not a time for the disciples to mourn and fast. They must open their hearts to receive the light of His glory so that they could shed light on those who sat in darkness and in the shadow of death.

## A Heavy Shadow

It was a bright picture, but across it lay a heavy shadow that Christ's eye alone could see. "The days will come when the bridegroom will be taken away from them; then they will fast." When they would see their Lord betrayed and crucified, the disciples would mourn and fast.

When He would come out from the tomb, their sorrow would turn to joy. After His ascension, He would still be with them through the Comforter, and they were not to spend their time mourning. Satan wanted them to give the impression that they had been deceived and disappointed. But by faith they were to look to the sanctuary above where Jesus was ministering for them. They were to open their hearts to the Holy Spirit and rejoice in the light of His presence. Yet days of trial would come. When Christ was not personally with them and they failed to recognize the Comforter, then it would be more fitting for them to fast.

The Scripture describes the fast that God has chosen—"To loose the bonds of wickedness, to undo the heavy burdens, to let the oppressed go free, and that you break every yoke"; to "extend your soul to the hungry and satisfy the afflicted soul." Isaiah 58:6, 10. This describes the character of the work of Christ. Whether fasting in the wilderness or eating with publicans, He was giving His life to redeem the lost. We find the true spirit of devotion in the surrender of self in willing service to God and humanity.

Continuing His answer to John's disciples, Jesus spoke a parable: "No one puts a piece of unshrunk cloth on an old garment; for the patch pulls away from the garment, and the tear is made worse." An attempt to blend the tradition and superstition of the Pharisees with the devotion of John would only make the gap between them more evident.

Nor could the principles of Christ's teaching unite with the forms of the Pharisees. Christ was to make the separation between the old and the new more distinct. "Nor do people put new wine into old wineskins, or else the wineskins break, the wine is spilled, and the wineskins are ruined. But they put new wine into new wineskins, and both are preserved." After a time, the skin bottles used as vessels for new wine became dry and brittle, and they were then worthless to serve the same purpose again. The Jewish leaders were set firmly in a rut of ceremonies and traditions. Their hearts had become like dried-up wineskins. Since they were satisfied with a legal religion, it was impossible for them to become the trusted holders of living truth. They did not want to have a new element brought into their religion. The faith that works by love and purifies the soul could find no common ground with the religion of the Pharisees, made up of ceremonies and human rules. To unite Jesus' teachings with the established religion would be futile. The vital truth of God, like wine, would burst the old decaying bottles of the Pharisees' tradition.

## New Bottles for New Wine

The Savior turned away from the Pharisees to find others who would receive the message of heaven. In uneducated fishermen, in the tax collector at the marketplace, in the woman of

Samaria, in the common people who heard Him gladly, He found His new bottles for the new wine. People who gladly receive the light that God sends are His agents to give truth to the world.

Christ's teaching, represented by new wine, was not new doctrine but what had been taught from the beginning. But to the Pharisees, His teaching was new in almost every respect, and they did not recognize it or acknowledge it.

"No one, having drunk old wine, immediately desires new; for he says, 'The old is better.' " The truth that had come through patriarchs and prophets was shining out in new beauty in the words of Christ. But the scribes and Pharisees did not want the precious new wine. Until they could be emptied of old traditions and practices, they had no place in mind or heart for the teachings of Christ.

### The Peril of Cherished Opinion

This proved to be the ruin of the Jews, and it will be the ruin of many in our day. Rather than give up some cherished idea or idol of opinion, many refuse the truth that comes from the Father of light. They insist on being saved in some way by which they may perform some important work. When they see that there is no way of weaving self into the work, they reject the salvation provided.

A legal religion is a loveless, Christless religion. Fasting or prayer, if it comes from a self-justifying spirit, is an abomination in the sight of God. Our own works can never purchase salvation. To those who do not know their spiritual bankruptcy comes the message, "Because you say, 'I am rich, have become wealthy, and have need of nothing'—and do not know that you are wretched, miserable, poor, blind, and naked—I counsel you to buy from Me gold refined in the fire, that you may be rich; and white garments, that you may be clothed, that the shame of your nakedness may not be revealed." Revelation 3:17, 18. Faith and love are the gold. But with many, the gold has become dim, the rich treasure lost. The righteousness of Christ is a robe unworn, a fountain untouched.

"The sacrifices of God are a broken spirit, a broken and a contrite heart— these, O God, You will not despise." Psalm 51:17. When we renounce self, then the Lord can make us new creatures. New bottles can contain new wine. The love of Christ will fill the believers with new life. The character of Christ will be evident in them.

# Jesus Rescues the Sabbath

The Sabbath was made holy at Creation. As something God planned for mankind, it had its origin when "the morning stars sang together, and all the sons of God shouted for joy." Job 38:7. Earth was in harmony with heaven. "God saw everything that He had made, and indeed it was very good"; and He rested in the joy of His completed work. Genesis 1:31.

Because He had rested on the Sabbath, "God blessed the seventh day and sanctified it" (Genesis 2:3)—set it apart for a holy use. It was a memorial of the work of Creation, and as such, it is a sign of God's power and love.

The Son of God created all things. "All things were made through Him, and without Him nothing was made that was made." John 1:3. And since the Sabbath is a memorial of the work of Creation, it is an example of the love and power of Christ.

The Sabbath brings us into fellowship with the Creator. In the song of the bird, the sighing of the trees, and the music of the sea, we may still hear the voice of the One who talked with Adam in Eden. And as we see His power in nature, we find comfort, for the Word that created all things is also the One who speaks life to the soul.

He "who commanded light to shine out of darkness . . . has shone in our hearts to give the light of the knowledge of the glory of God in the face of Jesus Christ." 2 Corinthians 4:6.

"Look to Me, and be saved, all you ends of the earth! For I am God, and there is no other." Isaiah 45:22. This is the message written in nature, which the Sabbath is designed to keep in memory. When the Lord told Israel to hallow His Sabbaths, He said, "They will be a sign between Me and you, that you may know that I am the Lord your God." Ezekiel 20:20.

The people of Israel knew about the Sabbath before they came to Sinai. On the way there, they kept the Sabbath. When some profaned it, the Lord reproved them, "How long do you refuse to keep My commandments and My laws?" Exodus 16:28.

The Sabbath was not just for Israel, but for the world. Like the other commands of the Decalogue, it is a permanent obligation. Christ says concerning that law, "Till heaven and earth pass away, one jot or one tittle will by no means pass from the law." Matthew 5:18. As long as the heavens and the earth endure, the Sabbath will continue as a sign of the Creator's power. And when Eden will bloom on earth again, everyone will honor God's holy rest day. " 'From one Sabbath to another' " the inhabitants of the glorified new earth will go up " 'to worship before Me, says the Lord.' " Isaiah 66:23.

## The Sign of True Conversion

But in order to keep the Sabbath holy, men and women must themselves be holy. Through faith they must receive the righteousness of Christ. When God gave the command to Israel, "Remember the Sabbath day, to keep it holy" (Exodus 20:8), the Lord also said to them, "You shall be holy men to Me." Exodus 22:31.

As the Jews departed from God and failed to make the righteousness of Christ their own by faith, the Sabbath lost its significance to them. Satan worked to corrupt the Sabbath, because it is the sign of the power of Christ. The Jewish leaders surrounded God's rest day with heavy requirements. In the days of Christ, Sabbath observance reflected the character of selfish and arbitrary people rather than the character of the loving heavenly Father. The rabbis virtually represented God as giving laws impossible to obey. They led the people to look on God as a tyrant and to think that the Sabbath made a person hardhearted and cruel. It was the work of Christ to clear away these misconceptions. Jesus did not follow the rabbis' requirements but went straight forward, keeping the Sabbath according to the law of God.

## A Sabbath Lesson

One Sabbath, as the Savior and His disciples passed through a field of ripening grain, the disciples began to gather the heads of grain and to eat the kernels after rubbing them in their hands. On any other day, this would have drawn no comment, for a person passing through a field, an orchard, or a vineyard was free to gather what he wanted to eat. See Deuteronomy 23:24, 25. But many believed that to do this on the Sabbath would profane the holy day. Gathering the grain was a kind of reaping, and rubbing it in the hands a kind of threshing.

The spies immediately complained to Jesus, "Look, why do they do what is not lawful on the Sabbath?" Mark 2:24.

When accused of Sabbath breaking at Bethesda, Jesus defended Himself by affirming His Sonship to God, declaring that He worked in harmony with the Father. Now that the disciples were attacked, He mentioned Old Testament examples of things people did on the Sabbath when they were in the service of God.

The Savior's answer to His accusers contained an implied rebuke for their ignorance of the Sacred Writings: "Have you not even read this, what David did when he was hungry, he and those who were with him: how he went into the house of God, took and ate the showbread, . . . which is not lawful for any but the priests to eat?" "And He said to them, 'The Sabbath was made for man, and not man for the Sabbath.' " "Or have you not read in the law that on the Sabbath the priests in the temple profane the Sabbath, and are blameless? But I say to you that in this place there is One greater than the temple." "The Son of man is Lord even of the Sabbath." Luke 6:3, 4; Mark 2:27; Matthew 12:5, 6, 8.

If it was right for David to satisfy his hunger by eating the bread set apart for a holy use, then it was right for the disciples to pluck grain on the Sabbath. Again, the priests in the temple had more work to do on the Sabbath than on other days. The same labor in secular business would be sinful, but they were performing rites that pointed to the redeeming power of Christ, and their labor was in harmony with the Sabbath.

The purpose of God's work in this world is to redeem mankind. So whatever is necessary to do on the Sabbath to accomplish this work is in harmony with the Sabbath law. Jesus then finished His argument by declaring Himself the "Lord of the Sabbath"—One above all questions and all law. This infinite Judge acquitted the disciples of blame, appealing to the very laws they were accused of violating.

Jesus declared that in their blindness, His enemies had mistaken the purpose of the Sabbath. He said, "If you had known what this means, 'I desire mercy and not sacrifice,' you would not have condemned the guiltless." Matthew 12:7. Their heartless rites could not make up for the lack of the integrity and tender love that characterize the true worshiper of God.

## Jesus Deliberately Heals on the Sabbath

In themselves, sacrifices were of no value. They were a means, not an end. Their purpose was to direct people to the Savior, to bring them into harmony with God. The service of love is what God values. Without this, mere ceremony is an offense to Him. It is the same with the Sabbath. When the mind is absorbed with tiresome rites, the purpose of the Sabbath is defeated. Just observing it outwardly is a mockery.

In the synagogue on another Sabbath, Jesus saw a man who had a withered hand. The Pharisees watched, eager to see what He would do. The Savior did not hesitate to break down the wall of traditional requirements that barricaded the Sabbath.

Jesus told the suffering man to step forward and asked, "Is it lawful on the Sabbath to do good or to do evil, to save life or to kill?" Mark 3:4. It was a common saying among the Jews that failure to do good when one had opportunity was to do evil; to neglect to save life was to kill. So Jesus met the rabbis on their own ground. "But they kept silent. So when He had looked around at them with anger, being grieved by the hardness of their hearts, He said to the man, 'Stretch out your hand.' And he stretched it out, and his hand was restored." Verses 4, 5.

When He was asked, "Is it lawful to heal on the Sabbath?" Jesus answered, "What man is there among you who has one sheep, and if it falls into a pit on the Sabbath, will not lay hold of it and lift it out? Of how much more value then is a man than a sheep? Therefore it is lawful to do good on the Sabbath." Matthew 12:10–12.

## Greater Care Shown Animals

The spies did not dare to answer Christ. They knew He had spoken the truth. Rather than violate traditions, they would allow a man to suffer, while they would relieve a work animal because neglecting it would bring loss to the owner. They showed greater care for the animals than for human beings. This illustrates how all false religions work. They originate in our human desire to exalt ourselves above God, but they result in degrading us below the animals. Every false religion teaches its followers to be careless of human needs, sufferings, and rights. The gospel places a high value on humanity as the purchase of Christ's blood, and it teaches us to regard human wants and distress with tenderness. See Isaiah 13:12.

The Pharisees were hunting Jesus' life with bitter hatred, while He was saving life and bringing happiness to large numbers of people. Was it better to kill on the Sabbath, as they were planning to do, than to heal the suffering ones, as He had done?

In healing the withered hand, Jesus condemned the custom of the Jews and left the fourth commandment standing as God had given it. "It is lawful to do good on the Sabbath," He declared. By sweeping away senseless restrictions, Christ honored the Sabbath, while those who complained about Him were dishonoring God's holy day.

Those who hold that Christ abolished the law teach that He broke the Sabbath and justified His disciples in doing the same. In this way, they are taking the same position as did the disapproving Jews. In doing so, they contradict Christ Himself, who declared, "I have kept My Father's commandments and abide in His love." John 15:10. Neither the Savior nor His followers broke the Sabbath. Looking at a nation of witnesses who were trying to find some way to condemn Him, He could say unchallenged, "Which of you convicts Me of sin?" John 8:46.

"The Sabbath was made for man, and not man for the Sabbath," Jesus said. God gave the Ten Commandments, including the Sabbath, to His people as a blessing. See Deuteronomy 6:24. Of all who keep "from defiling the Sabbath," the Lord declares, "Even them I will bring to My holy mountain, and make them joyful in My house of prayer." Isaiah 56:6, 7.

"The Son of man is Lord even of the Sabbath." For "all things were made through Him, and without Him nothing was made that was made." John 1:3. Since Christ made everything, He made the Sabbath. He is the One who set it apart as a memorial of Creation. It points to Him as both Creator and Sanctifier. It declares that He who created all things is the Head of the church and that by His power we are reconciled to God. He said, "I gave them My Sabbaths, to be a sign between them and Me, that they might know that I am the Lord who sanctifies them," or makes them holy. Ezekiel 20:12. The Sabbath is a sign of Christ's power to make us holy. And He has given it to all whom He makes holy, as a sign of His sanctifying power.

To all who receive the Sabbath as a sign of Christ's creative and redeeming power, it will be a delight. See Isaiah 58:13, 14. Seeing Christ in it, they delight themselves in Him. While it reminds us of the lost peace of Eden, it also tells us of peace restored through the Savior. And every object in nature repeats His invitation, "Come to Me, all you who labor and are heavy laden, and I will give you rest." Matthew 11:28.

# Christ Ordains Twelve Apostles*

A nd He went up on the mountain and called to Him those He Himself wanted. And they came to Him. Then He appointed twelve, that they might be with Him and that He might send them out to preach."

Beneath the sheltering trees of the mountainside, a little distance from the Sea of Galilee, Jesus called the Twelve to be His apostles, and He gave the Sermon on the Mount. In training His disciples, Jesus chose to leave the confusion of the city for the quiet of the fields and hills, which was more in harmony with the lessons of self-denial He wanted to teach. And during His ministry, He loved to gather the people around Him under the blue heavens, on some grassy hillside, or on the beach beside the lake. Here He could turn His hearers from the artificial things to the natural. In the growth and development of nature, they could learn precious lessons of divine truth.

Jesus was about to take the first step in organizing the church that was to be His representative on earth after His departure. They had no costly sanctuary, but the Savior led His disciples to the secluded place He loved, and in their minds the sacred experiences of that day were linked forever with the beauty of mountain, valley, and sea.

Jesus had called His disciples so that He could send them out to tell the world what they had seen and heard from Him. Their task, the most important to which human beings had ever been called, was second only to that of Christ Himself. They were to work with God for the saving of the world.

The Savior knew the character of the men He had chosen. Their weaknesses and errors were open before Him. He knew the dangers that they must pass through, and His heart went out to these chosen ones. Alone on a mountain, He spent the entire night in prayer for them, while they were sleeping at the foot of the mountain. With the first light of dawn, He called them to meet Him.

John and James, Andrew and Peter, with Philip, Nathanael, and Matthew, had been more closely connected with Jesus in active labor than the others. Peter, James, and John had an even closer relationship with Him, witnessing His miracles and hearing His words. The Savior loved them all, but John's spirit was the most receptive.

---

* This chapter is based on Mark 3:13–35; Luke 6:12–16.

Younger than the others, with more of a child's simple trust, he opened his heart to Jesus. In this way, he came more into harmony with Christ, and through him the Savior communicated His deepest spiritual teaching to His people.

## Slow to Believe

Philip was the first to whom Jesus spoke the distinct command, "Follow Me." He had heard John the Baptist announce Christ as the Lamb of God. He was a sincere seeker for truth but was slow to believe, as his announcement of Jesus to Nathanael shows. Though the Voice from heaven had proclaimed Christ as the Son of God, to Philip He was "Jesus of Nazareth, the son of Joseph." John 1:45. Again, when Jesus fed the five thousand, Philip showed his lack of faith. To test him, Jesus questioned, "Where shall we buy bread, that these may eat?" Philip's answer, on the side of unbelief, made Jesus sad: "Two hundred denarii worth of bread is not sufficient for them, that every one of them may have a little." John 6:5, 7. Philip had seen Jesus' works and felt His power, yet he did not have faith.

When the Greeks asked Philip concerning Jesus, he did not take the opportunity to introduce them to the Savior, but went to tell Andrew. Again, in those last hours before the Crucifixion, the words of Philip were the kind that discourage faith. When Thomas said, "Lord, . . . how can we know the way?" the Savior answered, "I am the way. . . . If you had known Me, you would have known My Father also." From Philip came the response of unbelief: "Lord, show us the Father, and it is sufficient for us." John 14:5–8.

In happy contrast to Philip's unbelief was the childlike trust of Nathanael, whose faith took hold of unseen realities. Yet Philip was a student in the school of Christ, and the divine Teacher bore patiently with his unbelief and dullness. When the Holy Spirit was poured out on the disciples, Philip became a godly teacher who taught with an assurance that carried conviction to the hearers.

While Jesus was preparing the disciples for ordination, one whom He had not called pressed in among them. Judas Iscariot, a professed follower of Christ, came forward, asking for a place in this inner circle. By joining the apostles, he hoped to gain a high place in the new kingdom. He looked like someone important, he had a keen mind and executive ability, and the disciples recommended him to Jesus as one who would help Him greatly in His work. If Jesus had turned Judas away, they would have questioned their Master's wisdom. However, the later history of Judas would show the danger of allowing worldly consideration to have weight in deciding someone's fitness for the work of God.

Yet Judas felt the influence of the divine power that was drawing people to the Savior. Jesus would not reject this man while even one desire was reaching toward the light. The Savior read Judas's heart. He knew the depths of sin to which he would sink, unless he was delivered by the grace of God. In connecting this man with Himself, He placed him where day by day he could come into contact with

His own unselfish love. If he would open his heart to Christ, even Judas might become a citizen of the kingdom of God.

God takes people as they are and trains them for His service, if they will be disciplined and learn from Him. Through knowing and practicing the truth, through the grace of Christ, they may be transformed into His image.

Judas had the same opportunities as the other disciples had. But to follow the truth was not what he wanted or intended, and he would not yield his ideas in order to receive wisdom from Heaven.

Tenderly the Savior dealt with the one who was to be His betrayer! Jesus showed Judas the hateful character of greed. Many times the disciple realized that Jesus had portrayed his character and pointed out his sin, but he would not confess and forsake his unrighteousness. He continued to follow his dishonest practices. Lesson after lesson fell in vain on the ears of Judas.

## Judas Without Excuse

With divine patience, Jesus allowed this erring man to continue with Him, even while giving him evidence that He read his heart like an open book. He presented before him the highest incentives for doing right. But Judas cherished evil desires, revengeful passions, and dark and sullen thoughts until Satan had full control.

If Judas had been willing to serve like Christ, he could have been among the greatest of the apostles. But he chose his own selfish ambitions, unfitting himself for the work God would have given him to do.

All the disciples had serious faults when Jesus called them. John and his brother were called the "Sons of Thunder." Any disrespect or contempt shown to Jesus made them angry. Evil temper, revenge, criticism, were all in John, the beloved disciple. But day by day he saw the tenderness and self-restraint of Jesus and heard His lessons of humility and patience. He opened his heart to the divine influence and learned to wear the yoke of Christ.

Jesus corrected and cautioned His disciples, but John and the others did not leave Him. They continued to the end to share His trials and to learn the lessons of His life. By beholding Christ, they became transformed in character.

The apostles differed widely in habits and character. There was the tax collector, Levi-Matthew; the fiery zealot Simon; generous, impulsive Peter; mean-spirited Judas; Thomas, truehearted, but timid and fearful; Philip, inclined to doubt; the ambitious, outspoken sons of Zebedee, with their fellow apostles. Jesus brought them together, all with inherited and cultivated tendencies to evil. But in Christ, they would learn to become one in faith, in doctrine, in spirit. They would have their differences of opinion, but while Christ was abiding in the heart, there could be no discord. The Master's lessons would lead them to harmonize all differences, till the disciples would be of one mind and one judgment. Christ is the great Center, and they would approach one another more and more as they approached the center.

## Ordained for Sacred Work

Jesus gathered the little group close around Him. Kneeling in the midst of them and laying His hands on their heads, He offered a prayer dedicating them to His sacred work.

To represent Him among us, Christ does not choose angels who have never fallen, but human beings who have the same nature as those they seek to save. Christ took humanity on Himself. It required both the Divine and the human to bring salvation to the world. The situation is similar with the servants and messengers of Christ. Humanity lays hold on divine power, Christ dwells in the heart by faith, and through cooperating with the Divine, human power becomes efficient for good.

He who called the fishermen of Galilee is still calling men and women to His service. However imperfect and sinful we may be, the Lord offers to make us apprentices of Christ. Uniting with Him, we may work the works of God.

"We have this treasure in clay jars, so that it may be made clear that this extraordinary power belongs to God and does not come from us." 2 Corinthians 4:7, NRSV. It becomes clear to everyone that the power that works through the weakness of humanity is the power of God. This enables us to believe that the power that can help others as weak as ourselves can help us.

Those who are "subject to weakness" (NRSV) themselves should be able to "have compassion on those who are ignorant and going astray." Hebrews 5:2. There are people who are perplexed with doubt, weak in faith, and unable to grasp the Unseen. But a friend, someone they can see, coming in Christ's place, can be a connecting link to fasten their trembling faith on Christ.

We must be the channel to communicate with other people. And when we give ourselves to Christ, angels rejoice that they may speak through our voices to reveal God's love.

# The Sermon on the Mount[*]

Christ seldom gathered His disciples alone to receive His words. It was His work to reach everyone, in words of warning, pleading, and encouragement, seeking to help all who would come to Him.

Jesus gave His Sermon on the Mount especially to the disciples, but He spoke it within the hearing of the crowds. After ordaining the apostles, Jesus went to the seaside. In the early morning, people had begun to assemble. "When they heard how many things He was doing," they "came to hear Him and be healed of their diseases, . . . power went out from Him and healed them all." Mark 3:8; Luke 6:17–19.

The narrow beach did not provide even standing room, and Jesus led the way back to the mountainside. Reaching a level space that featured a pleasant gathering place, He sat down on the grass, and the disciples and the crowd followed His example.

The disciples sat close beside Him, eager to understand the truths they were to take to all lands and all ages. They believed that Jesus would soon establish His kingdom.

A feeling of expectancy also swept through the crowd. As the people sat on the green hillside, their hearts were filled with thoughts of future glory. Scribes and Pharisees looked forward to the day when they would rule over the hated Romans and possess the riches and splendor of the world's great empire. Poor peasants and fishermen hoped to hear that they were going to exchange their small, poor homes, scanty food, and fear of having nothing for mansions and ease. They hoped that Israel would soon be honored before the nations as the Lord's chosen and Jerusalem be exalted as the head of a universal kingdom.

## Christ Disappointed the Hope of Worldly Greatness

In the Sermon on the Mount, Christ tried to undo the work that false education had done and to give His hearers a right understanding of His kingdom. Without combating their ideas of God's kingdom, He told them the conditions for entering it, leaving them to draw their own conclusions about its nature. "Happy are they," He said, "who recognize their spiritual poverty and feel their need of redemption." The gospel is revealed, not to the spiritu-

---

[*] *This chapter is based on Matthew 5–7.*

ally proud, but to those who are humble and repentant.

The proud heart tries to earn salvation, but both our title to heaven and our fitness for it are found in the righteousness of Christ. The Lord can do nothing toward our recovery until we yield ourselves to God's control. Then we can receive the gift God is waiting to bestow. From the person who feels his need, nothing is withheld. See Isaiah 57:15.

"Blessed are those who mourn, for they shall be comforted." The mourning that Christ speaks of does not consist in sadness and wailing. We often sorrow because our evil deeds bring unpleasant consequences, but real sorrow for sin is the result of the Holy Spirit's working. The Spirit brings us in repentance to the foot of the cross. Jesus is wounded again by every sin, and as we look on Him whom we have pierced, we mourn for sins that have brought anguish on Him. Such mourning will lead us to renounce sin. This sorrow binds the repentant sinner to the Infinite One. The tears of repentance are the raindrops that precede the sunshine of holiness, announcing a joy that will be a living fountain in the soul. See Jeremiah 3:12, 13; Isaiah 61:3.

There is comfort also for those who mourn in trial and sorrow. Through affliction God reveals to us the deadly spots in our characters, so that by His grace we may overcome. He opens to us unknown chapters about ourselves, and the test comes, revealing whether we will accept the reproof and counsel of God. When in such trials, we should not rebel or worry ourselves out of the hand of Christ. The ways of the Lord appear dark and joyless to our human nature. But God's ways are ways of mercy, and the result is salvation.

God's word for the sorrowing is, "I will turn their mourning to joy, [and] will comfort them." Jeremiah 31:13.

### A Calm Spirit Glorifies God

"Blessed are the meek." The meekness that hides itself in Christ will greatly reduce the difficulties we encounter. If we possess the humility of our Master, we will rise above scorn, snubs, and annoyances. These things will no longer cast sadness over the spirit. People who fail to keep a calm spirit when others treat them badly rob God of His right to reveal His own perfection of character in them. Humbleness of heart is the strength that gives victory to Christ's followers.

The world may look scornfully on those who reveal the meek and lowly spirit of Christ, but God values them greatly. The poor in spirit, the humble in heart, whose highest ambition is to do God's will—these will be among the saved who have washed their robes and made them white in the blood of the Lamb.

"Blessed are those who hunger and thirst for righteousness." The sense of unworthiness will lead us to hunger for righteousness. All who long to bear the likeness of God's character will be satisfied. Love will enlarge us spiritually, giving us a capacity for higher achievements, for increased knowledge of heavenly things, so that we will not rest short of the fullness—"For they shall be filled."

The merciful shall find mercy, and

the pure in heart shall see God. Every impure thought weakens the moral sense and tends to erase the impressions of the Holy Spirit. The Lord may and does forgive the repenting sinner, but though forgiven, the character is marred. Anyone who wants to have clear perceptions of spiritual truth must shun all impurity of speech or thought.

But the words of Christ cover more than freedom from fleshly impurity, more than freedom from that ceremonial defilement which the Jews so carefully shunned. Selfishness prevents us from beholding God. Until we have given up our self-seeking, we cannot understand Him who is love. Only the unselfish heart, the humble and trustful spirit, will see God as "merciful and gracious, longsuffering, and abounding in goodness and truth." Exodus 34:6.

"Blessed are the peacemakers." The world is hostile to the law of God; sinners are hostile to their Maker. As a result, they are hostile to one another. Human plans will fail to produce peace because they do not reach the heart. The only power that can create true peace is the grace of Christ. When this grace is implanted in the heart, it will banish the evil passions that cause conflicts and divisions.

### The Multitudes Were Amazed

The people had come to think that happiness consisted in possessing the things of this world and that fame and honor were something to covet. It was very pleasing to be called "Rabbi" and to be praised as wise and religious. But Jesus declared that earthly honor was all that such persons would ever receive. A convincing power accompanied His words. Many were convinced that the Spirit of God was working through this remarkable Teacher.

After explaining how to obtain true happiness, Jesus pointed out His disciples' duty. He knew that they would often be insulted and their testimony be rejected. The humble men who listened to His words would experience slander, torture, imprisonment, and death, and He continued:

"Blessed are those who are persecuted for righteousness' sake, for theirs is the kingdom of heaven. Blessed are you when they revile and persecute you, and say all kinds of evil against you falsely for My sake. Rejoice and be exceedingly glad, for great is your reward in heaven, for so they persecuted the prophets who were before you."

The world loves sin and hates righteousness, and this is what caused its hostility to Jesus. The light of Christ sweeps away the darkness that covers their sins, revealing the need for reform. Those who yield to the Holy Spirit begin war with themselves; those who cling to sin war against the truth and its representatives.

Because of this, people accuse Christ's followers of being troublers of the people. But it is fellowship with God that brings them the world's hatred. They are walking the path that the noblest of earth have walked. Each fiery trial is God's agent to refine them. Each conflict will add to the joy of their final triumph. When they keep this in mind, they will cheerfully accept the testing of their faith rather than dread it.

"You are the salt of the earth." "Do not withdraw yourselves from the world in order to escape persecution. You are to live among people, so that the distinctive quality of divine love may be like salt to preserve the world from corruption." If those who serve God were removed from the earth, this world would be left to destruction. The wicked owe even the blessings of this life to the presence in the world of God's people, whom they despise and oppress. But if Christians are Christians in name only, they are like salt that has lost its flavor. By misrepresenting God, they are worse than unbelievers.

"You are the light of the world." Salvation is like sunshine; it belongs to the whole world. We must not keep the religion of the Bible between the covers of a book nor just within the walls of a church. It must sanctify the daily life and reveal itself in all our interactions with people. We must cherish the principles of righteousness in our hearts. The consistent life, the unswerving integrity, the kindly spirit, the godly example—these are the mediums through which God conveys light to the world.

Jesus knew that spies stood ready to grasp every word that they could twist to serve their purpose. He said nothing to unsettle faith in the institutions committed to them through Moses. Christ Himself had given both the moral and the ceremonial law. He did not come to destroy confidence in His own instruction. While He set aside false interpretations of the law, He carefully guarded against surrendering the vital truths God had committed to the Hebrews.

To the Pharisees, the Savior's words sounded like heresy. As He swept away the rubbish under which truth had been buried, they thought He was sweeping away the truth itself. He read their thoughts and answered them, saying, "Do not think that I came to destroy the Law or the Prophets. I did not come to destroy but to fulfill." His mission was to vindicate the sacred claims of the law that they charged Him with breaking. If God could have revoked or changed His law, then Christ did not need to have suffered the consequences of our transgressions. He came to explain how the law related to us and to illustrate its principles by His life of obedience.

## Obedience Leads to Joy

God loves mankind. To shield us from the results of transgression, He has revealed the principles of righteousness. When we receive the law in Christ, it lifts us above the power of our natural desires and tendencies, above temptations that lead to sin. God gave us the commands of the law so that in obeying them, we could have joy.

At Sinai, God made known to the human family the holiness of His character so that by contrast they could see the sinfulness of their own. He gave the law to convict them of sin and reveal their need of a Savior. This is still its work. As the Holy Spirit reveals to us our need of Christ's cleansing blood and justifying righteousness, the law is still a means to bring us to Christ so that we may be justified by faith. "The law of the Lord is perfect, converting the soul." Psalm 19:7.

"Till heaven and earth pass away, one jot or one tittle will by no means pass from the law till all is fulfilled." The shining sun and the solid earth are God's witnesses that His law is eternal. Even if they might pass away, the divine principles will endure. The system of symbols that pointed to Jesus as the Lamb of God would come to an end at His death, but the Decalogue is as permanent as the throne of God.

The Savior's life of obedience proved that it was possible for a human being to keep the law, and it showed the excellence of character that obedience would develop. On the other hand, all who break God's commandments support Satan's claim that no one can obey the law. To allow them into heaven would bring in strife and rebellion again and would threaten the well-being of the universe. No one who willfully disregards one principle of the law will enter the kingdom of heaven.

The greatest deception of the human mind in Christ's day was that just agreeing with the truth makes a person righteous. All of human experience has proved that a theoretical knowledge of the truth is not enough to save the soul. It does not bring out the fruits of righteousness.

A jealous regard for what people call theological truth often accompanies a hatred of genuine truth that would show in the life. The darkest chapters of history are filled with the record of crimes committed by bigoted advocates of their religion. The Pharisees thought themselves to be the most religious people in the world, but their so-called orthodoxy led them to crucify the Lord of glory. Many claim a faith in the truth; but if it does not make them sincere, kind, patient, self-restrained, and heavenly minded, it is a curse to them, and through their influence it is a curse to the world.

## The Depth and Breadth of God's Law

Jesus talked about the commandments separately and showed how far-reaching their principles are. He said that we can violate the law of God by the evil thought or lustful look. The smallest injustice breaks the law. Those who give hatred a place in their hearts are setting their feet in the path of the murderer.

The Jews nurtured a spirit of retaliation. In their hatred of the Romans, they denounced them harshly, training themselves to do terrible deeds. Some kinds of indignation are justifiable, even in the followers of Christ. When they see God dishonored and the innocent oppressed, a righteous indignation stirs the soul. Such anger is not sin. But we must banish bitterness and animosity from the heart if we want to be in harmony with heaven.

God's ideal for His children is higher than the highest human thought can reach. "Be perfect, therefore, as your heavenly Father is perfect." NRSV. This command is a promise. The plan of redemption aims at our complete recovery from the power of Satan. Christ always separates the sorrowing one from sin. He has made provision to give the Holy Spirit to every repentant person, to keep him from sinning.

## Temptations Are Not Excuses

We should not think that Satan's temptations are an excuse for one wrong act. There is no excuse for sinning. A holy temper, a Christlike life, is within reach of every repenting, believing child of God.

As the Son of man was perfect in His life, so His followers are to be perfect in their lives. In all things Jesus was made like His brethren. He became flesh, the same as we are. He shared the condition of mankind, yet He was the blameless Son of God. He was God in the flesh. His character is to be ours.

Christ is the ladder that Jacob saw, with its base resting on the earth and the topmost rung reaching heaven. If that ladder had failed to reach the earth by even a single step, we would have been lost. But Christ reaches us where we are. He took our nature and overcame, so that we, through taking His nature, may overcome. Made "in the likeness of sinful flesh" (Romans 8:3), He lived a sinless life. Now He asks us by faith in Him to come up to the glory of God's character.

We are to be perfect, even as our "Father in heaven is perfect."

Jesus had shown what righteousness consists of and had pointed to God as its source. Now He turned to practical duties. "Do nothing to attract attention or win praise to self. Give in sincerity, to benefit the suffering poor. In prayer, talk with God. In fasting, do not let the heart be filled with thoughts of self."

Service given with a sincere heart has great rewards. "Your Father who sees in secret will Himself reward you openly." By the life we live through the grace of Christ, we form our character. Christ gives us the attributes of His character, and the divine image begins to shine out. Men and women who walk and work with God are surrounded with the atmosphere of heaven. For these souls the kingdom of God has begun.

"No one can serve two masters." Bible religion is not one influence among many others. It is to saturate the whole life.

"If therefore your eye is good, your whole body will be full of light. But if your eye is bad, your whole body will be full of darkness." Whoever wants to know the truth must be willing to accept all that it reveals. If we waver and are halfhearted in allegiance to truth, we are choosing error and Satan's delusions.

Worldly schemes and the principles of righteousness do not blend into each other, like the colors of the rainbow. God draws a clear line between the two. The likeness of Christ stands out distinctly from that of Satan, like noontime contrasts with midnight. And only those who live the life of Christ are His coworkers.

All who have chosen God's service are to rest in His care. Christ pointed to the birds flying in the heavens and to the flowers of the field, and He asked, "Are you not of more value than they?" God watches over the little brown sparrow. The flowers and the grass share the notice of our heavenly Father. The great Master Artist has taken thought for the lilies, making them outshine Solomon's glory. How much more does He care for His human creatures, who are the image and glory of God! As the sunbeam gives the flowers their delicate tints, so God gives us the beauty of His own character.

In the book of God's divine guidance, the volume of life, we are each given a page. That page contains every particular of our history. God's children are never absent from His mind. "Therefore do not worry about tomorrow." God does not give His children all the directions for their life journey at once. He tells them just as much as they can remember and perform. The strength and wisdom He gives are for the present emergency.

"Judge not, that you be not judged." "Do not think yourself better than others and set yourself up as their judge. You cannot see the motives. In criticizing another, you are passing sentence on yourself, because you show that you are a participant with Satan, the accuser of the brethren." See 2 Corinthians 13:5; 1 Corinthians 11:31.

The good tree will produce good fruit. So the fruit of our lives testifies about our character. Good works can never purchase salvation, but they are an evidence of the faith that works by love and purifies the soul. The reward we receive is not because of our merit, yet it will be in proportion to the work we have done through grace.

In this way, Christ laid out the principles of His kingdom. To impress the lesson, He added an illustration. "It is not enough," He said, "to hear My words. By obedience, you must make them the foundation of your character. If you build on human theories, your house will fall. It will be swept away by the winds of temptation and trial. But these principles that I have given will endure. Receive Me; build on My words."

"Therefore whoever hears these sayings of Mine, and does them, I will liken him to a wise man who built his house on the rock: and the rain descended, the floods came, and the winds blew and beat on that house; and it did not fall, for it was founded on the rock."

# An Army Officer Asks Help for His Servant[*]

Christ was sad that His own nation wanted outward signs that He was the Messiah. But He was amazed that the centurion who came to Him did not even ask Him to come in person to perform the miracle. "Only speak a word, and my servant will be healed."

The centurion's servant was paralyzed and at the point of death. Among the Romans, servants were slaves, bought and sold and treated with abuse and cruelty. But the centurion, tenderly attached to his servant, very much wanted him to recover. He believed that Jesus could heal him. The reports he heard had inspired him with faith.

This Roman was convinced that the Jews' religion was better than his own. He had broken through the prejudice and hatred that separated the conquerors from those they had conquered and had shown kindness to the Jews. The teaching of Christ met the needs of his heart. All that was spiritual within him responded to the Savior's words. But he felt unworthy to come into Jesus' presence, so he appealed to the Jewish elders to request the healing of his servant. They were acquainted with the Great Teacher

and would, he thought, know how to approach Him in a way to win His favor. As Jesus entered Capernaum, a delegation of the elders met Him. They urged that "the one for whom He should do this was worthy, 'for he loves our nation, and has built us a synagogue.' "

Jesus immediately set out for the officer's home, but the crowds pressed in on Him, and He advanced slowly. The centurion, in his self-distrust, sent Him the message, "Lord, . . . I am not worthy that You should enter under my roof." But the Savior kept on His way. Daring at last to approach Him, the centurion said, "I did not even think myself worthy to come to You." "Only speak a word, and my servant will be healed. For I also am a man under authority, having soldiers under me. And I say to this one, 'Go,' and he goes; and to another, 'Come,' and he comes; and to my servant, 'Do this,' and he does it."

"As I represent the power of Rome and my soldiers recognize my authority, so You represent the power of the Infinite God, and all created things obey Your word. You can command the disease to leave, and it will obey.

---

[*] *This chapter is based on Matthew 8:5-13; Luke 7:1-17.*

You can call heavenly messengers to give healing power. Just speak the word, and my servant will be healed."

"When Jesus heard these things, He marveled at him, and turned around and said to the crowd that followed Him, 'I say to you, I have not found such great faith, not even in Israel!' " And He said to the centurion, " 'As you have believed, so let it be done for you.' And his servant was healed that same hour."

In their self-righteousness, the Jewish elders recommended the centurion because of the favor he had shown to "our nation." But the centurion said of himself, "I am not worthy." He did not trust to his own goodness. His faith fastened onto Christ in His true character, the Friend and Savior of mankind.

When Satan tells you that you are a sinner, tell him that Christ came into the world to save sinners. The plea that we may urge now and always is our completely helpless condition that makes His redeeming power necessary.

In my hand no price I bring;
Simply to Thy cross I cling.

The Jews saw nothing to be desired in Jesus. But the centurion, educated in the idolatry of Rome, seemingly cut off from spiritual life by education and surroundings and shut out by the bigotry of the Jews—this man understood truth to which the children of Abraham were blind. The "Light which gives light to every man who comes into the world" (John 1:9) had been shining on him, and he had

recognized the glory of the Son of God. To Jesus, this was an advance assurance of the gathering of souls from all nations to His kingdom.

## A Dead Man Raised to Life

Jesus next made His way to Nain, a village more than twenty miles from Capernaum. All along the way the people came, bringing their sick for healing, and always hoping that He would make Himself known as the King of Israel. A glad, expectant group followed Him up the rocky path toward the gate of the mountain village.

As they came near, they saw a funeral procession going out to the place of burial. On an open pallet in front was the body of the dead. Filling the air with their wailing cries, the mourners gathered to show sympathy for the bereaved.

The one who had died was the only son of his mother, and she was a widow. The lonely mourner was following to the grave her only earthly support and comfort. "When the Lord saw her, He had compassion on her." As she moved on blindly, weeping, He came close beside her and gently said, "Do not weep."

"He came and touched the open coffin." Contact with death could bring no defilement to Jesus. The bearers stood still and the mourners gathered, hoping against hope. Someone was here who had vanquished demons. Was death also subject to His power?

In a clear, authoritative voice, Jesus spoke the words, "Young man, I say to you, arise." That Voice pierced the ears of the dead. The young man opened his eyes. Jesus took him by the hand and lifted him up, and mother and son united in a long, joyful embrace. The crowd looked on in silence, as if they were in the very presence of God. Then they "glorified God, saying, 'A great prophet has risen up among us'; and, 'God has visited His people.' " The line of mourners returned to Nain as a triumphal procession.

Jesus, who stood beside the sorrowing mother at Nain, is touched with sympathy for our grief. His word is no less powerful now than when He spoke to the young man of Nain. See Matthew 28:18. To all who believe on Him, He is still a living Savior.

Jesus awakened this mother's son to return to this earthly life, to endure its sorrows and to pass under the power of death again. But Jesus comforts our sorrow for the dead with a message of infinite hope: "I am He who lives, and was dead, and behold, I am alive forevermore. . . . And I have the keys of Hades and of Death." Revelation 1:18.

Satan cannot hold one person in spiritual death who by faith receives Christ's word of power. "Awake, you who sleep, arise from the dead." Ephesians 5:14. The word of God that called the first man to life still gives life. Christ's word, "Young man, I say to you, arise," gave life to the youth of Nain. In the same way that word, "Arise from the dead," is life to the one who receives it.

And "if the Spirit of Him who raised Jesus from the dead dwells in you, He who raised Christ from the dead will also give life to your mortal bodies." Romans 8:11; see 1 Thessalonians 4:16, 17. This is the word with which He tells us to comfort one another.

# How Jesus Related to Family Problems*

The sons of Joseph were far from being in sympathy with Jesus in His work. The reports about His life and labors filled them with concern. They heard that He devoted entire nights to prayer, that through the day He was surrounded by people and did not even take time to eat. His friends felt He was wearing Himself out. They were unable to find a reason for His attitude toward the Pharisees. Some even feared that He might be losing His mind.

His brothers keenly felt the disapproval that came on them through their relation to Jesus. They were offended and angry that He denounced the Pharisees. They thought someone must persuade Him to stop working in this way, and they got Mary to unite with them, thinking that through His love for her they might succeed in getting Him to be more cautious.

The Pharisees had repeated the charge, "He casts out demons by the ruler of the demons." Matthew 9:34. Christ told them that those who spoke against Him, not recognizing His divine character, could receive forgiveness; through the Holy Spirit they might see their error and repent. But

those who reject the work of the Holy Spirit are placing themselves where repentance cannot come to them. When people willfully reject the Spirit and declare it to be from Satan, they cut off the channel by which God can communicate with them.

The Pharisees did not actually believe the charge they brought against Jesus. Those religious leaders had heard the Spirit's voice in their own hearts declaring Him to be the Anointed One of Israel. In His presence, they had realized their unholiness and longed for righteousness. But after rejecting Him, it would be too humiliating to receive Him as the Messiah. To avoid acknowledging truth, they tried to dispute the Savior's teaching. They could not prevent Him from working miracles, but they did everything in their power to misrepresent Him. Still the convicting Spirit of God followed them, and they had to build up barriers to withstand the mightiest Agency that God can bring to bear on the human heart.

God does not blind people's eyes or harden their hearts. He sends them light to correct their errors. Rejecting this light blinds the eyes and hardens

---

* This chapter is based on Matthew 12:22–50; Mark 3:20–35.

the heart. Often the process is almost imperceptible. But when we disregard one ray of light, we numb our spiritual perceptions a little and don't recognize as clearly the second revealing of light. So the darkness increases, until it is night in the heart. This is what had happened with these Jewish leaders. They credited the work of the Holy Spirit to Satan. In doing this, they deliberately chose deception, and from that time on, they were controlled by Satan's power.

Closely connected with Christ's warning about the sin against the Holy Spirit is a warning against idle and evil words. Words are an indication of character. "Out of the abundance of the heart the mouth speaks." Words also have power to react on the character. People are influenced by their own words. Often under a sudden prompting by Satan, they say something that they do not really believe. But the expression reacts on the thoughts, and they come to believe what they spoke at Satan's prompting. Having once expressed an opinion or decision, often they are too proud to retract it. They try to prove themselves right, until they believe that they are.

It is dangerous to speak a word of doubt, dangerous to question and criticize light. Careless and irreverent criticism reacts on the character, strengthening irreverence and unbelief. Many people have gone on until they were ready to criticize and reject the Holy Spirit. Jesus said, "For every idle word men may speak, they will give account of it in the day of judgment. For by your words you will be justified, and by your words you will be condemned."

Then Jesus added a warning to those who had been impressed by His words but had not surrendered themselves for the Holy Spirit to live in them. "When an unclean spirit goes out of a man, he goes through dry places, seeking rest, and finds none. Then he says, 'I will return to my house from which I came.' And when he comes, he finds it empty, swept, and put in order. Then he goes and takes with him seven other spirits more wicked than himself, and they enter and dwell there."

Like today, through the grace of God many in Christ's day were set free from evil spirits that controlled their being. They rejoiced in the love of God, but then they did not surrender themselves to God daily to allow Christ to live in the heart. When the evil spirit returned, with "seven other spirits more wicked than himself," they were completely dominated by the power of evil.

## A New Power Takes Possession

When anyone surrenders to Christ, a new power takes possession of the heart. A change takes place that we can never accomplish for ourselves. The life that is yielded to Christ becomes His own fortress, which He holds in a world that has revolted, and He intends no authority to rule in it but His own. A life that heaven's agencies keep in this way cannot be conquered by Satan's assaults.

But unless we yield ourselves to the control of Christ, the wicked one will dominate us. It is not necessary to choose the kingdom of darkness deliberately in order to come under its rule.

We can simply neglect to unite ourselves with the kingdom of light. If we do not cooperate with heavenly agencies, Satan will make the heart his home. The only defense against evil is to have Christ living in the heart through faith in His righteousness. If we are not vitally connected with God, we can never resist self-love and temptation to sin. We may leave off bad habits for a time, but without moment-by-moment surrender to Christ and a continual relationship with Him, we are at the mercy of the enemy and will do what he says in the end.

"The last state of that man is worse than the first. So shall it also be with this wicked generation." There are none so hardened as those who have scorned the invitations of mercy. The most common evidence of the sin against the Holy Spirit is in persistently ignoring Heaven's invitation to repent.

In rejecting Christ, the Jewish people committed the unpardonable sin; and by refusing the invitation of mercy, we may commit the same error. We put the Prince of life to shame before Satan and before the heavenly universe when we refuse to listen to His appointed messengers, and instead listen to people who would draw our hearts away from Christ. As long as people do this, they can find no pardon, and they will finally lose all desire to be reconciled to God.

## Christ's Real Brethren

While Jesus was still teaching the people, His disciples brought the message that His mother and brothers were outside and wanted to see Him. "But He answered and said to the one who told Him, 'Who is My mother and who are My brothers?' And He stretched out His hand toward His disciples and said, 'Here are My mother and My brothers! For whoever does the will of My Father in heaven is My brother and sister and mother.' "

All who receive Christ by faith are united to Him by a tie closer than human family connections. As someone who believed and acted on His words, His mother was more nearly and savingly related to Him than she was through her natural relationship. His brothers would receive no benefit from their connection with Him unless they accepted Him as their personal Savior.

Their unbelief was a part of the bitterness of the cup of woe that He drank for us.

The opposition kindled in the human heart against the gospel was most painful to Jesus in His home. His brothers looked on Him as needing their counsel. They thought that if He would speak things that the Pharisees could accept, He would avoid disagreeable controversy. They thought He was mentally unbalanced in claiming divine authority. They knew that the Pharisees were looking for an opportunity to accuse Him, and they felt that He had given it to them.

They could not grasp the mission He came to fulfill, and so they could not sympathize with Him in His trials. Their coarse, unappreciative words showed that they had no true understanding of His character. Instead of comforting Him, their spirit and words wounded His heart. His sensitive nature was tortured, His motives misunderstood, His work uncomprehended.

His brothers often presumed to think that they could teach Him who understood all truth. They freely condemned things that they could not understand. They thought they were vindicating God, when God was with them in the flesh, and they did not recognize Him.

These things made Jesus' path thorny. Christ was so pained by being misunderstood in His own home that it was a relief to go where such misunderstanding did not exist. He loved to visit the home of Lazarus, Mary, and Martha, because in the atmosphere of faith and love, His spirit had rest. Yet often He could find relief only in being alone and communicating with His Father.

Those who are called to endure misunderstanding and distrust in their own homes for Christ's sake may find comfort in the thought that Jesus endured the same. He invites them to find companionship in Him and relief in sharing their hearts' concerns with the Father.

Those who accept Christ are not left as orphans, to bear trials alone. He invites them as members of the heavenly family to call His Father their Father. He has great tenderness for them, far more than what our father or mother felt toward us in our helplessness.

When a Hebrew had been forced to sell himself as a slave because of poverty, the duty of redeeming him fell to his nearest relative. See Leviticus 25:25, 47–49; Ruth 2:20. So the work of redeeming us fell on Him who is a "close relative" to us. Christ became our "redeeming relative." Closer than father, mother, brother, friend, or lover is the Lord our Savior. We cannot understand this love, but we can know it to be true in our own experience.

# His Yoke Is Easy and His Burden Light*

"Come to Me, all you who labor and are heavy laden, and I will give you rest." The Savior left none to feel shut out from His care and love. He looked on the distressed and heart-burdened, those whose hopes were crushed and who were trying to satisfy the longing of the soul with earthly joys, and He invited all to find rest in Him.

Tenderly He told the toiling people, "Take My yoke upon you and learn from Me, for I am gentle and lowly in heart, and you will find rest for your souls."

In these words, Christ is speaking to every human being. Whether they know it or not, all are weighed down with burdens that only Christ can remove. The heaviest burden is the burden of sin. If we were left to bear this, it would crush us. But the Sinless One has taken our place. "The Lord has laid on Him the iniquity of us all." Isaiah 53:6. He has carried the burden of our guilt. The burden of care and sorrow He will also bear.

The Elder Brother of the human race is by the eternal throne. He knows by experience the weaknesses of humanity, our wants, and the strength of our temptations, for He was in all points tempted like we are, yet without sin. Are you tempted? He will deliver. Are you weak? He will strengthen. Are you ignorant? He will enlighten. Are you wounded? He will heal. "He heals the broken-hearted and binds up their wounds." Psalm 147:3.

Whatever your anxieties and trials, present your case before the Lord. Your spirit will be braced for endurance. He will open the way for you to disentangle yourself from embarrassment and difficulty. The heavier your burdens, the more blessed the rest you will find in placing them on the Burden Bearer.

The rest that Christ offers depends on conditions, but the Bible plainly tells us what they are. Anyone can fulfill them.

"Take My yoke upon you." The yoke is an instrument of service. Cattle are yoked for labor, and the yoke is essential for them to work effectively. By this illustration, Jesus teaches that we are called to service. We are to take His yoke upon us.

The yoke is the law of God, in the new covenant written in the heart. It

---

* This chapter is based on Matthew 11:28–30.

binds the human worker to the will of God. If we were left to go just where our will would lead us, we would fall into Satan's ranks. So God confines us to His will.

Christ Himself has worn the yoke of service in humanity. He said, "I have come down from heaven, not to do My own will, but the will of Him who sent Me." John 6:38. Love for God, zeal for His glory, and love for fallen humanity brought Jesus to earth. This was the controlling power of His life. This principle He asks us to adopt.

## What Makes Us So Tired

Many whose hearts are aching under a load of care have chosen the world's service, accepted its perplexities, adopted its customs. Because of this, their life has become a burden. To gratify worldly desires, they injure the conscience and bring an additional burden of remorse on themselves. Our Lord wants them to lay aside this yoke of bondage. He says, "My yoke is easy and My burden is light." He calls them to seek first the kingdom of God and His righteousness. Worry is blind and cannot see the future, but in every difficulty, Jesus has His way prepared to bring relief. Our heavenly Father has a thousand ways to provide for us of which we know nothing. Those who make serving and honoring God their main goal will find perplexities vanish and a plain path before their feet.

"Learn from Me," says Jesus, "for I am gentle and lowly in heart, and you will find rest." We are to enter the school of Christ and learn from Him.

Redemption is the process that trains a person for heaven. This training means being freed from ideas, habits, and practices we have learned in the school of the prince of darkness.

In the heart of Christ, there was perfect peace. He was never elated by applause nor dejected by criticism or disappointment. Amid opposition and cruel treatment, He was still of good courage. But many of His followers have anxious, troubled hearts, because they are afraid to trust God. They fear the consequences of complete surrender to Him. But unless they make this surrender, they cannot find peace.

When we are born from above, we will have the same mind in us that was in Jesus. Then we will not be seeking the highest place. We will want to sit at Jesus' feet and learn from Him. We will understand that the value of our work is in proportion to how much of the Holy Spirit we have received. Trust in God brings holier qualities of mind, so that in patience we may possess our souls.

## How His Yoke Makes the Work Easy

The yoke is placed on the oxen to help them in pulling the load, to lighten the burden. This is also true with the yoke of Christ. When our will is swallowed up in the will of God, we will find life's burden light. Whoever walks in the path of God's commandments walks with Christ, and in His love the heart finds its rest. When Moses prayed, "Show me now Your way, that I may know You," the Lord answered, "My presence will go with you, and I will give you rest." Exodus 33:13, 14.

Those who take Christ at His word and surrender their lives to His plans will find peace. Nothing the world does can make them sad when Jesus makes them glad by His presence. "You will keep him in perfect peace, whose mind is stayed on You, because he trusts in You." Isaiah 26:3.

Our lives may seem tangled, but as we submit to the wise Master Worker, He will bring out the pattern of life and character that will be to His own glory. And this life that expresses the glory—the character—of Christ will be received into the Paradise of God.

As we enter into rest through Jesus, heaven begins here. We respond to His invitation, "Come, learn from Me," and so we begin the life eternal. Heaven is a constant approaching to God through Christ. The more we know of God, the more intense our happiness will be. As we walk with Jesus in this life, we may be filled with His love, satisfied with His presence. All that human nature can bear, we may receive here.

# The Stilling of the Storm *

It had been an eventful day. Beside the Sea of Galilee Jesus had spoken His first parables, explaining the nature of His kingdom and how it was to be established. He had compared His work to that of the sower and the development of His kingdom to the growth of the mustard seed and the effect of leaven in flour. He had pictured the final separation of the righteous and the wicked in the parables of the wheat and tares and the fishing net. The precious truths He taught had been illustrated by the hidden treasure and the pearl of great price.

As evening came on, the crowds still pressed in on Him. Day after day He had ministered to them, scarcely pausing for food or rest. Now the close of day found Him so completely weary that He went looking for rest in some solitary place across the lake. He asked His disciples to accompany Him there.

After He had sent the crowds away, the disciples took Him into the boat and quickly set off. But other fishing boats lying near the shore were soon crowded with people who followed Jesus, still eager to see and hear Him.

The Savior, overcome with weariness and hunger, lay down in the stern of the boat and soon fell asleep. The evening had been calm and pleasant, but suddenly darkness spread over the sky, and a fierce storm burst upon the lake.

The waves, lashed into fury by howling winds, dashed fiercely over the boat and threatened to sink it. Those strong fishermen had guided their boats safely through many a storm, but now their strength and skill were of no use. Helpless in the grasp of the storm, they saw their boat filling.

## Jesus Cared

Focused on their efforts to save themselves, they had forgotten that Jesus was on board. Now, seeing only death before them, they remembered who had commanded them to set out across the sea. Their only hope was in Jesus. "Master, Master!" But the roaring tempest drowned out their voices, and there was no reply. Doubt and fear overtook them. Jesus had conquered disease and demons, and even death. Was He powerless to help His disciples now? Was He unaware of their distress?

---

* *This chapter is based on Matthew 8:23–34; Mark 4:35–41; 5:1–20; Luke 8:22–39.*

Again they called, but there was no answer except the shrieking of the angry storm. Apparently, they were going to be swallowed up by the hungry waters.

Suddenly a flash of lightning pierced the darkness, and they saw Jesus lying asleep, undisturbed by the tempest. In amazement, they exclaimed, "Teacher, do You not care that we are perishing?"

Their cry awakened Jesus. As the lightning's glare revealed Him, they saw the peace of heaven in His face; they saw tender love in His glance, and they cried, "Lord, save us! We are perishing!"

Never did anyone utter that cry unheard. As the disciples grasped their oars to make a last effort, Jesus rose. While the storm raged and the waves broke over them, He lifted His hand and said to the angry sea, "Peace, be still!"

The waves sank, the clouds rolled away, and the stars came out. The boat rested on a quiet sea. Then Jesus asked sorrowfully, "Why are you so fearful? How is it that you have no faith?"

A hush fell on the disciples. Terror and despair had seized the occupants of the boats that had set out to accompany Jesus. The storm had driven the boats close together, and all on board saw the miracle. The people whispered among themselves, "Who can this be, that even the winds and the sea obey Him?"

When Jesus was awakened to meet the storm, He showed no trace of fear in word or look. But it was not His possession of almighty power that gave Him rest. It was not as "Master of earth and sea and sky" that He rested quietly. That power He had laid down. "I can of Myself do nothing." John 5:30. He trusted in the Father's might. It was in faith—faith in God's love and care—that Jesus rested, and the power of the word that stilled the storm was the power of God.

In the same way, we are to rest in the care of our Savior. The disciples' fear in time of danger revealed their unbelief. They forgot Jesus, and only when they turned to Him could He give them help.

When tempests of temptation gather, how often we battle with the storm alone. We trust to our own strength till we are ready to perish. Then we remember Jesus, and if we call on Him to save us, we will not cry out in vain. He never fails to give us the help we need. If we have the Savior in our hearts, we do not need to fear. The Redeemer will deliver us from danger in the way that He knows best.

"The wicked are like the troubled sea." Isaiah 57:20. Sin has destroyed our peace. No human power can control the ruling passions of the heart. We are as helpless here as the disciples were to quiet the raging storm. But however fierce the tempest, those who turn to Jesus with the cry, "Lord, save us," will find deliverance. His grace quiets the strife of human passion, and in His love the heart is at rest.

He made the storm be still,
and the waves of the sea were hushed.
Then they were glad because they had
    quiet,

and he brought them to their desired haven.

Psalm 107:29, 30, NRSV

"Having been justified by faith, we have peace with God through our Lord Jesus Christ." Romans 5:1.

In the early morning, the Savior and His companions came to shore. The light of the rising sun touched sea and land with the blessing of peace. But as they stepped on the beach, their eyes took in a sight more terrible than the fury of the tempest. Two madmen rushed on them as if to tear them to pieces. Hanging about these men were parts of chains they had broken in escaping from confinement. Their flesh was torn and bleeding. Their eyes glared out from under their long, matted hair. Demons possessed them, and they looked more like wild beasts than like men.

The disciples ran away in terror, but soon they turned to look for Jesus. He was standing where they had left Him. He who had stilled the storm did not run away. When the men, foaming at the mouth, approached Him, Jesus raised that hand whose gesture had quieted the waves, and the men could come no nearer.

With authority, Jesus commanded the unclean spirits to come out of them. His words penetrated the darkened minds of the unfortunate men. They realized dimly that One was near who could save them from the tormenting demons. But when they opened their lips to beg for His mercy, the demons spoke through them, crying furiously, "What have I to do with You, Jesus, Son of the Most High God? I beg You, do not torment me!"

Jesus asked, "What is your name?" And the answer was, "My name is Legion; for we are many." The demons begged Jesus not to send them out of the country. On a mountainside not far away, a large herd of swine was feeding. The demons asked to be allowed to enter these pigs. Immediately, the herd rushed madly down the cliff, plunged into the lake, and died.

Meanwhile, a marvelous change had come over the two demon-possessed men. Light had shone into their minds. Their eyes beamed with intelligence and their blood-stained hands were quiet. With glad voices, the men praised God for deliverance.

From the cliff, the keepers of the pigs had seen everything that had happened, and they hurried away to announce the news to their employers. In fear and amazement, the whole population flocked to meet Jesus. The demon-possessed men had been the terror of the country. No one had been safe to pass where they were. Now these men were clothed and in their right mind, listening to Jesus' words and glorifying Him who had made them whole. But the people did not rejoice. The loss of the pigs seemed greater to them than the deliverance of these captives of Satan.

The owners of the swine were absorbed in earthly things and did not care about the great interests of spiritual life. Jesus wanted to break the spell of selfish indifference, so that they might accept His grace. But resentment over their financial loss blinded their eyes to the Savior's mercy.

## Superstition Excited Fears

The demonstration of supernatural power raised the fears of the people. Further disasters might follow from having this Stranger among them. Those who had crossed the lake with Jesus told of their danger in the storm and how Jesus had stilled the wind and the sea. But their words had no effect. In terror the people pleaded with Jesus to go away, and He complied, taking ship at once for the opposite shore.

The people of Gergesa were so afraid of endangering their earthly interests that they treated Jesus, who had vanquished the prince of darkness before their eyes, like an intruder, turning away the Gift of heaven from their doors. There are still many people today who refuse to obey Christ's word because obedience would involve sacrificing some worldly interest. Fearful that His presence might cause them some monetary loss, many reject His grace and drive His Spirit from them.

But the men whom Jesus had restored wanted the company of their Deliverer. In His presence, they felt safe from the demons that had tormented their lives and wasted their best years. As Jesus was about to enter the boat, they kept close to His side and begged Him to keep them near Him. But Jesus told them to go home and tell what great things the Lord had done for them.

Here was a work for them to do— to go to a heathen home and tell of the blessing they had received from Jesus. It was hard for them to be separated from the Savior. Difficulties were sure to follow them. Long isolation from society seemed to disqualify them for the work He had given them. But as soon as Jesus pointed out their duty, they were ready to obey. They went throughout Decapolis, declaring everywhere His power to save and describing how He had freed them from the demons. In doing this work, they could receive a greater blessing than if they had remained in His presence. In working to spread the "good news" of salvation, we are brought near to the Savior.

The two restored men were the first missionaries Christ sent to preach in the region of Decapolis. These men had been privileged to hear the teachings of Christ for only a few moments. But in their own persons, they carried the evidence that Jesus was the Messiah. They could tell what they knew, what they had seen and heard and felt of the power of Christ. This is what everyone can do whose heart has been touched by the grace of God. See 1 John 1:1–3.

If we have been following Jesus step by step, we will have something to tell about the way in which He has led us—how we have tested His promise and found the promise true. This is the witness for which our Lord calls us.

Though the people of Gergesa had not received Jesus, He did not leave them to the darkness they had chosen. They had not heard His words. They were ignorant of what they were rejecting. So He again sent light to them by those to whom they would not refuse to listen.

The destruction of the swine alerted

the whole country as nothing else could have done and directed attention to Christ. The men He healed remained as witnesses to His power, channels of light, messengers of the Son of God. This experience opened a door throughout that region. When Jesus returned to Decapolis, thousands heard the message. God overrules even the working of evil to bring about good.

The demon-possessed men of Gergesa, dwelling among the graves, in slavery to uncontrolled passions and loathsome lusts, represent what humanity would become if left to Satan's rule. Satan constantly exerts his influence on people to control the mind and incite to violence and crime. He darkens the intellect and defiles the heart. Whenever people reject the Savior's invitation, they are yielding themselves to Satan. Many in the home, in business, and even in church are doing this today. Because of this, violence and crime blanket the earth, and moral darkness encloses the places where people live. Satan leads men and women to worse and worse evils, until complete wickedness and ruin are the result. The only safeguard against his power is the presence of Jesus. In the sight of men and angels, Satan has been revealed as our enemy and destroyer; Christ, as our Friend and Deliverer.

God has called us to be "conformed to the image of His Son." Romans 8:29. And people who have been degraded into instruments of Satan are still transformed through Christ into messengers of righteousness and sent out to tell "what great things the Lord has done for you."

# The Touch of Faith Brings Healing*

Returning from Gergesa to the western shore of Lake Galilee, Jesus found a crowd gathered to meet Him. He stayed by the seaside for a while, teaching and healing, and then went to the house of Levi-Matthew to meet the tax collectors at the feast. Jairus, the ruler of the synagogue, found Him there. In great distress he exclaimed, "My little daughter lies at the point of death. Come and lay Your hands on her, that she may be healed, and she will live."

Jesus set out immediately with the ruler for his home. The disciples were surprised that he agreed to the request of the proud rabbi, yet they accompanied their Master, and the people followed. Jesus and His companions advanced slowly, for the crowd pressed around Him on every side. The anxious father was impatient, but Jesus stopped now and then to relieve suffering or to comfort a troubled heart.

While they were on the way, a messenger pushed through the crowd, bearing the news that Jairus's daughter was dead. The word caught the ear of Jesus. "Do not be afraid; only believe, and she will be made well."

Together they hurried to the ruler's home. Already hired mourners and flute players were filling the air with their anguished noise. Jesus tried to silence them: "Why make this commotion and weep? The child is not dead, but sleeping." They were offended at the Stranger's words. They had seen the child in the grip of death. Requiring them all to leave, Jesus took the girl's father and mother with Peter, James, and John, and entered the chamber of death.

Jesus approached the bedside and, taking the child's hand in His own, said softly, in the familiar language of her home, "Little girl, I say to you, arise."

Instantly, a tremor passed through the unconscious form. The eyes opened widely as if from sleep, and the young girl looked with amazement at the group beside her. She got up, and her parents embraced her and wept for joy.

On the way to the ruler's house, Jesus had met a poor woman who had suffered for twelve years from a disease that made her life a burden. She had spent all her money on physicians

---

* This chapter is based on Matthew 9:18–26; Mark 5:21–43; Luke 8:40–56.

and medicines, only to be told that she was incurable. But her hopes revived when she heard of Christ. If she could only go to Him, she would be healed. In weakness and suffering, she came to the seaside where He was teaching and tried to press through the crowd, but without success. She followed Him from the house of Levi-Matthew, but still she was unable to reach Him. She had begun to give up hope when He came near where she was.

She was in the presence of the Great Physician! But in the confusion, she could not speak to Him or catch more than a quick glimpse of Him. Afraid that she might lose her one chance of relief, she pushed forward, saying to herself, "If only I may touch His clothes, I shall be made well." As He was passing by, she reached forward and succeeded in barely touching the border of His garment. In that one touch was concentrated the faith of her life, and instantly her pain and feebleness gave way to the vigor of perfect health.

With a grateful heart she tried to slip out of the crowd, but suddenly Jesus stopped. Looking around, He asked in a voice that everyone could hear above the confusion, "Who touched Me?" Jostled on all sides as He was, it seemed a strange question.

Peter, always ready to speak, said, "Master, the multitudes throng You and press You, and You say, 'Who touched Me?' " Jesus answered, "Somebody touched Me, for I perceived power going out from Me." The Savior could distinguish the touch of faith from the casual contact of the careless crowd. Such trust should not go by without

comment. He would speak words of comfort to the humble woman, words that would be a blessing to His followers to the close of time.

Looking toward the woman, Jesus insisted on knowing who had touched Him. Finding that she could not hide, she came forward, trembling. With grateful tears she told of her suffering and how she had found relief. Jesus said, "Daughter, . . . your faith has made you well. Go in peace." He gave no opportunity for superstition to claim healing by merely touching His garments. The cure happened through the faith that took hold of His divine power.

## Living Faith Brings Healing

To talk of religion in a casual way, to pray without soul hunger and living faith, accomplishes nothing. A theoretical faith, which accepts Christ merely as the Savior of the world, can never bring healing to the spiritual life. Faith is not agreeing with truth intellectually. It is not enough to believe *about* Christ; we must believe *in* Him. Saving faith is a transaction by which those who receive Christ join themselves in covenant relationship with God. Genuine faith means an increase of vigor, a deep and willing trust, by which our spirit becomes a conquering power.

After healing the woman, Jesus wanted her to acknowledge the blessing she had received. The gifts that the gospel offers are not to be enjoyed in secret. Our acknowledgement of His faithfulness is Heaven's chosen way for revealing Christ to the world. The testimony of our own experience is what will be most effective. See Isaiah 43:12. When we back them up by a Christlike life, our personal stories of His grace have irresistible power that works for the salvation of others.

When the ten lepers came to Jesus for healing, they were cleansed; but only one returned to give Him glory. The others went their way, forgetting Him who had made them whole. How many still do the same thing! The Lord raises up the sick, He delivers people from danger, He commissions angels to save them from disaster, to guard them from disease and destruction (Psalm 91:6), yet they do not remember His great love. By ingratitude they close their hearts against the grace of God.

It is for our own benefit to keep every gift of God fresh in our memory. This will strengthen faith. Let us, then, remember the loving-kindness of the Lord. And as we review God's dealings with us, let us declare, "What shall I render to the Lord for all His benefits toward me?" Psalm 116:12.

# The First Evangelists[*]

The apostles had accompanied Jesus on foot through Galilee. They had walked and talked with the Son of God and learned how to work for humanity. As Jesus ministered to the people, His disciples were eager to lighten His work. They helped in bringing the suffering ones to the Savior and promoting the comfort of all. They watched for interested hearers and explained the Scriptures to them.

But they needed an experience in working alone. They still needed much instruction and patience. Now, while He was personally with them to counsel and correct them, the Savior sent them out as His representatives.

The disciples had often been perplexed by the teaching of the priests and Pharisees, but they had brought their questions to Jesus. He had strengthened their confidence in God's Word and to a great degree had set them free from their slavery to tradition. When they were apart from Him, every look and word came back to them. Often when in conflict with enemies of the gospel, they repeated His words.

Calling the Twelve around Him, Jesus told them to go out two by two through the towns and villages. In this way, they could counsel and pray together, each one's strength making up for the other's weakness.

Evangelistic work would be far more successful if Christians followed this example.

The disciples were not to argue with anyone about whether Jesus was the Messiah; but in His name they were to "heal the sick, cleanse the lepers, raise the dead, cast out demons. Freely you have received, freely give."

Jesus devoted more time to healing the sick than to preaching. Wherever He went, the people who received His compassion were rejoicing in health. His voice was the first sound that many had ever heard, His name the first word they had ever spoken, His face the first they had ever seen. As He passed through the towns and cities, He was like a vital current, spreading life and joy.

The followers of Christ are to work as He did. We are to feed the hungry, comfort the suffering, and inspire hope in the hopeless. The love of Christ, shown in unselfish ministry, will be more effective in reforming the

---

[*] *This chapter is based on Matthew 10; Mark 6:7–11; Luke 9:1–6.*

evildoer than will the sword or court of justice. Often the heart will melt under the love of Christ. Through His servants, God wants to be a greater Comforter than the world has ever seen.

On their first missionary tour, the disciples were to go only to "the lost sheep of the house of Israel." If the Jews would receive the gospel, God intended to make them His messengers to the Gentiles. So they were first to hear the message.

On this first tour, the disciples were to go only where Jesus had been before them and had made friends. Their preparation for the journey was to be simple. They were not to adopt the dress of religious teachers nor use certain clothing to distinguish them from the humble peasants. They were not to call the people together for public meetings; their efforts were to be in house-to-house work. In every place, they were to accept the hospitality of those who would welcome them as if entertaining Christ Himself, entering the home with the beautiful salutation, "Peace to this house." Luke 10:5. That home would be blessed by their prayers, their songs of praise, and their opening of the Scriptures in the family circle. The message they had brought was the word of eternal life, and the destiny of men and women depended on whether they received or rejected it. See Matthew 10:14, 15.

"Behold," said Jesus, "I send you out as sheep in the midst of wolves. Therefore be wise as serpents and harmless as doves." Christ did not suppress one word of truth, but He always spoke it in love. He was never rude, never gave needless pain to a sensitive

soul. He did not scold human weakness. He fearlessly condemned hypocrisy and evil, but tears were in His voice as He spoke His sharpest rebukes. Every person was precious in His eyes.

The servants of Christ need to have close fellowship with God, or else when others irritate them self may rise up and they release a torrent of words that are not like the dew or the soft showers that refresh the withering plants. God's servants are to fasten their eyes on Christ's loveliness. Then they can present the gospel with divine tact. And the spirit that is kept gentle when dealing with difficult people or circumstances will speak more effectively in favor of truth than any argument, no matter how strong.

### We Must Meet Opposition

Continuing His instruction to His disciples, Jesus said, "Beware of men." They were not to put complete confidence in those who did not know God and open their plans to them, for this would give Satan's agents an advantage. Human ideas often work against God's plans. God's servants dishonor Him and betray the gospel when they depend on the counsel of those who are not under the Holy Spirit's guidance.

"They will deliver you up to councils. . . . You will be brought before governors and kings for My sake, as a testimony to them and to the Gentiles." The servants of Christ will be brought before the great men of the world who might never hear the gospel otherwise. Having listened to false charges concerning the faith of Christ's disciples, often their only way to learn its real character is through the testimony of those who are brought to trial for their faith. "It will be given to you," said Jesus, "in that hour what you should speak; for it is not you who speak, but the Spirit of your Father who speaks in you." Those who reject the truth will stand to accuse the disciples. But the Lord's children are to reveal the meekness of their Divine Example. In this way, rulers and people will see the contrast between Satan's agents and Christ's representatives.

The servants of Christ were not to prepare a set speech to present when brought to trial. The Holy Spirit would bring to their remembrance the very truths that they would need. The knowledge they had obtained by diligently searching the Scriptures would flash into the memory. But if any had neglected to acquaint themselves with the words of Christ, they could not expect the Holy Spirit to bring His words to their remembrance.

### What to Do When Persecution Comes

The disciples of Christ would be betrayed even by members of their own households. "You will be hated by all for My name's sake. But he who endures to the end will be saved." But He instructed them not to expose themselves to persecution unnecessarily. He Himself often left one field of labor for another in order to escape from those who wanted to take His life. So His servants were not to be discouraged by persecution, but to look for a place where they could still work for souls.

But whatever the danger, Christ's followers must not hide their principles. They cannot remain uncommitted until they are sure it is safe to profess the truth. Jesus said, "Whatever I tell you in the dark, speak in the light; and what you hear in the ear, preach on the housetops."

Jesus never purchased peace by compromise. His heart overflowed with love for the whole human race, but He never tolerated their sins. He was too much their Friend to remain silent while they were following a course that would ruin their souls. He worked to help people be true to themselves, true to their higher, eternal interest. The servants of Christ, called to the same work, should be careful that, in trying to prevent conflict, they do not surrender truth. We can never obtain real peace by compromising principle. And no one can be true to principle without stirring up opposition. Jesus told His disciples, "Do not fear those who kill the body but cannot kill the soul." Their only fear should be to surrender truth, betraying the trust with which God has honored them.

Satan works to fill our hearts with doubt. He tempts us to sin and then to regard ourselves as too evil to approach our heavenly Father. The Lord understands all this. Jesus assures His disciples of God's sympathy, that not a sigh is breathed, not a pain felt, not a grief pierces the soul, but the throb vibrates to the Father's heart.

The Bible shows us God in His high and holy place (Isaiah 57:15), not inactive, not in silence and solitude, but surrounded by thousands of holy beings waiting to do His will. Through channels we cannot understand, He is in active communication with every part of His domain, including this speck of a world. God is leaning forward from His throne to hear the cry of the oppressed. To every sincere prayer He answers, "Here I am." He lifts up the distressed and downtrodden. In every temptation and trial, the angel of His presence is near to deliver.

Jesus continued, "As you acknowledge Me before others, so I will acknowledge you before God and the holy angels. You are to be My witnesses on the earth; likewise I will be your Representative in heaven. The Father does not see your faulty character, but He sees you clothed in My perfection. And everyone who shares My sacrifice for the lost will share in the glory and joy of the redeemed."

Those who would witness for Christ must have Christ abiding in them. The disciples might speak fluently on doctrines, but unless they possessed Christlike meekness and love, they were not representing Him. A spirit contrary to the spirit of Christ would deny Him. People may deny Christ by speaking evil, by foolish talking, by words that are untruthful or unkind. They may deny Him by shunning life's burdens, by conforming to the world, by uncourteous behavior, by justifying self, by cherishing doubt,

and by borrowing trouble. And "whoever denies Me before men, him I will also deny before My Father who is in heaven."

The Savior said, "I did not come to bring peace but a sword." This strife is not the effect of the gospel, but comes from opposition to it. Of all persecution, the hardest to bear is in the home, the distancing of our dearest earthly friends. But Jesus said, "He who loves father or mother more than Me is not worthy of Me. And he who loves son or daughter more than Me is not worthy of Me. And he who does not take his cross and follow after Me is not worthy of Me.

"He who receives you receives Me, and he who receives Me receives Him who sent Me." Christ will not fail to reward any act of kindness shown in His name. He includes the feeblest and lowliest of the family of God. "Whoever gives one of these little ones only a cup of cold water in the name of a disciple, assuredly, I say to you, he shall by no means lose his reward."

And so the Savior ended His instruction. The chosen Twelve went out, as He had gone, "to preach the gospel to the poor; . . . to heal the brokenhearted, to preach deliverance to the captives and recovery of sight to the blind." Luke 4:18.

# Christ and the Twelve Take a Vacation[*]

When they returned from their missionary tour, "the apostles gathered to Jesus and told Him all things, both what they had done and what they had taught. And He said to them, 'Come aside by yourselves to a deserted place and rest a while.' "

The disciples' close relationship with Jesus encouraged them to tell Him about their good and bad experiences as evangelists. As they frankly told Christ of their experiences, He saw that they needed much instruction. He saw, too, that they needed rest.

But where they were then, they could not find privacy, "for there were many coming and going, and they did not even have time to eat." The people were crowding around Christ, anxious to be healed and eager to listen to His words. To many, He seemed to be the Fountain of all blessings.

But now Christ longed to be away from the crowds because He had much to say to His disciples. Sometimes in their work, they had been very troubled to know what to do. Now they needed to go to a place of seclusion where they could talk privately with Jesus and receive instruction for future work. They had been putting their whole souls into labor for the people, and this was exhausting their physical and mental strength. It was their duty to rest.

As the disciples had seen their work succeed, they were in danger of taking credit to themselves, of cherishing spiritual pride, and falling under Satan's temptations. They must learn that their strength was not in themselves but in God. They needed to spend time with Christ, with nature, and with their own hearts.

It was about this time that Jesus received the news of John the Baptist's death. This brought vividly to His mind the end to which His own steps were leading. Priests and rabbis were watching, spies followed Him closely, and plots for His destruction were multiplying.

News reached Herod of Jesus and His work. "This is John the Baptist," he said, "he is risen from the dead"; and he expressed a desire to see Jesus. Herod was in constant fear of a revolution that might overthrow him and break the Roman yoke from the

---

[*] *This chapter is based on Matthew 14:1, 2, 12, 13; Mark 6:30–32; Luke 9:7–10.*

Jewish nation. Among the people, the spirit of revolt was everywhere. It was evident that Christ's public work in Galilee could not continue long, and He yearned to get away from the confusion of the crowds for a little while.

With saddened hearts, the disciples of John had carried his mutilated body to its burial. Then they "went and told Jesus." These disciples had been envious of Christ and had doubted His divine mission because He did not set the Baptist free. But now they longed for consolation in their great sorrow and for guidance regarding their future work. They came to Jesus and united their cause with His.

At the northern end of the lake was a lonely region, beautiful with the fresh green of spring. They set out in their boat for this place. The scenes of nature were a rest in themselves, refreshing to the senses. Here they could listen to Christ without the angry interruptions, rebuttals, and accusations of the scribes and Pharisees.

### Rest Refreshed Them

Christ and His disciples did not devote the time they spent in seclusion to pleasure seeking. They talked together regarding the work of God and the possibility of greater effectiveness. Christ corrected their errors and made plain to them the right way of approaching the people. They were vitalized by divine power and inspired with hope and courage.

When Jesus said that the harvest was great and the laborers few, He did not urge endless work, but said, "Therefore pray the Lord of the harvest to send out laborers into His har-

vest." Matthew 9:38. God would not have a few workers crushed with responsibilities while others have no burden, no urgency of heart.

Christ's words of compassion apply to His workers today: "Come aside by yourselves . . . and rest a while." It is not wise to be always under the strain of ministering to other people's spiritual needs, for in this way, we neglect personal piety and overtax soul and body. God requires self-denial, but we must be careful that Satan does not take advantage of our human weakness, and the work of God be damaged.

As activity increases and we become successful in doing any work for God, there is a tendency to pray less and to have less faith. We lose sight of our dependence on God and seek to make a savior out of our activity. It is Christ's power that does the work. We must take time for meditation, prayer, and study of the Word. Only the work accomplished with much prayer and sanctified by Christ's merit will prove effective for good in the end.

### Never Too Busy to Talk With God

No other life was so crowded with work as was that of Jesus, yet how often He was found in prayer! Again and again we find records such as these: "Having risen a long while before daylight, He went out and departed to a solitary place; and there He prayed." "Great multitudes came together to hear, and to be healed by Him of their infirmities. So He Himself often withdrew into the wilderness and prayed." "Now it came to pass in those days that He went out to the mountain to pray, and continued all night in prayer to God." Mark 1:35; Luke 5:15, 16; 6:12.

The Savior found it necessary to turn aside from a life of endless activity and contact with human needs to seek unbroken fellowship with His Father. As one with us, He was entirely dependent on God. In the secret place of prayer, He sought divine strength so that He could go out braced for duty and trial. Jesus endured struggles and torture of soul. In fellowship with God, He could unburden the sorrows that were crushing Him. As a man, He brought His requests to the throne of God till His humanity was charged with a heavenly current that could connect humanity with Divinity. He received life from God in order to give life to the world. His experience is to be ours.

Today, if we would take time to go to Jesus and tell Him our needs, we would not be disappointed. He is the Wonderful Counselor. Isaiah 9:6. We are invited to ask wisdom of Him. He "gives to all liberally and without reproach." James 1:5.

Everyone needs a personal experience in obtaining a knowledge of the will of God. Individually we must hear Him speaking to the heart. When every other voice is hushed and in quietness we wait before Him, the silence of the heart makes more distinct the voice of God. See Psalm 46:10. Here alone we can find true rest. Those who are refreshed in this way will reveal a divine power that will reach people's hearts.

# "You Give Them Something to Eat"*

This rare season of peaceful quietude did not last long. The disciples thought they would not be disturbed, but as soon as the crowds missed the divine Teacher, they inquired, "Where is He?" Some had noticed the direction where He and His disciples had gone. Many went by land, others in their boats, to meet them. The Passover was near, and pilgrims on their way to Jerusalem gathered to see Jesus, until five thousand men were assembled, besides women and children.

From the hillside, Jesus looked at the crowd, and "was moved with compassion for them, because they were like sheep not having a shepherd." Leaving His refuge, He found a convenient place where He could minister to them.

The people listened to words of mercy from the Son of God, words that were like soothing medicine to their hearts. The healing from His divine hand brought life to the dying and relief and health to those suffering with disease. The day seemed like heaven on earth, and they were unaware of how long it had been since they had eaten anything.

Finally the sun was sinking in the west, and yet the people lingered. Jesus had worked all day without food or rest, but He could not take Himself away from the people that crowded around Him.

The disciples finally urged Jesus to send the people away for their own sake. Many had eaten nothing since morning. In surrounding towns they could buy food. But Jesus said, "You give them something to eat." Turning to Philip, He asked, "Where shall we buy bread, that these may eat?" He said this to test the faith of the disciple. Philip looked over the sea of heads and answered that two hundred pennyworth† of bread would not be nearly enough for each of them to have a little.

Jesus asked how much food they could find among the people. "There is a lad here," said Andrew, "who has five barley loaves and two small fish, but what are they among so many?"

---

* This chapter is based on Matthew 14:13–21; Mark 6:32–44; Luke 9:10–17; John 6:1–13.

† The "penny," or denarius, was equivalent to the daily wage of a common laborer. See Matthew 20:1, 2.

Jesus directed them to bring these to Him and that the disciples seat the people on the grass in parties of fifty or a hundred, so that all could witness what He was about to do. When this was done, Jesus "looked up to heaven, blessed and broke the loaves, and gave them to His disciples to set before them; and the two fish He divided among them all. So they all ate and were filled. And they took up twelve baskets full of fragments and of the fish." He who taught the people the way to find peace and happiness was just as thoughtful about their physical necessities as He was about their spiritual need.

Christ never worked a miracle except to meet a genuine need, and every miracle was meant to lead the people to the tree of life. The simple food passed around by the disciples contained a whole treasure of lessons. Jesus had provided a humble meal; the fish and barley loaves were the daily food of the fisherfolk. Christ could have spread a rich meal, but food prepared just to gratify appetite would have carried no lesson for their good. Never did people enjoy luxurious feasts as much as this people enjoyed the rest and simple food that Christ provided so far from human homes and resources.

If people today maintained simple habits, living in harmony with nature's laws, there would be an abundant supply for the needs of the human family. There would be fewer imaginary wants and more opportunities to work in God's ways. But selfishness and gratifying of unnatural taste have brought sin and misery into the world.

To that great assembly, weary and hungry, the simple food was an assurance not only of Jesus' power, but of His tender care for them in the common needs of life. The Savior has not promised His followers luxuries. Their food may be plain, even scarce; their lives may be shut in by poverty. But His word is pledged that their need will be supplied, and He has promised what is far better than worldly good—the comfort of His own presence.

In the production of earth's harvests, God is working a miracle every day. Through natural agencies, He accomplishes the same work that Jesus did in feeding the multitude. People prepare the soil and sow the seed, but life from God causes the seed to germinate. It is God who feeds millions from earth's harvest fields every day. People credit the working of His power to natural causes or to human instrumentality. They glorify man in place of God and make His gracious gifts a curse instead of a blessing. God wants us to recognize Him in His gifts. To accomplish this, Christ performed His miracles.

### A Valuable Lesson in Ecology

After that large group had eaten, an abundance of food was left. But Jesus said, "Gather up the fragments that remain, so that nothing is lost." The lesson had two parts. Nothing is to be wasted. Gather up everything that will relieve earth's hungry ones. And there should be the same carefulness in spiritual things. The people wanted their friends at home to share in the bread that Christ had blessed. So those who were at the feast were to give to others the bread that comes down from heaven, to satisfy the hunger of the heart. They were to repeat what they had learned of the wonderful things of God. Nothing was to be lost.

The miracle of the loaves teaches us to depend on God. When Christ fed the five thousand, there was no food nearby. Here He was, in the wilderness. But He knew that the large crowd would feel hungry and faint, for He was one with them in their need for food. They were far from home, and many had no money to purchase food. God's leading had placed Jesus where He was, and He depended on His heavenly Father for the means to meet the need.

We too are to depend on God. We are not to plunge into difficulties and misuse the abilities God has given us. But when, after following His directions, we are brought into tight places, we are to seek help from Him who has infinite resources at His command. He will help every person who comes into difficulty because of trying to keep the way of the Lord.

### How We Often Repeat Andrew's Unbelief

Christ has directed us, "Go into all the world and preach the gospel to every creature." Mark 16:15. But how often our faith fails us, as we see how great the need is and how small the resources in our hands. Like Andrew, we often hesitate, unwilling to give all that we have, afraid to spend and to be spent for others. But Jesus has instructed us, "You give them something to eat." Behind His command is the same power that fed the multitude beside the sea.

In Christ's act is wrapped up a deep spiritual lesson for all His workers. Christ received from the Father; He gave to the disciples; they distributed to the crowd, and the people to one another. So all who are united to Christ will receive from Him the bread of life and give it to others. Jesus took the little loaves, and although there was only a little portion for His own disciples, He did not invite them to eat, but began to distribute to them, instructing them serve the people. The food multiplied in His hands; and the hands of the disciples, reaching out to Christ, were never empty. After feeding the people, Christ and His disciples ate together of the Heaven-supplied food.

The disciples were the channel of communication between Christ and the people. The most intelligent, the most spiritual, can give only as they receive. We can share only what we receive from Christ, and we can receive only as we share with others. And the more we give, the more we will receive.

Too often the workers for Christ fail to realize their personal responsibility. They are in danger of shifting their burden on organizations instead of relying on Him who is the Source of all strength. Successful work for Christ depends not so much on talent as on earnest, dependent faith. Instead of shifting your responsibility on someone you think is more richly endowed than you are, work according to your ability. When the question comes home to your heart, "Where shall we buy bread, that these may eat?" do not let your answer be the response of unbelief. When people are completely lacking the bread of life, should we send for someone from far away to come and feed them? Christ said, "Make the people sit down," and He fed them there. So when you are surrounded by people in need, know that Christ is there. Bring your barley loaves to Jesus. The little that we use wisely in the service of the Lord will increase in the very act of sharing.

The Lord says, "Give, and it will be given to you." "He who supplies seed to the sower and bread for food will supply and multiply your seed for sowing and increase the harvest of your righteousness. You will be enriched in every way for your great generosity." Luke 6:38; 2 Corinthians 9:10, 11, NRSV.

# A Night on the Lake*

Seated on the grassy plain in the twilight of the spring evening, the people ate the food Christ provided. The miracle of the loaves appealed to everyone in that vast crowd. God had fed Israel with manna in the desert, and who was this that had fed them that day, if not the One whom Moses had foretold? They said one to another, "This is truly the Prophet who is to come into the world."

That crowning act was assurance that the long-looked-for Deliverer was among them. He was the One who would make Judea an earthly paradise, a land flowing with milk and honey. He could break the power of the hated Romans. He could heal the soldiers wounded in battle. He could supply whole armies with food. He could give to Israel the long-sought rulership!

The people were ready to crown Him king immediately. They saw that He made no effort to get honor for Himself, and they feared He would never assert His claim to David's throne. Consulting together, they agreed to take Him by force and proclaim Him the King of Israel. The disciples united with the crowd in declaring that the throne of David was the rightful inheritance of their Master. Let the arrogant priests and rulers be forced to honor Him who came clothed with the authority of God.

But Jesus saw what was happening and what would be the result. Violence and insurrection would follow, hindering the work of the spiritual kingdom. He must stop the movement at once. Calling His disciples, Jesus told them to take the boat and return right then to Capernaum, leaving Him to dismiss the people.

Never before had a command from Christ seemed so impossible. This seemed the golden opportunity to establish their beloved Master on the throne of Israel. It was hard for them to go away by themselves and leave Jesus alone on that desolate shore. They protested, but Jesus now spoke with an authority He had never before revealed toward them. In silence they turned toward the lake.

Jesus now commanded the crowd to disperse, and His manner was so decisive that they did not dare disobey. In the very act of coming to seize Him,

---

* This chapter is based on Matthew 14:22–33; Mark 6:45–52; John 6:14–21.

their steps were halted. The kingly bearing of Jesus and His few quiet words of command frustrated their plans. They recognized in Him a power greater than all earthly authority, and without question they submitted.

Left alone, Jesus "went up on a mountain by Himself to pray." For hours He prayed for power to reveal to the people the divine character of His mission, so that Satan would not blind their understanding and twist their judgment. He knew that His days on earth were nearly ended, and that few would receive Him. His disciples were to be severely tried, their long-cherished hopes disappointed. Instead of seeing Him exalted to the throne of David, they were to witness His crucifixion. This would indeed be His true coronation, but they did not understand this, and without the Holy Spirit, the faith of the disciples would fail. Jesus poured out His requests to God for them with bitter agony and tears.

The disciples had not immediately set out in the boat from land, hoping that Jesus would come. But as darkness was fast gathering, they "got into the boat, and went over the sea toward Capernaum." They complained because Jesus had not permitted them to proclaim Him King. They blamed themselves; if they had been more persistent, they might have accomplished their purpose.

Unbelief was taking possession of their minds and hearts. Love of honor had blinded them. They were eager to see Jesus exalted as they thought He should be. Were they always to be thought of as followers of a false prophet? Why did not Jesus, who pos-sessed such power, reveal Himself in His true character and make their lives less painful? Why had He not saved John the Baptist from a violent death? The disciples reasoned this way until they brought great spiritual darkness on themselves. They questioned, "Could Jesus be an impostor, as the Pharisees claimed?"

## The Storm Within the Disciples' Hearts

The memory of that precious, glorious day should have filled them with faith and hope, but they had forgotten it all. Their thoughts were stormy and unreasonable, and the Lord gave them something else to afflict their souls and occupy their minds. God often does this when people create burdens and troubles for themselves. The disciples had no need to make trouble. Already danger was fast approaching.

A violent storm had been silently coming their way, and they were unprepared for it. It was a sudden contrast, and when the gale struck they were afraid. They forgot their resentments, unbelief, and impatience. Everyone worked to keep the boat from sinking. In ordinary weather, the journey took only a few hours, but now they were driven farther from where they were going. They labored at the oars until around three o'clock in the morning. Then the weary men gave themselves up for lost. Helpless, they longed for the presence of their Master.

The Watcher on the shore saw those fear-stricken men battling with the tempest. With deepest care His eyes followed the storm-tossed boat with its precious burden, for these men were to be the light of the world. When their hearts were subdued and their unholy ambition silenced, and in humility they prayed for help, it was given them.

At the moment when they believed themselves lost, a gleam of light revealed a mysterious figure approaching on the water. But they thought that the One who had come for their help was an enemy. Terror overpowered them. Hands that had grasped the oars with muscles like iron let go. The boat rocked at the will of the waves; all eyes were riveted on this vision of a man walking on the white-capped billows of the foaming sea.

They thought it was a phantom that was a sign of their destruction, and they cried out in fear. Jesus kept walking as if He would pass them, but they recognized Him and begged for His help. His voice silenced their fear: "It is I; do not be afraid."

As soon as they could believe this wonderful fact, Peter called out, " 'Lord, if it is You, command me to come to You on the water.' So He said, 'Come.' "

## Peter's Self-Exaltation and His Fall

Looking to Jesus, Peter walked securely; but as he glanced back toward his companions in the boat, his eyes were turned from the Savior. The waves rolled high and he was afraid. For a moment Christ was hidden from view, and his faith gave way. He began to sink. But while the waves talked with death, Peter lifted his eyes from the angry waters and cried, "Lord, save me!" Jesus grasped the outstretched hand, saying, "O you of little faith, why did you doubt?"

Walking side by side, Peter's hand in his Master's, they stepped into the boat together. Peter was now subdued and silent. Through unbelief and pride he had nearly lost his life.

When trouble comes, how often we look at the waves instead of keeping our eyes on the Savior! The proud waters go over our souls. Jesus does not call us to follow Him and then forsake us. "Fear not," He says. "When you pass through the waters, I will be with you; and through the rivers, they shall not overflow you. . . . I am the Lord your God, the Holy One of Israel, your Savior." Isaiah 43:1–3.

In this incident on the sea, Jesus wanted to reveal to Peter that his only safety was in constantly depending on divine power. Amid the storms of temptation, he could walk safely only as he relied on the Savior. Where he thought himself strong, Peter was weak. If he had learned the lesson in that experience on the lake, he would not have failed when the great test came upon him.

Day by day God instructs His children. By the circumstances of daily life, He is preparing them to act their part on that wider stage to which His wisdom has appointed them. We may now think that our feet stand secure, and that we will never be moved. We may say with confidence, "Nothing can shake my faith in God and in His Word." But Satan is planning to take advantage of our hereditary and cultivated defects. We can only walk securely by realizing our own weakness and looking steadily to Jesus.

No sooner had Jesus taken His

place in the boat than the wind ceased, "and immediately the boat was at the land where they were going." The disciples and others on board bowed at the feet of Jesus with thankful hearts, saying "Truly You are the Son of God"!

# The Crisis in Galilee<sup>*</sup>

Christ knew that a turning point in His history was reached. Multitudes who wanted to exalt Him to the throne today would turn from Him tomorrow. Disappointment of their selfish ambition would turn love to hatred and praise to curses.

Yet Jesus did not try to avoid the crisis. From the beginning He had held out no hope of earthly rewards. Many of those now connected with Him had been attracted by hope of a worldly kingdom. These must be undeceived.

Early the next morning, the people flocked to Bethsaida in great numbers. Those who had left Jesus the preceding night returned, expecting to find Him still there, for there had been no boat by which He could pass to the other side. But their search was fruitless.

Meanwhile, He had arrived at the Sea of Galilee after an absence of only one day. Those who had come from Bethsaida learned from His disciples how He had crossed the lake. The disciples faithfully recounted everything to the astonished crowd: the fury of the storm, the many hours of adverse winds, Christ walking on water, His

reassuring words, the adventure of Peter, the sudden quieting of the storm, and the landing of the boat. But many were not content with this and hoped to receive from Christ's own lips a further account of the miracle.

Jesus did not gratify their curiosity. He sadly said, "You seek Me, not because you saw the signs, but because you ate of the loaves and were filled. Do not labor for the food which perishes, but for the food which endures to everlasting life." Do not look just for material benefit, but for spiritual food.

For the moment, this awakened the interest of the hearers. "What shall we do, that we may work the works of God?" Their question meant, "What shall we do that we may deserve heaven? What price are we required to pay in order to obtain the life to come?"

Jesus answered, "This is the work of God, that you believe in Him whom He sent." The price of heaven is Jesus. The way to heaven is through faith in the Lamb of God.

### Selfish Hopes Unfulfilled

Jesus had done the very work that prophecy had foretold the Messiah

---

<sup>*</sup> *This chapter is based on John 6:22–71.*

would do, but the people had not seen what their selfish hopes had pictured as His work. In the days of Moses, Israel had been fed with manna forty years, and they expected far greater blessings from the Messiah. Why could Jesus not give health, strength, and riches to all His people, free them from their oppressors, and exalt them to power and honor? He claimed to be the One sent from God, yet He refused to be Israel's King. This was a mystery they could not fathom. Did He dare not assert His claims because He Himself doubted the divine character of His mission?

Half-mockingly a rabbi questioned: "What sign will You perform then, that we may see it and believe You? What work will You do? Our fathers ate the manna in the desert; as it is written, 'He gave them bread from heaven to eat.'

"Then Jesus said to them, 'Most assuredly, I say to you, Moses did not give you the bread from heaven.' " The Giver of the manna was standing among them. Christ Himself had led the Hebrews and had fed them daily with the bread from heaven. That food was a symbol of the real Bread from heaven. The life-giving Spirit is the true Manna. "For the bread of God is He who comes down from heaven and gives life to the world."

Still thinking it was physical food, some exclaimed, "Lord, give us this bread always." Jesus then spoke plainly, "I am the bread of life."

Moses had said, "Man shall not live by bread alone; but man lives by every word that proceeds from the mouth of the Lord." Deuteronomy 8:3. And Jeremiah had written, "Your words were found, and I ate them, and Your word was to me the joy and rejoicing of my heart." Jeremiah 15:16. The teaching of the prophets made plain the spiritual lesson in the miracle of the loaves. If Christ's hearers in the synagogue had understood the Scriptures, they would have understood His words, "I am the bread of life." As the multitude had received physical strength from the bread He had given them the day before, so they could receive spiritual strength from Christ for eternal life. "He who comes to Me," He said, "shall never hunger, and he who believes in Me shall never thirst." But he added, "You have seen Me and yet do not believe."

They had seen Christ by the witness of the Holy Spirit, by the revelation of God to their hearts. The living evidences of His power had been before them day after day, yet they asked for still another sign. If they were not convinced by what they had seen and heard, it was useless to show them more marvelous works. Unbelief will always find excuse for doubt and will explain away the most positive proof.

Again Christ appealed to those stubborn hearts: "The one who comes to Me I will by no means cast out." All who received Him in faith, He said, would have eternal life. No longer did people need to mourn in hopeless grief over their dead. "This is the will of Him who sent Me, that everyone who sees the Son and believes in Him may have everlasting life; and I will raise him up at the last day."

But the leaders were offended. "Is not this Jesus, the son of Joseph, whose father and mother we know? How is it then that He says, 'I have come down from heaven'?" Referring scornfully to Jesus' lowly origin, with contempt they alluded to His family as being poor and lowly. The claims of this uneducated Carpenter, they said, were unworthy of their attention. Because of His mysterious birth, they insinuated that He was of doubtful parentage.

Jesus did not attempt to explain the mystery of His birth, as He had given no answer to the questions about His crossing the sea. Voluntarily He had made Himself of no reputation and taken the form of a servant. But His words and works revealed His character.

The prejudice of the Pharisees grew out of the stubbornness of their hearts. Every word and act of Jesus made them angry, for the spirit they cherished could find no answering chord in Him.

"No one can come to Me unless the Father who sent Me draws him. . . . It is written in the prophets, 'And they shall all be taught by God.' Therefore everyone who has heard and learned from the Father comes to Me." None will ever come to Christ except those who respond to the drawing of the Father's love. But God is drawing all hearts to Him, and only those who resist His drawing will refuse to come to Christ. Those who had learned from God had been listening to His Son, and they would recognize in Jesus of Nazareth the One who had declared the Father.

## When Heaven Begins

"Most assuredly, I say to you, he who believes in Me has everlasting life." And Jesus said, "I will raise him up at the last day." Christ became one flesh with us so that we could become one spirit with Him. As a result of this union, we will come out from the grave, because through faith His life has become ours. Those who see Christ and receive Him into the heart have everlasting life. Through the Spirit, Christ dwells in us; and the Spirit of God, received by faith, is the beginning of eternal life.

The manna that the fathers ate in the wilderness did not prevent their death nor insure immortality, but the bread of heaven would feed the soul for everlasting life. The Savior said, "This is the bread which comes down from heaven, that one may eat of it and not die." Only through dying could Christ give life to us, and He points to His death as the means of salvation: "The bread that I shall give is My flesh, which I shall give for the life of the world."

The Jews did not recognize the Lord's body in the symbol of the Passover lamb. The words of Christ taught the same truth, but the people still did not recognize it.

Now the rabbis exclaimed angrily, "How can this Man give us His flesh to eat?" To some extent they understood Jesus' meaning, but by misinterpreting His words, they hoped to prejudice the people against Him.

Christ repeated the truth in even stronger language. "Most assuredly, I say to you, unless you eat the flesh of the Son of Man and drink His blood, you have no life in you. Whoever eats My flesh and drinks My blood has eternal life, and I will raise him up at the last day. For My flesh is food indeed, and My blood is drink indeed. He who eats My flesh and drinks My blood abides in Me, and I in him."

What food is to the body, Christ must be to the soul. Food cannot benefit us unless it becomes a part of our being. And spiritually, a theoretical knowledge will do us no good. We must feed upon Christ. We must assimilate His life, His love, His grace.

"As the living Father sent Me, and I live because of the Father, so he who feeds on Me will live because of Me." Jesus was surrendered to the will of God so fully that the Father alone appeared in His life. Although tempted in all points as we are, He stood untainted by the evil that surrounded Him. In the same way, we also are to overcome as Christ overcame.

Are you a follower of Christ? Then by uniting yourself to Jesus you may attain all that the Bible promises concerning the spiritual life. Has your first love grown cold? Accept the love of Christ again. Eat of His flesh, drink of His blood, and you will become one with the Father and with the Son.

By ritual law, the Jews were forbidden to taste blood, and they now twisted Christ's language into sacrilegious speech. Even many of the disciples said, "This is a hard saying; who can understand it?"

The Savior answered them: "Does *this* offend you? What then if you should see the Son of Man ascend where He was before? It is the Spirit who gives life; the flesh profits nothing. The words that I speak to you are spirit, and they are life."

## Life in the Word

The life of Christ that gives life to the world is in His word. By His word Jesus healed disease and cast out demons; by His word He stilled the sea and raised the dead. The whole Bible is a revelation of Christ, and the Savior wanted to fasten the faith of His followers on the Word. When His visible presence would be withdrawn, the Word must be the source of their power.

As food sustains our physical life, so the Word of God sustains our spiritual life. As we must eat for ourselves, so we must receive the Word for ourselves. We should carefully study the Bible, asking God for the Holy Spirit's aid so that we may understand His Word. We should take one verse, discover the thought God has put in that verse for us, and dwell on the thought until it becomes our own.

In His promises and warnings, Jesus means me. God so loved the world that He gave His Son, that *I* by believing in Him might not perish, but have everlasting life. The experiences related in God's Word are to be *my* experiences. Prayer and promise are *mine*. "I have been crucified with Christ; it is no longer I who live, but Christ lives in me; and the life which I now live in the flesh I live by faith in the Son of God, who loved me and gave Himself for me." Galatians 2:20. As faith thus absorbs the principles of truth, they become a part of the being and the ruling power of the life. The Word molds the thoughts and enters into the development of character.

God will make precious revelations to His hungering, thirsting people. As they feed on His Word, they find it is spirit and life. The Word destroys the natural, earthly nature and gives a new life in Christ. The Holy Spirit comes as a Comforter. By God's grace, the disciple becomes a new creature. Love takes the place of hatred, and the heart receives the divine likeness. This is eating the Bread that comes down from heaven.

Christ knew the character of those who claimed to be His disciples, and His words tested their faith. He declared that they were to believe and act on His teaching and be molded in His character. This involved relinquishing their cherished ambitions. It required complete surrender to Jesus. They were called to become self-sacrificing, meek and humble in heart, to walk in the narrow path traveled by the Man of Calvary.

## Christ's Words Alienate Many

The test was too great. The enthusiasm of those who had wanted to take Jesus by force and make Him King grew cold. This speech had opened their eyes. No earthly rewards would come from connection with Him. They had welcomed His miracle-working power but would not come into agreement with His self-sacrificing life. If He would not regain their freedom from the Romans, they would have nothing to do with Him.

Jesus told them plainly, "There are some of you who do not believe," adding, "Therefore I have said to you that no one can come to Me unless it has been granted to him by My Father." If they were not drawn to Him, it was because their hearts were not open to the Holy Spirit.

By His public rebuke of their unbelief, these disciples were still further alienated from Jesus. Wanting to wound the Savior and gratify the hatred of the Pharisees, they turned their backs on Him and left Him with disdain. They had made their choice; they did not walk with Jesus any more.

By the words of truth, the chaff was being separated from the wheat. See Matthew 3:12. Many turned away because they were too self-righteous to receive reproof. People are tested today as those disciples were in the synagogue at Capernaum. When truth comes home to the heart, they see the need of an entire change but are not willing to take up the self-denying work. They go away offended, complaining, "This is a hard saying; who can understand it?"

## Truth Is Unwelcome

When the crowds follow and the multitudes are fed and people are shouting in triumph, their voices are loud in praise. But when God's Spirit reveals sin and calls them to leave it, they turn their backs on the truth.

As those alienated disciples turned away, a different spirit took control of them. They could see nothing attractive in Christ whom they had once found so interesting. They misinterpreted His words, falsified His statements, and attacked His motives, gathering up every item that they could turn against Him. These false reports stirred up such indignation that His life was in danger.

The news spread swiftly that by His own admission Jesus of Nazareth was not the Messiah. This caused the popular feeling in Galilee to turn against Him, as it had turned in Judea the year before. Israel rejected their Savior because they wanted the food that perishes, not that which endures to everlasting life.

With a yearning heart, Jesus saw His former disciples leave. His compassion was unappreciated, His love unreturned, His salvation rejected—these things filled Him with inexpressible sorrow. Such developments as these made Him "a Man of sorrows and acquainted with grief." Isaiah 53:3.

Without attempting to stop those who were leaving, Jesus turned to the Twelve and said, "Do you also want to go away?"

Peter replied by asking, "Lord, to whom shall we go? You have the words of eternal life. Also we have come to believe and know that You are the Christ, the Son of the living God."

"To whom shall we go?" The disciples had found more peace and joy since they had accepted Christ than in all their previous lives. How could they go back to those who scorned and persecuted the Friend of sinners?

"To whom shall we go?" To the darkness of unbelief, the wickedness of the world? Peter expressed the faith of the disciples—"You are the Christ." To be without a Savior was to be adrift on a dark and stormy sea.

Every word and act of Jesus had its definite purpose in the work of our redemption. While we cannot now comprehend the ways of God, we can recognize His great love that motivates all His dealings with humanity. He who lives near to Jesus will recognize the mercy that tests the character and brings to light the intentions of the heart.

## Love Under All His Dealings

Jesus knew what would be the result of His words. He foresaw that His agony in Gethsemane, His betrayal and crucifixion, would be a most trying ordeal to His beloved disciples. If there had been no previous test, many who were driven by merely selfish motives would still have been with Jesus and the disciples. When their Lord was condemned, when the multitude who had hailed Him as their King hissed at Him and reviled Him, when the jeering crowd cried, "Crucify Him!"—these self-seeking ones, by renouncing their allegiance to Jesus, would have brought a bitter, heart-burdening sorrow on the disciples in addition to their grief and disappointment in seeing their dearest hopes dashed. The example of those who turned from Him might have carried others with them. But Jesus brought this crisis on while He could still strengthen the faith of His true followers by His personal presence.

Compassionate Redeemer! Knowing fully the doom that awaited Him, He tenderly smoothed the way for the disciples, preparing them for their greatest trial and strengthening them for the final test!

# Christ Foretells a Great Uprooting[*]

The mission of the Twelve showed that Christ's work was expanding, and so it had reignited the jealousy of the leaders at Jerusalem. The spies they had sent to Capernaum in the early part of Christ's ministry had been no match for Jesus, but now they sent another delegation to watch His movements and find some accusation against Him.

As before, the basis of their complaint was that He disregarded the traditional rules supposedly designed to help people keep from breaking the law. Among the rules they enforced most strenuously was ceremonial purification. They claimed that neglecting the forms to be observed before eating was a terrible sin.

Those who tried to observe the rabbis' requirements found life to be one long struggle against ceremonial defilement. While the people were occupied with trivial observances, their attention was turned away from the great principles of God's law.

Christ and His disciples did not observe ceremonial washings. The spies, however, did not make a direct attack on Christ, but came to Him with criticism of His disciples: "Why do Your disciples transgress the tradition of the elders? For they do not wash their hands when they eat bread."

Jesus made no attempt to defend Himself or His disciples. He proceeded to show the spirit that drove these sticklers for human ceremonies. He gave them an example of what they were repeatedly doing: "All too well you reject the commandment of God," He said, "that you may keep your tradition. For Moses said, 'Honor your father and your mother'; and, 'He who curses father or mother, let him be put to death.' But you say, 'If a man says to his father or mother, "Whatever profit you might have received from me is Corban"—' (that is, a gift to God)"; and you no longer let him do anything for his father or his mother." An undutiful child only needed to pronounce the word *Corban* over his property, and he could keep it for his own use during his lifetime, and after his death it was donated for the temple service. In this way, he was free to dishonor and defraud his parents, under cover of a pretended devotion to God.

Jesus spoke well of the poor woman who gave her all to the temple treasury. But the priests and rabbis' appar-

* This chapter is based on Matthew 15:1–20; Mark 7:1–23.

ent zeal for God was just a show to cover a desire to exalt themselves. Even the disciples of Christ were not completely free from the yoke of inherited prejudice and rabbinical authority. By revealing the true spirit of the rabbis, Jesus was trying to free all who really wanted to serve God.

"Hypocrites! Well did Isaiah prophesy about you, saying:

'These people draw near to Me with
    their mouth,
And honor Me with their lips,
But their heart is far from Me.
And in vain they worship Me,
Teaching as doctrines the command-
    ments of men.' "

Christ declared that by placing their requirements above the divine laws, the rabbis were setting themselves above God. Jesus explained that defilement does not come from the outside, but from within. Purity and impurity are matters of the heart.

**The Rage of the Spies**

The disciples noticed the spies' rage and heard their half-muttered words of dissatisfaction and revenge. They told Christ, hoping that He would make peace with the enraged officials: "Do You know that the Pharisees were offended when they heard this saying?"

He answered, "Every plant which My heavenly Father has not planted will be uprooted." The customs and traditions that the rabbis valued so highly could not endure God's testing. Every human invention that people have substituted for the commandments of God will be found worthless in that day when "God will bring every work into judgment, including every secret thing, whether it is good or whether it is evil." Ecclesiastes 12:14.

Even among Christians, we can find institutions and practices that have no better foundation than the traditions of the fathers. People cling to their traditions and hate those who show them their error. In this day, when Heaven directs us to call attention to the commandments of God and the faith of Jesus, we see the same hatred as people expressed in the days of Christ. The Bible says about the remnant people of God, "The dragon was enraged with the woman, and he went to make war with the rest of her offspring, who keep the commandments of God and have the testimony of Jesus Christ." Revelation 12:17.

But "every plant which My heavenly Father has not planted will be uprooted." In place of the authority of the so-called fathers of the church, God asks us to accept the word of the eternal Father, the Lord of heaven and earth. Here alone we can find truth unmixed with error. "In vain they worship Me, teaching as doctrines the commandments of men."

# Christ Breaks Down Racial Barriers*

After the encounter with the Pharisees, Jesus left Capernaum and crossed Galilee to the hill country on the borders of Phoenicia. Looking westward, He could see the ancient cities of Tyre and Sidon with their heathen temples. Beyond was the Mediterranean, over which the messengers of the gospel were to carry its joyful news to the centers of the world's empire. The work before Him now was to prepare His disciples for their mission.

"Behold, a woman of Canaan came from that region and cried out to Him, saying, 'Have mercy on me, O Lord, Son of David! My daughter is severely demon-possessed.'" The people of this district were idol worshipers, despised and hated by the Jews. The woman who now came to Jesus was a heathen, and so she was excluded from the advantages the Jews daily enjoyed.

News of Christ's work had reached this region. This woman had heard of the Prophet who, it was reported, healed all kinds of diseases. Hope sprang up in her heart. Inspired by a mother's love, she determined to present her daughter's case to Him. He must heal her child. At times she was tempted to think, *What can this Jewish Teacher do for me?* But the word had come, He heals all kinds of diseases, whether those who come for help are rich or poor.

Christ knew that this woman was longing to see Him, and He placed Himself in her path. By ministering to her sorrow, He could give a living example of the lesson He intended to teach. This was why He had brought His disciples to this region. He wanted them to see the ignorance existing in cities and villages close to Israel. The people to whom God had given the truth made no effort to help others in darkness. The partition wall that Jewish pride had built shut even the disciples from sympathy with the heathen world. Jesus would break these barriers down.

Christ received this woman, representing a despised race, with the cold and heartless attitude with which the Jews would treat such a case. But the woman did not lose faith. As He passed by, as if not hearing her, she followed, continuing her appeals. Annoyed, the disciples asked Jesus to send her away. They saw that their Master treated her with indifference,

---

* This chapter is based on Matthew 15:21–28; Mark 7:24–30.

and they supposed that the prejudice of the Jews against the Canaanites was pleasing to Him.

But it was a pitying Savior who answered, "I was not sent except to the lost sheep of the house of Israel." Although this answer appeared to be in keeping with Jewish prejudice, it was an implied rebuke to the disciples. They understood this later as reminding them of what He had often told them—that He came to the world to save all who would accept Him.

The woman urged her case more earnestly, bowing at Christ's feet and crying, "Lord, help me!" Jesus, still apparently rejecting her appeals, answered, "It is not good to take the children's bread and throw it to the little dogs." This was virtually saying that it was not right to lavish on strangers and aliens from Israel the blessings given to the favored people of God. This answer would have completely discouraged a less-earnest seeker. But the woman saw that her opportunity had come.

Behind Jesus' apparent refusal, she saw a compassion He could not hide. "True, Lord, yet even the little dogs eat the crumbs which fall from their masters' table." Even dogs are not left unfed! So, while God had given many blessings to Israel, was there not also a blessing for her? She was looked on as a dog, so didn't she have at least a dog's claim to a crumb from His bounty? If she could just have the privilege of a dog, she was willing to be regarded as a dog, and she immediately acknowledged Jesus as the Redeemer, Someone who was able to do all that she asked from Him.

## Faith in Christ Gives Her a Tremendous Argument

The Savior was satisfied. He had tested her faith. He had shown that she whom others had regarded as an outcast from Israel was no longer an alien, but a child in God's household. As a child, it was her privilege to share in the Father's gifts. Christ now granted her request and finished the lesson to the disciples. Turning to her with a look of pity and love, He said, "O woman, great is your faith! Let it be to you as you desire." From that hour, her daughter was healed. The woman left, acknowledging her Savior, and happy that He had granted her prayer.

It was for this miracle that Jesus went to the borders of Tyre and Sidon. He wanted to help the afflicted woman and at the same time leave His disciples an example of mercy for the time when He would no longer be with them. He wanted to lead them to be interested in working for others besides their own people.

Jesus longed to reveal the deep mysteries of the truth, that the Gentiles should be fellow heirs with the Jews and "partakers of His promise in Christ through the gospel." Ephesians 3:6. In rewarding the faith of the centurion at Capernaum and preaching to the people of Sychar, He had already given evidence that He did not share the Jewish intolerance. But now Jesus brought the disciples in contact with a heathen who they thought would have no reason to expect favor from Him. He would show that His love was not to be limited to race or nation.

When He said, "I was not sent except to the lost sheep of the house of

Israel," He stated the truth. This woman was one of the lost sheep that Israel should have rescued. The work they had neglected, Christ was doing.

This act opened the disciples' minds more fully to the work ahead of them among the Gentiles. They saw people carrying sorrows that others, more highly favored, knew nothing about. They were longing for help from the mighty Healer, hungering for truth. Afterward, when the death of Christ had broken down the dividing wall between Jew and Gentile, this lesson had a powerful influence on Christ's representatives.

The Savior's visit to Phoenicia and the miracle He performed there had an even wider purpose. Today, the same pride and prejudice have built strong walls of separation between different classes of people. Many feel virtually shut away from the gospel. But we should not let them feel that they are shut away from Christ.

In faith the woman of Phoenicia flung herself against the barriers piled up between Jew and Gentile. Regardless of appearances and against discouragement that might have led her to doubt, she trusted the Savior's love. This is how Christ wants us to trust in Him. The blessings of salvation are for every human being. Nothing but his or her own choice can prevent anyone from becoming a partaker of the promise in Christ by the gospel.

Caste is hateful to God. In His sight all people are of equal value. He "has made from one blood every nation of men . . . that they should seek the Lord, in the hope that they might . . . find Him, though He is not far from each one of us." All are invited to come to Him and live. "The same Lord over all is rich to all who call upon Him. For 'whoever calls on the name of the Lord shall be saved.' " Acts 17:26, 27; Romans 10:12, 13.

# The True Sign[*]

In Decapolis, where Jesus had healed the demon-possessed men of Gergesa, the people had insisted that Jesus leave. But they had listened to the messengers He left behind. As He came into that region again, a crowd gathered, and a deaf, stammering man was brought to Him. Taking him aside, Jesus put His fingers in his ears and touched his tongue. He sighed when He thought of the ears that would not be open to the truth, the tongues that refused to acknowledge the Redeemer. At the command, "Be opened," the man's speech was restored.

Jesus went up on a mountain, and there the crowds flocked to Him, bringing their sick and lame. He healed them all; and the people, though they were heathen, glorified the God of Israel. For three days they swarmed around the Savior, sleeping at night in the open air, and through the day pressing close to hear the words of Christ and see His works.

At the end of three days, their food was gone. Jesus would not send them away hungry, and He called on His disciples to give them food. At Bethsaida they had seen how their small supply of food became enough to feed the large crowd, yet they did not bring all they had to Him now, trusting His power to multiply it for the hungry crowds. Again the disciples revealed their unbelief. The people He fed at Bethsaida were Jews; these were Gentiles and heathen. Jewish prejudice was still strong in the disciples' hearts. "Where could we get enough bread in the wilderness to fill such a great multitude?"

But obedient to His word, they brought Him what they had—seven loaves and two fish. He fed the multitude, and they had seven large baskets of fragments remaining. Four thousand men, besides women and children, were refreshed in this way.

Then with His disciples, Jesus crossed the lake to Magdala. In the border country of Tyre and Sidon, the remarkable trust of the Phoenician woman had refreshed His spirit. The heathen people of Decapolis had received Him gladly. Now as He landed once more in Galilee, where He had performed most of His deeds of mercy, He was met with unbelieving contempt.

---

[*] *This chapter is based on Matthew 15:29–39; 16:1–12; Mark 7:31–37; 8:1–21.*

## The Aristocracy of the Nation Challenge Christ

The two sects—Pharisees and Sadducees—had been bitter enemies, but now they united against Christ, asking for a sign from heaven. When Israel went out to battle with the Canaanites at Beth Horon, the sun had stood still at Joshua's command. The leaders demanded some such sign from Jesus. But no mere external evidence could benefit them.

"Hypocrites!" said Jesus. "You know how to discern the face of the sky"—by studying the sky they could foretell the weather—"but you cannot discern the signs of the times." Christ's own words, spoken with the power of the Holy Spirit, were the sign God had given. The song of the angels to the shepherds, the star that guided the wise men, the Voice from heaven at His baptism, were witnesses for Him.

"But He sighed deeply in His spirit, and said, 'Why does this generation seek a sign?' " "No sign shall be given to it except the sign of the prophet Jonah." As the preaching of Jonah was a sign to the Ninevites, so Christ's preaching was a sign to His generation. But what a contrast in how these two groups had received the word! The people of the great heathen city humbled themselves. The high and lowly together cried to the God of heaven, and He granted them His mercy. "The men of Nineveh will rise in judgment with this generation," Christ had said, "and condemn it, because they repented at the preaching of Jonah; and indeed a greater than Jonah is here." Matthew 12:41.

Every miracle Christ performed was a sign of His divinity, but to the Pharisees, these works of mercy were a great offense. The Jewish leaders looked with heartless indifference on human suffering. In many cases, their oppression had caused the suffering that Christ relieved. So His miracles were a rebuke to them.

## The True Evidence That Christ Came From God

What led the Jews to reject the Savior was the highest evidence of His divine character: His miracles were for the blessing of humanity. His life revealed the character of God. He did the works and spoke the words of God. A life such as this is the greatest of all miracles.

Many in our day, like the Jews, say, "Show us a sign; work a miracle." Christ does not grant us power to prove our claims or satisfy the demands of unbelief and pride. But is it not a miracle that we can break from the bondage of Satan? Opposition to Satan is not natural to the human heart. It is implanted by the grace of God. When one who has been controlled by a stubborn, wayward will yields to the gentle pull of God's heavenly agencies, a miracle has happened. So also when someone who has been under strong delusion comes to understand moral truth. The change in human hearts, the transformation of human characters, is a miracle that reveals an ever-living Savior. In preaching the Word of God, the sign that should be evident now and always is the presence of the Holy Spirit, to make the Word a renewing power to those who hear.

The people who asked for a sign from Jesus had hardened their hearts. They refused to see that His mission fulfilled the Scriptures. "If they do not hear Moses and the prophets, neither will they be persuaded though one rise from the dead." Luke 16:31.

Turning from the group of critics, Jesus got into the boat with His disciples. In sorrowful silence, they again crossed the lake. When they reached the other side, Jesus said, "Take heed and beware of the leaven of the Pharisees and the Sadducees." The Jews had been taught to regard leaven as a symbol of sin. In leaving Magdala so suddenly, the disciples had forgotten to take bread. They understood Christ to be warning them not to buy bread from a Pharisee or Sadducee. Their lack of spiritual insight often led them to misunderstand His words.

Now Jesus reprimanded them for thinking that, in that solemn warning, He who had fed thousands with a few fish and barley loaves could have referred to merely temporal food. There was danger that the crafty reasoning of the Pharisees and Sadducees would leaven His disciples with unbelief.

The disciples were inclined to think that their Master should have granted the demand for a sign in the heavens. He was able to do this, and such a sign would silence His enemies. They did not recognize the hypocrisy of the critics. Months later, Jesus repeated the same teaching. "Beware of the leaven of the Pharisees, which is hypocrisy." Luke 12:1.

## Self-deception of Self-centered Motives

Leaven works without being no-ticed, changing the dough to its own nature. So if we allow hypocrisy in the heart, it permeates the character and life. A striking example was the practice of Corban, by which people concealed a neglect of duty to parents under a pretense of liberality to the temple. The scribes and Pharisees concealed the real tendency of their doctrines, instilling them skillfully but deceitfully into the minds of their hearers. This deceptive teaching made it hard for the people to receive the words of Christ.

The same influences are working through those who try to explain the law of God to make it conform to what they do. Such people do not attack the law openly. They put forward speculative theories that undermine its principles. They explain it in a way that destroys its force.

The Pharisees' hypocrisy was the product of their self-seeking. This led them to twist and misapply the Scriptures. Even the disciples of Christ were in danger of cherishing this subtle evil. The reasoning of the Pharisees, who often wavered between faith and unbelief, influenced the followers of Jesus to a great degree. In their hearts, even the disciples had not stopped seeking great things for themselves. This spirit stirred up the strife over who would be greatest. This put them so much out of sympathy with Christ's mission of self-sacrifice. As leaven will cause corruption, so the self-seeking spirit, if we cherish it, brings about our defilement and ruin.

Today, as long ago, how widespread is this subtle, deceptive sin! How often our service to Christ is marred by the secret desire to exalt self! How ready the thought of self-praise and the longing for human approval! The love of self, the desire for an easier way than God has appointed, leads us to substitute human theories and traditions for the divine principles.

The religion of Christ is sincerity itself. Zeal for God's glory is the motive that the Holy Spirit implants, and only the power of God can banish self-seeking and hypocrisy. This change is the sign that He is working. When the faith we accept destroys selfishness and falsehood, when it leads us to seek God's glory and not our own, we may know that it is from the right source. "Father, glorify Your name" (John 12:28) was the keynote of Christ's life, and if we follow Him, this will be the keynote of our life.

# The Foreshadowing of the Cross *

Even before Christ took humanity upon Himself, He saw the whole length of the path He must travel to save the lost. Every grief that tore His heart, every insult heaped on His head, every deprivation He was called to endure He saw clearly before He laid aside His crown and royal robe and stepped down from the throne to clothe His divinity with humanity. He knew the anguish that would come upon Him, and yet He said, "Behold, I come; in the scroll of the Book it is written of me. I delight to do Your will, O My God, and Your law is within My heart." Psalm 40:7, 8.

His earthly life was full of labor and self-sacrifice, but He was cheered by the possibility that by giving His life, He would win the world back to its loyalty to God. Although He must first receive the baptism of blood, although the sins of the world were to press on His innocent soul, although the shadow of an unspeakable distress was upon Him, yet for the joy set before Him, He chose to endure the cross.

The time was near when His chosen companions in ministry must see the One they loved and trusted hung on the cross of Calvary. Soon He must leave them to face the world without the comfort of His visible presence. Bitter hate and unbelief would persecute them, and He wanted to prepare them for their trials.

Jesus and His disciples had now come into one of the towns near Caesarea Philippi. They were beyond Galilee, in a region where idol worship was widespread. Around them they saw forms of superstition that existed in all parts of the world. Jesus wanted their exposure to these things to lead the disciples to feel their responsibility to the heathen.

He was about to tell them of the suffering in store for Him. But first He prayed that their hearts would be prepared to receive His words. He did not tell them immediately what He wanted to share with them, but He gave them opportunity to confess their faith in Him. He asked, "Who do men say that I, the Son of Man, am?"

Sadly the disciples acknowledged that Israel had failed to recognize their Messiah. The crowds at Bethsaida had wanted to proclaim Him King of Israel. Many were ready to accept Him as a

---

* This chapter is based on Matthew 16:13–28; Mark 8:27–38; Luke 9:18–27.

prophet, but they did not believe that He was the Messiah.

Jesus now asked a second question, relating to the disciples themselves: "But who do you say that I am?" Peter answered, "You are the Christ, the Son of the living God."

From the first, Peter had believed that Jesus was the Messiah. Many others who had accepted Christ began to harbor doubts about John's mission when he was imprisoned and put to death, and they now doubted that Jesus was the Messiah. Many who had expected Jesus to take His place on David's throne left Him when they saw that He had no such intention. But the shifting behavior of those who praised yesterday and condemned today did not destroy the faith of the Savior's true follower. Peter declared, "You are the Christ, the Son of the living God." He did not wait for kingly honors to crown his Lord, but accepted Him in His humiliation.

Peter had expressed the faith of the Twelve. Yet the opposition of the priests and rulers still troubled them greatly. They did not see their way clearly. Their early training, the teaching of the rabbis, the power of tradition still blocked their view of truth. Precious rays of light were shining on them, yet often they were like people groping among shadows. But on this day, the Holy Spirit rested on them in power. Beneath the appearance of humanity, they discerned the glory of the Son of God.

Jesus answered Peter, "Blessed are you, Simon Bar-Jonah, for flesh and blood has not revealed this to you, but My Father who is in heaven."

The truth that Peter had spoken is the foundation of the believer's faith. But God had not revealed it to Peter because of any wisdom or goodness of his own. The fact that Peter recognized the glory of Christ was an evidence that he had been "taught by God." John 6:45; see also Psalm 25:14.

Jesus continued, "I also say to you that you are Peter, and on this rock I will build My church, and the gates of Hades shall not prevail against it." The word *Peter* signifies a stone—a rolling stone. Peter was not the rock on which the church was founded. The gates of Hades, or hell, did prevail against him when he denied his Lord with cursing and swearing. The church was built on One against whom the gates of hell could not prevail.

### Christ Is the Rock

Moses had pointed to the Rock of Israel's salvation. See Deuteronomy 32:4. The psalmist had sung of "the rock of my strength." Psalm 62:7. Isaiah had written, "Thus says the Lord God: 'Behold, I lay in Zion a stone for a foundation, a tried stone, . . . a sure foundation.' " Isaiah 28:16. Peter himself applies this prophecy to Jesus: "You have tasted that the Lord is gracious. Coming to Him as to a living stone, rejected indeed by men, but chosen by God and precious, you also, as living stones, are being built up a spiritual house." 1 Peter 2:3–5. "No other foundation can anyone lay than that which is laid, which is Jesus Christ." 1 Corinthians 3:11. "On this rock," said Jesus, "I will build My church." Christ founded His church on the living Rock—Himself, His own body, broken and bruised for us. The gates of hell will not prevail against the church built on this foundation.

How feeble the church appeared when Christ spoke these words! There was only a handful of believers. Demons and men would direct their power against them, yet they were not to fear. They could not be overthrown.

Peter had expressed the truth that is the foundation of the church's faith, and Jesus now honored him as the representative of the body of believers. "I will give you the keys of the kingdom of heaven, and whatever you bind on earth will be bound in heaven, and whatever you loose on earth will be loosed in heaven."

"The keys of the kingdom of heaven" are the words of Christ. All the words of Holy Scripture are His. These words have power to open and shut heaven. The work of those who preach God's Word is an aroma of life unto life or of death unto death. 2 Corinthians 2:16.

The Savior did not commit the work of the gospel to Peter individually. Later, repeating the words spoken to Peter, He applied them to the church and also to the Twelve as representatives of the body of believers. If Jesus had delegated any special authority to one disciple above the others, we would not find them arguing so often over who would be the greatest. They would have honored the one Jesus chose. Instead of appointing one of them to be their head, Christ said, "Do not be called 'Rabbi.' " "And do not be called teachers; for One is your Teacher, the Christ." Matthew 23:8, 10.

"The head of every man is Christ." God, who put all things under the Savior's feet, "gave Him to be head over all things to the church, which is His body, the fullness of Him who fills all in all." 1 Corinthians 11:3; Ephesians 1:22, 23. The church is built on Christ as its Foundation. It is not to depend on any person or be controlled by human wisdom or power. Many claim that a position of trust in the church gives them authority to dictate what others must believe and do. The Savior declares, "You are all brethren." Matthew 23:8. We cannot depend on any finite being for guidance. The Rock of faith is the living presence of Christ in the church. Those who think that they are the strongest will prove to be the weakest, unless they make Christ their Source of power. See Jeremiah 17:5; Psalm 2:12.

Jesus instructed the disciples to tell no one that He was the Christ. The people, and even the disciples, had such a false concept of the Messiah that a public announcement would give them no true idea of His character or work.

## The Disciples Had Not Envisioned a Cross to Come

The disciples still expected Christ to reign as an earthly prince. They believed that He would not always remain unknown and that the time was near when He would establish His kingdom. The disciples had never entertained the thought that Christ would be rejected by His own nation, condemned as a deceiver, and crucified as a criminal. Jesus must alert His disciples to the conflict before them. He was sad as He anticipated the ordeal to come.

Until then, He had held back from telling them anything about His sufferings and death. In His conversation with Nicodemus, He had said, "As Moses lifted up the serpent in the wilderness, even so must the Son of Man be lifted up, that whoever believes in Him should not perish but have eternal life." John 3:14, 15. But the disciples did not hear this. Now the time had come for Him to pull back the veil that hid the future. "From that time Jesus began to show His disciples that He must go to Jerusalem, and suffer many things from the elders and chief priests and scribes, and be killed, and be raised again the third day."

The disciples listened, speechless with grief and amazement. Christ had accepted Peter's acknowledgment of Him as the Son of God, and now His words pointing to His suffering and death seemed incomprehensible. Peter could not keep silent. He took hold of his Master, as if to draw Him back from His approaching doom: "Far be it from You, Lord; this shall not happen to You!"

Peter loved his Lord, but Jesus did not praise him for the desire to shield Him from suffering. Peter's words were not a help and comfort to Jesus in the great test ahead of Him. They were not in harmony with God's plan of grace toward a lost world nor with the lesson of self-sacrifice that Jesus had come to teach by His own example. The impression Peter's words would make was directly opposed to the one that Christ wanted to make on the minds of His followers, and the

Savior was moved to speak one of the sternest rebukes that ever fell from His lips: "Get behind Me, Satan! You are an offense to Me, for you are not mindful of the things of God, but the things of men."

## Satan Was Trying to Get at Christ

Satan was trying to discourage Jesus and turn Him from His mission, and Peter was the one speaking the temptation! The prince of evil, the author of the thought, was behind Peter's impulsive appeal. Satan had offered Christ the rulership of the world, if He would only forsake the path of humiliation and sacrifice. Now he was trying to fasten Peter's gaze on earthly glory, so that he would not see the cross. Through Peter, he was again pressing the temptation on Jesus.

But the Savior did not respond to the temptation. His thought was for His disciple. Satan had come between Peter and his Master. Christ spoke to the one trying to separate Peter from his Redeemer: "Get behind Me, Satan!" "Let Me come face to face with Peter, so that I may reveal to him the mystery of My love."

It was a bitter lesson, and Peter learned it slowly: the path of Christ led through agony and humiliation. But in the heat of the furnace fire, the disciple was to learn the blessing of that path. Long afterward, he wrote, "Rejoice insofar as you are sharing Christ's sufferings, so that you may also be glad and shout for joy when his glory is revealed." 1 Peter 4:13, NRSV.

Jesus now explained to His disciples that His own life of self-denial was an example of what theirs should be:

"If anyone desires to come after Me, let him deny himself, and take up his cross, and follow Me." The cross, associated with the power of Rome, was the most cruel and humiliating form of death. Criminals were required to carry the cross to the place of execution. Often when it was laid on their shoulders, they resisted with desperate violence until the soldiers overpowered them. The disciples only dimly comprehended Jesus' words, but they recognized that He spoke of their submission to death for the sake of Christ.

The Savior's words could not have pictured any more complete self-surrender. But all this He had accepted for them. He left heaven for a life of reproach and insult and a death of shame. He was rich in heaven's priceless treasure, but He became poor so that through His poverty we could be rich. We are to follow in the path He walked.

Love for others means crucifixion of self. Those who are children of God should look on themselves as links in the chain let down to save the world, one with Christ, going forth with Him to seek and save the lost. Christians have consecrated themselves to God, and in character they are to reveal Christ to the world.

"Whoever desires to save his life will lose it, but whoever loses his life for My sake and the gospel's will save it." Selfishness is death. The heart that fails to send its lifeblood to the hand and the head would quickly lose its power. So is the love of Christ spread through every part of His spiritual body. We are members one of another, and whoever refuses to give will

perish. "What will it profit a man," said Jesus, "if he gains the whole world, and loses his own soul? Or what will a man give in exchange for his soul?"

Christ pointed the disciples to His coming in glory with the angels of heaven. Then He said, "He will reward each according to his works." And for their encouragement, He promised, "Assuredly, I say to you, there are some standing here who shall not taste death till they see the Son of Man coming in His kingdom."

But the disciples did not grasp His words. They were focused on the poverty, humiliation, and suffering. Did this mean that they would not see their Lord exalted to the throne of David? Could it be that Christ would be despised, rejected, and put to death? Sadness filled their hearts, for it seemed unbelievable that the Son of God would suffer such cruel humiliation. Why should He voluntarily go to Jerusalem to meet the treatment He would receive there? How could He resign Himself to such a fate and leave them in greater darkness than they were groping in before He revealed Himself to them?

The disciples reasoned that in the region of Caesarea Philippi Christ had nothing to fear from the hatred of the Jews or from the power of the Romans. Why not work there? Why give Himself up to death? If He were to die, how could He establish His kingdom so firmly that the gates of hell would not prevail against it? This was indeed a mystery.

Even now they were traveling toward the city where all their hopes were going to be crushed. They talked together in low, sorrowful tones about the future. Perhaps some unforeseen event might avert the doom that seemed in store for their Lord. In this way, they doubted, hoped, and feared for six long, gloomy days.

# Jesus Transfigured[*]

Evening was approaching when Jesus called Peter, James, and John to join Him and led them far up a lonely mountainside. They had spent the day traveling and teaching, and the climb added to their weariness. Soon the sun disappeared, and the travelers were wrapped in darkness. The gloom of their surroundings seemed in harmony with their sorrowful lives, around which clouds were gathering.

The disciples did not dare to ask Christ where He was going or for what purpose. He had often spent entire nights in the mountains in prayer. He was at home with nature and enjoyed its quiet. Yet the disciples wondered why their Master would lead them up this steep climb when they were tired and when He, too, needed rest.

Soon Christ told them that they should not go farther. Stepping aside a little distance from them, the Man of Sorrows poured out His prayer with tears. He prayed for strength to endure the test in behalf of humanity. He must gain a fresh hold on Omnipotence, for only then could He contemplate the future. And He poured out His heart-longings for His disciples,

that their faith would not fail. The dew was heavy on His bowed form, but He paid no attention to it. So the hours passed slowly by.

At first the disciples united their prayers with His, but after a time they fell asleep. Jesus had told them about His sufferings and had longed to lighten their grief by assuring them that their faith had not been misplaced. Not all, even of the Twelve, could receive the revelation He wanted to give. He had chosen only the three disciples who would witness His anguish in Gethsemane to be with Him on the mountain. Now He prayed that they might witness a scene that would comfort them at the time of His supreme agony with the knowledge that He was truly the Son of God and that His shameful death was part of the plan of redemption.

God heard His prayer. Suddenly the heavens opened and holy radiance came down on the mountain, covering the Savior's form. Divinity from within flashed through humanity and met the glory coming from above. Arising from His position facedown on the ground, Christ stood in godlike majesty. His face was shining "like the sun," and His

---

[*] *This chapter is based on Matthew 17:1–8; Mark 9:2–8; Luke 9:28–36.*

garments were "white as the light."

The disciples woke up and gazed in fear and amazement on the radiant form of their Master. As they became able to endure the supernatural light, they saw two heavenly beings beside Jesus—Moses, who on Sinai had talked with God, and Elijah, who experienced the high privilege of never coming under the power of death.

Because of his sin at Meribah, Moses was not allowed to enter Canaan. The joy of leading Israel into the inheritance of their fathers was not for him. A wilderness grave was his after forty years of toil and heart-burdening care. Moses passed under the dominion of death, but he did not remain in the tomb. Christ Himself called him back to life. See Jude 9.

On the mount of transfiguration, Moses represented those who will come out from the grave in the resurrection of the just. Elijah, who had been translated to heaven without seeing death, represented people living at Christ's second coming, who will be "changed—in a moment, in the twinkling of an eye, at the last trumpet." 1 Corinthians 15:51, 52. Jesus was clothed as He will appear when He comes the second time "in the glory of His Father with the holy angels." Mark 8:38; see Hebrews 9:28. On the mountain the disciples saw the future kingdom of glory in miniature—Christ the King, Moses a representative of the risen redeemed, and Elijah representing the translated ones.

## Peter Seriously Misunderstands

The disciples rejoiced to see the favored ones of heaven honor the meek and lowly One, who had wandered this earth as a helpless stranger. They believed that Elijah had come to announce that the kingdom was about to be set up on earth. They longed to linger here. Peter exclaimed, "Rabbi, it is good for us to be here; and let us make three tabernacles: one for You, one for Moses, and one for Elijah." The disciples were confident that God had sent Moses and Elijah to protect their Master and establish His authority as king.

But the cross must come before the crown. Bearing the weakness of humanity, burdened with its sorrow and sin, Jesus walked alone among us. As the darkness of the coming ordeal pressed in on Him, His spirit was lonely in a world that did not know Him. Even His loved disciples had not understood His mission. In the world He had created, He was alone. Now heaven had sent messengers—not angels, but men who had endured suffering and sorrow and could sympathize with the Savior.

Moses and Elijah had been colaborers with Christ. They had shared His longing for the salvation of the lost. Moses had pleaded for Israel, "Yet now, if You will forgive their sin—but if not, I pray, blot me out of Your book which You have written." Exodus 32:32. Elijah had known loneliness of spirit, as for three and a half years of famine he had endured the nation's hatred and woe. He had run away to the desert alone in anguish and despair. These men had come to talk deeply with Jesus concerning His suffering and to comfort Him. The topic of their conversation was the salvation of every human being.

Overcome with sleep, the disciples

heard little of what happened between Christ and the heavenly messengers. They had not received what God wanted to give them—a knowledge of Christ's sufferings and the glory that would follow. They lost the blessing that could have been theirs. Yet the experience assured them that all heaven knew of the Jewish nation's sin in rejecting Christ. They received a clearer insight into the work of the Redeemer. They were "eyewitnesses of His majesty" (2 Peter 1:16) and realized that Jesus was indeed the Messiah and that the heavenly universe recognized Him as such.

While they were still gazing at the scene, "a bright cloud overshadowed them; and suddenly a voice came out of the cloud, saying, 'This is My beloved Son, in whom I am well pleased. Hear Him!' " As they heard the voice of God speak in fearful majesty that caused the mountain to tremble, the disciples fell stricken to the earth, their faces hidden, till Jesus came near, dispelling their fears with His well-known voice, "Arise, and do not be afraid." The heavenly glory had faded away, and the forms of Moses and Elijah had disappeared. They were alone with Jesus.

# A Battle With Satan's Spirits[*]

As the sun arose, Jesus and His disciples went down the mountain to the plain. Absorbed in thought, the disciples were awed and silent. They would gladly have lingered in that holy place, but there was work to be done.

At the foot of the mountain a large group of people had gathered. As the Savior came near to them, He instructed His three companions to keep silent about what they had witnessed, saying, "Tell the vision to no one until the Son of Man is risen from the dead." To relate the revelation to the crowds would stir up only ridicule or idle wonder. Even the three favored disciples were slow to understand, as we can see from the fact that they questioned among themselves what the rising from the dead might mean. Yet they asked no explanation from Jesus.

As the people on the plain caught sight of Jesus, they ran to greet Him. Yet His quick eye recognized that something had happened that had caused the disciples bitter disappointment and humiliation. A father had brought his son to be delivered from a mute spirit that tormented him. Jesus had given His disciples authority to cast out unclean spirits when He sent them to preach through Galilee. As they went out, strong in faith, the evil spirits had obeyed their word. Now in the name of Christ they commanded the torturing spirit to leave his victim, but the demon only mocked them. The disciples could not find a reason for their defeat. They felt they were bringing dishonor on themselves and their Master. And in the crowd were scribes who were trying to prove that they and their Master were deceivers. Here was an evil spirit that neither the disciples nor Christ Himself could conquer! A feeling of contempt and scorn swept through the crowd.

But suddenly the crowd saw Jesus and the three disciples approaching. The night of fellowship with heavenly glory had left a light on their faces that awed the onlookers. The Savior came to the scene of conflict, and looking intently at the scribes He inquired, "What are you discussing with them?"

But the voices so bold and defiant before were silent. Now the afflicted father made his way through the crowd, and falling at the feet of Jesus,

---

* This chapter is based on Matthew 17:19–21; Mark 9:9–29; Luke 9:37–45.

he poured out the story of his trouble and disappointment.

"Master," he said, "I brought to You my son, who has a mute spirit. And wherever it seizes him, it throws him down. . . . So I spoke to Your disciples, that they should cast it out, but they could not."

Jesus read the unbelief in every heart, and exclaimed, "O faithless generation, how long shall I be with you? How long shall I bear with you?" Then He told the distressed father, "Bring your son here."

The father brought him, and the evil spirit threw him to the ground in convulsions of agony. He lay wallowing and foaming, filling the air with unearthly shrieks.

Again the Prince of life and the prince of darkness met on the field of battle—Christ to "proclaim liberty to the captives . . . , to set at liberty those who are oppressed" (Luke 4:18), Satan seeking to hold his victim under his control. For a moment, Jesus permitted the evil spirit to display his power.

Jesus asked, "How long has this been happening to him?" The father told the story of long years of suffering, and then, as if he could endure no more, exclaimed, "If You can do anything, have compassion on us and help us." "If You can"! Even now the father questioned Christ's power.

Jesus answered, "All things are possible to him who believes." With a burst of tears, realizing his own weakness, the father threw himself on Christ's mercy: "I believe; help my unbelief!"

Jesus turned to the suffering one and said, "Deaf and dumb spirit, I command you, come out of him and enter him no more!" There was a cry, an agonized struggle. Then the boy lay motionless, apparently lifeless. The crowd whispered, "He is dead." But Jesus took him by the hand, lifted him up, and presented him to his father in perfect health of mind and body. Father and son praised their Deliverer, while the scribes, defeated and crestfallen, turned away sullenly.

## Faith Connects Us With Heaven

"If You can do anything, have compassion on us and help us." How many a sin-burdened soul has echoed that prayer! And to all the answer is, "All things are possible to him who believes." In Christ, God has provided means for subduing every sinful trait and resisting every temptation, no matter how strong. But many feel that they lack faith, and therefore they remain away from Christ. Let these people not look to themselves, but to Christ. Faith comes by the Word of God. Grasp His promise, "The one who comes to Me I will by no means cast out." John 6:37. Throw yourself at His feet with the cry, "I believe; help my unbelief." You can never perish while you do this—never!

In a brief space of time, the three favored disciples had seen humanity as transfigured into the image of God and as debased into the likeness of Satan. They had seen Jesus proclaimed the Son of God and had seen Him meet the demon-possessed boy gnashing his teeth in agony. This mighty Redeemer had stood glorified a few hours before. Now He stooped to lift the victim of Satan from the earth and restore him to his father and home.

It was an illustration of redemption —the Divine One stooping to save the lost. It also represented the disciples' mission. Christ's servants are not to spend their lives alone on the mountaintop with Jesus. Down in the plain, people whom Satan has enslaved are waiting for the word of faith and prayer to set them free.

When Jesus was alone with the nine disciples once more, they questioned, "Why could not we cast it out?" Jesus answered, "Because of your unbelief; for assuredly, I say to you, if you have faith as a mustard seed, you will say to this mountain, 'Move from here to there,' and it will move; and nothing will be impossible for you. However, this kind does not go out except by prayer and fasting." Their unbelief, which shut them out from deeper sympathy with Christ, and the carelessness with which they regarded the sacred work committed to them had caused their failure. Jealous of the three disciples selected to go with Jesus to the mountain, they had been dwelling on their discouragements and personal grievances. In this state of darkness, they had attempted the conflict with Satan.

In order to succeed in such a conflict, their faith must be strengthened by earnest prayer, fasting, and humiliation of heart. They must be emptied of self and be filled with the Spirit and power of God. Only faith that leads to entire dependence on God and unreserved dedication to His work can bring the Holy Spirit's aid in the battle against wicked spirits.

Lay hold on God's word and all the helpful agencies He has appointed. In this way your faith will strengthen. The obstacles Satan piles across your path, apparently as impossible to scale as the eternal hills, will disappear when you exercise such faith. "Nothing will be impossible for you."

# Who Is the Greatest?*

Returning to Capernaum, Jesus quietly went to the house that was to be His temporary home. During the rest of His stay in Galilee, He intended to instruct the disciples rather than labor for the crowds.

Christ had told them again that He would be put to death and rise again. And He added that He would be betrayed into the hands of His enemies. The disciples did not comprehend His words even now. Although the shadow of a great sorrow came over them, they argued among themselves about who would be greatest in the kingdom. They tried to conceal this strife from Jesus. He read their thoughts and longed to counsel them, but He waited for a quiet time to do this, when their hearts would be open to receive His words.

Soon after they reached town, the collector of the temple revenue questioned Peter, "Does your Teacher not pay the temple tax?" This religious contribution every Jew was required to pay each year. A refusal to pay would be a grievous sin, in the opinion of the rabbis. Now Jesus' enemies saw an opportunity to discredit Him. They

found a ready ally in the collector of the tax.

Zealous for his Master's honor, Peter was quick to answer that Jesus would pay the tax. But some classes were exempt from paying the tax. The priests and Levites, still considered to be especially devoted to the temple, were not required to make the annual contribution for its support. Prophets also were exempt. In requiring the tax from Jesus, the rabbis were setting aside His claim as a prophet and were dealing with Him as with any ordinary person. If He refused to pay, they would represent this as disloyalty to the temple. On the other hand, if He paid, they would take this as justifying their rejection of Him as a prophet. Peter's answer to the collector virtually endorsed the false idea that the priests and rulers were trying to promote.

When Peter entered the house, the Savior made no reference to what had taken place, but inquired, "What do you think, Simon? From whom do the kings of the earth take customs or taxes, from their sons or from strangers?" Peter answered, "From strangers." And Jesus said, "Then the sons are free." While

* This chapter is based on Matthew 17:22–27; 18:1–20; Mark 9:30–50; Luke 9:46–48.

the people are taxed for the mainte-
nance of their king, the monarch's
own children are exempt. So Israel,
the people of God, were required to
maintain His service, but Jesus, the
Son of God, was under no such obligation.

If Jesus had paid the tax without a
protest, in effect He would have acknowledged the justice of the claim
and thus denied His divinity. But He
denied the claim on which the demand
was based. In providing for the pay-
ment, He gave evidence of His divine
character, and therefore He was not
under obligation as a mere subject of
the kingdom.

"Go to the sea," He directed Peter,
"cast in a hook, and take the fish that
comes up first. And when you have
opened its mouth, you will find a piece
of money; take that and give it to them
for Me and you."

While Jesus made it plain that He
was under no obligation to pay the
tax, He entered into no controversy
over the matter. So that He would not
give offense by withholding the tax,
He did what He could not justly be required to do. This lesson would be of
great value to His disciples. They were
not to place themselves needlessly in
opposition to established order. Christians are not to sacrifice one principle
of truth, but they should avoid controversy whenever possible. While Peter
was gone to the sea, Jesus called the
other disciples to Him and asked,
"What was it you disputed among
yourselves on the road?" Shame and
self-condemnation kept them silent.
Jesus had told them that He was going
to die for their sake, and their selfish

ambition made a painful contrast with
His unselfish love. But although He
had spoken so plainly of what awaited
Him, His mention of the fact that He
was soon to go to Jerusalem kindled
their hopes again that He was about
to set up His kingdom. This had led to
their dispute about who would fill the
highest offices. At last one of them
dared to ask Jesus, "Who then is greatest in the kingdom of heaven?"

## Strife for the Highest Place

The Savior said to them, "If anyone desires to be first, he shall be last
of all and servant of all." They did not
understand the nature of Christ's kingdom, and this was the apparent cause
of their conflict. But the real cause lay
deeper. Even after they had received
the fullest knowledge, any question of
rank or position might have started
the trouble again. This would bring disaster to the church after Christ's departure. The battle for the highest
place was the outworking of that same
spirit that had started the great controversy in the worlds above and had
brought Christ from heaven to die.
There rose up before Him a vision of
Lucifer, who had said, "I will be like
the Most High." Isaiah 14:14. This desire to exalt himself had brought strife
into the heavenly courts. Lucifer wanted God's power but not His character.
He sought the highest place, and every being moved by his spirit will do
the same. The kingdom of Satan is a
kingdom of force. Every individual re-
gards every other as an obstacle in the
way of his own advancement or a step-
ping-stone on which to climb to a
higher place.

While Lucifer wanted to be equal with God, Christ "made Himself of no reputation, taking the form of a bond-servant, and coming in the likeness of men. And being found in appearance as a man, He humbled Himself and became obedient to the point of death, even the death of the cross." Philippians 2:7, 8. Now the cross was just before Him, and His own disciples were so filled with self-seeking that they could not enter into sympathy with their Lord or even understand Him when He spoke of His humiliation for them.

Jesus tried to correct the evil. He showed what the principle is that prevails in the kingdom of heaven and what makes for true greatness. Those who were controlled by pride and love of distinction were thinking of themselves and the rewards they would have. There would be no place for them in the kingdom of heaven, for they belonged to the ranks of Satan.

Before honor is humility. To fill a high place before others, Heaven chooses the worker who takes a lowly place before God. The most childlike disciple is the most efficient in labor for God. Those who feel their need of divine aid will plead for it. From communion with Christ they will go out to work, anointed for their mission, and they succeed where many of the intellectually wise would fail.

But when people exalt themselves, feeling that they are necessary for God's plan to succeed, the Lord causes them to be set aside. The work does not stop but goes forward with greater power.

It was not enough for the disciples of Jesus to be instructed about the nature of His kingdom. What they needed was a change of heart. Calling a little child to Him, Jesus set him in the midst of them. Then tenderly wrapping the little one in His arms, He said, "Unless you are converted and become as little children, you will by no means enter the kingdom of heaven." The simplicity, self-forgetfulness, and trusting love of a little child are the attributes that Heaven values, the characteristics of real greatness. At the feet of Jesus, earthly dignity and display are forgotten. Rich and poor, the educated and the ignorant, meet together as blood-bought souls, with no thought of social levels or worldly superiority.

God places His own mark of ownership on us, not by rank, not by wealth, not by intellectual greatness, but by our oneness with Christ. "You have also given me," said David, "the shield of Your salvation; . . . Your gentleness"—as an element in the human character—"has made me great." Psalm 18:35.

The Savior's words awakened a feeling of self-distrust in the disciples. John began to question whether his actions in a certain case had been right. "Teacher," he said, "we saw someone . . . casting out demons in Your name, and we forbade him because he does not follow us."

James and John thought that in stopping this man they were defending their Lord's honor. Now they began to see that they were jealous for their own. They acknowledged their error and accepted Jesus' reproof, "Do not forbid him, for no one who works a miracle in My name can soon

HUMBLE HERO

afterward speak evil of Me." Many had been deeply moved by the character and work of Christ, and their hearts were opening to Him in faith. The disciples must be careful not to discourage these people. They must show the same far-reaching sympathy they had seen in their Master.

Christ is the Great Teacher. We are to sit at His feet and learn from Him. Every individual whom God has made willing is a channel through whom Christ will reveal His pardoning love. How careful we should be not to discourage one of God's light bearers and thus intercept the rays He wants to have shine to the world!

Actions like John's in forbidding someone to work miracles in Christ's name might result in causing that person to lose salvation. Rather than for anyone to do this, said Jesus, "It would be better for him if a millstone were hung around his neck, and he were thrown into the sea."

Why this strong language? Because "the Son of Man has come to seek and to save that which was lost." Luke 19:10. Should His disciples show less regard for the salvation of others than the Majesty of heaven has shown? How terrible the sin of turning one person away, so that for him the Savior's love and agony will have been in vain.

"Woe to the world because of stumbling blocks! Occasions for stumbling are bound to come." NRSV. The world will surely oppose the followers of Christ, but woe to anyone who has taken Christ's name and yet is found doing this work. Many are deceived and led into false paths by those who claim to serve Him but misrepresent His character.

## Anything That Leads to Sin Must Be Put Away

One sin cherished is enough to degrade the character and mislead others. If we would be willing to cut off a foot or a hand or even pluck out an eye to save the body from death, how earnest should we be to put away sin that brings death to the soul!

In the ritual service, salt was added to every sacrifice. Like the offering of incense, this signified that only the righteousness of Christ could make the service acceptable to God. Jesus referred to this when He said, "Have salt in yourselves, and have peace with one another." All must receive the saving salt, the righteousness of our Savior. Then they become "the salt of the earth," restraining evil among those they meet, as salt preserves from corruption. Matthew 5:13. But if "the salt loses its flavor," the life can exert no saving influence on the world. Jesus says, "You must be partakers of My grace in order to be 'an aroma of life leading to life.' " 2 Corinthians 2:16. Then there will be no rivalry, no self-seeking, no desire for the highest place.

When we see Jesus, a Man of Sorrows and acquainted with grief, working to save the lost, disregarded, scorned, driven from city to city till His mission was accomplished; when we behold Him in Gethsemane, sweating great drops of blood, and on the cross dying in agony—when we see this, self will no longer demand recognition. We will rejoice to carry the cross after Jesus, to endure trial, shame, or persecution for His sake.

No one who believes in Christ is to be treated as unimportant. Everything that has given us advantage over another —education, refinement, nobility of character, religious experience—puts us in debt to those less favored. If we are strong, we are to support the hands of the weak. Angels are always at the side of those who have the hardest battle with self to fight, who have many objectionable traits of character, and whose surroundings are the most discouraging. Christ's true followers will cooperate in this ministry.

"What do you think?" said Jesus. "If a man has a hundred sheep, and one of them goes astray, does he not leave the ninety-nine and go to the mountains to seek the one that is straying? And if he should find it, assuredly, I say to you, he rejoices more over that sheep than over the ninety-nine that did not go astray. Even so it is not the will of your Father who is in heaven that one of these little ones should perish."

### Need of the Delicate Touch

When others have done wrong, do not put them to shame by exposing their faults to others nor bring dishonor on Christ by making public the sins of those who bear His name. We must lead the wrongdoers to see their errors so that they may reform, but we are not to judge or condemn. In treating the spiritual wounds, we must have the most delicate touch. Only the love that flows from the Suffering One of Calvary will achieve good results here. If you succeed, you will "save a soul from death," and "cover a multitude of sins." James 5:20.

But even this effort may not succeed. Then Jesus said, "Take one or two others along with you." NRSV. If the sinner will not hear them, then, and not till then, the matter is to be brought before the whole body of believers. Let the members of the church unite in prayer and loving appeals that the offender may be restored. The Holy Spirit will speak through His servants, pleading with the wanderer to return to God: "We implore you in Christ's behalf, be reconciled to God." 2 Corinthians 5:20. Anyone who rejects this united plea has broken the tie that binds him to Christ and so has cut himself off from the fellowship of the church. From that time on, said Jesus, "Let him be to you like a heathen and a tax collector." But the sinner's former brothers and sisters in the church should not despise or neglect him, but treat him with tenderness and compassion.

If we neglect the duty Christ has given us, of trying to restore those who are in error and sin, we become partakers in the sin. See Leviticus 19:17. For evils that we might have stopped, we are just as responsible as if we were guilty of the acts ourselves.

We are not to make someone else's wrong a matter of comment and criticism among ourselves nor repeat it to others. While we try to correct the errors of a brother or sister, we will shield that person as far as possible from the criticism of fellow church members, and how much more from condemnation by the unbelieving world. As we wish Christ to deal with us, He asks us to deal with one another. "Whatever you bind on earth will be bound in heaven, and whatever you loose on earth will be loosed in heaven." Matthew 16:19. The results of your work are for eternity!

But we are not to carry this great responsibility alone. Wherever people obey His word with a sincere heart, there Christ lives. In the assemblies of the church and wherever even a few disciples meet in His name, there He will also be. "If two of you agree on earth concerning anything that they ask, it will be done for them by My Father in heaven." By His humanity Jesus shares with His disciples in their trials and sympathizes with them in their sufferings. At the same time, by His divinity He is connected with the throne of the Infinite.

Wonderful assurance! All the power of heaven combines with human ability in drawing people to Christ.

# "If Anyone Thirsts, Let Him Come!"*

Three times a year the Jews were required to come to Jerusalem for religious purposes. The Feast of Tabernacles was the last gathering of the year. The harvest had been gathered from the valleys and plains of Palestine. The olives had been picked and pressed for their oil. The palm trees had yielded their fruits. The people had trodden the purple clusters of the vine in the wine press.

The feast continued for seven days, and the inhabitants of Palestine, with many from other lands, came to Jerusalem to celebrate it. Old and young, rich and poor, all brought some gift as an offering of thanksgiving to Him who had crowned the year with His goodness. The people brought from the woods everything that could give expression to the universal joy. The city resembled a beautiful forest.

The feast was not only the harvest thanksgiving but the memorial of God's care over Israel in the wilderness. To commemorate their tent life, during the feast the Israelites lived in tabernacles, or shelters, of green branches set up in the streets, in the courts of the temple, or on the housetops. The hills and valleys surrounding Jerusalem were dotted with these leafy dwellings. With sacred song and thanksgiving the worshipers celebrated this occasion.

A little before the feast was the Day of Atonement, when the people were declared to be at peace with Heaven. "O give thanks to the Lord . . . For His mercy endures forever" (Psalm 106:1) rose triumphantly, while all kinds of music accompanied the united singing.

The temple was the center of the universal joy. On either side of the sacred building's white marble steps, the Levite choir led the service of song. Voices near and far took up the melody until the encircling hills rang with praise.

At night the temple blazed with artificial light. The music, the waving of palm branches, the great gathering of people with the light streaming over them from the hanging lamps, and the majesty of the ceremonies deeply impressed the onlookers. But the most impressive ceremony was one that commemorated an event in the wilderness journey.

At dawn the priests sounded a long blast on their silver trumpets, and

---

* This chapter is based on John 7:1–15, 37–39.

the glad shouts of the people from their shelters welcomed the festal day. Then the priest dipped a container of water from the flowing waters of the Brook Kidron. Lifting it to his shoulder, while the trumpets were sounding, he went up the broad steps of the temple, keeping time with the music with a slow and measured step.

At the altar in the court of the priests, there were two silver basins. The priest poured the water into one, and a similar amount of wine was poured into the other, and the contents of both flowed into the Kidron and on to the Dead Sea. This consecrated water represented the fountain that gushed from the rock at God's command to quench the thirst of the children of Israel.

As the sons of Joseph made their preparations to attend the feast, they saw that Christ gave no sign that He intended to go. Since the healing at Bethesda, He had not attended the national gatherings. To avoid useless conflict at Jerusalem, He had been working only in Galilee. His apparent neglect of the great religious assemblies and the hatred shown Him by the priests and rabbis perplexed even His own disciples and His family. In His teachings He presented the blessings of obedience, yet He Himself seemed indifferent to the service that God had established.

He mingled with tax collectors, disregarded rabbinical observances, and freely set aside traditional requirements concerning the Sabbath—all these seemed to place Him in conflict with the religious authorities. His brothers thought it was a mistake to alienate the great and scholarly men of the nation. They felt that these men must be in the right. But they had witnessed Jesus' blameless life, and His works had deeply impressed them. They still hoped He would lead the Pharisees to see that He was the Messiah, the Prince of Israel! They cherished this thought with proud satisfaction.

They were so anxious about this that they urged Christ to go to Jerusalem. "Depart from here," they said, "and go into Judea, that Your disciples also may see the works that You are doing. For no one does anything in secret while he himself seeks to be known openly. If You do these things, show Yourself to the world." If He knew He was the Messiah, why this strange reserve? Why not go boldly to Jerusalem and perform the wonderful works reported about Him in Galilee? Do not hide in secluded provinces, they said. Present yourself at the capital, win the support of the priests and rulers, and establish the new kingdom.

## Selfish Motives Exposed

These brothers of Jesus reasoned from the selfish motive of people who long for attention. "Then Jesus said to them, 'My time has not yet come, but your time is always ready. The world cannot hate you, but it hates Me because I testify of it that its works are evil. You go up to this feast. I am not yet going up to this feast, for My time is not yet fully come.' When He had said these things to them, He remained in Galilee." His brothers had spoken to Him in a tone of authority.

He threw their rebuke back to them, not classing them with His self-denying disciples but with the world. The world does not hate those who are like it in spirit. It loves them as its own.

Christ was not to be presumptuous, not to rush into danger, not to hurry a crisis. He knew that He was going to receive the world's hatred; He knew that His work would result in His death. But to expose Himself to danger prematurely would not be the will of His Father.

Many from all parts of the world had come to the Feast of Tabernacles in hopes of seeing Christ. The Pharisees and rulers looked for Him, hoping for an opportunity to condemn Him. They anxiously inquired, "Where is He?" but no one knew. None dared acknowledge Him as the Messiah, but everywhere there was quiet, earnest discussion concerning Him. Many defended Him as one sent from God, while others denounced Him as a deceiver.

Meanwhile Jesus quietly arrived at Jerusalem by a less-traveled route. If He had joined the caravans, this would have attracted public attention to Him, and a popular demonstration would have stirred up the authorities against Him.

In the middle of the feast, He entered the temple courtyard in the presence of the crowds. People had been saying that He did not dare to place Himself in the power of the priests and rulers. Everyone was surprised at His presence. Every voice was hushed.

Standing there as the center of attraction to that vast assembly, Jesus spoke to them as no man had ever done. His words showed that He knew the sacrificial service and the teachings of the prophets far better than the priests and rabbis did. As one who saw the Unseen, He spoke with positive authority about both earthly and heavenly things. As at Capernaum, the people were astonished at His teaching, "for His word was with authority." Luke 4:32. He made every possible effort to bring them to repentance. He did not want to be rejected and murdered by His own nation if He could save them from the guilt of such a deed.

The question passed from one to another, "How does this Man know letters, having never studied?" Both Jesus and John the Baptist had been described as ignorant because they had not received training in the rabbinical schools. Those who heard them were astonished at their knowledge of the Scriptures, but the God of heaven was their teacher. As Jesus spoke in the temple courtyard, His words held the people spellbound. Those who were most violent against Him felt powerless to do Him harm.

## Weariness of the Worshipers Recognized

On the morning of the last day of the feast, the people were tired from the long festivity. Suddenly Jesus lifted up His voice: "If anyone thirsts, let him come to Me and drink. He who believes in Me, as the Scripture has said, out of his heart will flow rivers of living water." The people had participated in a continued scene of pomp and festivity, their eyes dazzled with light and color and their ears filled with the richest music, but there had been nothing to meet the wants of the spirit, nothing to satisfy the thirst of the soul.

That morning the priest had performed the ceremony commemorating the time that Moses struck the rock in the wilderness. That rock symbolized Him who by His death would cause living streams of salvation to flow. There in the presence of the multitude Christ set Himself apart to be struck, so that the Water of Life could flow to the world. As Jesus spoke, their hearts thrilled with a strange awe. Many were ready to exclaim, with the woman of Samaria, "Give me this water, that I may not thirst." John 4:15.

Many who heard Jesus were mourning over disappointed hopes, nourishing a secret grief, or seeking to satisfy their restless longing with the things of the world, but among the glitter of the joyful scene they stood dissatisfied and sad. That sudden cry, "If anyone thirsts," startled them, and as they listened to the words that followed, their minds lit up with a new hope. In the symbol before them they saw the offer of the priceless gift of salvation.

The cry of Christ to the thirsty ones is still going out, and it appeals to us with even greater power than to those who heard it in the temple on the last day of the feast. "Let him who thirsts come. Whoever desires, let him take the water of life freely." Revelation 22:17.

# Among Snares*

All during the feast Jesus was shadowed by spies. Day after day brought new attempts to silence Him. The priests and rulers were planning to stop Him by violence. On the first day at the feast they demanded by what authority He taught.

"My teaching is not mine," said Jesus, "but his who sent me. Anyone who resolves to do the will of God will know whether the teaching is from God or whether I am speaking on my own." John 7:16, 17, NRSV. Understanding and appreciating truth, He said, depends less on the mind than on the heart. Truth claims the allegiance of the will. We can receive it only through the work of grace in the heart, and its reception depends on our renouncing every sin that the Spirit of God reveals. There must be a conscientious surrender of every habit and practice opposed to its principles. Those who yield themselves to God in this way will be able to distinguish between someone who speaks for God and someone who speaks merely from himself. The Pharisees were not seeking to know the truth but to find some excuse to evade it. This was why they did not understand Christ's teaching.

"Those who speak on their own seek their own glory; but the one who seeks the glory of him who sent him is true, and there is nothing false in him." NRSV. The spirit of self-seeking reveals its own origin. But Christ was seeking the glory of God. This was the evidence of His authority as a teacher of the truth.

Jesus gave the rabbis an evidence of His divinity by showing that He read their hearts. They had been plotting His death, and so they were breaking the law that they claimed to be defending. "Did not Moses give you the law," He said, "yet none of you keeps the law? Why do you seek to kill Me?"

Like a swift flash of light, these words revealed the pit of ruin into which they were about to fall. For an instant they saw that they were fighting against Infinite Power. But they refused to be warned. They determined to conceal their murderous plans. Evading the question, they exclaimed, "You have a demon. Who is seeking to kill You?"

Christ ignored the insinuation that an evil spirit had prompted His wonderful works. He went on to show that the Jews' own interpretation of the

---

* This chapter is based on John 7:16–36, 40–53; 8:1–11.

Sabbath law justified His work of healing at Bethesda. According to the law, every male child must be circumcised on the eighth day. If the appointed time fell on the Sabbath, the rite must be performed then. How much more must it be in harmony with the spirit of the law to make a man "completely well on the Sabbath." He warned them, "Do not judge according to appearance, but judge with righteous judgment." His reasoning silenced the rulers.

## Erroneous Ideas of the Messiah and His Coming

Many who lived at Jerusalem felt drawn to Christ by an irresistible power. The conviction grew on them that He was the Son of God. But Satan was ready to suggest doubt. People generally believed that Christ would be born at Bethlehem, but that after a time He would disappear, and when He appeared again no one would know where He came from. Many held that the Messiah would have no natural relationship to humanity.

While the people were wavering between doubt and faith, Jesus spoke about their thoughts: "You both know Me, and you know where I am from; and I have not come of Myself, but He who sent Me is true, whom you do not know." Christ's words repeated the claim He had made in front of the Sanhedrin many months before, when He declared that He was the Son of God.

Among the people, many believed on Him and said, "When the Christ comes, will He do more signs than these which this Man has done?" The leaders of the Pharisees, watching the course of events, caught the expressions of sympathy among the crowds. Hurrying to the chief priests, they made plans to arrest Him when He was alone, because they did not dare seize Him in the presence of the people.

The false reasoning of the priests and rabbis misled many who were convinced that Jesus was the Son of God. These teachers had impressed the people by repeating the prophecies concerning the Messiah, that He would "reign on Mount Zion and in Jerusalem and before His elders, gloriously," that He would "have dominion also from sea to sea, and from the River to the ends of the earth." Isaiah 24:23; Psalm 72:8. Then with contempt they contrasted the glory pictured in such verses with the humble appearance of Jesus. If the people had studied the Word for themselves, they would not have been misled. Isaiah 61 testifies that Christ was to do the very work He did. Chapter 53 portrays His rejection, and chapter 59 describes the character of the priests and rabbis.

## Power to Discriminate Between Right and Wrong

God does not compel people to give up their unbelief. He wants them to decide not from impulse but from the weight of evidence, carefully comparing scripture with scripture. If the Jews had compared written prophecy with the facts, they would have recognized a beautiful harmony between the prophecies and their fulfillment in the life and ministry of the humble Galilean.

Many are deceived today in the same way as the Jews were. Religious teachers read the Bible in the light of their traditions, and the people do not search the Scriptures for themselves. They give up their own judgment and commit their destiny to their leaders. Whoever will prayerfully study the Bible in order to obey it will receive divine enlightenment. He will understand the Scriptures. "Anyone who resolves to do the will of God will know whether the teaching is from God or whether I am speaking on my own." NRSV.

On the last day of the feast, the officers who had been sent to arrest Jesus returned without Him. The leaders angrily asked, "Why have you not brought Him?" They answered, "No man ever spoke like this Man!"

Even hearts as hard as theirs were melted by His words. While He was speaking, they had lingered near to catch something to turn against Him. But as they listened, Christ revealed Himself to their hearts. They saw what priests and rulers would not see—humanity flooded with the glory of divinity.

The priests and rulers had felt the same conviction when they first came into Christ's presence. Their hearts were deeply moved and the thought came forcibly to them, "No man ever spoke like this Man!" But they had stifled the Holy Spirit's conviction. Now, enraged, they cried, "Are you also deceived? Have any of the rulers or the Pharisees believed in Him? But this crowd that does not know the law is accursed."

Those who hear the message of truth seldom ask, "Is it true?" but instead ask, "Who supports it?" Many people judge it by the numbers who accept it, and the question arises, "Have any of the educated men or religious leaders believed?" It is no argument against the truth that large numbers are not ready to accept it, or that it is not received by the world's great men or even by the religious leaders.

Again some of the rulers argued that if Jesus were left free, He would draw the people away from the established leaders, and the only safe course was to silence Him immediately. In the full tide of their discussion, they were suddenly stopped. Nicodemus questioned, "Does our law judge a man before it hears him and knows what he is doing?" Silence fell on the assembly. They could not condemn a man unheard. But the haughty rulers were startled and distressed that one of their own members had been so impressed by Jesus that he would now speak a word in His defense. "Surely you are not also from Galilee, are you? Search and you will see that no prophet is to arise from Galilee." NRSV.

Yet because of the protest, the rulers were defeated for the time, and "everyone went to his own house."

## Jesus Deals With a Case of Adultery

Jesus turned from the confusion of the city, from eager crowds and treacherous rabbis, to the quiet of the olive groves where He could be alone with God. But in the early morning, He returned to the temple, and the people gathered around Him.

Soon He was interrupted. A group of Pharisees and scribes approached, dragging a terror-stricken woman. With hard, eager voices they accused her of violating the seventh commandment. They pushed her into the presence of Jesus and said, "Moses, in the law, commanded us that such should be stoned. But what do You say?"

They had grasped this opportunity to trap and condemn Him, thinking that whatever decision He might make, they would use it to accuse Him. If He would acquit the woman, they could charge Him with despising the law of Moses. If He would declare her worthy of death, they could accuse Him to the Romans as having assumed authority that belonged only to Rome.

Jesus looked on the scene—the trembling victim in her shame, the hard-faced dignitaries devoid of pity. He read the heart and knew the character and life history of every one. Giving no indication that He had heard their question, He stooped and began to write in the dust.

The accusers drew nearer, impatient with His delay and apparent indifference. But as their eyes fell on the pavement at His feet, their faces changed. There, written before them, were the guilty secrets of their own lives. The people saw the sudden change of expression and pressed forward to discover what it was they were looking at with such astonishment and shame.

With all their claims to reverence the law, these rabbis were disregarding its provisions. It was the husband's duty to take action against the woman, and the guilty parties were to be punished equally. The action of these accusers was unauthorized. Jesus, however, met them on their own ground. The law specified that the witnesses in the case should be the first to cast a stone. Standing up and looking intently at the plotting elders, Jesus said, "He who is without sin among you, let him throw a stone at her first." And then He continued writing on the ground.

Now the accusers were defeated, with their robe of pretended holiness torn from them. They stood guilty and condemned in the presence of Infinite Purity. One by one, with bowed heads and downcast eyes, they slipped away, leaving their victim with the pitying Savior.

Jesus got up again, looked at the woman, and said, " 'Woman, where are those accusers of yours? Has no one condemned you?' She said, 'No one, Lord.' And Jesus said to her, 'Neither do I condemn you; go and sin no more.' "

The woman had stood before Jesus, cowering with fear. His words, "He who is without sin among you, let him throw a stone at her first," had come to her as a death sentence. Silently she awaited her doom. In astonishment she saw her accusers leave speechless and confused. Then those words of hope fell on her ear, "Neither do I condemn you; go and sin no more." Her heart melted, and sobbing out her grateful love, with bitter tears she confessed her sins.

For her, this was the beginning of a life of purity and peace. In lifting up this fallen soul, Jesus performed a greater miracle than in healing the most severe physical disease. He cured the spiritual illness that leads to everlasting death. This repentant woman became one of His most faithful followers.

Jesus does not excuse sin nor lessen the sense of guilt, but He seeks to save. The Sinless One pities the sinner's weakness and extends a helping hand. It is not Christ's follower who leaves sinners unhindered to pursue their downward course. Most people hate the sinner, while they love the sin. Christ hates the sin, but loves the sinner. This will be the spirit of all who follow Him. Christian love is slow to condemn, quick to discern repentance, ready to forgive, to encourage, and to set the wanderer on the path of holiness.

# "The Light of Life"*

I am the light of the world. He who follows Me shall not walk in darkness, but have the light of life."

It was morning. The sun had just risen above the Mount of Olives, and its rays fell with dazzling brightness on the marble palaces and lighted up the gold of the temple walls when Jesus pointed to it and said, "I am the light of the world." Long afterward the apostle John re-echoed these words in that sublime passage, "In Him was life, and the life was the light of men. And the light shines in the darkness, and the darkness did not comprehend it. . . . That was the true Light which gives light to every man coming into the world." John 1:4, 5, 9. God is light, and in the words, "I am the light of the world," Christ declared His oneness with God and His relation to the whole human family. It was He who had caused the "light to shine out of darkness" at the beginning. 2 Corinthians 4:6. He is the light of sun, moon, and stars. As the sunbeams penetrate to the farthest corners of the earth, so does the light of the Sun of Righteousness shine on every person.

"That was the true Light which gives light to every man coming into the world." People of giant intellect and wonderful research, whose words have opened vast fields of knowledge, have been honored as benefactors of the human race. But One stands higher than all of them. "As many as received Him, to them He gave the right to become children of God. . . . No one has seen God at any time. The only begotten Son, who is in the bosom of the Father, He has declared Him." John 1:12, 18. We can trace the line of the world's great teachers as far back as human records extend, but the Light was before them. As the moon and the planets of the solar system reflect the light of the sun, so (as far as their teaching is true) do the world's great thinkers reflect the rays of the Sun of Righteousness. The true "higher education" is what Jesus gives, "in whom are hidden all the treasures of wisdom and knowledge." Colossians 2:3. "He who follows Me shall not walk in darkness, but have the light of life."

When Jesus said, "I am the light of the world," the people could not fail to recognize His claim to be the Messiah, the Promised One. To the Pharisees and rulers this claim seemed arrogant. They could not tolerate that a mere

---

* This chapter is based on John 8:12–59; 9.

Man like themselves would make such bold claims. They demanded, "Who are You?" They were determined to force Him to declare that He was the Christ. His sly enemies believed that His appearance and work were so different from the people's expectations that a direct announcement of Himself as the Messiah would cause them to reject Him as an impostor.

But Jesus replied, "Just what I have been saying to you from the beginning." He was the embodiment of the truths He taught. "I do nothing on my own," He continued, "but I speak these things as the Father instructed me. And the one who sent me is with me." NRSV. He did not attempt to prove His Messianic claim but showed His unity with God.

Many of His hearers were drawn to Him in faith. To them He said, "If you abide in My word, you are My disciples indeed. And you shall know the truth, and the truth shall make you free."

These words offended the Pharisees. "We are Abraham's descendants, and have never been in bondage to anyone. How can You say, 'You will be made free?'" Jesus looked on these men, slaves of hatred, and sadly answered, "Most assuredly, I say to you, whoever commits sin is a slave of sin." They were in the worst kind of slavery—ruled by the spirit of evil.

All who refuse to give themselves to God are under the control of another power. They are in the deepest slavery, their minds under the control of Satan. Christ came to break the chains of sin-slavery from the heart and mind. "If the Son makes you free,

you shall be free indeed."

In the work of redemption there is no forced obedience. We are left free to choose whom we will serve. When we surrender to Christ, there is the highest sense of freedom. Expelling sin is the act of the soul itself. When we desire to be set free from sin, and we cry out for a power outside of and above ourselves, the powers of the soul receive the energy of the Holy Spirit, and they obey the instructions of the will to fulfill the will of God.

The only condition on which our freedom is possible is that we must become one with Christ. Sin can triumph only by destroying the liberty of the soul. Submitting ourselves to God is what restores to us our very self—restored to our true glory and dignity. The divine law, to which we are brought into subjection, is "the law of liberty." James 2:12.

The Pharisees had declared themselves the children of Abraham. The true children would not try to kill One who was speaking the truth that God gave Him. A mere ancestry that goes back to Abraham was of no value. Without possessing the same spirit and doing the same works, they were not his children.

## The Question of Apostolic Succession

As descent from Abraham was proved not by name and genealogy but by likeness of character, so apostolic succession rests not on the transmission of church governing authority but on spiritual relationship. A life actuated by the apostles' spirit, that believes and teaches the truth they taught—this is the true evidence of having received the apostles' authority.

Jesus said, "You do the deeds of your father" In mockery the Jews answered, "*We* were not born of fornication; we have one Father—God." These words, in implying evil about the circumstances of His birth, were intended to discredit Christ in the presence of those who were beginning to believe on Him. Jesus paid no attention to this low insinuation, but said, "If God were your Father, you would love Me, for I proceeded forth and came from God."

"You are of your father the devil," said Jesus. "The desires of your father you want to do. He was a murderer from the beginning, and does not stand in the truth, because there is no truth in him. . . . If I tell the truth, why do you not believe Me?" The fact that Jesus spoke the truth with certainty was why the Jewish leaders did not receive Him. The truth offended these self-righteous men. The truth exposed why error was wrong, it condemned their teaching and practice, and it was unwelcome. They did not love truth.

**No Sin in Jesus**

"Which of you convicts Me of sin? And if I tell the truth, why do you not believe Me?" Day by day for three years Christ's enemies had been trying to find some stain in His character. Satan had been looking for a way to overcome Him but had found nothing to take advantage of in Him. Even the devils were forced to confess, "You are—the Holy One of God!" Mark 1:24. Jesus lived the law in the sight of heaven, in the sight of unfallen worlds, and in the sight of sinful humanity. He

had spoken, unchallenged, words that would have been blasphemy from any other lips: "I always do those things that please Him."

The Jews did not recognize God's voice in the message of His Son. They thought that they were passing judgment on Christ, but they were pronouncing sentence on themselves. "He who is of God," said Jesus, "hears God's words; therefore you do not hear, because you are not of God."

Many who love to quibble, to criticize, looking for something to question in the Word of God, think that this is evidence of independent thought and a sharp mind. But hunting for sticks and straws reveals a narrow and earthly nature, a heart that is quickly losing its ability to appreciate God. As a flower turns to the sun so that the bright rays may touch it with tints of beauty, the heart will turn to the Sun of Righteousness so that heaven's light may beautify the character with the graces of Christ.

Jesus continued, "Your father Abraham rejoiced to see My day, and he saw it and was glad." Abraham offered up the most earnest prayer, asking to see the Messiah before he died. And God gave him a supernatural light, a view of the divine sacrifice for sin. He had an illustration of this sacrifice in his own experience. The command came to Him, "Take now your son, your only son Isaac, whom you love, . . . and offer him there as a burnt offering." Genesis 22:2. Upon the altar he laid the son of promise. Then, with the knife upraised to obey God, he heard a Voice from heaven saying, "Do not lay your hand on the lad, or do anything to him; for now I know that you fear God, since you have not withheld your son, your only son, from Me." Genesis 22:12. God imposed this terrible ordeal on Abraham so that he could see the day of Christ and realize God's great love for the world, so great that He gave His only Son to raise the world from its degradation.

By making an entire surrender, Abraham saw that when God gave His only Son to save sinners from eternal ruin, He was making a greater and more wonderful sacrifice than any human could ever make.

When God provided a sacrifice instead of Isaac, He was declaring that no one could atone for his own guilt, that the pagan system of sacrifice was wholly unacceptable to God. No father was to offer up his son or daughter for a sin offering. The Son of God alone can bear the guilt of the world.

Christ's words concerning Abraham did not seem deeply significant to His hearers. The Pharisees saw in them only fresh ground for arguing. They retorted with a sneer, as if they would prove Jesus to be a madman, "You are not yet fifty years old, and have You seen Abraham?"

With solemn dignity Jesus answered, "Most assuredly, I say to you, before Abraham was, I AM."

Silence fell on the large gathering. This Galilean Rabbi had claimed the name of God, given to Moses to express the idea of the eternal presence. He had announced Himself to be the self-existent One, He "whose goings forth are from of old, from everlasting." Micah 5:2.

Again the priests and rabbis cried out against Jesus as a blasphemer. Because He was, and proclaimed Himself to be, the Son of God, they were bent on destroying Him. Many of the people sided with the priests and rabbis and picked up stones to throw at Him. "But Jesus hid Himself and went out of the temple."

## The Man Born Blind

"As Jesus passed by, He saw a man who was blind from birth. And His disciples asked Him, saying, 'Rabbi, who sinned, this man or his parents, that he was born blind?' Jesus answered, 'Neither this man nor his parents sinned, but that the works of God should be revealed in him. . . .'

"When He had said these things, He spat on the ground and made clay with the saliva; and He anointed the eyes of the blind man with the clay. And He said to him, 'Go, wash in the pool of Siloam' (which is translated, Sent). So he went and washed, and came back seeing."

The Jews generally believed that sin is punished in this life. Satan, the author of sin and its results, had led people to look on disease and death as proceeding from God. If some great affliction had fallen on anyone, that person had the burden of being considered a great sinner. This viewpoint prepared the way for the Jews to reject Jesus. They looked on the One who "has borne our griefs and carried our sorrows" as Someone "stricken, smitten by God, and afflicted," and they hid their faces from Him. Isaiah 53:4.

Christ's disciples held the same belief about the connection between sin and suffering that the Jews held. After anointing the blind man's eyes, Jesus sent him to wash in the pool of Siloam, and the man's sight was restored. In doing this, Jesus answered the disciples' question in a practical way. The disciples were not to discuss about who had sinned or had not sinned. They were to understand God's mercy in giving sight to the blind. There was no healing virtue in the clay or in the pool where the blind man was sent to wash. The virtue was in Christ.

## A Miracle on the Sabbath

The Pharisees were astonished at the cure and were filled with hatred more than ever, for Jesus had performed the miracle on the Sabbath day.

The neighbors who knew the young man when he was blind looked on him with doubt, because when his eyes were opened, his face was changed and brightened, and he appeared like another man. Some said, "This is he"; others said, "He is like him." But he settled the question by saying, "I am he." He then told them of Jesus and how Jesus had healed him, and they inquired, "Where is He?" He said, "I do not know."

A council of the Pharisees summoned the man and asked him how he had received his sight. "He said to them, 'He put clay on my eyes, and I washed, and I see.' Therefore some of the Pharisees said, 'This Man is not from God, because He does not keep the Sabbath.' " The Pharisees appeared wonderfully zealous for Sabbath observance, yet they were plan-

ning murder on that very day. But many were convicted that the One who had opened the eyes of the blind was more than a common man. They said, "How can a man who is a sinner do such signs?"

Again the rabbis questioned the blind man. " 'What do you say about Him because He opened your eyes?' He said, 'He is a prophet.' " The Pharisees then claimed that he had not been born blind. They called for his parents and asked them, saying, "Is this your son, who you say was born blind?"

There was the man himself, declaring that he had been blind and had had his sight restored. But the Pharisees would rather deny the evidence of their own senses than admit that they were wrong. Prejudice is that powerful, pharisaical righteousness that distorting.

The Pharisees had one hope left: to intimidate the man's parents. They asked, "How then does he now see?" The parents feared to compromise themselves, for it had been declared that whoever would acknowledge Jesus as the Christ would be "put out of the synagogue," that is, excluded for thirty days. People thought that this sentence was a great calamity. The great work accomplished for their son had brought conviction to the parents, yet they answered, "We know that this is our son, and that he was born blind; but by what means he now sees we do not know, or who opened his eyes we do not know. He is of age; ask him. He will speak for himself." In this way they shifted all responsibility to their son.

## The Miracle Could Not Be Denied

The Pharisees' questioning and prejudice, their unbelief in the facts of the case, were opening the eyes of the people. The question in many minds was, Would God do such mighty works through an impostor, as the Pharisees insisted that Jesus was?

The Pharisees could not deny the miracle. The blind man, filled with joy and gratitude, freely told his experience. Again the Pharisees tried to silence him. "Give God the glory! We know that this Man is a sinner." That is, Do not say again that this Man gave you sight. It is God who has done this.

The blind man answered, "Whether He is a sinner or not I do not know. One thing I know: that though I was blind, now I see."

As these hypocrites tried to make him disbelieve, God helped him to show, by the vigor and pointedness of his replies, that he would not be caught in any trap of theirs. He answered, " 'I told you already, and you did not listen. Why do you want to hear it again? Do you also want to become His disciples?'

"Then they reviled him and said, 'You are His disciple; but we are Moses' disciples. We know that God spoke to Moses; as for this fellow, we do not know where He is from.' "

The Lord gave the man grace and clarity so that he became a witness for Christ in words that were a cutting rebuke to his questioners. Here was One performing miracles, and they were admittedly ignorant about the source of His power. "Why, this is a marvelous thing, that you do not know where He is from; yet He has opened my eyes! Now we know that God does not hear sinners; but if anyone is a worshiper of God and does His will, He hears him. Since the world began it has been unheard of that anyone opened the eyes of one who was born blind. If this Man were not from God, He could do nothing."

The man's reasoning was unanswerable. The Pharisees were spellbound at his pointed, determined words. For a few moments there was silence. Then the frowning priests and rabbis gathered their robes about them, as though they feared contamination from contact with him. "You were completely born in sins, and are you teaching us?" And they excommunicated him.

Jesus heard what had happened, and finding him soon afterward, said, "Do you believe in the Son of God?"

For the first time, the blind man looked on the face of his Restorer. He had seen his parents troubled and perplexed; he had looked on the frowning faces of the rabbis; now his eyes rested on the loving, peaceful face of Jesus. Already, at great cost to himself, he had acknowledged Him as One entrusted with divine power. Now a higher revelation was granted him.

To the Savior's question, the blind man replied by asking, "Who is He, Lord, that I may believe in Him?" And Jesus said, "You have both seen Him and it is He who is talking with you." The man threw himself at the Savior's feet in worship. Christ had been revealed to his heart, and he received Him as the One sent by God.

A group of Pharisees had gathered

near, and the sight of them brought to Jesus' mind the contrast always evident in the effect of His words and works. "For judgment I have come into this world, that those who do not see may see, and that those who see may be made blind." At the Savior's advent, the people had the privilege of a fuller revelation of the divine presence than the world had ever enjoyed before. But in this very revelation, judgment was passing on men and women. Their character was tested, their destiny determined.

Feeling that Christ's words applied to them, some of His hearers inquired, "Are we blind also?" Jesus answered, "If you were blind, you would have no sin." If God had made it impossible for you to see the truth, your ignorance would involve no guilt. "But now you say, 'We see.' " You believe yourselves able to see, and you reject the only means through which you could receive sight. The Pharisees refused to come to Christ, and so they were left in blindness. Jesus said, "Therefore your sin remains."

# The Divine Shepherd*

"I am the good shepherd. . . . And I lay down My life for the sheep." John 10:14, 15.

Jesus found access to His hearers by the pathway of their familiar associations. In a beautiful picture of sheep and shepherd, He represents His relationship to those who believe on Him. No picture was more familiar to His hearers than this. Remembering the Savior's lesson, the disciples would see Christ in each faithful shepherd and themselves in each helpless, dependent flock.

The Pharisees had just driven one from the fold because he dared to bear witness to the power of Christ. They had cut off someone whom the True Shepherd was drawing to Himself. In doing this they had shown themselves unworthy of their trust as shepherds of the flock. Now Jesus pointed to Himself as the real Keeper of the Lord's flock.

"He who does not enter the sheepfold by the door, but climbs up some other way, the same is a thief and a robber. But he who enters by the door is the shepherd of the sheep." When the Pharisees reasoned silently about what He meant, Jesus told them plainly,

"I am the door. If anyone enters by Me, he will be saved, and will go in and out and find pasture. The thief does not come except to steal, and to kill, and to destroy. I have come that they may have life, and that they may have it more abundantly."

Christ is the door to the fold of God. From earliest times, all His children have found entrance through this door. Whether in shadowy symbols, or disclosed in the revelation of the prophets, or unveiled in the lessons Jesus gave to His disciples and in miracles, they have seen "the Lamb of God who takes away the sin of the world." John 1:29. People have devised ceremonies and systems by which they hope to receive justification and peace with God. But all who introduce something to take the place of Christ, to enter the fold in some other way, are thieves and robbers.

The priests and rulers, the scribes and Pharisees, destroyed the living pastures and defiled the wellsprings of the Water of Life. Inspiration describes these false shepherds: "The weak you have not strengthened, nor have you healed those who were sick, nor bound up the broken, nor brought back what

---

was driven away, nor sought what was lost; but with force and cruelty you have ruled them." Ezekiel 34:4.

Every heathen nation has had its great teachers and religious systems offering some other means of redemption than Christ, turning people's eyes away from the Father's face and filling their hearts with fear. Millions are burdened down under false religions, without hope or joy here and with only a dull fear of the hereafter. Only the gospel of God's grace can lift up the soul. The love of God as seen in His Son will stir the heart and arouse the powers of our being as nothing else can. Whoever turns people away from Christ is turning them away from the Source of true development, depriving them of the hope and glory of life. He is a thief and a robber.

### Responsibility of a Faithful Shepherd

In the East, a shepherd's care for the flock was untiring and constant. Raiding thieves or beasts of prey lay in wait to steal the sheep. Shepherds watched their flocks at the peril of their own lives. Jacob, who kept Laban's flocks, said, "In the day the drought consumed me, and the frost by night, and my sleep departed from my eyes." Genesis 31:40. While guarding his father's sheep, the boy David singlehandedly rescued the stolen lamb from the lion and the bear.

A strong and tender attachment unites shepherds to the sheep in their care. Every sheep has its name and responds to the shepherd's call. Likewise the divine Shepherd knows His flock that are scattered throughout the world. Jesus says, "I have called you by your name; you are Mine." Isaiah 43:1. Jesus knows us individually and can sympathize with our weaknesses. He knows the very house in which we live. At times He has given directions to His servants to go to a certain street in a certain city, to such a house, to find one of His sheep.

Jesus knows every person as fully as if he were the only one for whom the Savior died. The distress of each one touches His heart. He came to draw all to Himself. He knows all who gladly hear His call and are ready to come under His shepherding care. He says, "My sheep hear My voice, and I know them, and they follow Me."

### Why His Sheep Gladly Follow Him

Eastern shepherds do not drive their sheep. They do not depend on force or fear, but going ahead of them, they call the sheep. The Savior-Shepherd does the same with His sheep. He declares, "I have loved you with an everlasting love; therefore with lovingkindness I have drawn you." Jeremiah 31:3.

It is not fear of punishment or hope of everlasting reward that leads the disciples of Christ to follow Him. They see the Savior's matchless love revealed from the manger of Bethlehem to Calvary's cross, and the sight of Him attracts, softens, and subdues them. Love awakens in their hearts. They hear His voice, and they follow Him.

The shepherd goes ahead of the sheep, encountering the perils first. So does Jesus with His people. The way to heaven is made holy by the Savior's footprints.

Though now He shares the throne of the universe, Jesus has lost none of His compassion. Today His pierced hand reaches out to bless His people in the world. "And they shall never perish; neither shall anyone snatch them out of My hand." The person who has come to Christ in faith is more precious in His sight than the whole world. He will never abandon one for whom He has died. Unless His followers choose to leave Him, He will hold them securely.

### Christ Is Still Our Personal Shepherd

Our never-failing Helper does not leave us alone to struggle with temptation and finally be crushed with burdens and sorrow. Though now He is hidden from mortal sight, the ear of faith can hear His voice saying, "Fear not; I am with you. I have endured your sorrows, experienced your struggles, encountered your temptations. I know your tears; I have also wept. I know the griefs that lie too deep to be breathed into any human ear. You are not forsaken. Though your pain may touch no responsive cord in any heart on earth, look to Me and live." See Isaiah 54:10.

Because we are the gift of His Father and the reward of His work, Jesus loves us as His children. He loves you.

Heaven itself can bestow nothing greater, nothing better. So trust.

Jesus thought about people all over the earth who were misled by false shepherds, scattered among wolves, and He said, "I have other sheep that do not belong to this fold. I must bring them also, and they will listen to my voice. So there will be one flock, one shepherd." NRSV.

"Therefore My Father loves Me, because I lay down My life that I may take it again. . . . I have power to lay it down, and I have power to take it again." As a member of the human family Jesus was mortal; as God He was the Fountain of life for the world. He could have withstood death's approach, but He laid down His life voluntarily so that He could bring life and immortality to light.

He was wounded for our transgressions,
He was bruised for our iniquities;
The chastisement of our peace was upon Him,
And by His stripes we are healed.
All we like sheep have gone astray;
We have turned, every one, to his own way;
And the Lord has laid on Him the iniquity of us all.

Isaiah 53:5, 6

# The Last Journey From Galilee[*]

Near the close of His ministry, there was a change in the way Christ worked. Up to then He had tried to shun publicity, refused the adoration of the people, and had commanded that no one should declare Him to be the Christ.

At the time of the Feast of Tabernacles, He had made His way to Jerusalem unnoticed and entered the city unannounced. But it was not this way with His last journey. He now traveled in the most public manner, preceded by such an announcement of His coming as He had never made before. He was going to the scene of His great sacrifice, and He must direct the attention of the people to it.

"As Moses lifted up the serpent in the wilderness, even so must the Son of Man be lifted up." John 3:14. All eyes must be drawn to Christ, the Sacrifice that brought salvation to the lost world.

The disciples would have prevented Him from making the journey to Jerusalem. They knew the deadly hostility of the religious leaders. It was a bitter task for Christ to lead His beloved disciples to the anguish and despair that waited for them at Jerusalem. And Satan was close by to press his temptations. Why should He now go to Jerusalem, to certain death? All around Him there were suffering ones waiting for healing. He was full of the vigor of manhood's prime. Why not go to the vast fields of the world with the words of His grace, the touch of His healing power? Why not give light and gladness to those darkened and sorrowing millions? Why face death now and leave the work in its infancy? The enemy attacked Christ with fierce and subtle temptations. If Jesus had changed His course in the smallest way to save Himself, the world would have been lost.

But Jesus had "steadfastly set His face to go to Jerusalem." The one law of His life was the Father's will. In His boyhood, He had said to Mary, "Did you not know that I must be about My Father's business?" Luke 2:49. But in God's great plan, the hour for Him to offer Himself for our sins was soon to strike. He would not fail nor hesitate. His enemies had long plotted to take His life; now He would lay it down.

And He "sent messengers before His face. And as they went, they entered a village of the Samaritans, to

* This chapter is based on Luke 9:51–56; 10:1–24.

prepare for Him." But the people refused to receive Him, because He was on His way to Jerusalem. Little did they realize that they were turning away from their doors the best gift of heaven. The Samaritans lost all this because of their prejudice and bigotry.

James and John, Christ's messengers, were greatly annoyed at the insult; they were filled with indignation because the Samaritans had treated Him so rudely. They reported to Christ that the people had even refused to give Him a night's lodging. Seeing Mount Carmel in the distance, where Elijah had killed the false prophets, they said, "Do You want us to command fire to come down from heaven and consume them?" They were surprised at Jesus' rebuke: "You do not know what manner of spirit you are of. For the Son of Man did not come to destroy men's lives but to save them." And He went to another village.

It is no part of Christ's mission to compel people to receive Him. He wants only voluntary service, the willing surrender of the heart moved by love. There can be no more conclusive evidence that we possess the spirit of Satan than the desire to hurt and destroy those who do not appreciate our work, who act contrary to our ideas. Nothing can be more offensive to God than, through religious bigotry, bringing suffering on those who are the purchase of the Savior's blood.

Christ spent a significant part of the closing months of His ministry in Perea, the province beyond the Jordan from Judea. See Mark 10:1. Here the people crowded around Him, and He repeated much of His former teaching.

As He had sent out the Twelve, so He "appointed seventy others and sent them on ahead of Him in pairs to every town and place where he himself intended to go." NRSV. For some time these disciples had been in training for their work. They had had the privilege of close association with Him and direct personal instruction.

Jesus did not give the same command to the Seventy that He had given to the Twelve—not to enter into any city of the Gentiles or the Samaritans. Though the Samaritans had rudely rejected Christ, His love toward them was unchanged. In His name, the Seventy visited, first of all, the cities of Samaria.

## Samaritans Responded to Christ's Love

In His commission to the disciples just before His ascension, Jesus mentioned Samaria with Jerusalem and Judea as the places where they were to preach the gospel first. When they went to Samaria, they found the people ready to receive them. The Samaritans saw that, despite their rude treatment of Him, Jesus had only thoughts of love toward them, and He won their hearts. After His ascension the disciples gathered a precious harvest from among those who had once been their bitterest enemies.

"A bruised reed He will not break,
And smoking flax He will not quench;
He will bring forth justice for truth."
                                    Isaiah 42:3

In sending out the Seventy, Jesus instructed them not to urge their presence where they were unwelcome.

"Whatever city you enter, and they do not receive you," He said, "go out into its streets and say, 'The very dust of your city which clings to us we wipe off against you. Nevertheless know this, that the kingdom of God has come near you.' " They were not to do this from resentment or wounded dignity, but to show how serious it is to refuse the Lord's message. To reject the Lord's servants is to reject Christ Himself.

### Religious Leaders Turned Many Against Christ

"I say to you," Jesus added, "that it will be more tolerable in that Day for Sodom than for that city." Then His mind went back to the Galilean towns where He had spent so much of His ministry. Day after day the Prince of life had gone in and out among them. The glory of God had been shining on the multitudes that crowded the Savior's steps. Yet they had refused the heavenly Gift.

The rabbis had warned against receiving the doctrines that this new Teacher taught. Instead of trying to understand the Word of God for themselves, the people honored the priests and rulers, rejected the truth, and kept their traditions. Many had been almost persuaded, but they did not act on their convictions. In this way many rejected the truth that would have been their salvation.

The True Witness says, "Behold, I stand at the door and knock." Revelation 3:20. Every appeal in the Word or through God's messengers is a knock at the door of the heart. It is the voice of Jesus asking entrance. With every

knock unheeded, the willingness to open becomes weaker. If we disregard the impressions of the Holy Spirit today, they will not be as strong tomorrow. The heart becomes less impressible, and it lapses into a dangerous lack of awareness of how short life is and of eternity beyond. Condemnation in the judgment will not result from the fact that we have been in error, but from the fact that we have neglected heaven-sent opportunities for learning what is truth.

When their work was completed, the Seventy returned with joy, saying, "Lord, even the demons are subject to us in Your name." Jesus answered, "I saw Satan fall like lightning from heaven." Beyond the cross of Calvary, with its agony and shame, Jesus looked forward to the great final day when Satan will meet his destruction in the earth that has been marred so long by his rebellion.

From that time onward, Christ's followers were to look on Satan as a conquered foe. On the cross, Jesus would gain the victory for them. He wanted them to accept that victory as their own. "Behold," He said, "I give you the authority to trample on serpents and scorpions, and over all the power of the enemy, and nothing shall by any means hurt you."

The omnipotent power of the Holy Spirit is the defense of every repentant sinner. Christ will not permit one who in penitence and faith has claimed His protection to fall under the enemy's power. When temptations and trials come, look to Jesus, your Helper. Thank God, we have a mighty Savior, who threw out the evil one from heaven.

Why not talk of Him? God will never forsake His people in their struggle with evil.

## Secret of Personal Power

Jesus added, "Nevertheless do not rejoice in this, that the spirits are subject to you, but rather rejoice because your names are written in heaven." Be careful not to let self-sufficiency come in, leading you to work in your own strength. Self is always ready to take the credit if any success follows the work. When we realize our weakness, we learn to depend on a power that is not our own. See 2 Corinthians 12:10. Nothing reaches down to our deepest motives of conduct as fully as a sense of Christ's pardoning love. We are to come in touch with God. Then His Holy Spirit will fill us, enabling us to come in touch with those around us. The more closely you connect yourself with the Source of light and power, the greater power you will have to work for God.

As the Seventy listened to Christ, the Holy Spirit was writing truth on their hearts. Though crowds surrounded them, it was as though they were shut in with God.

Knowing that they had caught the inspiration of the hour, Jesus "rejoiced in the Spirit and said, 'I thank You, Father, Lord of heaven and earth, that You have hidden these things from the wise and prudent and revealed them to babes. Even so, Father, for so it seemed good in Your sight.' "

The honored of the world, the so-called great and wise men, could not comprehend Christ's character. But fishermen and tax collectors were enabled to see the Invisible. From time to time, as they surrendered to the Holy Spirit's power, God illuminated the disciples' minds. They realized that the mighty God had wrapped Himself in humanity and was among them. Often as Jesus had presented the Old Testament scriptures and showed how they applied to Himself, they had been lifted into a heavenly atmosphere. They had a clearer understanding of these things than the original writers themselves had. Ever afterward, they would read the Old Testament scriptures as a new revelation from God. They saw Him "whom the world cannot receive, because it neither sees Him nor knows Him." John 14:1.

The only way for us to gain a more perfect grasp of truth is by keeping the heart tender and subdued by the Spirit of Christ. Human science is too limited to understand the plan of redemption. Philosophy cannot explain it. But we can know the science of salvation by experience. Only those who see their own sinfulness can discern how precious the Savior is.

The lessons Christ taught as He slowly made His way toward Jerusalem were full of instruction. In Perea the people were less under the control of Jewish bigotry than in Judea, and His teaching found a response in their hearts.

Christ spoke many of His parables during the last months of His ministry. The priests and rabbis could not mistake His meaning, yet they could find no basis on which to accuse Him. Christ repeated the beautiful parable of the lost sheep. And He carried its lesson still further, as He told of the lost piece of silver and the prodigal son. After the Holy Spirit was poured out, as the disciples went out in their Master's name facing criticism, poverty, and persecution, they often strengthened their hearts by repeating what He said on this last journey: "Do not fear, little flock, for it is your Father's good pleasure to give you the kingdom. Sell what you have and give alms; provide yourselves money bags which do not grow old, a treasure in the heavens that does not fail, where no thief approaches nor moth destroys. For where your treasure is, there your heart will be also." Luke 12:32–34.

# The Good Samaritan[*]

As Christ was teaching the people, "a certain lawyer stood up and tested him, saying, 'Teacher, what shall I do to inherit eternal life?' " The priests and rabbis had thought they would entangle Christ by having the lawyer ask this question. But the Savior entered into no controversy. "What is written in the law?" He said. "What is your reading of it?" He turned the question of salvation on the keeping of God's commandments.

The lawyer said, "You shall love the Lord your God with all your heart, with all your soul, with all your strength, and with all your mind," and "your neighbor as yourself." Jesus said, "You have answered rightly; do this and you will live."

The lawyer had been studying the Scriptures to learn their real meaning. In his answer about the law's requirements, he claimed no value for the mass of ceremonial and ritualistic instructions but presented the two great principles on which hang all the law and the prophets. This answer, which Christ commended, gave the Savior an advantage with the rabbis.

"Do this and you will live," Jesus said. He presented the law as a divine unity. It is not possible to keep one commandment and break another, because the same principle runs through them all. Supreme love to God and impartial love to others are the principles to be lived out in the life.

The lawyer was convicted under Christ's uncompromising words. He had not shown love toward others within his reach. But instead of repenting, he tried to justify himself, saying, "Who is my neighbor?"

Among the Jews, this question caused endless dispute. The heathen and Samaritans were strangers and enemies, but where should the distinction be made among people of their own nation and different classes of society? Were they to regard the ignorant and careless crowds, the "unclean," as neighbors?

## Dispel Darkness by Admitting Light

Jesus did not denounce the bigotry of those who were watching His words to condemn Him. But by a simple story He held up such a picture of heaven-born love flowing out to others that it touched all hearts and drew from the lawyer a confession of the truth. The best way to deal with error is to present

---

[*] *This chapter is based on Luke 10:25–37.*

truth. "A certain man," Jesus said, "went down from Jerusalem to Jericho, and fell among thieves, who stripped him of his clothing, wounded him, and departed, leaving him half dead. Now by chance a certain priest came down that road. And when he saw him, he passed by on the other side. Likewise a Levite, when he arrived at the place, came and looked, and passed by on the other side." This was an actual occurrence, known to be exactly as Jesus told it. The priest and Levite were in the group that listened to Christ's words.

From Jerusalem to Jericho, the road led down a wild, rocky ravine infested by robbers. It was often the scene of violence. Here the robbers attacked the traveler and left him half dead. The priest merely glanced toward the wounded man. The Levite was convicted of what he ought to do, but he persuaded himself that the case was no concern of his.

Both of these men were of the class specially chosen to represent God to the people. They were to "have compassion on those who are ignorant and going astray." Hebrews 5:2.

Angels of heaven look on the distress of God's family on earth and are prepared to cooperate with men and women in relieving oppression and suffering. All heaven watched to see if the priest and the Levite would be touched with pity for human misery. The Savior had instructed the Hebrews in the wilderness, teaching a very different lesson from the one the people were now receiving from their priests and teachers. He had given the message through Moses that the Lord

their God "administers justice for the fatherless and the widow, and loves the stranger. . . . Therefore love the stranger." "You shall love him as yourself." Deuteronomy 10:18, 19; Leviticus 19:34.

But, trained in the school of national bigotry, the priest and Levite had become selfish, narrow, and exclusive. When they looked at the wounded man, they could not tell whether he was Jewish. They thought he might be a Samaritan, and they turned away.

But now a Samaritan came where the sufferer was and had compassion on him. The Samaritan knew very well that, if their conditions were reversed, the stranger, a Jew, would pass him by with contempt. He himself might be in danger of violence by spending extra time in the place. But it was enough that here before him was a human being in need and suffering. He took off his own garment to cover him. The oil and wine he had brought for his own journey he used to heal and refresh the wounded man. He lifted him on his own beast and moved slowly along at an even pace, so that the stranger might not be jarred and suffer increased pain. He brought him to an inn and cared for him through the night, watching him tenderly.

Before going on his way in the morning, the Samaritan placed the man in the care of the innkeeper, paid the charge, and left a deposit for his benefit. Not satisfied even with this, he made provision for any further need, saying, "Take care of him; and whatever more you spend, when I come again, I will repay you."

When the story ended, Jesus fixed His eyes on the lawyer and said, "Which of these three do you think was neighbor to him who fell among the thieves?" The lawyer answered, "He who showed mercy on him." Jesus said, "Go and do likewise."

So the question, "Who is my neighbor?" is forever answered. Our neighbor is every person who needs our help, every soul wounded and bruised by the enemy, everyone who is the property of God.

In the story of the good Samaritan, Jesus gave a picture of Himself and His mission. Humanity had been bruised, robbed, and left to die by Satan. But the Savior left His glory to come to our rescue. He healed our wounds. He covered us with His robe of righteousness. He made complete provision for us at His own expense. Pointing to His own example, He says to His followers, "As I have loved you, . . . love one another." John 13:34.

The Samaritan had obeyed the dictates of a kind and loving heart. In doing this he had proved himself to be a doer of the law. Christ told the lawyer, "Go and do likewise."

The lesson is no less needed today.

Selfishness and cold formality have nearly extinguished the fire of love and dispelled the graces that should make the character fragrant. Many who profess Jesus' name have forgotten that Christians are to represent Christ. Unless we show practical self-sacrifice for the good of others wherever we may be, we are not Christians, no matter what we profess to be.

Christ asks us to unite with Him to save humanity. "Freely you have received," He says, "freely give." Matthew 10:8. Many have gone astray and feel their shame and foolishness. They are hungry for encouragement. They look at their mistakes until they are driven almost to desperation. If we are Christians, when we see human beings in distress, whether through affliction or through sin, we will never say, "This does not concern me."

The story of the good Samaritan and the character of Jesus reveal the true significance of the law and what it means to love our neighbor as ourselves. And when the children of God show love toward all mankind, they also are witnessing to the character of heaven's laws. "If we love one another, God abides in us, and His love has been perfected in us." 1 John 4:12.

# Not With Outward Show *

More than three years had passed since John the Baptist gave the message, "The kingdom of heaven is at hand!" Matthew 3:2. Many of those who rejected John and had opposed Jesus at every step were suggesting that His mission had failed.

Jesus answered, "The kingdom of God does not come with observation ["things that can be observed," NRSV], nor will they say, 'See here!' or 'See there!' For indeed, the kingdom of God is within you." The kingdom of God begins in the heart. Do not expect earthly power to mark its coming.

"The days will come," Jesus said, turning to His disciples, "when you will desire to see one of the days of the Son of Man, and you will not see it." You do not realize what a great privilege is now yours in having among you the One who is the Life and Light of humanity. You will look back with longing on the opportunities you now enjoy to walk and talk with the Son of God.

Not until after Christ's ascension and the outpouring of the Holy Spirit did the disciples fully appreciate the Savior's character and mission. They began to realize that they had been in the very presence of the Lord of glory. See John 1:14. Their minds were opened to comprehend the prophecies and to understand the miracles He had performed. They were like people awakened from a dream. The disciples never tired of going over Christ's words and works. His lessons now came as a fresh revelation. The Scriptures became a new book to them.

As the disciples searched the prophecies that testified about Christ, they came into fellowship with the Deity. They learned from Him who had ascended to heaven to complete the work He had begun on earth. With amazement they reread the prophetic descriptions of His character and work. How dimly had they understood the prophetic scriptures! Looking on Him as He walked as a Man among them, they had not understood the mystery of His incarnation. They did not fully recognize divinity in humanity. But after the Holy Spirit shed light into their minds, how they longed to see Him again! And how they wished they could have Him explain the Scriptures that they could not comprehend! What had Christ meant when He said, "I still

---

* This chapter is based on Luke 17:20–22.

have many things to say to you, but you cannot bear them now"? John 16:12. They grieved that their faith had been so feeble, that they had so failed of comprehending the reality.

The wonderful Person whom John had announced had been among them for more than thirty years, and they had not really known Him as the One sent from God. The disciples had allowed the prevailing unbelief to cloud their understanding. They often repeated His conversations and said, "Why did we allow the opposition of the priests and rabbis to confuse our senses so that we did not comprehend that Someone greater than Moses was among us, that One wiser than Solomon was instructing us? How dull were our ears!"

When they were brought before councils and put into prison, the followers of Christ rejoiced "that they were counted worthy to suffer shame for His name." Acts 5:41. They recognized the glory of Christ, and they chose to follow Him even if it meant losing all things.

The kingdom of God does not come with outward show. The gospel, with its spirit of self-denial, can never be in harmony with the spirit of the world. But today many people want to make our Lord the ruler of the kingdoms of this world, the ruler in its courts, legislative halls, palaces, and marketplaces. They expect Him to rule through legal enactments, enforced by human authority. Since Christ is not here in person now, they themselves will act in His place. Such

a kingdom is what the Jews wanted in the days of Christ. But He said, "My kingdom is not of this world." John 18:36.

The government under which Jesus lived was corrupt and oppressive. Everywhere were terrible abuses—extortion, intolerance, and grinding cruelty. Yet the Savior attempted no civil reforms, attacked no national abuses, nor condemned the national enemies. He did not interfere with the authority of those in power. He who was our example kept His distance from earthly governments, not because He was indifferent to human woe, but because the remedy did not lie in merely human and external measures. The cure must regenerate the heart.

The kingdom of Christ is not established by courts, councils, or legislative assemblies but by implanting Christ's nature in humanity through the work of the Holy Spirit. Here is the only power that can elevate mankind. And the human agency to accomplish this work is the teaching and practicing of the Word of God.

Now, as in Christ's day, the work of God's kingdom does not lie with those who clamor for recognition and support from earthly rulers and human laws. Rather, it lies with those who declare to the people in Christ's name the spiritual truths that produce in the receivers the experience of Paul: "I have been crucified with Christ; it is no longer I who live, but Christ lives in me." Galatians 2:20.

# Jesus' Love for Children[*]

Jesus loved children. He accepted their childish sympathy and open, sincere love. The grateful praise from their lips refreshed His spirit when contact with crafty and hypocritical men oppressed Him. Wherever He went, His gentle, kindly manner won their confidence.

It was customary for parents to bring their children to some rabbi, so that he could lay his hands on them in blessing. But when the mothers came to Jesus with their little ones, the disciples were not receptive. They thought these children were too young to benefit from a visit to Jesus, and they concluded that He would be displeased. But it was the disciples with whom He was displeased. The Savior understood the burden of the mothers who were trying to train their children. He Himself had drawn them into His presence.

Several mothers came together with their little ones to have Jesus bless their children. Jesus heard with sympathy their timid, tearful request. But He waited to see how the disciples would treat them. When He saw them send the mothers away, He showed them their error, saying, "Let the little children come to Me, and do not forbid them; for of such is the kingdom of heaven." He took the children in His arms and gave them the blessing for which they came.

The words of Christ strengthened the mothers and encouraged them to take up their burden with new cheerfulness. The mothers of today are to receive His words with the same faith. Christ is a personal Savior. He is as truly the helper of mothers today as when He gathered the little ones in His arms in Judea.

Jesus knows the burden of every mother's heart. He made a long journey to relieve the anxious heart of a Canaanite woman. He gave back to the widow of Nain her only son, and in His agony on the cross He remembered His own mother. He is touched today by the mother's sorrow. In every grief and need, He will give comfort and help.

He who said, "Let the little children come to Me, and do not forbid them" still invites mothers to lead their little ones to Him for blessing. Even the baby in its mother's arms may live

---

* This chapter is based on Matthew 19:13–15; Mark 10:13–16; Luke 18:15–17.

under the shadow of the Almighty through the faith of the praying mother. John the Baptist was filled with the Holy Spirit from his birth. If we will live in communion with God, we too may expect the divine Spirit to mold our little ones, even from their earliest moments.

Jesus saw that some of the children who were brought in contact with Him would become martyrs for His sake. These children would accept Him as their Redeemer far more readily than many grown-up people would. The Majesty of heaven answered their questions and simplified His important lessons to meet their childish understanding.

### An Example to Mothers and Fathers

Children are still the most receptive to the teachings of the gospel. Their hearts are strong to retain the lessons they receive. Little children may be Christians, in keeping with their years.

Fathers and mothers should look on their children as younger members of the Lord's family whom God has committed to them to educate for heaven. The Christian home becomes a school, with the parents as under-teachers and Christ Himself the Chief Instructor. We should teach our children to bring their sins to Jesus, asking forgiveness and believing that He pardons them, just as He received the children when He was personally on earth.

As the mother teaches her children to obey her because they love her, she is teaching them the first lesson in the Christian life. The mother's love represents to the child the love of Christ, and the little ones who trust and obey their mother are learning to trust and obey the Savior.

Jesus was also the father's example. His word had power, yet even with rude and violent men He did not use one unkind or discourteous expression. The grace of Christ in the heart will soften whatever is harsh and subdue everything that is coarse and unkind. It will lead fathers and mothers to treat their children as they themselves would like to be treated.

Parents, in training your children, study the lessons God has given in nature. If you want to train a rose or lily, how do you do it? Ask the gardener how he makes every branch and leaf develop in symmetry and loveliness. He will tell you: it was by no harsh touch, no violent effort. This would only break the delicate stems. It was by little attentions, often repeated. He moistened the soil and protected the growing plants from the fierce winds and scorching sun, and God caused them to blossom into loveliness. By gentle touches, seek to fashion the characters of your children after the pattern of the character of Christ.

Encourage the expression of love toward God and toward one another. The reason why there are so many hard-hearted men and women in the world is that true affection has been discouraged and repressed. Parents and perhaps others stifled the better nature of these persons in childhood. Unless divine love melts away their cold selfishness, their happiness will be forever ruined. If we want our children to possess the tender spirit of Jesus, we must encourage the generous, loving impulses of childhood.

Teach the children to see Christ in nature. Take them out into the open air, under the noble trees, into the garden. In all the wonderful works of creation, teach them to see His love. He made the laws that govern all living things, and He has made laws for our happiness and joy. Do not weary them with long prayers and tiresome lectures, but through nature's object lessons teach them to obey the law of God.

As you try to make plain the truths of salvation, point the children to Christ as a personal Savior. Angels will be by your side. The Lord will give grace to fathers and mothers to interest their little ones in the precious story of the Baby in Bethlehem.

Do not keep the little ones away from Jesus by being cold and harsh. Never give them cause to feel that heaven will not be a pleasant place if you are there. Do not speak of religion as something that children cannot understand. Do not give the false impression that the religion of Christ is a religion of gloom, and that in coming to the Savior they must give up everything that makes life joyful.

As the Holy Spirit moves on the hearts of the children, cooperate with His work. The Savior is calling them. Nothing can give Him greater joy than for them to give themselves to Him in the bloom and freshness of their years. His heart is drawn out, not only to the best-behaved children, but to those who have inherited objectionable traits of character. Many parents do not have the tenderness and wisdom to deal with the misbehaving children whom they have made what they are. But Jesus looks on these children with pity.

Be Christ's agent in drawing these children to the Savior. By wisdom and tact give them courage and hope. Through the grace of Christ they may be transformed in character, so that it may be said about them, "Of such is the kingdom of God."

# The Rich Young Ruler Lacked One Thing*

Now as He was going out on the road, one came running, knelt before Him, and asked Him, 'Good Teacher, what shall I do that I may inherit eternal life?' "

This young man, a ruler, had many possessions and a position of responsibility. He saw the love that Christ showed toward the children, and his heart burned with love for the Savior. He was so deeply moved that He ran after Christ and, kneeling at His feet, asked sincerely and earnestly the question so important to his life and to every human being.

"Why do you call Me good?" said Christ. "No one is good but One, that is, God." Jesus wanted to draw from him in what way he regarded Him as good. Did he realize that the One to whom he was speaking was the Son of God? What was the true feeling of his heart?

This ruler had a high opinion of his own righteousness, yet he felt the lack of something he did not possess. Could Jesus bless him and satisfy his heart's craving?

In reply, Jesus told him that obedience to the commandments of God was necessary if he wanted to obtain eternal life. The ruler's answer was positive: "All these things I have kept from my youth. What do I still lack?"

Christ looked into the face of the young man as if reading his life and searching his character. He loved him and hungered to give him peace and joy. "One thing you lack: Go your way, sell whatever you have and give to the poor, and you will have treasure in heaven; and come, take up the cross, and follow Me."

Christ was drawn to this young man. The Redeemer longed to create in him the power to see the necessity of heart devotion. He longed to see in him a humble and repentant heart, hiding its shortcomings in the perfection of Christ.

In this ruler Jesus saw just the help He needed in the work of salvation. If he would place himself under Christ's guidance, he would be a power for good. Christ, seeing into his character, loved him. Love for Christ was awakening in the ruler's heart, for love produces love. Jesus longed to see him become a coworker with Him. He longed to develop the excellence of his

---

* This chapter is based on Matthew 19:16–22; Mark 10:17–22; Luke 18:18–23.

character and to sanctify it to the Master's use. If the ruler had then given himself to Christ, how different would have been his future!

"You still lack one thing," Jesus said. "Sell all that you have and distribute to the poor, and you will have treasure in heaven; and come, follow Me." Christ read the ruler's heart. Only one thing he lacked, but that was a vital principle. He needed the love of God at the core of his life. If this lack went unfilled, it would prove fatal. His whole nature would become corrupted. In order for him to receive the love of God, he must surrender his supreme love of self.

Christ called for him to choose between heavenly treasure and worldly greatness. Self must yield; he must give his will into Christ's control. The young ruler had the privilege of becoming a co-heir with Christ to the heavenly treasure. But he must take up the cross and follow the Savior in the path of self-denial.

The choice was left with him. Jesus had shown him the fatal spot in his character. If he decided to follow Christ, he must obey His words in everything. He must turn from his ambitious projects. With earnest, anxious longing, the Savior looked at the young man, hoping he would yield to the invitation of the Spirit of God.

Christ's words were words of wisdom, though they appeared severe. The ruler's only hope of salvation was in accepting and obeying them. His position and possessions were exerting a subtle influence for evil on his character. If he cherished them, they would replace God in his affections.

## Did Jesus Demand Too Much?

The ruler, quick to understand all that Christ's words involved, became sad. He was a member of the honored council of the Jews, and Satan was tempting him with flattering prospects for the future. He wanted the heavenly treasure, but he also wanted the advantages his riches would bring. He desired eternal life, but the sacrifice seemed too great, and he went away sorrowful, "for he had great possessions."

His claim that he had kept the law of God was a deception. He showed that riches were his idol. He loved the gifts of God more than he loved the Giver. Christ had offered the young man fellowship with Himself. "Follow Me," He said. But the Savior was not as valuable to him as his own name in society or his possessions. To give up the seen for the unseen was too great a risk. He refused the offer of eternal life and went away. Ever after the world would receive his worship. Thousands pass through this ordeal, weighing Christ against the world, and many choose the world.

Christ's dealing with the young man contains lessons for us all. God has given us the rule of conduct that His servants must follow. It is obedience to His law—not merely a legal obedience, but an obedience that enters into the life and shows in the character. Only those who will say, "Lord, all I have and all I am is Yours," will God acknowledge as His sons and daughters. Think of what it means to say No to Christ. The Savior offers to share with us the work that God has given us to do. Only in this way can He save us.

God entrusts us with money, talents, and opportunities, that we may be His agents in helping the poor and the suffering. Those who use their entrusted gifts as God designs become co-workers with the Savior.

To those like the young ruler who are in high positions and have great possessions, it may seem too great a sacrifice to give up all in order to follow Christ. But God can accept nothing short of obedience. Self-surrender is the essence of Christ's teachings. There is no other way to save us than to cut away those things which, if we cling to them, will demoralize the whole being.

When Christ's followers give back to the Lord His own, they are accumulating treasure that they will receive when they hear the words, "Well done, good and faithful servant. . . . Enter into the joy of your lord." Matthew 25:23. The joy of seeing people eternally saved is the reward of all who put their feet in the footprints of Him who said, "Follow Me."

# The Raising of Lazarus*

Among the most faithful of Christ's disciples was Lazarus of Bethany, and the Savior loved him greatly. Christ performed the greatest of His miracles for Lazarus. The Savior loves all the human family, but He is bound to some by especially tender associations.

At the home of Lazarus, Jesus often found rest. The Savior had no home of His own. When tired, thirsting for human fellowship, He had been glad to escape to this peaceful household. Here He found a sincere welcome and pure, holy friendship.

As the crowds followed Christ through the open fields, He unfolded to them the beauties of the natural world. But they were slow to understand, and in the home at Bethany Christ found rest from the weary conflict of public life. Here He did not need to speak in parables.

As Christ gave His wonderful lessons, Mary sat at His feet, a reverent and devoted listener. On one occasion, Christ's first visit to Bethany, Martha was preparing the meal. She went to Jesus, saying, "Lord, do You not care that my sister has left me to serve alone? Therefore tell her to help

me." Jesus answered her with mild and patient words: "Martha, Martha, you are worried and troubled about many things. But one thing is needed, and Mary has chosen that good part, which will not be taken away from her." Mary was storing in her mind words from the Savior's lips, words more precious to her than earth's most costly jewels.

Martha needed less anxiety for the things that pass away and more for those things that endure forever. The cause of Christ needs Marthas, with their zeal in active religious work, but let them first sit with Mary at the feet of Jesus. Let diligence and energy be sanctified by the grace of Christ.

Sorrow entered the peaceful home where Jesus had rested. Lazarus was struck with sudden illness, and his sisters sent a message to the Savior, saying, "Lord, behold, he whom You love is sick." They saw the violence of the disease that had seized their brother, but they knew that Christ had shown that He was able to heal all kinds of diseases. They made no urgent demand for Him to come immediately but thought He would be with them as soon as He could reach Bethany.

---

* This chapter is based on Luke 10:38–42; John 11:1–44.

They waited anxiously. As long as the spark of life was in their brother, they prayed and watched for Jesus to come. But the messenger returned without Him. Yet he brought the message, "This sickness is not unto death," and they clung to the hope that Lazarus would live. When he died, they were bitterly disappointed, but they felt the sustaining grace of Christ.

When Christ heard the message, He gave no sign of the sorrow the disciples expected Him to show. He said, "This sickness is not unto death, but for the glory of God, that the Son of God may be glorified through it." For two days Jesus remained in the place where He was. This delay was a mystery to the disciples, for His strong affection for the family at Bethany was well known.

During the two days, Christ seemed to have dismissed the message from His mind. The disciples thought of John the Baptist. With the power to perform miracles, why had Jesus permitted John to languish in prison and die a violent death? The Pharisees presented this question as an unanswerable argument against Christ's claim to be the Son of God. The Savior had warned His disciples of trials, losses, and persecution. Would He forsake them in trial? They were all deeply troubled.

After waiting two days, Jesus said, "Let us go to Judea again." If Jesus were going to Judea, the disciples questioned why He had waited two days. But anxiety for Christ and for themselves was now uppermost in their minds. They could see nothing but danger in the course He was about to pursue. " 'Rabbi,' " they said, " 'lately the Jews sought to stone You, and are You going there again?' Jesus answered, 'Are there not twelve hours in the day?' " "I am under the guidance of My Father. As long as I do His will, My life is safe. I have entered on the last part of My day; but while any of this time remains, I am safe."

"If anyone walks in the day, he does not stumble, because he sees the light of this world." The light of God's guiding Spirit gives him a clear understanding of his duty and leads him until the close of his work. "But if one walks in the night, he stumbles, because the light is not in him." He who walks in a path of his own choosing will stumble. Wherever he may be, he is not secure.

"These things He said, and after that He said to them, 'Our friend Lazarus sleeps, but I go that I may wake him up.' " In thinking of the danger their Master was about to be in by going to Jerusalem, the disciples had almost forgotten the mourning family at Bethany. But not so with Christ. The disciples had been tempted to think that Jesus did not have the tender love for Lazarus and his sisters that they thought He had. But the words, "Our friend Lazarus sleeps," awakened right feelings in their minds. Christ had not forgotten His suffering friends.

"Then His disciples said, 'Lord, if he sleeps he will get well.' However, Jesus spoke of his death, but they thought He was speaking of taking rest in sleep." Christ describes death as a sleep to His believing children. Their life is hid with Christ in God, and until the last trumpet shall sound,

those who die will sleep in Him. See
1 Corinthians 15:51-54.

"Then Jesus said to them plainly,
'Lazarus is dead. And I am glad for
your sakes that I was not there, that
you may believe. Nevertheless let us
go to him.' "

The disciples were amazed at
Christ's words when He said, "Lazarus
is dead. And I am glad . . . that I was
not there." Did the Savior avoid the
home of His suffering friends by His
own choice? But Christ saw the whole
scene, and His grace upheld the
mourning sisters. Jesus witnessed the
sorrow of their aching hearts as their
brother wrestled with death. But Christ
had to think of not only the loved ones
at Bethany. He had His disciples'
training to consider. They were to be
His representatives to the world. For
their sake He permitted Lazarus to
die. If He had restored him from illness to health, the miracle that is the
most positive evidence of His divine
character would not have happened.

If Christ had been in the sickroom,
death could not have aimed his javelin
at Lazarus. Therefore Christ remained
away. He permitted the suffering sisters to see their brother put in the
grave. He suffered every pang of sorrow that they endured. He loved them
no less because He delayed, but He
knew that for them, for Lazarus, for
Himself, and for His disciples, there
was a victory to gain.

For all who are reaching out to feel
the guiding hand of God, the moment
of greatest discouragement is the time
when divine help is nearest. They will
look back thankfully on the darkest
part of their way. Through every

temptation and trial God will bring
them out with firmer faith and a richer
experience.

Christ had delayed so that by raising Lazarus from the dead He could
give His stubborn, unbelieving people
another evidence that He was truly
"the resurrection and the life." He was
unwilling to give up all hope for the
people of Israel, and He determined to
give them one more evidence that He
was the only One who could bring life
and immortality to light. This was the
reason that He delayed in going to
Bethany.

When He reached Bethany, Jesus
sent a messenger to the sisters with
the news that He had arrived, but He
remained in a quiet place along the
way. The Jews' great outward display
when friends or relatives died was not
in harmony with the spirit of Christ.
He heard the wailing from the hired
mourners and did not want to meet
the sisters in that scene of confusion.
Some of Christ's bitterest enemies
were among the mourning friends.
Christ knew their plans, and so He did
not make His presence known immediately.

The message was given to Martha
so quietly that others, even Mary, did
not hear. Martha went out to meet her
Lord, but Mary sat still in her sorrow,
making no sound.

Martha's heart was troubled with
conflicting emotions. In Christ's expressive face she read the same tenderness and love that had always been
there, but she thought of the brother
she had loved so much. With grief
surging in her heart because Christ
had not come before, she said, "Lord,

if You had been here, my brother would not have died." Over and over again, the sisters had repeated these words.

Martha had no desire to go over the past, but looking into the face of love, she added, "But even now I know that whatever You ask of God, God will give You."

Jesus encouraged her, saying, "Your brother will rise again." His answer fastened Martha's thoughts on the resurrection of the just, so that in the resurrection of Lazarus she could see a pledge of resurrection for all the righteous dead.

Martha answered, "I know that he will rise again in the resurrection at the last day." Seeking to give a true direction to her faith, Jesus declared, "I am the resurrection and the life." In Christ is life—original, unborrowed, underived. "He who has the Son has life." 1 John 5:12. Jesus said, "He who believes in Me, though he may die, he shall live. And whoever lives and believes in Me shall never die. Do you believe this?" In this statement, Christ looked forward to the time of His second coming. Then the righteous dead will be raised incorruptible, and the living righteous will be translated to heaven without seeing death. The raising of Lazarus would represent the resurrection of all the righteous dead. By His word and His works Jesus asserted His right and power to give eternal life.

To the Savior's words, "Do you believe?" Martha responded, "Yes, Lord, I believe that You are the Christ, the Son of God, who is to come into the world." She confessed her faith in His divinity and her confidence that He was able to do whatever He chose.

"When she had said these things, she went her way and secretly called Mary her sister, saying, 'The Teacher has come and is calling for you.' " She delivered her message as quietly as possible, since the priests and rulers were prepared to arrest Jesus whenever they could. The mourners' cries prevented others from hearing her words.

When Mary heard the message, she rose quickly and left the room. The mourners thought that she had gone to the grave to weep, so they followed her. When she reached the place where Jesus was waiting, she said with quivering lips, "Lord, if You had been here, my brother would not have died." The cries of the mourners were painful to her, for she longed for a few quiet words alone with Jesus.

"Therefore, when Jesus saw her weeping, and the Jews who came with her weeping, He groaned in the spirit and was troubled." He saw that for many of them, what passed as grief was only for show. Some who now were putting on a hypocritical sorrow would plan the death of not only the mighty Miracle Worker, but also the one He would raise from the dead. "Where have you laid him?" He asked. "Lord, come and see." Together they went on to the grave. Many people had loved Lazarus, and his sisters wept with breaking hearts while his friends mingled their tears with those of the sorrowing sisters. In view of this human distress and of the fact that the grieving friends could mourn while the Savior of the world stood by, "Jesus wept." The Son of God had taken human nature on Himself and was moved by human sorrow. Suffering always awakens sympathy in His tender, pitying heart.

But Jesus wept not only out of sympathy with Mary and Martha. Christ wept because the weight of the grief of ages was on Him. He saw the terrible results of breaking God's law. He saw that the conflict between good and evil had been constant. He saw the suffering and sorrow, tears, and death that were to afflict the human family through all the ages in all lands. The troubles of the sinful race were heavy on His heart, and His tears flowed freely as He longed to relieve all their distress.

Lazarus had been placed in a cave, and a massive stone had been rolled in front of the entrance. "Take away the stone," Christ said. Thinking that He only wanted to look upon the dead, Martha objected, saying that the body had been buried four days, and corruption had already begun its work. This statement, made before Jesus raised Lazarus, left no room for Christ's enemies to say that He had carried out a deception. When Christ raised the daughter of Jairus, He had said, "The child is not dead, but sleeping." Mark 5:39. Because she had been raised immediately after her death, the Pharisees declared that the child had not been dead, that Christ Himself said she was only asleep. They had tried to make it appear that His miracles were not genuine. But in this case, no one could deny that Lazarus was dead.

When the Lord is about to do a work, Satan prompts someone to object. Martha was unwilling for the decomposing body to be seen. Her faith had not grasped the true meaning of Jesus' promise. Christ reproved Martha in the gentlest way: "Did I not say to you that if you would believe you would see the glory of God?" "You have My word. Natural impossibilities cannot prevent the work of the Omnipotent One." Unbelief is not humility. Unquestioning belief in Christ's word is true humility, true self-surrender.

"Take away the stone," Christ could have commanded the angels close by His side to remove the stone. But He wanted to show that humanity is to cooperate with divinity. What human power can do, divine power is not summoned to do.

Those standing near obeyed Jesus' command and rolled away the stone. Everything was done openly and deliberately. Everyone saw that there was no deception. They saw the body of Lazarus, cold and silent in death. Surprised and expectant, the people stood around the tomb, waiting to see what would happen.

A sacred solemnity came over everyone there. Christ stepped closer to the tomb. Lifting His eyes to heaven, He said, "Father, I thank You that You have heard Me." Christ's enemies had accused Him of blasphemy because He claimed to be the Son of God. But here, with perfect confidence, Christ declared that He was the Son of God.

Christ was careful to make it clear that He did not work independently of His Father. It was by faith and prayer that He worked His miracles. Christ wanted everyone to know His relationship with His Father. "Father," He said, "I thank You that You have heard Me. And I know that You always hear Me, but because of the people who are standing by I said this, that they may believe that You sent Me." Here the disciples and the people would see that Christ's claim was not a deception.

"Now when He had said these things, He cried with a loud voice, 'Lazarus, come forth!' " Divinity flashed through humanity. In His face, which was lighted up by the glory of God, the people saw the assurance of His power. Every eye was fastened on the cave, every ear listening to catch the slightest sound. With intense interest all waited for the evidence that was to prove Christ's claim to be the Son of God or to extinguish the hope forever.

There was a stir in the silent tomb, then he who was dead stood at the door of the sepulchre. The grave-clothes restricted his movements, so Christ said to the astonished spectators, "Loose him, and let him go." Again they were shown that humanity is to work for humanity. They set Lazarus free, and he stood before the crowd, not as someone wasted by disease but as a man in the prime of life. His eyes beamed with intelligence and love for His Savior. In adoration he threw himself at Jesus' feet.

At first the onlookers were speechless with amazement; then indescribable rejoicing followed. The sisters received their brother back to life as the gift of God, and then brokenly, with joyful tears, they expressed their thanks to the Savior. But while everyone was rejoicing in this reunion, Jesus quietly left the scene. When they looked for the Life-Giver, He was not to be found.

# Priests and Rulers Continue Plotting*

News of the raising of Lazarus soon arrived at Jerusalem. Spies quickly supplied the Jewish rulers with the facts. They called a meeting of the Sanhedrin at once to decide what to do. This mighty miracle was the crowning evidence God offered that He had sent His Son into the world for their salvation. It was a demonstration of divine power sufficient to convince every mind that was under the control of reason and an enlightened conscience.

But the priests were only enraged by this new miracle. Jesus had raised the dead in the full light of day and before a crowd of witnesses. No trick could explain away such evidence. For this reason the priests were more determined than ever to put a stop to Christ's work.

The Sadducees had not been so full of hatred toward Christ as the Pharisees were, but now they were thoroughly alarmed. They did not believe in a resurrection of the dead, reasoning that it would be impossible for a dead body to be brought to life. But by a few words from Christ, they were shown to be ignorant of both the Scriptures and the power of God.

How could they turn people away from One who had successfully robbed the grave of its dead? They could not deny the miracle, and they did not know how to counteract its effect. After the resurrection of Lazarus, the Sadducees decided that only Jesus' death could stop His fearless denunciations against them.

The Pharisees believed in the resurrection, and they could not avoid seeing that this miracle was evidence that the Messiah was among them. But from the beginning, they had hated Him because He had torn aside the cloak hiding their moral deformity. The pure religion that He taught had condemned their hollow claims to piety. They thirsted for revenge for His pointed rebukes. Several times they had tried to stone Him, but He had quietly slipped away.

To stir up the Romans against Him, the Pharisees had claimed that He was trying to undermine Roman authority. They had tried every false accusation to cut Him off from influencing the people. But their attempts had failed. The crowds who witnessed His works and heard His pure teachings knew that these were not the

---

* This chapter is based on John 11:47–54.

deeds and words of a Sabbath breaker or blasphemer. In desperation, the Jews had finally passed a decree that anyone who professed faith in Jesus would be expelled from the synagogue.

So Pharisees and Sadducees were more nearly united than ever before. They became one in their opposition to Christ.

At this time the Sanhedrin was not a legal assembly. It existed only by tolerance. Some of its members questioned the wisdom of putting Christ to death. They feared that this would stir up a revolt. The Sadducees, united with the priests in hating Christ, wanted to be cautious, fearing that the Romans would take away their high standing.

### How the Holy Spirit Tried to Help Them

In this council, assembled to plan the death of Christ, the Witness who had heard the boastful words of Nebuchadnezzar and witnessed the idol-worshiping feast of Belshazzar was now impressing the rulers with the work they were doing. Events in the life of Christ rose up before their minds so distinctly that they were alarmed. They remembered when Jesus, as a child of twelve, stood before the educated doctors of the law, asking questions that amazed them. The miracle Jesus had just performed bore witness that He was none other than the Son of God. Perplexed and troubled, the rulers asked, "What shall we do?" There was a division in the council.

While the council was in its greatest perplexity, Caiaphas, the high priest, arose. Proud and cruel, arrogant and intolerant, he spoke with great authority and assurance: "You know nothing at all, nor do you consider that it is expedient for us that one man should die for the people, and not that the whole nation should perish." Even if Jesus were innocent, He must be put out of the way. He was lessening the authority of the rulers, and if the people were to lose confidence in their rulers, the national power would be destroyed. After this miracle, the followers of Jesus would likely rise in revolt. "The Romans would then come," he said, "close our temple, and destroy us as a nation. What is the life of this Galilean compared with the nation? Is it not doing God a service to remove Him? Better that one man perish than that the whole nation be destroyed."

The policy Caiaphas recommended was based on a principle borrowed from heathenism. The dim consciousness that one was to die for the human race had led to human sacrifices. So by the sacrifice of Jesus, Caiaphas proposed to save the guilty nation, not *from* transgression, but *in* transgression, so that they could continue in sin.

At this council Christ's enemies had come under deep conviction. The Holy Spirit had impressed their minds. But Satan reminded them of the grievances they had suffered because of Christ. How little He had honored their righteousness! Paying no regard to their forms and ceremonies, He had encouraged sinners to go directly to God as a merciful Father and tell Him their wants. He had refused to acknowledge the theology of the rabbinical schools and hurt the priests' influence beyond repair by exposing their evil practices.

Except for a few who did not dare to speak their minds, the Sanhedrin received the words of Caiaphas as the words of God. Relief came to the council; the discord ended. They resolved to put Christ to death at the first good opportunity. These priests and rulers had come entirely under Satan's control, yet they were so deceived that they were well pleased with themselves. They thought of themselves as patriots seeking the nation's salvation.

To prevent the people from becoming incensed and bringing on them the violence they were planning for Jesus, the council delayed carrying out the sentence they had pronounced. The Savior knew that they would soon accomplish what they intended, but it was not His role to hurry the crisis, and He left that region, taking the disciples with Him.

Jesus had now given three years of public labor to the world. Everyone knew His self-denial, selfless kindness, purity, and devotion. Yet this short period was as long as the world could endure the presence of its Redeemer. He who was always touched by human suffering, who healed the sick, fed the hungry, and comforted the sorrowful, was driven away from the people He had worked so hard to save. He who broke the sleep of the dead and held thousands spellbound by His words of wisdom was unable to reach the hearts of those who were blinded by prejudice and hatred and who stubbornly rejected light.

# What Is the Highest Position?*

Passover was approaching, and again Jesus turned toward Jerusalem. In His heart He had the peace of perfect oneness with the Father's will, and with eager steps He pressed on toward the place of sacrifice. But a sense of mystery, of doubt and fear, came over the disciples. The Savior "was going before them; and they were amazed. And as they followed they were afraid."

Again Christ opened to the Twelve His betrayal and sufferings: " 'Behold, we are going up to Jerusalem, and all things that are written by the prophets concerning the Son of Man will be accomplished. For He will be delivered to the Gentiles and will be mocked and insulted and spit upon. They will scourge Him and kill Him. And the third day He will rise again.' But they understood none of these things; this saying was hidden from them, and they did not know the things which were spoken."

Had they not just been proclaiming everywhere, "The kingdom of heaven is at hand"? Had not Christ Himself given to the Twelve the special promise of positions of high honor in His kingdom? And had not the prophets foretold the glory of the Messiah's reign? In the light of these thoughts, His words about betrayal, persecution, and death seemed vague and shadowy. Whatever difficulties might come, they believed that He was soon to establish His kingdom.

John and his brother James had been among the first group who had left home and friends to be with Him. Their hearts seemed linked with His, and in the warmth of their love, they longed to be nearest to Him in His kingdom. Whenever he could, John took his place next to the Savior, and James longed to be honored with an equally close connection with Him.

Their mother had provided for Christ freely from her funds. With a mother's love and ambition for her sons, she coveted the most honored place for them in the new kingdom. Together mother and sons came to Jesus.

"What do you wish?" He questioned.

"Grant that these two sons of mine may sit, one on Your right hand and the other on the left, in Your kingdom."

Jesus read their hearts. He knew the depth of their attachment to Him.

---

* *This chapter is based on Matthew 20:20–28; Mark 10:32–45; Luke 18:31–34.*

Their love, though defiled by the earthliness of its human channel, flowed from the fountain of His own redeeming love.

"Are you able to drink the cup that I am about to drink, and be baptized with the baptism that I am baptized with?" They recalled His mysterious words, pointing to trial and suffering, yet they answered confidently, "We are able."

"You will indeed drink My cup, and be baptized with the baptism that I am baptized with," He said. John and James were to share with their Master in suffering: James, the first of the disciples to die by the sword; John, the longest of all to endure toil and persecution.

"But to sit on My right hand and on My left is not Mine to give, but it is for those for whom it is prepared by My Father." In the kingdom of God, we do not gain high position through favoritism nor receive it through arbitrary grants. It is the result of character. The crown and the throne are indications of a condition we reach through our Lord Jesus Christ. The one who stands nearest to Christ will be the one who on earth has drunk most deeply of the His spirit of self-sacrificing love—love that moves the disciple to give all, to live and work and sacrifice, even to death, for the saving of humanity.

The other ten disciples were greatly displeased. The highest place in the kingdom was just what every one of them was seeking for himself, and they were angry that the two disciples seemed to have gained an advantage over them.

Jesus said to the offended disciples, "You know that those who are considered rulers over the Gentiles lord it over them, and their great ones exercise authority over them. Yet it shall not be so among you."

In the kingdoms of the world, position meant exalting oneself. The people existed for the benefit of the ruling classes. Wealth and education were ways to gain control of the masses. The higher classes were to think, decide, and rule; the lower, to obey and serve. Like everything else, religion was a matter of authority.

## A Kingdom of Different Principles

Christ was establishing a kingdom on different principles. He called people not to authority, but to service, the strong to help the infirmities of the weak. Power, position, talent, education, placed those who possessed them under greater obligation to serve.

"The Son of Man did not come to be served, but to serve, and to give His life a ransom for many." The principle on which Christ acted is to motivate the members of the church, His body. The greatest ones in the kingdom of Christ are those who follow the example He has given.

The words of Paul reveal the true dignity and honor of the Christian life: "Though I am free from all men, I have made myself a servant to all," "not seeking my own profit, but the profit of many, that they may be saved." 1 Corinthians 9:19; 10:33.

In matters of conscience, no one is to control another's mind or dictate his duty. God gives everyone freedom to think and to follow his own convictions. In matters where principle is involved, "let each be fully convinced in his own mind." Romans 14:5. The angels of heaven do not come to earth to rule and to demand honor, but to cooperate with men and women in uplifting humanity.

The principles and words of the Savior's teaching lived in John's memory to his final days. The burden of his testimony was, "This is the message that you heard from the beginning, that we should love one another. . . . By this we know love, because He laid down His life for us. And we also ought to lay down our lives for the brethren." 1 John 3:11, 16.

This spirit characterized the early church. After the outpouring of the Holy Spirit, "the multitude of those who believed were of one heart and soul. . . . And with great power the apostles gave witness to the resurrection of the Lord Jesus." Acts 4:32, 33.

# The Little Man Who Became Important*

The city of Jericho was surrounded by lush tropical plants and trees. Running springs watered it, and it gleamed like an emerald in the setting of limestone hills and desolate ravines. The city was a great center of commerce, and Roman officials and soldiers, with strangers from many places, were found there. The collection of customs on the transport of goods made it the home of many tax collectors.

The "chief tax collector," Zacchaeus, was a Jew, and his countrymen detested him. His rank and wealth were the reward of a profession that they regarded as another name for injustice and extortion. Yet this wealthy customs officer was not entirely the hardened man that he seemed. Zacchaeus had heard of Jesus. The report had spread far and wide that He had treated society's outcasts with kindness and courtesy. John the Baptist had preached at the Jordan, and Zacchaeus had heard of his call to repentance. Now, hearing the words reported to have come from the Great Teacher, he felt that he was a sinner in God's sight. Yet what he had heard of Jesus kindled hope in his heart. Repentance,

reformation of life, was possible, even for him. Was not one of the new Teacher's most trusted disciples a tax collector? Zacchaeus immediately began to follow the conviction that had taken hold of him and to make restitution to those he had wronged.

When the news spread through Jericho that Jesus was entering the town, Zacchaeus determined to see Him. The tax collector longed to look on the face of the One whose words had brought hope to his heart.

The streets were crowded, and Zacchaeus, who was small, could see nothing over the heads of the people. So, running a little ahead of the crowd to a wide-spreading fig tree, he climbed to a seat among the branches. As the procession passed below, Zacchaeus scanned the crowd eagerly to locate the one Person he longed to see.

Suddenly, just beneath the fig tree, the people came to a standstill, and One looked upward whose glance seemed to read his heart. Almost doubting his senses, the man in the tree heard Jesus say, "Zacchaeus, make haste and come down, for today I must stay at your house."

Walking as if in a dream, Zac-

---

* This chapter is based on Luke 19:1–10.

chaeus led the way toward his own home. But the rabbis, with scowling faces, complained in scorn that "He has gone to be a guest with a man who is a sinner."

Zacchaeus had been overwhelmed at Christ's condescension in paying any attention to him, so unworthy. Now love to his newfound Master prompted him to speak. He would make his repentance public. In the presence of the crowd, "Zacchaeus stood and said to the Lord, 'Look, Lord, I give half of my goods to the poor; and if I have taken anything from anyone by false accusation, I restore fourfold.' And Jesus said to him, 'Today salvation has come to this house, because he also is a son of Abraham.' "

Now the disciples had a demonstration of the truth of Christ's words, "The things which are impossible with men are possible with God." Luke 18:27. They saw how, through the grace of God, a rich man could enter into the kingdom.

Before Zacchaeus had even seen the face of Christ, he had confessed his sin. He had begun to carry out the teaching written for ancient Israel as well as for us: "If any of your kin fall into difficulty and become dependent on you, you shall support them; they shall live with you as though resident aliens. Do not take interest in advance or otherwise make a profit from them, but fear your God." "You shall not cheat one another, but you shall fear your God; for I am the Lord your God." Leviticus 25:35, 36, 17, NRSV. The very first response of Zacchaeus to Christ's love was to show compas-

sion toward the poor and suffering.

The tax collectors cooperated with one another to oppress the people and support each other in their fraudulent practices. But as soon as Zacchaeus yielded to the Holy Spirit, he put aside every shady practice.

No repentance is genuine that does not result in reformation. The righteousness of Christ is not a cloak to cover unconfessed and unforsaken sin. It is a principle of life that transforms the character and controls the conduct. Holiness is wholeness for God, entire surrender of heart and life to the principles of heaven to live within us.

In business life Christians are to represent to the world the way in which our Lord would conduct business. In every transaction, we are to show that God is our teacher. "Holiness to the Lord" is to be written on ledgers, deeds, receipts, and bills of sale. By abandoning unrighteous practices, every converted person will show that Christ has entered his heart. Like Zacchaeus, he will give proof of his sincerity by making restitution. "If the wicked restores the pledge, gives back what he has stolen, and walks in the statutes of life without committing iniquity, he shall surely live." Ezekiel 33:15.

If we have injured others, been deceptive in trade, or defrauded anyone, even though it might be within the letter of the law, we should confess our wrong and make restitution as far as it lies in our power. It is right to restore not only what we have taken, but all that it would have accumulated if wisely used during the time we had it.

To Zacchaeus, the Savior said, "Today salvation has come to this house." Christ went to his home to give him lessons of truth and to instruct his household in the things of the kingdom. Shut out from the synagogues by the contempt of rabbis and worshipers, now they gathered in their own home around the divine Teacher and heard the words of life.

When we receive Christ as a personal Savior, salvation comes to our lives. Zacchaeus had received Jesus, not merely as a passing guest, but as One to live in the temple of the heart. The scribes and Pharisees accused him as a sinner, but the Lord recognized him as a son of Abraham. See Galatians 3:7, 29.

# Mary Anoints Jesus*

Simon of Bethany was one of the few Pharisees who had openly joined Christ's followers. He hoped that Jesus might be the Messiah, but had not accepted Him as a Savior. His character was not transformed. His principles were unchanged.

Jesus had healed Simon of leprosy, and Simon wanted to show his gratitude. At the time of Christ's last visit to Bethany, he made a feast for the Savior and His disciples. This feast brought together many of the Jews, who watched His movements closely, some with unfriendly eyes.

As He usually did, the Savior had sought rest at the home of Lazarus. Many of the people flocked to Bethany, some out of sympathy with Jesus, and others from curiosity to see Lazarus, who had been raised from the dead. With assurance and power, Lazarus declared that Jesus was the Son of God.

The people were eager to see whether Lazarus would go with Jesus to Jerusalem and whether the Prophet would be crowned king at the Passover. The priests and rulers could hardly wait for the opportunity to re-move Him forever from their way. They remembered how often He had evaded their murderous plots, and they were afraid that He would remain away. They questioned among themselves, "What do you think—that He will not come to the feast?"

They called a council. Since the raising of Lazarus the people were so favorable to Christ that it would be dangerous to arrest Him openly. So the authorities decided to take Him secretly and carry out the trial as quietly as possible. They hoped that when people heard about His condemnation, the fickle tide of public opinion would turn in their favor.

But as long as Lazarus lived, the priests and rabbis knew they were not secure. The existence of a man who had been in the grave four days and had been restored by a word from Jesus would cause a reaction. The people would avenge themselves on their leaders for taking the life of One who could perform such a miracle. The Sanhedrin therefore decided that Lazarus also must die.

While this plotting was going on at Jerusalem, Jesus and His friends were

---

* This chapter is based on Matthew 26:6–13; Mark 14:3–11; Luke 7:36–50; John 11:55–57; 12:1–11.

invited to Simon's feast. At the table, Simon sat on one side of the Savior and Lazarus on the other. Martha served, but Mary was earnestly listening to every word from the lips of Jesus. In His mercy, Jesus had pardoned her sins and called her brother from the grave, and gratitude filled Mary's heart. She had heard Jesus speak of His approaching death, and she had longed to honor Him in some special way.

At great personal sacrifice she had purchased an alabaster box of "ointment of spikenard, very costly," with which to anoint His body. But now many were declaring that He was about to be crowned king. Her grief was turned to joy, and she was eager to be the first to honor her Lord. Breaking her box of ointment, she poured its contents on the head and feet of Jesus. Then, as she knelt weeping, moistening them with her tears, she wiped His feet with her long, flowing hair. Her movements might have gone unnoticed, but the ointment filled the room with its fragrance and announced her act to everyone there.

## Why Judas Was Annoyed

Judas witnessed this act with great displeasure. He began to whisper his complaints to those near him, blaming Christ for allowing such waste. Judas, the treasurer for the disciples, had secretly taken funds for his own use from their little supply of money, in this way reducing their resources to almost nothing. He was eager to put into the money-bag all that he could get. When one of their group bought something that he did not think was essential, he would

say, "Why was not the cost of this put into the bag that I carry for the poor?"

Mary's act was in such dramatic contrast to his selfishness that he was put to shame. He tried to claim a worthy motive for objecting to her gift: " 'Why was this fragrant oil not sold for three hundred denarii and given to the poor?' This he said, not that he cared for the poor, but because he was a thief." If Mary's ointment had been sold and the proceeds come into his possession, the poor would have received no benefit.

As a financier, Judas thought of himself as far above his fellow disciples, and he had gained a strong influence over them. His professed sympathy for the poor deceived them. The murmur went round the table, "Why this waste? For this fragrant oil might have been sold for much and given to the poor."

Mary heard the criticism. Her heart trembled within her. She was afraid that her sister would criticize her for extravagance. The Master, too, might think her wasteful. She was about to shrink away, when she heard the voice of her Lord, "Let her alone. Why do you trouble her?" He knew that in this act she had expressed her gratitude for the forgiveness of her sins. Lifting His voice above the rumblings of criticism, He said, "She has done a good work for Me. For you have the poor with you always, and whenever you wish you may do them good; but Me you do not have always. She has done what she could. She has come beforehand to anoint My body for burial."

The fragrant gift that Mary had

thought to lavish on the dead body of the Savior she poured on His living form. At His burial its sweetness could only have filled the tomb; now it gladdened His heart. She was pouring out her love while the Savior was conscious of her devotion, even as she was anointing Him for the burial. When He went down into the darkness of His great trial, He carried with Him the memory of that deed, a foretaste of the love that would be His from His redeemed ones forever.

### Mary Had Obeyed the Holy Spirit's Promptings

Mary did not know the full significance of her deed of love. She could not explain why she had chosen that occasion to anoint Jesus. The Holy Spirit had planned for her, and she had obeyed His promptings. Inspiration is not obligated to give its reasons. An unseen presence, it moves the heart to action. It is its own justification.

Christ told Mary the meaning of her act: "In pouring this fragrant oil on My body, she did it for My burial." As the alabaster box was broken and filled the house with fragrance, so Christ's body was to be broken; but He was to rise from the tomb, and the fragrance of His life was to fill the earth. "Christ also has loved us and given Himself for us, an offering and a sacrifice to God for a sweet-smelling aroma." Ephesians 5:2.

"Assuredly, I say to you," Christ declared, "wherever this gospel is preached in the whole world, what this woman has done will also be told as a memorial to her." The Savior spoke with certainty about His gospel that was to be preached throughout the world. And as far as the gospel extended, Mary's gift would spread its fragrance, and hearts would be blessed through her generous, spontaneous act. Kingdoms would rise and fall, the names of conquerors would be forgotten, but this woman's deed would live forever on the pages of sacred history. Until time is no more, that broken alabaster box will tell the story of God's abundant love for a fallen race.

What a sharp lesson Christ could have given to Judas! He who reads the motives of every heart might have revealed to those at the feast the dark chapters in Judas's experience. Instead of sympathizing with the poor, he was robbing them of the money intended for their relief. But if Christ had unmasked Judas, this would have seemed like a reason for the betrayal. Judas would have gained sympathy, even among the disciples. The Savior avoided giving him an excuse for his evil bargain.

### Judas Goes From the Feast to Negotiate Jesus' Betrayal

But the look that Jesus gave Judas convinced him that the Savior saw through his hypocrisy and read his corrupt character. And in praising Mary's action, Christ rebuked Judas. The reproof stirred up resentment in his heart, and he went directly to the palace of the high priest and offered to betray Jesus into their hands.

The leaders of Israel had been given the privilege of receiving Christ as their Savior, without money and without price. But they refused the precious Gift and bought their Lord for thirty pieces of silver.

Judas resented Mary's gift of costly ointment to Jesus. His heart burned with envy that the Savior received a gift suitable for the kings of the earth. For an amount far less than the ointment cost, he betrayed his Lord.

The disciples were not like Judas. They loved the Savior but did not rightly understand His character. The wise men from the East, who knew so little of Jesus, had shown that they understood more truly the honor due Him.

Christ values acts of heartfelt courtesy. He did not refuse the simplest flower that a child plucked and offered to Him in love. He accepted the offerings of children, and He blessed the givers. The Scriptures mention Mary's anointing of Jesus as a way to distinguish her from the other Marys. Acts of love and reverence for Jesus are an evidence of faith in Him as the Son of God.

Christ accepted Mary's wealth of pure affection which His disciples did not, would not, understand. It was the love of Christ that drove her to action. That ointment was a symbol of the giver's heart, the outward demonstration of a love fed by heavenly streams until it overflowed.

The disciples never appreciated, as they should have, the loneliness of Christ in living the life of humanity. He was often sad because He knew that if they were under the influence of the heavenly angels that accompanied Him, they too would think no offering to be valuable enough to declare their hearts' affection.

## Jesus Was Never Really Appreciated

When Jesus was no longer with them and they felt like sheep without a shepherd, they began to see how they could have brought gladness to His heart. They no longer heaped blame on Mary, but on themselves. Oh, if they could have taken back their criticism, presenting the poor as more worthy of the gift than Christ! They felt the reproof keenly as they took the bruised body of their Lord from the cross.

Today, few appreciate all that Christ is to them. If they did, they would express the great love of Mary. They would think that nothing was too costly to give for Christ, no self-denial or self-sacrifice too great to endure for His sake.

The words spoken in indignation, "Why this waste?" brought vividly before Christ the greatest sacrifice ever made—the gift of Himself as the atoning sacrifice for a lost world. From a human point of view, the plan of salvation is a reckless waste of mercies and resources. The heavenly universe properly looks with amazement on the human family who refuse the riches of the boundless love expressed in Christ. Well may they exclaim, "Why this great waste?"

But the atonement for a lost world was to be full, abundant, and complete. Christ's offering could not be restricted to just the number of people who would accept the Gift. The plan of redemption is not a waste because it does not accomplish all that its liberality has provided for. There must be enough, and more than enough.

Simon the host was surprised at Jesus' response, and he said in his heart, "This man, if He were a prophet, would know who and what manner of woman this is who is touching Him, for she is a sinner."

Because Christ allowed this woman to approach Him, because He did not reject her indignantly as someone whose sins were too great to be forgiven, because He did not show that He realized she had fallen, Simon was tempted to think that Christ was not a prophet. But it was Simon's ignorance of God and of Christ that led him to think as he did.

## How God Really Acts

Simon did not realize that God's Son must act in God's way, with compassion, tenderness, and mercy. Simon's way was to ignore Mary's repentant service. Her act of kissing Christ's feet and anointing them with ointment was exasperating to his hardheartedness. He thought that Christ should recognize sinners and rebuke them.

To this unspoken thought, the Savior answered, " 'Simon, I have something to say to you. . . . There was a certain creditor who had two debtors. One owed five hundred denarii, and the other fifty. And when they had nothing with which to repay, he freely forgave them both. Tell Me, therefore, which of them will love him more?' Simon answered and said, 'I suppose the one whom he forgave more.' And He said to him, 'You have rightly judged.' "

As Nathan did with David (2 Samuel 12:1–7), Christ gave His host the burden of pronouncing sentence on himself. Simon had led into sin the woman he now despised. He had

deeply wronged her. By the two debtors of the parable, Jesus represented Simon and the woman. Jesus did not intend to teach that the two of them should feel different degrees of obligation, for each owed a debt of gratitude that they could never repay. But Jesus wanted to show Simon that his sin was as much greater than hers as a debt of five hundred denarii exceeds a debt of fifty.

Simon now began to see himself in a new light. He saw how Jesus, who was more than a prophet, regarded Mary. Shame overcame him, and he realized that he was in the presence of One superior to himself.

"I entered your house," Christ continued, "you gave Me no water for My feet, [but with tears of repentance Mary has washed My feet and wiped them with the hair of her head.] You gave Me no kiss, but this woman, [whom you despise,] has not ceased to kiss My feet since the time I came in." Christ recounted the opportunities Simon had had to show his appreciation for what his Lord had done for him.

The Heart Searcher read the motive that led to Mary's action; He also saw the spirit that prompted Simon's words. "Do you see this woman?" He said to him. "I say to you, her sins, which are many, are forgiven, for she loved much. But to whom little is forgiven, the same loves little."

Simon had thought he honored Jesus by inviting Him to his house. But now he saw himself as he really was. He saw that his religion had been a robe of Pharisaism. He had despised the compassion of Jesus. He had not recognized Him as God's representative. Mary was a sinner pardoned; he was a sinner unpardoned.

## How Simon's Pride Was Humbled

Simon was touched by Jesus' kindness in not openly rebuking him in front of his guests. Jesus had not treated him as he desired Mary to be treated. He saw that Jesus had tried by pitying kindness to subdue his heart. Stern denunciation would have hardened him against repentance, but patient correction convinced him of his error. He saw how large was the debt he owed his Lord. He repented, and the proud Pharisee became a humble, self-sacrificing disciple.

Christ knew the circumstances that had shaped Mary's life. He could have extinguished every spark of hope in her soul, but He did not. He had lifted her from despair and ruin. Seven times she had heard Him rebuke the demons that controlled her heart and mind. She had heard His strong cries to the Father in her behalf. She knew how offensive sin is to His unblemished purity, and in His strength she had overcome.

When her case seemed hopeless to human eyes, Christ saw capabilities for good in Mary. The plan of redemption has granted great possibilities to humanity, and these would be realized in Mary. Through His grace she became a partaker of the divine nature. The one who had fallen, whose mind had been a home for demons, came near to the Savior in fellowship and ministry. Mary sat at His feet and learned from Him. Mary poured the precious anointing oil on His head and bathed His feet with her tears. Mary stood beside the cross and followed Him to the sepulchre. Mary was first at the tomb after His resurrection. Mary first proclaimed a risen Savior.

Jesus knows the circumstances of every person. You may say, "I am sinful, very sinful." You may be; but the worse you are, the more you need Jesus. He turns no weeping, repentant one away. He freely pardons everyone who comes to Him for forgiveness and restoration.

Those who turn to Him for refuge, Christ unites to His own divine-human nature. No human being or evil angel can condemn them. They stand beside the great Sin Bearer in the light streaming from the throne of God. "Who shall bring a charge against God's elect? It is God who justifies. Who is he who condemns? It is Christ who died, and furthermore is also risen, who is even at the right hand of God, who also makes intercession for us." Romans 8:33, 34.

# Jesus Acclaimed as Israel's King*

Five hundred years before Christ's birth, the prophet Zechariah foretold the coming of the King to Israel:

"Rejoice greatly, O daughter of Zion!
Shout, O daughter of Jerusalem!
Behold, your King is coming to you;
He is just and having salvation,
Lowly and riding on a donkey,
A colt, the foal of a donkey."
                              Zechariah 9:9

He who had refused royal honors for so long now came to Jerusalem as the Promised Heir to David's throne.

On the first day of the week, Christ made His triumphal entry. Crowds who had flocked to see Him at Bethany went with Him. Many who were on their way to keep the Passover joined the assembly. All nature seemed to rejoice. The trees were clothed in green, and their blossoms gave off a delicate fragrance. The hope of the new kingdom was again springing up.

Jesus had sent two disciples to bring Him a donkey and its colt. Although "the cattle on a thousand hills" (Psalm 50:10) are His, He was dependent on a stranger's kindness for an animal on which to enter Jerusalem as its King. But again His divinity was revealed, even in the detailed directions given. As He foretold, the request, "The Lord has need of them," was readily granted. The disciples spread their garments on the donkey and seated their Master on it. Jesus had always traveled on foot, and the disciples were amazed that He would now choose to ride. But hope brightened in their hearts with the thought that He was about to enter the capital, proclaim Himself King, and assert His royal power. Excitement spread far and near, raising the expectations of the people to the highest pitch.

Christ was following the Jewish custom for a royal entry. Prophecy had foretold that the Messiah would come to His kingdom in this way. No sooner was He seated on the colt than the crowd proclaimed Him as Messiah, their King. In imagination, the disciples and the people saw the Roman armies driven from Jerusalem and Israel once more an independent nation. They all tried to outdo one another in paying Him honor and the respect of royalty. Unable to present

---

* This chapter is based on Matthew 21:1–11; Mark 11:1–10; Luke 19:29–44; John 12:12–19.

Him with costly gifts, they spread their outer garments as a carpet in the path and strewed the leafy branches of the olive and the palm in the way. With no royal banners to wave, they cut down the spreading palm fronds, nature's emblem of victory, and waved them high in the air.

Spectators mingling with the crowds asked, "Who is this? What does all this commotion signify?" They knew that Jesus had discouraged all efforts to place Him on the throne, and they were astonished to learn that this was He. What had brought about this change in Him who had declared that His kingdom was not of this world?

From the great numbers gathered to attend the Passover, thousands greeted Him with palm branches waving and with a burst of sacred song. The priests at the temple sounded the trumpet for evening service, but few responded, and the rulers said to one another in alarm, "The world has gone after Him!"

## Why Jesus Permitted This Demonstration

Never before had Jesus permitted such a demonstration. He clearly foresaw the result. It would bring Him to the cross. But He wanted to call attention to the sacrifice that was to crown His mission to a fallen world. He, the One who fulfilled the symbol of the Lamb, voluntarily set Himself apart as a sacrifice. His church in all the ages to follow must make His death a subject of deep thought and study. Every fact connected with it should be verified beyond a doubt. The events that preceded His great sacrifice must call attention to the sacrifice itself. After

such a demonstration as the one that marked His entry into Jerusalem, all eyes would follow His rapid progress to the final scene. This triumphal ride would be the talk of every tongue and bring Jesus before every mind. After His crucifixion, many would remember these events and be led to search the prophecies. They would be convinced that Jesus was the Messiah.

This day, which seemed to the disciples like the crowning day of their lives, would have been shadowed with clouds if they had known it was only a prelude to the death of their Master. He had told them repeatedly about His sacrifice, yet in the glad triumph they had forgotten His sorrowful words.

With few exceptions, all who joined the procession caught the inspiration of the hour. The shouts went up continually,

"Hosanna to the Son of David!
'Blessed is He who comes in the name of the Lord!'
Hosanna in the highest!"

## No Train of Mourning in This Triumph

Never had the world seen such a triumphal procession. All around the Savior were the glorious trophies of His loving labors for sinful man. These were the captives rescued from Satan's power. Leading the way were the blind He had restored to sight. Those who had been mute, whose tongues He had loosed, shouted the loudest hosannas. Cripples whom He had healed leaped with joy. Lepers He had cleansed spread their uncontaminated garments in His path. Awakened from the sleep of death, Lazarus led the donkey on which the Savior rode.

Many Pharisees, burning with envy, tried to silence the people, but their appeals and threats only increased the enthusiasm. As a last resort they confronted the Savior with condemning and threatening words: "Teacher, rebuke Your disciples." They declared that such noisy demonstrations were unlawful. But Jesus' reply silenced them: "I tell you that if these should keep silent, the stones would immediately cry out." The prophet Zechariah had foretold that scene of triumph. If human beings had failed to carry out the plan, God would have given voice to inanimate stones, and they would have hailed His Son with praise. As the silenced Pharisees drew back, hundreds of voices took up the words of Zechariah:

"Rejoice greatly, O daughter of Zion!
Shout, O daughter of Jerusalem!
Behold, your King is coming to you;
He is just and having salvation,
Lowly and riding on a donkey,
A colt, the foal of a donkey."

When the procession reached the top of the hill, Jesus and all the multitude stopped. Before them lay Jerusalem in its glory, bathed in the light of the setting sun. In regal grandeurs, the temple towered above all else, the pride and glory of the Jewish nation for many centuries. The Romans also took pride in its magnificence. Its strength and richness had made it one of the wonders of the world.

While the setting sun made the heavens glow, its radiant glory lighted up the pure white marble of the temple walls and sparkled on its goldcapped pillars. From the hill where Jesus stood, it had the appearance of a massive structure of snow, set with golden pinnacles, shining as if with glory borrowed from heaven.

## Jesus Breaks Down in Tears

Jesus gazed on the scene, and the crowds hushed their shouts, spellbound by the sudden vision of beauty. All eyes turned to the Savior. They were surprised and disappointed to see His eyes fill with tears and His body rock back and forth like a tree in a storm. A wail of anguish burst from His quivering lips, as if from a broken heart. What a sight for angels to witness! What a sight for the glad throng of people escorting Him to the glorious city, where they hoped He was about to reign! This sudden sorrow was like a note of wailing in a grand triumphal chorus. Israel's King was in tears; not silent tears of gladness, but of uncontrollable agony. The crowd was struck with a sudden gloom. Many wept in sympathy with a grief they could not comprehend.

Just ahead of Jesus was Gethsemane, where soon the horror of a great darkness would overshadow Him. The sheepgate also was in sight, through which for centuries the animals for sacrificial offerings had been led. This gate was soon to open for Him, the great Fulfillment, toward whose sacrifice all these offerings had pointed. Nearby was Calvary, the scene of His approaching agony. Yet His was no selfish sorrow. The thought of His own agony did not affect that noble, self-sacrificing soul. It was the sight of Jerusalem that pierced the heart of Jesus—Jerusalem that had rejected the Son of God, scorned His love, and was about to take His life. He saw what she could have been if she had accepted Him who alone could heal her wound. How could He give her up?

Israel had been a favored people. God had made their temple His dwelling place; it was "beautiful in elevation, the joy of the whole earth." Psalm 48:2. In it Jehovah had revealed His glory, the priests had officiated, and the pomp of symbol and ceremony had gone on for ages. But all this must come to an end. Jesus waved His hand toward the doomed city, and in grief He exclaimed, "If you had known, even you, especially in this your day, the things that make for your peace!" The Savior left unsaid what could have been the condition of Jerusalem if she had accepted the help that God wanted to give her—the gift of His Son. Jerusalem could have stood out in the pride of prosperity, the queen of kingdoms, free in the strength of her God-given power, with no Roman banners waving from her walls. The Son of God saw that she could have been liberated from bondage and established as the leading city of the earth. From her walls the dove of peace would have gone forth to all nations. She would have been the world's crown of glory.

But the Savior realized she now was under the Roman rule, doomed to God's punishing judgment: "But now they are hidden from your eyes. For days will come upon you when your enemies will build an embankment around you, surround you and close you in on every side, and level you, and your children within you, to the ground; and they will not leave in you one stone upon another, because you did not know the time of your visitation."

Jesus saw the doomed city surrounded with armies, the besieged inhabitants driven to starvation and death, mothers feeding on the dead bodies of their children, and parents and children snatching the last morsel of food from one another—natural affection destroyed by the gnawing pangs of hunger. He saw that the stubbornness of the Jews would lead them to refuse to submit to the invading armies. He saw Calvary set with crosses as thickly as forest trees. He saw the beautiful palaces destroyed, the temple in ruins, and not one stone of its massive walls left on another, while the city was plowed like a field.

As a tender father mourns over a wayward son, so Jesus wept over the beloved city. "How can I give you up? How can I see you devoted to destruction?" When the setting sun would pass from sight, Jerusalem's day of grace would be over. While the procession was standing still on the Mount of Olives, it was not yet too late for Jerusalem to repent. While the last rays of sunlight were lingering on temple, tower, and pinnacle, would not some good angel lead her to the Savior's love? Beautiful, unholy city, that had stoned the prophets and rejected the Son of God—her day of mercy was almost gone!

Yet again the Spirit of God would speak to Jerusalem. Before the day was done, another testimony to Christ would be heard. If Jerusalem would receive the Savior entering her gates, she might yet be saved!

But the rulers in Jerusalem had no welcome for the Son of God. As the procession was about to descend the Mount of Olives, they intercepted it, asking the reason for the commotion. As they questioned, "Who is this?" the disciples, filled with the spirit of inspiration, repeated the prophecies concerning Christ.

Adam will tell you: It is the Seed of the woman that will bruise the serpent's head. See Genesis 3:15.

Abraham will tell you: It is Melchizedek, King of Salem, King of Peace. See Genesis 14:18.

Isaiah will tell you: "Immanuel," "Wonderful Counselor, Mighty God, Everlasting Father, Prince of Peace." Isaiah 7:14; 9:6, NRSV.

Jeremiah will tell you: The Branch of David, "THE LORD OUR RIGHTEOUSNESS." Jeremiah 23:6.

Daniel will tell you: He is the Messiah. See Daniel 9:24–27.

John the Baptist will tell you: He is "the Lamb of God who takes away the sin of the world!" John 1:29.

The great Jehovah has proclaimed: "This is My beloved Son." Matthew 3:17.

We, His disciples, declare, "This is Jesus, the Messiah, the Prince of life, the Redeemer of the world."

And the prince of the powers of darkness acknowledges Him: "I know who You are—the Holy One of God!" Mark 1:24.

# A Doomed People*

The last appeal to Jerusalem had been fruitless. The priests and rulers had heard the prophetic voice that the people echoed in answer to the question, "Who is this?" but they did not accept it as the voice of Inspiration. In anger they tried to silence the people. To Roman officers in the crowd, Jesus' enemies denounced Him as the leader of a rebellion. They claimed that He was about to take possession of the temple and reign as king in Jerusalem.

But in a calm voice Jesus again declared that He had not come to establish an earthly rule. He would soon ascend to His Father, and His accusers would see Him no more until He would come again in glory. Then, too late, they would acknowledge Him.

Jesus spoke these words with sadness and with noteworthy power. The Roman officers were quiet and subdued. Their hearts were moved as they had never been moved before. They read love and quiet dignity in the solemn face of Jesus. Stirred by a sympathy they could not understand, they were inclined to pay Him honor and respect. Turning on the priests and rulers, they charged them with creating the disturbance.

Meanwhile Jesus went unnoticed to the temple. All was quiet there, for the scene on the Mount of Olives had called the people away. For a short time Jesus remained, looking at the temple with sorrow. Then He returned to Bethany. When the people looked for Him to place Him on the throne, they could not find Him.

Jesus spent the entire night in prayer, and in the morning He came to the temple again. On the way He was hungry, "and seeing from afar a fig tree having leaves, He went to see if perhaps He would find something on it. When He came to it, He found nothing but leaves, for it was not the season for figs."

On the highlands around Jerusalem it could truly be said, "It was not the season for figs." But in the orchard to which Jesus came, one tree appeared to be ahead of all the others. It was already covered with leaves, giving promise of well-developed fruit. But its appearance was deceptive. Jesus found "nothing but leaves." It was a mass of showy foliage, nothing more.

Christ pronounced a withering curse

---

* This chapter is based on Matthew 21:17–19; Mark 11:11–14, 20, 21.

on it. "May no one ever eat fruit from you again," He said. NRSV. Next morning, as the Savior and His disciples were again on their way to the city, the dead branches and drooping leaves attracted their attention. "Rabbi," said Peter, "look! The fig tree which You cursed has withered away."

To the disciples, Christ's cursing of the fig tree seemed unlike what He would usually do. They remembered His words, "The Son of Man did not come to destroy men's lives but to save them." Luke 9:56. He had always worked to restore, never to destroy. This act stood alone. "What was its purpose?" they questioned.

" 'As I live,' says the Lord God, 'I have no pleasure in the death of the wicked.' " Ezekiel 33:11. To Him the work of destruction and the pronouncing of judgment is a "strange work." Isaiah 28:21, KJV. But in mercy and love He lifts the veil from the future and reveals the results of a course of sin.

The barren fig tree, making a great show of foliage in the face of Christ, was a symbol of the Jewish nation. The Savior wanted to make plain the cause of Israel's doom and its certainty. To do this, He made the tree the teacher of divine truth. The Jews claimed righteousness above every other people. But the love of the world and the greed of gain corrupted them. They made a show of spreading their branches high, appearing lush and beautiful to the eye, but they yielded "nothing but leaves." The Jewish religion, with its magnificent temple and impressive ceremonies, was indeed impressive in outward appearance,

but it lacked humility, love, and benevolence.

## Why This One Tree Was Cursed

The leafless trees raised no expectation and caused no disappointment. These represented the Gentiles, who had no more godliness than the Jews, but who made no boastful claims to goodness. With them "the season for figs" was not yet. They were still waiting for light and hope. God held the Jews, who had received greater blessings from Him, accountable for their abuse of these gifts. The privileges of which they boasted only increased their guilt.

Jesus had come to Israel, hungering to find the fruits of righteousness in them. He had granted them every privilege, and in return He longed to see in them self-sacrifice, compassion, and a deep yearning for the salvation of others. But pride and self-sufficiency eclipsed love to God and humanity. They did not give to the world the treasures of truth that God had committed to them. In the barren tree they might read both their sin and its punishment. Withered, dried up by the roots, the fig tree showed what the Jewish people would be when the grace of God was removed from them. Refusing to give blessing, they would no longer receive it. "O Israel," the Lord says, "thou hast destroyed thyself." Hosea 13:9, KJV.

Christ's act in cursing the tree that His own power had created stands as a warning to all churches and all Christians. There are many who do not live out Christ's merciful, unselfish life. Time is of value to them only so that they can use it to gather for themselves. In all the affairs of life, this is their aim. God planned for them to help others in every possible way. But self is so large that they cannot see anything else. Those who live for self in this way are like the fig tree. They follow the forms of worship without repentance or faith. They claim to honor the law of God, but they lack obedience. In the sentence pronounced on the fig tree Christ declares that the open sinner is less guilty than someone who professes to serve God but bears no fruit to His glory.

The parable of the fig tree, which Christ spoke before His visit to Jerusalem, had a direct connection with the lesson He taught by cursing the fruitless tree. In the parable the gardener pleaded for the barren tree, "Sir, let it alone this year also, until I dig around it and fertilize it. And if it bears fruit, well. But if not, after that you can cut it down." Luke 13:8, 9. It was to have every advantage. The parable did not predict the result of the gardener's work. The outcome depended on the people to whom Christ spoke those words, whom the fruitless tree represented. It was up to them to decide their own destiny. God had given them every advantage, but they did not profit by their increased blessings. Christ's act in cursing the barren fig tree showed what the result would be. They had determined their own destruction.

For more than a thousand years the Jewish nation had rejected God's warnings and killed His prophets. When the people of Christ's day followed the same course, they made themselves responsible for these sins.

They were fastening on themselves the chains that the nations had been forging for centuries.

There comes a time when mercy makes her last appeal. Then the sweet, winning voice of the Spirit no longer pleads with the sinner.

That day had come to Jerusalem. Jesus wept in anguish over the doomed city, but He could not deliver her. He had exhausted every resource. In rejecting the warnings of God's Spirit, Israel had rejected her only means of help.

The Jewish nation was a symbol of the people of all ages who scorn the pleadings of Infinite Love. When Christ wept over Jerusalem, His tears were for the sins of all time.

In this generation many are walking the same path as the unbelieving Jews. The Holy Spirit has spoken to their hearts, but they are not willing to confess their errors. They reject God's message and His messenger.

Today Bible truth, the religion of Christ, struggles against a strong tide of moral impurity. Prejudice is stronger now than in Christ's day. The truth of God's Word does not harmonize with natural human preferences, and thousands reject its light and choose their independent judgment. But they do so at the peril of their eternal life.

Those who tried to pick flaws with the words of Christ found ever-increasing cause for doing so, until they turned from the Truth and the Life. God does not propose to remove every objection that the carnal heart may bring against His truth. To those who refuse light that would illuminate the darkness, the mysteries of God's

Word remain mysteries forever. The truth is hidden from them.

Christ's words apply to everyone who treats the pleadings of divine mercy lightly. Christ is shedding bitter tears for you who have no tears to shed for yourself. And every evidence of the grace of God, every ray of divine light, is either melting and subduing the heart or confirming it in hopeless rebellion.

Christ foresaw that Jerusalem would remain unrepentant, yet all the guilt lay at her own door. It will be this way with everyone who follows the same course. The Lord declares, "O Israel, thou hast destroyed thy self." Hosea 13:9, KJV.

"Hear, O earth!
Behold, I will certainly bring calamity
    on this people—
The fruit of their thoughts,
Because they have not heeded My
    words
Nor My law, but rejected it."
                                    Jeremiah 6:19

# The Temple Cleansed Again*

At the beginning of His ministry, Christ had driven from the temple those who defiled it by their unholy business dealings. His stern and godlike bearing had struck terror in the scheming traders.

At the close of His mission, He came to the temple again and found it still profaned like it was before—with the cries of animals, the sharp chinking of coin, and the sound of angry disputes. The dignitaries of the temple themselves were buying and selling. They were so completely controlled by greed for gain that they were no better than thieves in the sight of God.

At every Passover and Feast of Tabernacles, thousands of animals were killed, their blood caught by the priests and poured on the altar. The Jews had almost lost sight of the fact that sin was what made all this shedding of blood necessary. They did not recognize that it prefigured the blood of God's dear Son that would be shed for the life of the world.

Jesus saw how the Jews had made these great gatherings into scenes of bloodshed and cruelty. They had multiplied the sacrifice of animals, as if God could be honored by a heartless service. The priests and rulers had made the symbols pointing to the Lamb of God a way of making money. To a great degree, this had destroyed the sacredness of the sacrificial service. Jesus knew that the priests and elders would not appreciate His blood, so soon to be shed for the sins of the world, just as they had little appreciation for the blood of animals!

Through the prophets, Christ had spoken against these practices. In prophetic vision Isaiah saw the apostasy of the Jews and addressed them:

"To what purpose is the multitude of
    your sacrifices to Me?"
Says the Lord.
"I have had enough
    of burnt offerings of rams
And the fat of fed cattle.
I do not delight in the blood of bulls,
Or of lambs or goats.". . .

"Wash yourselves, make yourselves
    clean;
Put away the evil of your doings from
    before My eyes."
                  Isaiah 1:11, 16

---

* This chapter is based on Matthew 21:12–16, 23–46; Mark 11:15–19, 27–33; 12:1–12; Luke 19:45–48; 20:1–19.

He who had given these prophecies Himself now repeated the warning for the last time. In fulfillment of prophecy the people had proclaimed Jesus king of Israel. He had received their homage and accepted the office of king. He must now act like the king He was. He knew that His efforts to reform a corrupt priesthood would be futile. Even so, He must give an unbelieving people the evidence of His divine mission.

Again the piercing look of Jesus swept over the profaned court of the temple. All eyes turned toward Him. Divinity flashed through His humanity, filling Christ with a dignity and glory He had never manifested before. Those nearest Him moved as far away as the crowd would permit. Except for a few of His disciples, the Savior stood alone. The deep silence seemed unbearable. Christ spoke with a power that shook the people like a mighty storm: " 'It is written, "My house is a house of prayer," but you have made it a 'den of thieves.' " His voice rang like a trumpet through the temple. "Take these things away!" John 2:16.

Three years before, the rulers of the temple had been ashamed of having fled before the command of Jesus. They had felt it impossible that they would ever repeat their undignified surrender. Yet they were now more terrified than before and in a greater hurry to obey His command. Priests and traders fled, driving their cattle ahead of them.

On the way from the temple, they were met by a crowd who came with their sick, inquiring for the Great Healer. The report that the fleeing people gave made some of these turn back, but a large number pushed on through the crowd, eager to reach Him. Again the sick and the dying filled the temple court, and once more Jesus ministered to them.

After a while the priests and rulers cautiously returned to the temple. They expected Jesus to take the throne of David. When they entered the temple, they stopped short and stared in amazement. They saw the sick healed, the blind restored to sight, the deaf receive their hearing, and the crippled leap for joy. Children were first in the rejoicing. Jesus had healed their sicknesses and embraced them in His arms. Now with glad voices the children called out His praise. They repeated the hosannas of the day before and waved palm branches triumphantly before the Savior.

The sound of these happy, unrestrained voices was offensive to the rulers of the temple. They told the people that the house of God was desecrated by the feet of the children and the shouts of rejoicing. The rulers appealed to Christ: " 'Do You hear what these are saying?' And Jesus said to them, 'Yes. Have you never read, "Out of the mouth of babes and nursing infants you have perfected praise"?' " Prophecy had foretold that Christ would be proclaimed as king, and God impressed the children to be His witnesses. Had the voices of the children been silent, the very pillars of the temple would have shouted the Savior's praise.

The Pharisees were thrown into utter confusion. Never before had Jesus assumed such kingly authority. He had done marvelous works, but never before in a manner so solemn and impressive. Though enraged and frustrated, the priests and rulers were unable to accomplish anything further that day. The next morning the Sanhedrin again considered what to do about Jesus. For three years the rulers had evidences that He was the Messiah. They now decided to demand no sign of His authority but to get Him to make some admission or declaration by which they could condemn Him.

In the temple they proceeded to question Him: "By what authority are You doing these things? And who gave You this authority?" Jesus met them with a question apparently relating to another subject, and He made His reply conditional on their answering this question: "The baptism of John—where was it from? From heaven or from men?"

The priests saw they were in a dilemma from which no deceptive argument could provide escape. If they said that John's baptism was from heaven, Christ would say, "Why then did you not believe him?" John had testified of Christ, "Behold! The Lamb of God who takes away the sin of the world!" John 1:29. If the priests believed John's testimony, how could they deny that Jesus was the Messiah?

If they declared their real belief, that John's ministry was only human, they would bring on themselves a storm of resentment, for the people believed that John was a prophet. The onlookers knew that the priests had professed to accept John, and they expected them to acknowledge that he was sent from God. But after conferring secretly together, the priests decided not to commit themselves. Hypocritically claiming ignorance, they said, "We do not know." "Neither will I tell you," said Christ, "by what authority I do these things."

## Priests and Rulers Silenced

Baffled and disappointed, scribes, priests, and rulers all stood scowling, not daring to press further questions on Christ. The people stood by, amused to see these proud, self-righteous men defeated.

All these sayings and doings of Christ were important. After His crucifixion and ascension they would have an ever-increasing influence. Many who would finally become His disciples had first been drawn by His words on that eventful day. The contrast between Jesus and the high priest as they talked together was obvious. The proud dignitary of the temple wore rich and costly garments. On his head was a glittering tiara, his bearing was majestic, his hair and beard silvery with age. Facing this important-looking person stood the Majesty of heaven, without adornment or display, His garments travel-stained, His face pale, expressing a patient sadness. Yet dignity and benevolence were written there. Many who witnessed the words and deeds of Jesus in the temple enshrined Him in their hearts as a prophet of God from that time on. But as the popular feeling turned in His favor, the priests' hatred toward Jesus increased.

It was not Christ's intention to humiliate His opponents. He had an important lesson to teach. The acknowledged ignorance of His enemies regarding John's baptism gave Him opportunity to speak, presenting before them their real position and adding another warning to the many He had already given.

"What do you think?" He said. "A man had two sons, and he came to the first and said, 'Son, go, work today in my vineyard.' He answered and said, 'I will not,' but afterward he regretted it and went. Then he came to the second and said likewise. And he answered and said, 'I go, sir,' but he did not go. Which of the two did the will of his father?"

This abrupt question threw His hearers off guard. They immediately answered, "The first." Looking intently at them, Jesus responded in stern and solemn tones: "Assuredly, I say to you that tax collectors and harlots enter the kingdom of God before you. For John came to you in the way of righteousness, and you did not believe him; but tax collectors and harlots believed him; and when you saw it, you did not afterward relent and believe him."

The priests and rulers had no alternative but to give a correct answer to Christ's question, and so He got their opinion in favor of the first son, who represented the tax collectors. When John came, preaching repentance and baptism, the tax collectors received his message and were baptized.

The second son represented the leading men of the Jewish nation who would not acknowledge that John came from God. They "rejected the will of God for themselves, not having

been baptized by him." Luke 7:30. Like the second son, the priests and rulers professed obedience, but acted disobedience.

The priests and rulers remained silent. But Christ said, "Hear another parable: There was a certain landowner who planted a vineyard and set a hedge around it, dug a winepress in it and built a tower. And he leased it to vinedressers and went into a far country. Now when vintage-time drew near, he sent his servants to the vinedressers, that they might receive its fruit. And the vinedressers took his servants, beat one, killed one, and stoned another. Again he sent other servants, more than the first, and they did likewise to them. Then last of all he sent his son to them, saying, 'They will respect my son.' But when the vinedressers saw the son, they said among themselves, 'This is the heir. Come, let us kill him and seize his inheritance.' So they took him and cast him out of the vineyard and killed him. Therefore, when the owner of the vineyard comes, what will he do to those vinedressers?"

The priests and rulers answered, "He will destroy those wicked men miserably, and lease his vineyard to other vinedressers who will render to him the fruits in their seasons." The speakers now saw that they had pronounced their own condemnation. As the vinedressers were to return to the owner a due proportion of the vineyard's fruits, so God's people were to honor Him by a life that reflected their sacred privileges. But as the vinedressers had killed the servants whom the owner sent to them for fruit, so the

Jews had put to death the prophets whom God sent to call them to repentance.

Up to that point no one could question the parable's application, and in what followed it was just as clear. In the beloved son whom the vineyard's owner finally sent to his disobedient servants, and whom they seized and killed, the priests and rulers saw a distinct picture of Jesus and His approaching fate. The punishment inflicted on the ungrateful vinedressers portrayed the doom of those who would put Christ to death.

### The Strange Stone That Prefigured Christ

Looking at them with pity, the Savior continued, "Have you never read in the Scriptures:

'The stone which the builders rejected Has become the chief cornerstone. This was the Lord's doing, And it is marvelous in our eyes?'

"Therefore I say to you, the kingdom of God will be taken from you and given to a nation bearing the fruits of it. And whoever falls on this stone will be broken; but on whomever it falls, it will grind him to powder."

The Jews had often repeated this prophecy in the synagogues, applying it to the coming Messiah. Christ was the Cornerstone of the Jewish system and of the whole plan of salvation. The Jewish builders were now rejecting this Foundation Stone. By every means in His power, the Savior tried to make plain the nature of the deed they were about to do. His warnings would seal their doom if they failed to

bring them to repentance. He intended to show them God's justice in withdrawing their national privileges, which would end not only in the destruction of their temple and their city, but in the scattering of the nation among the Gentiles.

The hearers recognized the warning, but despite the sentence they themselves had pronounced, the priests and rulers were ready to complete the picture by saying, "This is the heir. Come, let us kill him." "But when they sought to lay hands on Him, they feared the multitudes," for the public sentiment was in Christ's favor.

In quoting the prophecy of the rejected stone, Christ referred to an actual incident connected with the building of the first temple. It had a special lesson at Christ's first advent, but it also has a lesson for us. When the temple of Solomon was constructed, the immense stones were prepared entirely at the quarry. After they were brought to the building site, the workmen only had to place them in position. One stone of unusual size and peculiar shape had been brought for the foundation, but the workmen could find no place for it. It annoyed them as it lay unused in their way. For a long time it remained a rejected stone.

But when the builders came to the laying of the corner, they searched for a long time to find a stone of sufficient size and strength and of the proper shape to bear the great weight that would rest on it. If they were to make an unwise choice, it would endanger the safety of the entire building. They tried several stones, but under the pressure of immense weights these had crumbled to pieces.

But finally someone called attention to the stone so long rejected. It had been exposed to sun and storm without revealing the slightest crack. It had borne every test but one—the test of severe pressure. They put it through the trial. The stone passed the test and was accepted. When they brought it to its assigned position, they found it to be an exact fit. This stone was a symbol of Christ. Isaiah says,

"He will be as a sanctuary,
But a stone of stumbling and a rock of offense
To both the houses of Israel. . . .
And many among them shall stumble;
They shall fall and be broken,
Be snared and taken."
Isaiah 8:14, 15

The chief cornerstone in the temple of Solomon was symbolic of the trials and tests Christ was to bear.

"Behold, I lay in Zion a stone for a foundation,
A tried stone, a precious cornerstone, a sure foundation;
Whoever believes will not act hastily."
Isaiah 28:16

God chose the Foundation Stone and called it "a sure foundation." The entire world may lay their burdens and griefs on it. They may build on it with perfect safety. He never disappoints those who trust in Him. He has passed every test. He has carried the burdens placed on Him by every repenting sinner. All who make Him their dependence rest in perfect security.

Christ is both "a sure foundation" and "a stone of stumbling." "Therefore, to you who believe, He is precious; but to those who are disobedient, 'The stone which the builders rejected has become the chief cornerstone,' and 'A stone of stumbling and a rock of offense.' They stumble, being disobedient to the word." 1 Peter 2:7, 8.

## How to Be Built Up by Being Broken

To those who believe, Christ is the sure foundation. They fall on the Rock and are "broken." To fall on the Rock and be broken is to give up our self-righteousness, to go to Christ with the humility of a child, repenting of our sins and believing in His forgiving love. So also by faith and obedience we build on Christ as our foundation.

Jews and Gentiles alike may build on this Living Stone. It is broad enough for all and strong enough to hold the weight and burden of the whole world. By connecting with Christ, all who build on this foundation become living stones. See 1 Peter 2:5.

To those who "stumble, being disobedient to the word," Christ is a Rock of offense. Like the rejected stone, Christ had experienced neglect and abuse. He was

despised and rejected by men,
A Man of sorrows and acquainted with grief. . . .
He was despised, and we did not esteem Him.
Isaiah 53:3

But by the resurrection from the dead He would be declared the "Son of God with power." Romans 1:4. At His second coming, He would be revealed as Lord of heaven and earth. In the sight of the whole universe, the rejected stone would become the head of the corner.

And on "whomever it falls, it will grind him to powder." The people who rejected Christ would soon see their city and nation destroyed and their glory scattered as the dust before the wind. And what was it that destroyed the Jews? The Rock that would have been their security, if they had built on it. It was the goodness of God despised, mercy slighted. The people set themselves in opposition to God, and everything that would have been their salvation was turned to their destruction.

The destruction of Jerusalem was involved in the Jews' crucifixion of Christ. The blood shed on Calvary was the weight that sank them to ruin.

It will be like that in the great final day, when judgment will fall on those who reject God's grace. Christ, their Rock of offense, will then appear like an avenging mountain. The glory of His face, which is life to the righteous, will be a consuming fire to the wicked. Because of love rejected, grace despised, the sinner will be destroyed. The profaned temple, the disobedient son, the false vinedressers, and the contemptuous builders have their counterpart in the experience of every sinner. Unless the sinner repents, the doom that they foreshadowed will be his.

# Christ Confounds His Enemies[*]

The priests and rulers could not refute Christ's charges. But this made them only the more determined to entrap Him. They sent spies, "who pretended to be honest, in order to trap him by what he said, so as to hand him over to the jurisdiction and authority of the governor." NRSV. These young men, eager and zealous, were accompanied by Herodians who were to hear Christ's words so that they could testify against Him at His trial.

The Pharisees had always chafed under Roman taxes, holding that paying them was contrary to the law of God. Now the spies came to Jesus as though they were wanting to know their duty: "Teacher, we know that You say and teach rightly, and You do not show personal favoritism, but teach the way of God in truth: Is it lawful for us to pay taxes to Caesar or not?"

Those who put the question to Jesus thought they had disguised their intentions, but Jesus read their hearts like an open book. "Why do you test Me?" He said, showing that He read their hidden purpose. They were still more confused when He added, "Show me a denarius." They brought it, and He asked them, " 'Whose image and inscription does it have?' They answered and said, 'Caesar's.' " Pointing to the coin, Jesus said, "Render therefore to Caesar the things that are Caesar's, and to God the things that are God's."

The spies felt baffled and defeated. The brief, decisive way in which Jesus had settled their question left them nothing further to say. Christ's reply was no evasion, but a candid answer to the question. Holding in His hand the Roman coin, He declared that since they were living under the protection of the Roman power, they should give that power the support it claimed. But while they were peaceably subject to the laws of the land, they should at all times give their first allegiance to God.

If the Jews had fulfilled their obligations to God faithfully, they would not have come under a foreign power's control. No Roman banner would have waved over Jerusalem, no Roman governor would have ruled within her walls.

The Pharisees marveled at Christ's

---

* *This chapter is based on Matthew 22:15–46; Mark 12:13–40; Luke 20:20–47.*

answer. He had not only rebuked their hypocrisy but had stated a great principle that clearly defines the limits of duty to the civil government and duty to God. And although many went away dissatisfied, they saw that Jesus had clearly set forth the principle underlying the question, and they marveled at His farseeing discernment.

No sooner had Jesus silenced the Pharisees than the Sadducees came forward with sly questions. As a group they were bigoted, yet there were persons of genuine piety among them who accepted Christ's teachings. The Sadducees professed to believe the greater portion of the Scriptures, but in practical terms they were skeptics and materialists.

### The Resurrection, a Subject of Controversy

The resurrection was especially a subject of controversy between the Pharisees and Sadducees. The Pharisees had been firm believers in the resurrection, but their views about the future state became confused. Death became a mystery beyond explanation. The discussions between the two parties usually resulted in angry disputes.

The Sadducees did not have so strong a hold on the common people, but many had the influence that wealth gives. The high priest was usually chosen from among them. The fact that they were eligible for such a high office gave influence to their errors.

The Sadducees rejected the teaching of Jesus; His teaching about the future life contradicted their theories. They believed that, having created human beings, God had left them to themselves, independent of a higher influence. They held that people were free to control their own lives and to shape the events of the world; their destiny was in their own hands.

### Ideas of God Mold Character

Their ideas of God molded their own character. Just as, in their view, He had no interest in mankind, so they had little regard for one another. Refusing to acknowledge the influence of the Holy Spirit, they lacked His power in their lives. They boasted of their birthright as children of Abraham, but they were destitute of the faith and kindness of Abraham. Their hearts were not touched by the needs and sufferings of others. They lived for themselves.

By His words and works, Christ bore witness to a divine power that produces supernatural results, to a future life, to God as a Father of the human family, always mindful of their true interests. He taught that God moves on the heart by the Holy Spirit. He showed how wrong it was to trust in human power to transform character, when only the Spirit of God can do it.

In seeking a controversy with Jesus, the Sadducees felt confident that they could damage His reputation, if not condemn Him. The resurrection was the subject on which they chose to question Him. If He would agree with them, He would offend the Pharisees. If He would differ with them, they intended to hold His teaching up to ridicule. The Sadducees reasoned that if the immortal body is to be composed of the same particles of matter as it was in its mortal state, then it must have flesh and blood and resume in the eternal world the life interrupted on earth. Husband and wife would be reunited, marriages formed, and all things go on the same as before death.

In answer to their questions, Jesus lifted the veil from the future life. "In the resurrection," He said, "they neither marry nor are given in marriage, but are like angels of God in heaven." The Sadducees were wrong. "You are mistaken," He added, "not knowing the Scriptures nor the power of God." He did not charge them with hypocrisy, but with error in their beliefs.

He declared their ignorance of the Scriptures and the power of God to be the cause of their confusion of faith and darkness of mind. Christ called on them to open their minds to those sacred truths that would broaden the understanding. Thousands become unbelievers because they cannot understand the mysteries of God. The only key to the mysteries that surround us is to acknowledge in them the presence and power of God. People need to recognize God as the Creator of the universe, One who commands and performs all things.

Christ told His hearers that if there were no resurrection of the dead, the Scriptures that they professed to believe would be of no value. He said, "But concerning the resurrection of the dead, have you not read what was spoken to you by God, saying, 'I am the God of Abraham, the God of Isaac, and the God of Jacob'? God is not the God of the dead, but of the living." God sees the result of His work

as though it were now accomplished. The precious dead will hear the voice of the Son of God and come out from the grave to immortal life. There will be a close and tender relationship between God and the resurrected redeemed. He sees this condition as if it were already existing. The dead live unto Him.

The Sadducees were left with nothing to say. He had not spoken a word that they could take the least advantage of to condemn Him.

The Pharisees, however, did not despair yet. They convinced a certain learned scribe to question Jesus about which of the ten commandments was the most important. They had exalted the first four commandments, which point out our duty to our Maker, as of far greater significance than the other six, which define our duty to others. Jesus had been charged with exalting the last six commandments above the first four.

The lawyer approached Jesus with a direct question, "Which is the first commandment of all?" Christ's answer was direct: "The first of all the commandments is . . . 'you shall love the Lord your God with all your heart, with all your soul, with all your mind, and with all your strength.' " "The second is like the first," said Christ, "for it flows out of it." " 'You shall love your neighbor as yourself.' There is no other commandment greater than these." "On these two commandments hang all the Law and the Prophets."

Both of these commandments are an expression of the principle of love. We cannot keep the first and break the second, nor can we keep the second while we break the first. Only as we love God supremely is it possible for us to love our neighbor impartially.

Christ taught His hearers that the law of God is a divine unit, not so many separate laws, some of them highly important and others only slightly important. We show our love to God by obeying all His commandments.

The scribe who had questioned Jesus was astonished. In the presence of the assembled priests and rulers he honestly acknowledged that Christ had given the right interpretation to the law.

The scribe had some sense of how worthless were mere ceremonial offerings and the faithless shedding of blood for cleansing from sin. Love and obedience to God and unselfish regard for others appeared to him to be more valuable than all these rites. His firm and prompt response before the people showed a spirit entirely different from that of the priests and rulers. Jesus' heart went out in pity to the honest scribe who had dared to speak his true convictions. "Now when Jesus saw that he answered wisely, He said to him, 'You are not far from the kingdom of God.' "

The Pharisees had gathered close around Jesus as He answered the scribe. Now He asked them a question: "What do you think about the Christ? Whose Son is He?" He intended this question to show whether they regarded Him simply as a man or as the Son of God. A chorus of voices answered, "The Son of David." When Jesus revealed His divinity by His mighty miracles, when He healed the sick and raised the dead, the people had inquired among themselves, "Could this be the Son of David?" But many who called Jesus the Son of David did not recognize His divinity. The Son of David was also the Son of God.

In reply, Jesus said, " 'How then does David in the Spirit [the Spirit of Inspiration from God] call Him "Lord," saying:

"The Lord said to my Lord,
'Sit at My right hand,
Till I make Your enemies Your
    footstool' "?

" 'If David then calls Him "Lord," how is He his son?' And no one was able to answer Him a word, nor from that day on did anyone dare question Him anymore."

# Jesus' Last Visit to the Temple*

It was the last day of Christ's teaching in the temple. There stood the young Galilean, with no earthly honor or royal badge. Surrounding Him were priests in rich clothing, rulers with robes and badges, and scribes with scrolls in their hands, to which they frequently referred. Jesus stood calmly, as one holding the authority of heaven. He looked unflinchingly upon His adversaries who thirsted for His life. Their schemes to trap Him had failed. He had met challenge after challenge, presenting pure, bright truth in contrast to the darkness and errors of the priests and Pharisees. He had faithfully given the warning. Yet another work remained for Christ to do.

The people were charmed with His teaching, but they were greatly perplexed. They had respected the priests and rabbis, yet now they saw these men trying to discredit Jesus, whose virtue and knowledge appeared brighter with every assault. They marveled that the rulers would not believe on Jesus when His teachings were so plain and simple. They themselves did not know what course to take.

Christ's purpose in the parables was to warn the rulers and instruct the people. But He needed to speak even more plainly. The people were enslaved through their blind faith in a corrupt priesthood. These chains Christ must break. "The scribes and the Pharisees," He said, "sit in Moses' seat. Therefore whatever they tell you to observe, that observe and do, but do not do according to their works; for they say, and do not do."

The scribes and Pharisees claimed to take Moses' place as expounders of the law, but they did not practice their own teaching. And much of what they taught was contrary to the Scriptures: "They bind heavy burdens, hard to bear, and lay them on men's shoulders; but they themselves will not move them with one of their fingers." Certain portions of the law they explained in such a way as to impose regulations on the people that they themselves secretly ignored or from which they even claimed exemption.

"All their works they do to be seen by men. They make their phylacteries broad and enlarge the borders of their garments. They love the best places at feasts, the best seats in the synagogues,

* This chapter is based on Matthew 23; Mark 12:41–44; Luke 20:45–47; 21:1–4.

greetings in the marketplaces, and to be called by men, 'Rabbi, Rabbi.' But you, do not be called 'Rabbi,' for One is your Teacher, the Christ, and you are all brethren. Do not call anyone on earth your father; for One is your Father, He who is in heaven. And do not be called teachers; for One is your Teacher, the Christ."

In such plain words the Savior revealed the selfish ambition that was always reaching for place and power, displaying a mock humility, while the heart was filled with greed and envy. The Pharisees were constantly scheming to secure the places of honor and special favors. Jesus rebuked this practice.

He also reproved the leaders' vanity in coveting the title of rabbi, or teacher. Priests, scribes, and rulers were all brethren, children of one Father. The people were to give no man a title of honor indicating his control of their conscience or their faith.

If Christ were on earth today, surrounded by those who bear the title of "Reverend" or "Right Reverend," would He not repeat His saying, "Do not be called teachers; for One is your Teacher, the Christ"? The Scripture declares of God, "Holy and awesome ["reverend," KJV] is His name." Psalm 111:9. How many who assume this title misrepresent the name and character of God! How often have worldly ambition and the lowest sins been hidden under the ornate garments of a high and holy office!

The Savior continued, "He who is greatest among you shall be your servant. And whoever exalts himself will be humbled, and he who humbles him-

self will be exalted." Again and again Christ had taught that true greatness is measured by moral worth. In heaven's view, greatness of character consists in living for the benefit of others. Christ the King of glory was a servant to fallen humanity.

"You lock people out of the kingdom of heaven. For you do not go in yourselves, and when others are going in, you stop them." NRSV. By perverting the Scriptures, the priests and lawyers blinded the minds of those who otherwise would have received a knowledge of Christ's kingdom.

You "devour widows' houses, and for a pretense make long prayers. Therefore you will receive greater condemnation." The Pharisees gained the confidence of devout widows and then presented it as a duty for them to give their property for religious purposes. Having gained control of their money, the wily schemers used it for their own benefit. To cover their dishonesty, they offered long prayers in public and made a great show of being religious. The same rebuke falls on many in our day. Their lives are stained by selfishness and greed, yet over it all they throw a garment of pretended holiness.

### The Priceless Gift of the Poor Widow

Christ severely condemned abuses, but He was careful not to lessen obligation. Someone else's abuse of the gift could not turn God's blessing from the giver.

Jesus was in the court and watched those who came to deposit their gifts. Many of the rich brought large sums with great show. Jesus looked at them sadly but made no comment on their liberal offerings. Soon His face lit up as He saw a poor widow approach hesitatingly, as though afraid of being observed. She looked at the gift in her hand. It was very small in comparison with the gifts of those around her, yet it was everything she had. She quickly threw in her two mites ["small copper coins," NRSV] and turned to hurry away. But in doing this she caught the eye of Jesus, which was fastened earnestly on her.

The Savior told His disciples to notice the widow's poverty. Then His words of approval fell on her ear: "Truly I say to you that this poor widow has put in more than all." Tears of joy filled her eyes as she felt that her act was appreciated. Many would have advised her to keep her tiny offering for her own use; it would disappear among the many costly gifts brought to the treasury. But she believed the service of the temple to be established by God, and she was anxious to do all in her power to sustain it. She did what she could, and her act was to be a monument to her memory through all time and her joy in eternity.

She "has put in more than all." The large donations of the rich had required no sacrifice. They could not compare in value with the widow's mites.

Motive gives character to our acts, stamping them with disgrace or with high moral worth. Little duties cheerfully done, little gifts that make no show, often stand highest in God's sight. The poor widow deprived herself of food in order to give those two copper coins to the cause she loved. And she did it in faith, believing that

her heavenly Father would not overlook her need. This unselfish spirit and childlike faith won the Savior's approval.

Many among the poor long to show their gratitude to God for His grace and truth. Let them deposit their mites in the bank of heaven. If given from a heart filled with love for God, these seemingly insignificant gifts become priceless offerings that God smiles on and blesses.

When Jesus said of the widow, she "has put in more than all," His words were true, not only of the motive, but of the results of her gift. The "two small copper coins, which are worth a penny" (NRSV) have brought to God's treasury an amount of money far greater than the contributions of those rich Jews. That little gift has been like a stream, widening and deepening through the ages. In a thousand ways it has contributed to the relief of the poor and the spread of the gospel. Her example of self-sacrifice has acted and reacted on thousands of hearts in every land and in every age. God's blessing on the widow's mite has made it the source of great results. So it is with every gift given with a sincere desire for God's glory. No one can measure its results for good.

"Woe to you, scribes and Pharisees, hypocrites! For you pay tithe of mint and anise and cummin, and have neglected the weightier matters of the law: justice and mercy and faith. These you ought to have done, without leaving the others undone." Christ did not set aside the obligation itself. The tithing system, established by God, was observed from earliest times. Abraham paid tithes of all that he possessed. As God gave it, the system was fair and reasonable, but the priests and rabbis had made it a wearisome burden.

The Pharisees were very exact in tithing garden herbs such as mint, anise, and rue. This cost little and gave them a reputation for exactness and sanctity. At the same time, they neglected the weightier matters of the law, justice, mercy, and truth. "These," Christ said, "you ought to have done, without leaving the others undone."

The rabbis had perverted other laws in a similar way. In the directions God gave through Moses, the use of swine's flesh and of certain other animals was prohibited, because they were likely to fill the blood with impurities and to shorten life. But the Pharisees went to unjustified extremes. They required the people to strain all the water used, in case it might contain the smallest insect that could be classed with the unclean animals. Contrasting these trivial requirements with the magnitude of actual sins, Jesus said to the Pharisees, "Blind guides, who strain out a gnat and swallow a camel!"

"You are like whitewashed tombs which indeed appear beautiful outwardly, but inside are full of dead men's bones and all uncleanness." The whited and beautifully decorated tomb concealed the putrefying remains within. Similarly, the outward holiness of the priests and rulers concealed iniquity.

Jesus continued, "You build the tombs of the prophets and adorn the monuments of the righteous, and say, 'If we had lived in the days of our fathers, we would not have been partakers with them in the blood of the prophets.' Therefore you are witnesses against yourselves that you are sons of those who murdered the prophets."

People at that time cherished a superstitious regard for the tombs of the dead and lavished vast sums of money on decorating them. In the sight of God this was idolatry. It showed that they did not love God supremely nor their neighbor as themselves. Today, many neglect the widows and the fatherless, the sick and the poor, in order to build expensive monuments for the dead. Duties to the living—duties which Christ has plainly commanded—they leave undone.

The Pharisees said one to another, "If we had lived in the days of our fathers, we would not have united with them in shedding the blood of God's servants." At the same time they were planning to take the life of His Son. This should open our eyes to the power of Satan to deceive any mind that turns away from the light of truth. Many are amazed at the blindness of the Jews in rejecting Christ. If we had lived in His day, they declare, we would never have been guilty of rejecting the Savior. But when obedience to God requires self-denial and humiliation, these very people refuse obedience. They reveal the same spirit as did the Pharisees.

Little did the Jews realize the terrible responsibility involved in rejecting Christ. In every age, prophets had lifted up their voices against the sins of kings, rulers, and people, obeying God's will at the risk of their lives. A terrible punishment had been building up for the rejecters of light and truth. By rejecting the Savior, the priests and rulers were making themselves responsible for the blood of all the righteous killed from Abel to Christ. They were about to fill their cup of iniquity to overflowing. And soon it was to be poured on their heads in their just punishment. Jesus warned them about this:

"That on you may come all the righteous blood shed on the earth, from the blood of righteous Abel to the blood of Zechariah, son of Berechiah, whom you murdered between the temple and the altar. Assuredly, I say to you, all these things will come upon this generation."

The scribes and Pharisees knew how the prophet Zechariah had been killed. While God's words of warning were on his lips, a satanic fury came over the rebellious king, and at his command the prophet was put to death. See 2 Chronicles 24:18–22. His blood had stained the very stones of the temple court and remained to bear witness against rebellious Israel. As long as the temple stood, there would be the stain of that righteous blood, crying to God to be avenged. As Jesus referred to these fearful sins, a chill of horror ran through the crowd.

Looking forward, Jesus declared that the Jews would be as unrepentant in the future as they had been in the past:

"Therefore, indeed, I send you prophets, wise men, and scribes: some of them you will kill and crucify, and some of them you will scourge in your synagogues and persecute from city to city." With hand uplifted to heaven and a divine light surrounding Him, Christ spoke as a judge, in rebuke and condemnation. The listeners shuddered. The impression that His words and His look made would never fade away.

Christ directed His indignation against the major sins by which the leaders were destroying their own souls, deceiving the people, and dishonoring God. But He spoke no words of retaliation. He showed no irritated temper. The face of the Son of God revealed divine pity as He took one lingering look at the temple and then at His hearers. In a voice choked by anguish and bitter tears He exclaimed, "O Jerusalem, Jerusalem, the one who kills the prophets and stones those who are sent to her! How often I wanted to gather your children together, as a hen gathers her chicks under her wings, but you were not willing!" In Christ's lament the very heart of God poured forth. It was the mysterious farewell of the Deity's long-suffering love.

Pharisees and Sadducees alike were silenced. Jesus called His disciples to Him and prepared to leave the temple, not as someone defeated, but as someone whose work was done. He withdrew from the contest as the victor.

In many hearts that eventful day, new thoughts started into life and a new history began. After the Crucifixion and Resurrection, these persons came forward with wisdom and zeal. They bore a message that appealed to hearts. In the light of their testimony, human theories and philosophies became like idle fables.

But Israel as a nation had divorced herself from God. Looking for the last time on the interior of the temple, Jesus said with mournful tones, "See! Your house is left to you desolate; for I say to you, you shall see Me no more till you say, 'Blessed is He who comes in the name of the Lord!' " When the Son of God went out from those walls, God's presence would be withdrawn forever from the temple built for His glory. Its ceremonies would be meaningless, its services a mockery.

# When the Greeks Wished to "See Jesus"*

Now there were certain Greeks among those who came up to worship at the feast. Then they came to Philip . . . and asked him, saying, 'Sir, we wish to see Jesus.' . . . Andrew and Philip told Jesus."

At this time Christ's work looked as though it had suffered cruel defeat. He had been the victor in the controversy with the priests and Pharisees, but it was clear that they would never accept Him as the Messiah. The final separation had come. The case seemed hopeless. But the great event that concerned the whole world was about to take place. When Christ heard the eager request, "We wish to see Jesus," echoing the hungering cry of the world, His face lit up, and He said, "The hour has come that the Son of Man should be glorified."

These men came from the West to find the Savior at the close of His life. The wise men had come from the East at the beginning. These Greeks represented the nations, tribes, and peoples of the world. People of all lands and all ages would be drawn by the Savior's cross.

The Greeks longed to know the truth about Christ's mission. When they said, "We wish to see Jesus," He was in that part of the temple that excluded everyone except Jews, but He went out to the Greeks in the outer court and had a personal interview with them.

The inquiry of the Greeks showed Christ that the sacrifice He was about to make would bring many sons and daughters to God. He knew that the Greeks would soon see Him in a position they did not dream of then. They would see Him placed beside Barabbas, a robber and a murderer. To the question, "What . . . shall I do with Jesus?" the people would answer, "Let Him be crucified!" Matthew 27:22. By making this sacrifice for sin Christ knew that His kingdom would be perfected and would extend throughout the world. He would work as the Restorer, and His Spirit would prevail.

For a moment He heard voices proclaiming in all parts of the earth, "Behold! The Lamb of God who takes away the sin of the world!" John 1:29. In these strangers He saw the pledge of a great harvest. He expressed His anticipation of this, the fulfillment of His hopes, in His words, "The hour has come that the Son of Man should

---

* This chapter is based on John 12:20–43.

be glorified." But He never forgot the way in which this glorification must take place. The world could be saved only by His death. Like a grain of wheat, the Son of man must be put into the ground and die, and be buried out of sight; but He was to live again.

"Most assuredly, I say to you, unless a grain of wheat falls into the ground and dies, it remains alone; but if it dies, it produces much grain." When the grain of wheat falls into the ground and dies, it springs up and bears fruit. Likewise the death of Christ would result in fruit for the kingdom of God. In accordance with the law of the vegetable kingdom, life was to be the result of His death.

Year by year, the farmer preserves his supply of grain by apparently throwing away the best part. For a time it must be hidden under the furrow, to be watched over by the Lord. Then appears the blade, then the ear, and then the grain in the ear.

The seed buried in the ground produces fruit, and in turn this is planted. In this way the harvest is multiplied. So the death of Christ on the cross will bear fruit for eternal life. Contemplating this sacrifice will be the glory of those who live through eternal ages as the fruit of it.

Christ could save Himself from death if He chose. But if He were to do this, He must "remain alone." Only by falling into the ground to die could He become the seed for that huge harvest—the great multitude redeemed to God.

Everyone should learn this lesson of self-sacrifice: "He who loves his life will lose it, and he who hates his life in this world will keep it for eternal life." The life must be thrown into the furrow of the world's need. Self-love, self-interest, must die. And the law of self-sacrifice is the law of self-preservation. To give is to live. The life that will be preserved is the life that is freely given in service to God and others.

The life spent on self is like the grain that is eaten. There is no increase. We may gather all we can; we may live, think, and plan for self; but our life passes away, and we have nothing. The law of self-serving is the law of self-destruction.

"If anyone serves Me," said Jesus, "let him follow Me; and where I am, there My servant will be also. If anyone serves Me, him My Father will honor." All who have carried the cross of sacrifice with Jesus will share with Him in His glory. They are workers together with Christ, and the Father will honor them as He honors His Son.

The message of the Greeks brought to Jesus' mind the work of redemption from the time when the plan was formed in heaven to His death that was now so close. A mysterious cloud seemed to enclose the Son of God. He sat, deep in thought. At last His mournful voice broke the silence: "Now My soul is troubled, and what shall I say? 'Father, save Me from this hour'?" Christ's humanity recoiled from the hour of abandonment, when everyone would see Him stricken, smitten by God, and afflicted. He shrank from being treated as the worst of criminals, from a shameful, dishonored death. A sense of the awful burden of human sin and the Father's wrath because of sin made the spirit of

Jesus faint and the paleness of death come over His face.

## Voice of God Heard

Then He yielded divine submission to His Father's will. "For this purpose," He said, "I came to this hour. Father, glorify Your name." Only through His death could Christ overthrow Satan's kingdom, redeem humanity, and glorify God. Jesus accepted the sacrifice; He agreed to suffer as the Sin Bearer. A response came from the cloud that hovered above His head: "I have both glorified it and will glorify it again." In the coming ordeal Christ's divine-human sufferings would indeed glorify His Father's name.

As the Voice was heard, a light encircled Christ, as if the arms of Infinite Power were thrown around Him like a wall of fire. No one dared to speak. All stood looking intently at Jesus. When the Father had finished giving His testimony, the cloud lifted and scattered in the heavens.

The inquiring Greeks saw the cloud, heard the Voice, understood its meaning, and recognized the truth about Christ. He was revealed to them as the One sent by God. The voice of God had spoken at Jesus' baptism and again at His transfiguration. Now a larger number of people heard it on this third occasion. Jesus had just made His last appeal and pronounced the doom of the Jews. Now God again recognized the One whom Israel had rejected. "This voice did not come because of Me," said Jesus, "but for your sake." It was the signal from the Father that Jesus had spoken the truth and was the Son of God.

" 'Now is the judgment of this world,' " Christ continued, " 'now the ruler of this world will be cast out. And I, if I am lifted up from the earth, will draw all peoples to Myself.' This He said, signifying by what death He would die." If I become the atoning sacrifice for human sin, the world will be lighted up. Satan's hold on men and women will be broken. The defaced image of God will be restored in humanity, and a family of believing saints will finally inherit the heavenly home. The Savior saw the cross, the cruel, shameful cross with all its attending horrors, blazing with glory.

But human redemption is not all that the cross accomplishes. The love of God is displayed to the universe. The accusations of Satan against heaven are forever answered. Angels as well as fallen human beings are drawn to the Redeemer. "I, if I am lifted up from the earth," He said, "will draw all peoples to Myself."

Many people were standing around Christ as He spoke these words. But "although He had done so many signs before them, they did not believe in Him." He had given them countless signs, but they had closed their eyes and hardened their hearts. Now that the Father Himself had spoken and they could ask for no further sign, they still refused to believe.

"Nevertheless even among the rulers many believed in Him, but because of the Pharisees they did not confess Him, lest they should be put out of the synagogue." To save themselves from condemnation and shame, they denied Christ and rejected the offer of eternal life.

How terrible for those who did not recognize the time of their opportunity!

Slowly and regretfully Christ left the temple courts forever.

# Signs of the Second Coming of Christ*

Christ's words to the priests and rulers, "See! Your house is left to you desolate" (Matthew 23:38), had struck terror in their hearts. The question kept rising in their minds about what these words might mean. Could it be that the magnificent temple, the nation's glory, was soon to be a heap of ruins?

The disciples also shared this sense of approaching evil. As they walked out of the temple with Jesus, they called His attention to its strength and beauty. The stones of the temple were of the purest marble, some of almost incredible size. A portion of the wall had withstood the siege by Nebuchadnezzar's army. In its perfect masonry it appeared like one solid stone dug whole from the quarry.

The view Christ saw was indeed beautiful, but He said with sadness, "I see it all. You point to these walls as apparently indestructible, but listen: The day will come when 'not one stone shall be left upon another, that shall not be thrown down.' "

When He was alone, Peter, John, James, and Andrew came to Him. "Tell us, when will these things be? And what will be the sign of Your com-ing, and of the end of the age?" Jesus did not answer by speaking separately of the destruction of Jerusalem and the great day of His coming. He mingled the description of these two events. If He had opened to His disciples the future events as He saw them, they would have been unable to endure the sight. In mercy, He blended the description of the two great crises, leaving the disciples to study out the meaning for themselves. When He referred to the destruction of Jerusalem, His prophetic words reached beyond that event to that day when the Lord will come to punish the world for their iniquity. Jesus gave this entire discourse not just for the disciples but for those who would live in the last scenes of this earth's history.

Christ said, "Take heed that no one deceives you. For many will come in My name, saying, 'I am the Christ,' and will deceive many." Many false messiahs will appear, declaring that the time of deliverance for the Jewish nation has come. These will mislead many. Christ's words were fulfilled. Between His death and the siege of Jerusalem many false messiahs appeared. The same deceptions will arise again.

---

* This chapter is based on Matthew 24; Mark 13; Luke 21:5–38.

"And you will hear of wars and rumors of wars. See that you are not troubled; for all these things must come to pass, but the end [of the Jewish nation as a nation] is not yet. For nation will rise against nation, and kingdom against kingdom. And there will be famines, pestilences, and earthquakes in various places. All these are the beginning of sorrows." The rabbis will declare that these signs are announcing the advent of the Messiah. Don't be deceived. The signs that they say are indicators of their release from oppression are signs of their destruction.

"Then they will deliver you up to tribulation and kill you, and you will be hated by all nations for My name's sake. And then many will be offended, will betray one another, and will hate one another." All this the Christians experienced. Fathers and mothers betrayed their children, children their parents. Friends betrayed friends to the Sanhedrin. The persecutors killed Stephen, James, and other Christians.

Through His servants, God gave the Jewish people a last opportunity to repent. He revealed Himself in their arrest and trial, yet their judges pronounced the death sentence on them. By killing them, the Jews crucified the Son of God anew. It will be this way again. The authorities will make laws to restrict religious liberty. They will think they can force the conscience, which God alone should control. They will continue this work until they reach a boundary over which they cannot step. God will intervene in behalf of His loyal, commandment-keeping people.

When persecution comes, many stumble and fall, renouncing the faith they once advocated. Those who leave their faith in difficult times will bear false witness and betray their brethren in order to secure their own safety. Christ has warned us of this so that we will not be surprised at the unnatural, cruel behavior of those who reject the light.

Christ told His disciples how to escape the ruin that was coming on Jerusalem: "When you see Jerusalem surrounded by armies, then know that its desolation is near. Then let those who are in Judea flee to the mountains, let those who are in the midst of her depart, and let not those who are in the country enter her." Jesus gave this warning to be heeded forty years after, at the destruction of Jerusalem. The Christians obeyed the warning, and not one died in the fall of the city.

"Pray that your flight may not be in winter or on the Sabbath," Christ said. He who made the Sabbath did not abolish it. His death did not cancel the Sabbath. Forty years after His crucifixion His followers were still to hold it sacred.

## Dark Centuries of Persecution

From the destruction of Jerusalem, Christ turned rapidly to the last link in the chain of this earth's history—the coming of the Son of God in majesty and glory. Between these two events, long centuries of darkness for His church lay open to Christ's view, centuries marked with blood, tears, and agony. Jesus passed these scenes by with a brief mention. "Then there will be great tribulation," He said, "such as has not been since the beginning of the world until this time, no, nor ever shall be. And unless those days were shortened, no flesh would be saved; but for the elect's sake those days will be shortened."

For more than a thousand years, persecution such as the world had never before known was to come upon Christ's followers. Millions of His faithful witnesses would be killed. If God's hand had not been stretched out to preserve His people, all of them would have lost their lives.

Now, in unmistakable language, our Lord speaks of His second coming: "If anyone says to you, 'Look, here is the Christ!' or 'There!' do not believe it. For false christs and false prophets will rise and show great signs and wonders to deceive, if possible, even the elect. . . . If they say to you, 'Look, He is in the desert!' do not go out; or 'Look, He is in the inner rooms!' do not believe it. For as the lightning comes from the east and flashes to the west, so also will the coming of the Son of Man be." From thousands of gatherings where people profess to hold communication with departed spirits, is not the call now heard, "Look, He is in the inner rooms"? This is the claim that spiritism makes. But what does Christ say? "Do not believe it."

### Signs in the Heavens

The Savior gives signs of His coming and sets the time when the first of these signs will appear: "Immediately after the tribulation of those days the sun will be darkened, and the moon will not give its light; the stars will fall from heaven, and the powers of the heavens will be shaken. Then the sign of the Son of Man will appear in heaven, and then all the tribes of the earth will mourn, and they will see the Son of Man coming on the clouds of heaven with power and great glory. And He will send His angels with a great sound of a trumpet, and they will gather together His elect from the four winds, from one end of heaven to the other."

At the close of the great papal persecution, Christ declared the sun would be darkened and the moon not give her light. Next, the stars would fall from heaven. And He says, "When you see all these things, you know that he is near, at the very gates." Matthew 24:33, NRSV. Christ says of those who see these signs, "This generation will by no means pass away till all these things take place." These signs have appeared. Now we know with certainty that the Lord's coming is near.

Christ is coming with great glory. A multitude of shining angels will come with Him. He will come to raise the dead and to change the redeemed who are living, to honor those who have loved Him and kept His commandments, and to take them to Himself. When we look on our dead, we may think of the morning when "the dead will be raised incorruptible, and we shall be changed." 1 Corinthians 15:52. The King will wipe all tears from our eyes and present us "faultless before the presence of His glory with exceeding joy." Jude 24. "When these things begin to happen, look up and lift up your heads, because your redemption draws near."

But Christ stated plainly that He Himself could not reveal the day or the hour of His second appearing. The exact time of the second coming is God's mystery.

## The Overwhelming Wickedness of the Last Days

Christ continues, "As the days of Noah were, so also will the coming of the Son of Man be. For as in the days before the flood, they were eating and drinking, marrying and giving in marriage, until the day that Noah entered the ark, and did not know until the flood came and took them all away, so also will the coming of the Son of Man be."

How was it in Noah's day? "The Lord saw that the wickedness of man was great in the earth, and that every intent of the thoughts of his heart was only evil continually." Genesis 6:5. The inhabitants of the world before the Flood followed their own unholy imagination and perverted ideas. Because of their evil, they were destroyed. Today the world is going the same way. Those who break God's law are filling the earth with wickedness. Their gambling, drunkenness, lustful practices, and untamed passions are quickly filling the world with violence.

Christ said, "Because lawlessness will abound, the love of many will grow cold. But he who endures to the end shall be saved. And this gospel of the kingdom will be preached in all the world as a witness to all the nations, and then the end will come." Before the fall of Jerusalem, Paul declared that the gospel had been preached to "every creature under heaven." Colossians 1:23. Similarly now, the everlasting gospel is to be preached "to every nation, tribe, tongue, and people." Revelation 14:6. Christ does not say that all the world will be converted, but that "this gospel of the kingdom will be preached in all the world as a witness to all the nations, and then the end will come." By giving the gospel to the world it is in our power to speed our Lord's return. We are not only to look for but to hasten the coming of the day of God. See 2 Peter 3:12. If the church had done her appointed work as the Lord intended, before now the whole world would have been warned, and Jesus would have come.

## Something to Live For!

Because we do not know the exact time of His coming, Jesus has commanded us to watch. See Luke 12:37. Those who watch for the Lord's coming are not waiting in idle anticipation. They are purifying their hearts by obedience to the truth. They combine vigilant watching with earnest working. Their zeal is stirred to cooperate with divine intelligences in working for the salvation of others. They are declaring the truth that has special application just now. As Enoch, Noah, Abraham, and Moses each declared the truth for his time, so Christ's servants now will give the special warning for their generation.

But Christ mentions another group: "If that evil servant says in his heart, 'My master is delaying his coming,' and begins to beat his fellow servants, and to eat and drink with the drunkards, the master of that servant will come on a day when he is not looking for him."

The evil servant does not say that Christ will not come. But by his actions and words he declares that the Lord's coming is *delayed*. He banishes from the minds of others the conviction that the Lord is coming quickly. His influence confirms them in their worldliness and unconcern. Earthly passions, corrupt thoughts, take possession of the mind. The evil servant beats his fellow servants, accusing and condemning those who are faithful to their Master. He mingles with the world, and with the world he is caught in the trap. "The master of that servant will come . . . at an hour that he is not aware of, and will cut him in two and appoint him his portion with the hypocrites."

The coming of Christ will surprise the false teachers. The day of God will come like a snare, like a prowling thief on all who make this world their home. Full of rioting, full of godless pleasure, the world is asleep in godless security. People laugh at warnings. "Tomorrow will be as today, and much more abundant." Isaiah 56:12. We will go deeper into pleasure loving. But Christ says, "I am coming as a thief." Revelation 16:15. When the scoffer has become shameless, when people follow the routine of money making without regard to principle, when the student is eagerly seeking knowledge of everything but his Bible, Christ comes as a thief.

The signs of the times are ominous. Coming events cast their shadows ahead of time. The Spirit of God is withdrawing from the earth, and calamity follows calamity. Where is security? There is assurance in nothing human or earthly.

There are those who are waiting, watching, and working for our Lord's appearing. Another class are falling into line under the leadership of the first great apostate. The crisis is creeping gradually upon us. The sun shines in the heavens, following its usual circuit. People are still eating and drinking, planting and building. Merchants are still buying and selling. People are competing for the highest place. Pleasure lovers are crowding to theaters, horse races, gambling establishments. The highest excitement prevails, yet probation's hour is quickly closing, and every case is about to be decided for eternity. Satan has set all his agencies at work to deceive people and keep them occupied and fascinated until the door of mercy is shut forever.

"Watch therefore, and pray always that you may be counted worthy to escape all these things that will come to pass, and to stand before the Son of Man."

# Christ Identifies With the Poor and Suffering*

When the Son of Man comes . . . , then He will sit on the throne of His glory. All the nations will be gathered before Him, and He will separate them one from another." In this way Christ pictured the scene of the great Judgment Day. When the nations are gathered before Him, there will be only two classes, and their eternal destiny will depend on what they have done or have neglected to do for Him in the person of the poor and suffering.

In that day Christ does not present before men and women the great work He has done for them in giving His life; He presents the faithful work they have done for Him. " 'Come, you blessed of My Father, inherit the kingdom prepared for you from the foundation of the world: for I was hungry and you gave Me food; I was thirsty and you gave Me drink; I was a stranger and you took Me in; I was naked and you clothed Me; I was sick and you visited Me; I was in prison and you came to Me.' " But those whom Christ commends do not realize that they have been ministering to Him. To their perplexed inquiries He answers, " 'Inasmuch as you did it to one of the least of these My brethren, you did it to Me.' "

"In all who suffer for My name," said Jesus, "you are to recognize Me. As you would minister to Me, so you are to minister to them." All who have been born into the heavenly family are in a special sense the brothers and sisters of our Lord. The love of Christ binds the members of His family together. "Everyone who loves is born of God and knows God." 1 John 4:7.

Those whom Christ approves in the judgment may have known little of theology, but they have cherished His principles. Even among the heathen there are those who have cherished the spirit of kindness. Before the words of life had fallen on their ears, they befriended the missionaries, even at the risk of their own lives. Those who worship God ignorantly, those to whom no human ever brings the light, will not perish. Though ignorant of the written law of God, they have done the things that the law required. Their works are evidence that the Holy Spirit has touched their hearts, and God recognizes them as His children.

How surprised the lowly people among the nations will be to hear from the Savior's lips, "Inasmuch as you did

---

* This chapter is based on Matthew 25:31–46.

it to one of the least of these My brethren, you did it to Me"!

But Christ's love is not restricted to any class. He is the Son of man, and so He is a brother to every son and daughter of Adam. His followers are not to feel detached from the dying world around them. They are a part of the great web of humanity, family to sinners as well as to saints. Christ's love embraces the fallen and the sinful. Every kindness we do to uplift a fallen human being is accepted as something done to Him.

God sends the angels of heaven to minister to those who are to be heirs of salvation. It is not yet evident who will share the inheritance of the saints in light, but angels are moving throughout the earth seeking to comfort the sorrowing, protect those in danger, and win men and women to Christ. They do not pass by even one person. God shows no partiality.

As you open your door to Christ's needy, suffering ones, you are welcoming unseen angels. They bring a sacred atmosphere of joy and peace. Every act of mercy makes music in heaven. The Father on His throne counts unselfish workers among His most precious treasures.

Those on the left hand of Christ, those who had neglected Him in the person of the poor and suffering, were unaware of their guilt. They had been self-absorbed and did not care about others' needs.

To the rich, God has given wealth so that they may relieve His suffering children, but too often they are indifferent to the needs of others. They do not understand the temptations and struggles of the poor, and mercy dies out of their hearts. The resources that God has given to bless the needy are spent in pampering their own pride and selfishness. They rob the poor of the education they should have concerning the tender care of God, for He has made ample provision for them to have the comforts of life's necessities. They feel the poverty that pinches life, and they are often tempted to become envious and full of evil suspicions.

### How to Ignore Christ

But Christ sees it all, and He says, "It was I who was hungry and thirsty. It was I who was a stranger. While you were feasting at your abundant table, I was famishing in a shack. While you were comfortable in your luxurious home, I had nowhere to lay My head. While you enjoyed your pleasures, I languished in prison. When you doled out the crusts of bread to the starving poor, when you gave those flimsy garments to shield them from the biting frost, did you remember that you were giving them to the Lord of glory? All the days of your life I was near you in the person of these needy ones, but you did not seek Me. You would not enter into fellowship with Me. I do not know you."

Many visit the scenes of Christ's life on earth, to look on the lake beside which He loved to teach and the hills and valleys on which His eyes rested. But we do not need to go to Nazareth or Bethany in order to walk in Jesus' steps. We will find His footprints beside the sickbed, in the ghettos of poverty, in every place where there are human hearts in need of consolation.

Everyone may find something to do. Millions of people caught in ignorance and sin have never even heard of Christ's love for them. Christ's rule of life, by which every one of us will stand or fall in the judgment, is, "whatever you want men to do to you, do also to them." Matthew 7:12.

The Savior gave His life to establish a church capable of caring for tempted men and women. Believers may be poor, uneducated, and unknown, yet in Christ they may do a work in the neighborhood and even in "the regions beyond" whose results will reach to eternity. Because they neglect this work, many young disciples never advance beyond the mere alphabet of Christian experience. They could have directed the restless energy that is so often a source of danger into streams of blessing. They would forget self in earnest work to do others good. Those who minister to others will not be longing for exciting amusements or for some change in their lives. The great topic of interest will be how to save those who are ready to perish.

To make us children of one family, the King of glory became one with us. "Love one another as I have loved you." John 15:12. When we love the world as He has loved it, then for us His mission is accomplished. We are fitted for heaven, for we have heaven in our hearts. In the great Judgment Day, those who have not worked for Christ, who have drifted along thinking of themselves, will be placed by the Judge of the whole earth with those who did evil.

To every person God has given a trust. The Chief Shepherd will demand from everyone, "Where is the flock that was given to you, your beautiful sheep?" Jeremiah 13:20.

# A Servant of Servants*

Christ and His disciples had gathered to celebrate the Passover. The Savior knew that His hour had come. He Himself was the true Passover Lamb, and on the day the feast was eaten He was to be sacrificed. Only a few quiet hours remained for Him to spend for the benefit of His disciples.

Christ's life had been one of unselfish service. "Not come to be served, but to serve" (Matthew 20:28) had been the lesson of everything He did. But the disciples had not learned the lesson yet. At this last Passover, Jesus was troubled. A shadow came over His face. The disciples sensed that something weighed heavily on His mind.

As they were gathered around the table, He said, " 'With fervent desire I have desired to eat this Passover, with you before I suffer; for I say to you, I will no longer eat of it until it is fulfilled in the kingdom of God.' Then He took the cup, and gave thanks, and said, 'Take this and divide it among yourselves; for I say to you, I will not drink of the fruit of the vine until the kingdom of God comes.' "

Christ was now in the shadow of the cross, and the pain was torturing His heart. He knew that the disciples would desert Him. He knew that He would be put to death by the most humiliating process inflicted on criminals. He knew how ungrateful and cruel the people He had come to save could be. He knew that for many the sacrifice He must make would be in vain. Knowing all that was before Him, He might naturally have been overwhelmed with the thought of His own humiliation and suffering. But He did not think of Himself. His care for His disciples was uppermost in His mind.

On this last evening, Jesus had much to tell them. But He saw that they could not bear what He had to say. As He looked into their faces, the words remained unspoken on His lips. Moments passed in silence. The disciples were uneasy. The looks they gave each other told of jealousy and conflict.

There was "a dispute among them, as to which of them should be considered the greatest." This strife grieved and wounded Jesus. Each of them still longed for the highest place in the kingdom. James and John had dared to ask for the highest position, and

---

*This chapter is based on Luke 22:7–18, 24; John 13:1–17.*

this angered the ten so much that it threatened to split the group. Judas was the most severe on James and John.

When the disciples entered the upper room, Judas pushed his way next to Christ on the left side; John was on the right. If there was a highest place, Judas was determined to have it.

Another cause of conflict had arisen. It was customary for a servant to wash the feet of the guests. On this occasion the pitcher, the basin, and the towel were in place and ready, but no servant was present, and it was the disciples' duty to perform the task. But each determined not to act the part of a servant. All of them put on the appearance of unconcern. By their silence they refused to humble themselves.

How was Christ to bring these poor followers where Satan would not gain a clear victory over them? How could He show them that merely professing to be His disciples did not make them disciples? How could He kindle love in their hearts and enable them to comprehend what He longed to tell them?

Jesus waited for a time to see what they would do. Then He, the divine Teacher, rose from the table. Laying aside the outer garment that would have restricted His movements, He took a towel. In silence the disciples waited to see what would happen. "After that, He poured water into a basin and began to wash the disciples' feet, and to wipe them with the towel with which He was girded." This action opened the eyes of the disciples. Bitter shame filled their hearts, and they

saw themselves in a new light.

Christ gave them an example they would never forget. His love for them was not easily disturbed. He had full consciousness of His divinity, but He had laid aside His royal crown and had taken the form of a servant. One of the last acts of His life on earth was to clothe Himself like a servant and perform a servant's role.

Before the Passover Judas had made the arrangements to deliver Jesus into the hands of the priests and scribes. The disciples knew nothing of Judas's intentions. Jesus alone could read his secret, yet He did not expose him. He felt such a burden for Judas as He had felt for Jerusalem when He wept over the doomed city.

Judas felt the drawing power of that love. When the Savior's hands were washing those soiled feet and wiping them with the towel, the heart of Judas throbbed with the impulse to confess his sin. But he would not humble himself. He hardened his heart against repentance, and the old impulses again controlled him. Now Judas became offended at Christ's act in washing the feet of His disciples. If Jesus could so humble Himself, he thought, He could not be Israel's king. After seeing Him degrade Himself, as he thought, Judas was confirmed in his decision to disown Jesus and admit that he had been deceived. Possessed by a demon, he resolved to complete the work he had agreed to do in betraying his Lord.

## The Great Miracle of Changed Hearts

Judas, in choosing his position at the table, had tried to place himself first, and Christ as a Servant served him first. John was left till last. But John did not take this as a rebuke or any cause to be offended. When Peter's turn came he exclaimed with astonishment, "Lord, are You washing my feet?" Christ's condescension broke his heart. He was filled with shame to think that one of the disciples was not performing this service. "What I am doing," Christ said, "you do not understand now, but you will know after this." Peter could not bear to see his Lord, the Son of God, acting the part of a servant. His whole soul rose up against this humiliation. With great emphasis he exclaimed, "You shall never wash my feet!"

Christ said, "If I do not wash you, you have no part with Me." Christ had come to wash the heart from the stain of sin. Peter was refusing the higher cleansing included in the lower. He was really rejecting his Lord. It is not humiliating to the Master to allow Him to work to purify us.

Peter surrendered his pride. Separation from Christ would have been like death to him. " 'Not my feet only,' " he said, " ' but also my hands and my head!' Jesus said to him, 'He who is bathed needs only to wash his feet, but is completely clean.' "

These words mean more than bodily cleanliness. Christ is speaking of the higher cleansing as illustrated by the lower. Someone coming from the bath was clean, but the sandaled feet soon needed to be washed again. So Peter and his brethren had been washed in the great fountain opened for sin and uncleanness. But temptation had led them into evil, and they still needed Christ's cleansing grace.

Jesus wanted to wash the division, jealousy, and pride from their hearts. This was far more important than washing their dusty feet. With the spirit they had, not one of them was prepared for communion with Christ. Until brought into a state of humility and love, they were not prepared to share in the memorial service Christ was about to establish. Pride and self-seeking create strife, but Jesus washed all this away in washing their feet. He brought about a complete change of feeling. Jesus could say, "You are clean." Now there was union of heart, love for one another. Except Judas, each was ready to yield the highest place to another. Now they could receive Christ's words.

We, too, have been washed in the blood of Christ, yet often the heart's purity is soiled. We must come to Christ for cleansing grace. How often we bring our sinful, polluted hearts in contact with the heart of Christ! How painful to Him is our evil temper, our vanity, our pride! Yet we must bring all our infirmity and defilement to Him. He alone can wash us clean.

## Why Christ Instituted This Religious Service

After Christ had washed the disciples' feet, He said, "Do you know what I have done to you? You call Me Teacher and Lord, and you say well, for so I am. If I then, your Lord and Teacher, have washed your feet, you also ought to wash one another's feet. For I have given you an example, that you should do as I have done to you. Most assuredly, I say to you, a servant is not greater than his master; nor is he who is sent greater than he who sent him."

So that His people might not be misled by the selfishness that lives in the natural heart, Christ Himself set the example of humility. He Himself, equal with God, acted as a servant to His disciples. He to whom every knee shall bow bowed down to wash the feet of those who called Him Lord. He washed the feet of His betrayer.

God does not live for Himself. He is constantly meeting the needs of others. Jesus was given to stand at the head of humanity so that by His example He could teach what it means to minister. He served all, ministered to all. In this way He lived the law of God and showed by His example how we are to obey it.

Having washed the disciples' feet, Jesus said, "I have given you an example, that you should do as I have done to you." In these words Christ was establishing a religious service. The act of our Lord made this humbling ceremony a holy ordinance. The disciples were to observe it, so that they would always keep in mind His lessons of humility and service.

This ordinance is Christ's appointed preparation for the Communion service. While we cherish pride, divisiveness, and strife for supremacy, we are not prepared to receive the communion of His body and His blood. Therefore Jesus appointed the memorial of His humiliation for us to observe first.

In the human heart there is a disposition to think of ourselves more highly than our brother, to work for self, to seek the highest place. Often this results in evil suspicions and bitterness.

The service preceding the Lord's Supper is to bring us out of our selfishness, down from self-exaltation to the humility of heart that will lead us to serve our brother or sister. The Holy Watcher from heaven is present to make this occasion a time of heart searching, conviction of sin, and the assurance of sins forgiven. Christ is there to change the flow of thoughts that have been running in selfish channels.

As we remember the Savior's humiliation for us, a chain of memories comes to mind, memories of God's goodness and of the attentions and tenderness of earthly friends. We recall blessings forgotten and kindnesses ignored. Defects of character, neglect of duties, ingratitude, coldness, all come to remembrance. The mind is energized to break down every barrier that has caused division. Sins are confessed; they are forgiven. The subduing grace of Christ draws hearts together. We begin to desire a higher spiritual life. The soul will be uplifted. We can partake of the Communion with the sunshine of Christ's righteousness filling the temple of the heart.

To those who receive the spirit of this service, it can never become merely ceremonial. Whenever the children of God celebrate this ordinance correctly, they pledge themselves to give their lives to unselfish ministry for one another. The world is full of people who need our ministry. Those who have fellowshiped with Christ in the upper chamber will go out to minister as He did.

"If you know these things, blessed are you if you do them."

# The Lord's Supper Instituted*

The Lord Jesus on the same night in which He was betrayed took bread; and when He had given thanks, He broke it and said, 'Take, eat; this is My body which is broken for you; do this in remembrance of Me.' In the same manner He also took the cup after supper, saying, 'This cup is the new covenant in My blood. This do, as often as you drink it, in remembrance of Me.' For as often as you eat this bread and drink this cup, you proclaim the Lord's death till He comes." 1 Corinthians 11:23–26.

Christ, the Lamb of God, was about to bring to an end the system of types and ceremonies that for four thousand years had pointed to His death. The Passover, the Jews' national festival, was to pass away forever. The service that Christ established in its place was to be observed by His followers in all lands and through all ages.

God gave the Passover to commemorate Israel's deliverance from Egyptian slavery. The Lord's Supper was given to commemorate the great deliverance that Christ's death brought about. This ordinance is God's way of keeping His great work for us fresh in our minds.

In Christ's time, the people ate the Passover supper in a reclining position. The guests lay on couches placed around the table. They rested on the left arm, keeping the right hand free for use in eating. In this position a guest could lay his head on the chest of the one who sat next above him. And the feet, at the outer edge of the couch, could be washed by someone moving around the outside of the circle.

Christ was still at the table on which the Passover supper had been spread. The unleavened loaves were in front of Him. The Passover wine, untouched by fermentation, was on the table. Christ used these emblems to represent His own unblemished sacrifice. See 1 Peter 1:19.

"And as they were eating, Jesus took bread, blessed and broke it, and gave it to the disciples and said, 'Take, eat; this is My body.' Then He took the cup, and gave thanks, and gave it to them, saying, 'Drink from it, all of you. For this is My blood of the new covenant, which is shed for many for the remission of sins. But I say to you, I will not drink of this fruit of the vine from now on until that day when I

---

* This chapter is based on Matthew 26:20–29; Mark 14:17–25; Luke 22:14–23; John 13:18–30.

drink it new with you in My Father's kingdom.' "

Judas, the betrayer, received from Jesus the symbols of His broken body and spilled blood. Sitting in the very presence of the Lamb of God, the betrayer brooded on his dark plans and clung to his revengeful thoughts.

At the feet washing, Christ had given convincing proof that He understood Judas's character. "You are not all clean," He said. John 13:11. Now Christ spoke out more plainly: "I do not speak concerning all of you. I know whom I have chosen; but that the Scripture may be fulfilled, 'He who eats bread with Me has lifted up his heel against Me.' "

Even now the disciples did not suspect Judas. But a cloud settled over them, a premonition of some terrible calamity. As they ate in silence, Jesus said, "Assuredly, I say to you, one of you will betray Me." This alarmed and confused them. How could any one of them deal treacherously with their divine Teacher? Betray Him? To whom? Surely not one of the favored Twelve!

As they remembered how true His sayings were, fear and self-distrust came over them. With painful emotion, one after another inquired, "Lord, is it I?" But Judas sat silent. Finally John inquired, "Lord, who is it?" And Jesus answered, "He who dipped his hand with Me in the dish will betray Me." Judas's silence drew all eyes to him. Amid the confusion of questions and astonishment, Judas had not heard Jesus' words in answer to John's question. But now, to divert the attention of the others from himself, he asked as they had done, "Rabbi, is it

I?" Jesus solemnly replied, "You have said it."

Surprised and confused at having his plans exposed, Judas quickly got up to leave the room. Then Jesus said, " 'What you do, do quickly.' . . . Having received the piece of bread, he then went out immediately. And it was night." Night it was as the traitor turned from Christ into the outer darkness.

Until this step, Judas had not gone beyond the possibility of repentance. But when he left his Lord and his fellow disciples, he had passed the boundary line. Jesus had left nothing undone that could be done to save Judas. After he had twice agreed to betray his Lord, Jesus still gave him opportunity to repent. By reading the secret plan in the traitor's heart, Christ gave Judas the final, convincing evidence of His divinity. This was the last call to repent. From the sacred supper, Judas went out to complete the work of betrayal.

In pronouncing the woe on Judas, Christ also had a merciful purpose toward His disciples. "I tell you before it comes," He said, "that when it does come to pass, you may believe that I am He." If Jesus had remained silent, the disciples might have thought that their Master did not have divine foresight and had been surprised. A year before, Jesus had told the disciples that He had chosen twelve, and that one was a devil. Now His words to Judas would strengthen the faith of Christ's true followers during His humiliation. When Judas would come to his dreadful end, they would remember the woe that Jesus had pronounced on the betrayer.

And the Savior had still another purpose. He gave the disciples something to consider regarding the patience and mercy of God toward those who have committed some of the worst wrongs. The betrayer was privileged to unite with Christ in partaking of the Lord's Supper. This example is for us. When we suppose someone to be in error and sin, we should not divorce ourselves from him, leave him to suffer temptation, or drive him onto Satan's battleground. It was because the disciples made mistakes and were faulty that Christ washed their feet, and in this way He brought all but one to repentance.

## Christ's Example Forbids Exclusiveness

It is true that open sin excludes the guilty at the Lord's Supper. See 1 Corinthians 5:11. But beyond this none are to judge. Who can read the heart or distinguish weeds from wheat? "Let a man examine himself, and so let him eat of the bread and drink of the cup." "Whoever eats this bread or drinks this cup of the Lord in an unworthy manner will be guilty of the body and blood of the Lord. . . . He who eats and drinks in an unworthy manner eats and drinks judgment to himself, not discerning the Lord's body." 1 Corinthians 11:28, 27, 29.

When believers assemble to celebrate the ordinances of the Lord's Supper, there may be a Judas in the group. If so, messengers from the prince of darkness are there, for they accompany all who refuse to be controlled by the Holy Spirit. Heavenly angels are also present. People may come to the meeting who are not servants of truth and holiness, but who want to take part in the service. We should not refuse them. There are witnesses present who were there when Jesus washed the feet of the disciples.

Through the Holy Spirit, Christ is there to convict and soften the heart. Not a thought of sorrow for sin escapes His notice. He is waiting for the repentant, brokenhearted one. He who washed the feet of Judas longs to wash every heart from the stain of sin.

None should exclude themselves from Communion because some who are unworthy may be present. Christ Himself has made these appointments, and He meets His people there and energizes them by His presence. Hearts and hands that are unworthy may even administer the service, yet all who come with their faith set firmly on Christ will be greatly blessed. All who neglect these special times will suffer loss. The administration of the Lord's Supper was to remind the disciples often of the infinite sacrifice Jesus made for each of them individually as part of the great whole of fallen humanity.

## The Reasons for Celebrating the Lord's Supper

But the Communion service was not to be a time of sorrowing. As the Lord's disciples gather around His table, they are not to mourn over their shortcomings. They are not to recall differences between them and their brethren. The foot-washing service has included all this. Now they come to meet with Christ. They are not to stand in the shadow of the cross, but in its saving light. They are to open the heart to the bright beams of the Sun of Righteousness. They are to hear His words, "Peace I leave with you, My peace I give to you; not as the world gives do I give to you." John 14:27.

Our Lord says, "When oppressed and afflicted for My sake and the gospel's, remember My love. That love is so great that I gave My life for you. When your duties appear hard, your burdens too heavy to bear, remember that for your sake I endured the cross, despising the shame. Your Redeemer lives to make intercession for you."

The Communion service points to Christ's second coming. It was designed to keep this hope vivid in the mind. "As often as you eat this bread and drink this cup, you proclaim the Lord's death till He comes." 1 Corinthians 11:26.

Christ instituted this service so that it could speak to our senses about God's love. There can be no union between us and God except through Christ. And nothing less than the death of Christ could make His love effective for us. Only because of His death can we look joyfully to His second coming. Our senses need to be awakened to lay hold of the mystery of godliness, to comprehend, far more than we do, the atoning sufferings of Christ.

Our Lord has said, "Unless you eat the flesh of the Son of Man and drink His blood, you have no life in you. . . . For My flesh is food indeed, and My blood is drink indeed." John 6:53–55. We owe even this earthly life to the death of Christ. The bread we eat comes at the expense of His broken body; the water we drink, of His spilled blood. Never one, saint or sinner, eats his daily food, but he is nourished by the body and blood of Christ. The cross of Calvary is stamped on every loaf; it is reflected in every water spring. The light shining from that Communion service makes the provisions for our daily life sacred. The family food becomes like the table of the Lord, and every meal a sacred service.

Concerning our spiritual nature Jesus declares, "Whoever eats My flesh and drinks My blood has eternal life." By receiving His word, by doing the things that He has commanded, we become one with Him. "He who eats My flesh," He says, "and drinks My blood abides in Me, and I in him. As the living Father sent Me, and I live because of the Father, so he who feeds on Me will live because of Me." John 6:54, 56, 57. As faith contemplates our Lord's great sacrifice, we receive the spiritual life of Christ. Every Communion service forms a living connection to bind the believer to Christ, and through Him to the Father.

As we receive the bread and grape juice symbolizing Christ's broken body and spilled blood, in imagination we witness the struggle that enabled us to be reconciled to God. Christ is presented crucified among us. The thought of Calvary awakens living and sacred emotions in our hearts. Pride and self-worship cannot flourish in the heart that keeps the scenes of Calvary fresh in the memory. Whoever looks intently at the Savior's matchless love will be transformed in character. He will go out to be a light to the world, to reflect in some degree this mysterious love.

# "Let Not Your Heart Be Troubled"*

Judas had left the upper room, and Christ was alone with the eleven. He was about to speak of His approaching separation from them, but before this He pointed to the great purpose of His mission. He always kept freshly in mind His joy that all His humiliation and suffering would glorify the Father's name. This is where He first directed the thoughts of His disciples.

Their Master and Lord, their beloved Teacher and Friend, was dearer to them than life. Now He was going to leave them. Dark forebodings filled their hearts.

But the Savior's words were full of hope. He knew that Satan's craftiness is most successful against those who are depressed by difficulties. So He turned their thoughts to the heavenly home: "Let not your heart be troubled. . . . In My Father's house are many mansions; if it were not so, I would have told you. I go to prepare a place for you. And if I go and prepare a place for you, I will come again and receive you to Myself; that where I am, there you may be also." When I go away, I will still work earnestly for you. I go to the Father to cooperate with

Him on your behalf.

Christ's departure was the opposite of what the disciples feared—it did not mean a final separation. He was going to prepare a place for them so that He could receive them to Himself. While He was building mansions for them, they were to build characters in God's likeness.

Thomas was troubled by doubts. " 'Lord, we do not know where You are going, and how can we know the way?' Jesus said to him, 'I am the way, the truth, and the life. No one comes to the Father except through Me. If you had known Me, you would have known My Father also; and from now on you know Him and have seen Him.' "

There are not many ways to heaven. Each person may not choose his own way. Christ was the way by which patriarchs and prophets were saved. He is the only way by which we can have access to God.

But the disciples did not yet understand. "Lord, show us the Father, and it is sufficient for us," exclaimed Philip. Christ asked with pained surprise, "Have I been with you so long, and yet you have not known Me, Philip?" Is it possible that you do not see the Father

---

* This chapter is based on John 13:31–38; 14–17.

in the works He does through Me? "How can you say, 'Show us the Father'?" "He who has seen Me has seen the Father." Christ had not stopped being God when He became human; the Godhead was still His own. Christ's work testified to His divinity. Through Him the Father had been revealed.

If the disciples believed this vital connection between the Father and the Son, their faith would not leave them when they saw Christ's suffering and death. How persistently our Savior worked to prepare His disciples for the storm of temptation that would soon beat upon them. Everyone there felt a sacred awe as they listened to His words with breathless attention. And as their hearts were drawn to Christ in greater love, they were drawn to one another. They felt that heaven was very near.

The Savior was anxious for His disciples to understand why His divinity was united to humanity. He came to the world to display the glory of God so that He could lift us up by its restoring power. Jesus revealed no qualities and exercised no powers that we may not have through faith in Him. His perfect humanity is what all His followers may possess if they will submit to God as He did.

"Greater works than these he will do, because I go to My Father." By this Christ meant that under the influence of the Holy Spirit the disciples' work would have greater extent. After the Lord ascended to heaven, the disciples experienced the fulfillment of His promise. They knew that the divine Teacher was all that He had claimed to be. As they lifted high the love of God, hearts were touched and multitudes believed on Jesus.

## The Wonderful Privilege of Prayer

The Savior explained that the secret of their success would be to ask for strength and grace in His name. He presents the prayer of the humble petitioner to the Father as His own desire in that person's behalf. Sincere prayer may not be fluently expressed, but it will ascend to the sanctuary where Jesus ministers. He will present it to the Father without one awkward, stammering word, fragrant with the incense of His own perfection.

The path of sincerity and integrity is not free from obstacles, but in every difficulty we are to see a call to prayer. "Whatever you ask in My name," said Jesus, "that I will do, that the Father may be glorified in the Son. If you ask anything in My name, I will do it."

In Christ's name His followers are to stand before God. Because of the righteousness of Christ credited to them, they are regarded as precious. The Lord does not see the vileness of the sinner in them. He recognizes in them the likeness of His Son, in whom they believe.

The Lord is disappointed when His people place a low estimate on themselves. God wanted them, or He would not have sent His Son on such an expensive mission to redeem them. He is well pleased when they make the very highest demands on Him in order to glorify His name. They may expect large things if they have faith in His promises.

But to pray in Christ's name means

that we are to accept His character, reveal His spirit, and work His works. The Savior saves us, not in sin, but from sin. Those who love Him show their love by obedience.

All true obedience comes from the heart. It was heart work with Christ. And if we consent, He will blend our hearts and minds in conformity to His will so completely that when we obey Him we will be simply carrying out our own impulses. The will finds its highest delight in doing His service. Our life will be a life of continual obedience. Sin will become hateful to us.

As Christ lived the law in humanity, so we may do if we will take hold of the Strong One for strength. But we cannot depend on humanity for counsel. The Lord will teach us our duty just as willingly as He will teach someone else. If we come to Him in faith, He will speak His mysteries to us personally. Our hearts will often burn within us as One draws near to talk with us as He did with Enoch. Those who decide to do nothing in any line that will displease God will know, after presenting their case before Him, just what course to pursue. And God will give power to them for obedience and for service, as Christ has promised.

## How the Holy Spirit Makes Christ's Work for Us Effective

Before offering Himself as the sacrificial victim, Christ thought of the most essential gift to bestow on His followers. "I will pray the Father," He said, "and He will give you another Helper, that He may abide with you forever—the Spirit of truth, whom the world cannot receive, because it neither sees Him nor knows Him; but you know Him, for He dwells with you and will be in you. I will not leave you orphans; I will come to you." While Christ was on earth, the disciples had desired no other helper. Only when they were deprived of His presence would they feel their need of the Spirit, and then He would come.

The Holy Spirit is Christ's representative, but without the personality of humanity, and independent of it. Restricted by His humanity, Christ could not be in every place personally. It was in their best interest that He should go and send the Spirit to be His successor on earth. No one then could have any advantage because of his location. By the Spirit the Savior would be within reach of all.

Jesus read the future of His disciples. He saw one brought to the execution scaffold, one to the cross, one to exile among the lonely rocks of the sea, others to persecution and death. But in every ordeal, He would be with them. When for the truth's sake, believers stand at the judgment bar of unrighteous courts, Christ stands by their side. The reproaches that fall on them fall on Christ. When one is locked away behind prison walls, Christ fills the heart with His love.

At all times and in all places, when we feel helpless and alone, Jesus will send the Comforter in answer to the prayer of faith. Circumstances may separate us from every earthly friend, but no circumstance can separate us from the heavenly Comforter. He is always at our side to sustain and cheer.

The disciples still failed to understand Christ's words, so again He explained by the Spirit He would reveal Himself to them. "The Helper, the Holy Spirit, whom the Father will send in My name, He will teach you all things." No more will you say, I cannot comprehend.

Through the disciples Christ was to speak to all the people on the face of the earth. But in the death of Christ the disciples would suffer great disappointment. So that after this experience their word would be accurate, Jesus promised that the Comforter would "bring to your remembrance all things that I said to you." "When He, the Spirit of truth, has come, He will guide you into all truth; for He will not speak on His own authority, but whatever He hears He will speak; and He will tell you things to come. He will glorify Me, for He will take of what is Mine and declare it to you."

Jesus' disciples had been taught to accept the teaching of the rabbis as the voice of God, and it still held a power over their minds. Earthly ideas still had a large place in their thoughts. They did not understand the spiritual nature of Christ's kingdom. Many of His lessons seemed almost lost on them. Jesus promised that the Holy Spirit would bring these sayings back to their minds.

The Comforter is called "the Spirit of truth." His work is to define and uphold truth. He first lives in the heart as the Spirit of truth, and in this way He becomes the Comforter. There is comfort in truth but no real comfort in falsehood. Through false traditions Satan gains his power over the mind.

False standards misshape the character. The Holy Spirit exposes such error and expels it from the heart. By the Spirit of truth, working through the Word of God, Christ subdues His chosen people to Himself.

## The Chief Purpose of the Spirit

Jesus worked to inspire His disciples with the joy and hope that inspired His own heart. He rejoiced because the Holy Spirit was the highest of all gifts He could ask from His Father for His people. God would give the Spirit to regenerate us. Without this, the sacrifice of Christ would not have accomplished its purpose. The power of evil had been strengthening for centuries, and the submission of men and women to satanic captivity was amazing. They could resist sin and overcome it only through the mighty agency of the Third Person of the Godhead, who would come with all divine power. The Spirit makes effective what the world's Redeemer worked out. The Spirit makes the heart pure. Christ has given His Spirit to overcome all hereditary and cultivated tendencies to evil and to imprint His own character on His church. The very image of God is to be reproduced in humanity. The honor of God, the honor of Christ, is at stake in His people's perfection of character.

"When He [the Spirit of truth] has come, He will convict the world of sin, and of righteousness, and of judgment." The preaching of the Word will be of no use without the presence of the Holy Spirit. Truth will awaken the conscience or transform the life only when the Spirit accompanies it to the heart. Unless the Holy Spirit impresses the truth on hearts, no sinner will fall on the Rock and be broken. No advantages, however great, can make anyone a channel of light.

Christ has promised the gift of the Holy Spirit to His church, and the promise belongs to us as much as to the first disciples. But like every other promise, it is given on conditions. Many who profess to claim the Lord's promise talk about Christ and about the Holy Spirit, yet they receive no benefit. They do not surrender their lives to be guided by the divine agencies. We cannot use the Holy Spirit. The Spirit is to use us. But many want to manage themselves. God gives the Spirit only to those who wait humbly on Him. This promised blessing, claimed by faith, brings all other blessings along with it. Christ is ready to supply every person according to the capacity to receive.

Before leaving the upper room, the Savior led His disciples in a song of praise. He lifted His voice, not in the strains of some mournful lament, but in the joyful notes of the Passover hallel:

Praise the Lord, all you nations!
    Extol Him, all you peoples!
For great is His steadfast love toward
        us,
    And the faithfulness of the Lord
        endures forever.
Praise the Lord!
                    Psalm 117, NRSV

After the hymn, they made their way out of the city gate toward the Mount of Olives. Slowly they walked along, each busy with his own thoughts. As they began to descend toward the mount, Jesus said, "All of you will be made to stumble because of Me this night, for it is written: 'I will strike the Shepherd, and the sheep of the flock will be scattered.' " Matthew 26:31. In the upper chamber, Jesus had said that one of the Twelve would betray Him and that Peter would deny Him. But now His words included them all.

## Peter's Buried Sin

Then Peter spoke, protesting, "Even if all are made to stumble, yet I will not be." Jesus had warned him that he would deny his Savior that very night. Now He repeated the warning: "Asssuredly, I say to you that today, even this night, before the rooster crows twice, you will deny Me three times." But Peter only "spoke more vehemently, 'If I have to die with You, I will not deny You!' And they all said likewise." Mark 14:29–31.

When Peter said he would follow his Lord to prison and to death, he meant every word of it, but he did not know himself. Hidden in his heart were elements of evil that circumstances would fan into life. Unless he became conscious of his danger, these things would result in his eternal ruin. The Savior saw a self-love in him that would be stronger even than his love for Christ. Peter needed to distrust himself and to have a deeper faith in Christ. When on the Sea of Galilee he was about to sink, he cried, "Lord, save me!" So now if he had cried, "Save me from myself," Jesus would have kept him secure. But Peter thought it was cruel that Jesus seemed to distrust him, and he became more persistent in his self-confidence.

Jesus could not save His disciples from the test, but He did not leave them comfortless. Before the denial, they had the assurance of forgiveness. After His death and resurrection, they knew that they were forgiven and were dear to the heart of Christ.

Jesus and the disciples were on the way to Gethsemane, at the foot of the Mount of Olives. The moon was shining brightly, revealing a flourishing grapevine. Drawing His disciples' attention to it, Jesus said, "I am the true vine." The vine with its clinging tendrils represents Himself. The palm tree, the cedar, and the oak stand alone, requiring no support. But the vine entwines around the trellis, and in this way it climbs toward heaven. So Christ in His humanity had to depend on divine power. "I can of Myself do nothing." John 5:30.

"I am the true vine, and My Father is the vinedresser." On the hills of Palestine, our heavenly Father had planted this goodly Vine. Many were attracted by the beauty of this Vine, declaring its heavenly origin. But the leaders in Israel trampled the plant under their unholy feet. After they thought they had killed it, the heavenly Vinedresser took it and replanted it on the other side of the wall. The Vine Stock was to be no longer visible. It was hidden from the violent assaults of men. But the Vine's branches hung over the wall, and through them grafts could still be united to the Vine.

"The connection of the branch with the Vine," Jesus said, "represents the relation His followers are to maintain with Him." The branch is engrafted into the Living Vine, and fiber by fiber, vein by vein, it grows into the Vine Stock. So the Christian receives life through connection with Christ. The sinner unites His weakness to Christ's strength, his emptiness to Christ's fullness. Then he has the mind of Christ. The humanity of Christ has touched our humanity, and our humanity has touched divinity.

We must keep this union unbroken. Christ said, "Abide in Me, and I in you. As the branch cannot bear fruit of itself, unless it abides in the vine, neither can you, unless you abide in Me." This is no off-and-on connection. The branch becomes a part of the Living Vine. "The life you have received from Me," Jesus said, "can be preserved only by continual fellowship. Without Me, you cannot overcome sin or resist temptation." We are to cling to Jesus and by faith receive from Him the perfection of His own character.

The root sends its nourishment through the branch to the farthest twig. "He who abides in Me," Jesus said, "and I in him, bears much fruit; for without Me you can do nothing." When we live by faith on the Son of God, the fruits of the Spirit will show in our lives; not one will be missing.

"My Father is the vinedresser. Every branch in Me that does not bear fruit He takes away." There may be an apparent connection with Christ without a real union with Him by faith. A profession of religion places us in the church, but the character shows whether we are connected with Christ. If we bear no fruit, we are false branches. "If anyone does not abide in Me," Christ said, "he is cast out as a branch and is withered; and they gather them and throw them into the fire, and they are burned."

"Every branch that bears fruit He prunes, that it may bear more fruit." From the Twelve who had followed Jesus, one, a withered branch, was about to be taken away. The rest would pass under the pruning knife of bitter trial. The pruning will cause pain, but it is the Father who applies the knife. He does not work with a reckless hand. Excessive foliage requires pruning to keep it from drawing away the life current from the fruit. Overgrowth must be cut out to give room for the healing beams of the Sun of Righteousness. The Vinedresser prunes away the harmful growth so that the fruit may be more abundant.

"By this My Father is glorified," Jesus said, "that you bear much fruit." Through you, God desires to reveal the holiness, kindness, and compassion of His own character. Yet the Savior does not ask the disciples to work to bear fruit. He tells them to abide in Him. Through the Word, Christ abides in His followers. The life of Christ in you produces the same fruits as in Him. Living in Christ, clinging to Christ, supported by Christ, drawing nourishment from Christ, you bear fruit after the likeness of Christ.

Jesus' very first instruction when He was alone with His disciples in the upper chamber was, "A new commandment I give to you, that you love one another; as I have loved you, that you also love one another." This commandment was new to the disciples, for they had not loved one another as Christ had loved them. But through His life and death they would receive a new understanding of love. The command to love one another had a new meaning in the light of His self-sacrifice.

When people are bound together not by force or self-interest, but by love, they show the working of an influence that is more than human. It is evidence that God is restoring His image in humanity. This love, visible in the church, will surely stir Satan's anger. "If the world hates you," Jesus said, "you know that it hated Me before it hated you. If you were of the world, the world would love its own. Yet because you are not of the world, but I chose you out of the world, therefore the world hates you. Remember the word that I said to you, 'A servant is not greater than his master.' If they persecuted Me, they will also persecute you. If they kept My word, they will keep yours also. But all these things they will do to you for My name's sake, because they do not know Him who sent Me." You are to carry the gospel forward in the midst of opposition, peril, loss, and suffering.

As the world's Redeemer, Christ was constantly confronted with apparent failure. He seemed to do little of the work He longed to do. Satanic influences were constantly working to oppose His way. But He would not be discouraged. Through Isaiah He declares,

" 'I have labored in vain,
I have spent my strength for nothing

and in vain;
Yet surely my just reward is with the
  Lord,
And my work with my God.' "
                              Isaiah 49:4

Jesus rested on this word, and He gave Satan no advantage. When the deepest sorrow was closing in on His heart, He said to His disciples, "The ruler of this world is coming, and he has nothing in Me." "The ruler of this world is judged." Now shall he be thrown out. John 12:31.

Christ knew that when He would exclaim, "It is finished!" all heaven would triumph. His ear caught the distant music and the shouts of victory in the heavenly realm. He knew that the name of Christ would be praised from world to world throughout the universe. He knew that truth, armed with the Holy Spirit, would conquer in the contest with evil. He knew that the life of His trusting disciples would be like His, a series of uninterrupted victories, not appearing that way to human sight, but recognized as such in the great hereafter.

Christ did not fail, neither was He discouraged, and His followers are to exhibit a faith of the same enduring nature. They are to live as He lived and work as He worked. Instead of complaining about difficulties, they are to overcome them, to despair of nothing.

Christ intends that heaven's order and divine harmony will be represented in His church and on earth. In this way, through His people He will receive a large revenue of glory. Filled with the righteousness of Christ, the church is His storehouse, in which the riches of His grace and love are to appear in full display. Christ looks on His people in their purity and perfection as the reward of His humiliation and the supplement of His glory.

With strong, hopeful words, the Savior ended His instruction. He had finished the work God had given Him to do. He had revealed the Father's character and gathered out those who were to continue His work on earth.

As a consecrated High Priest, Christ interceded for His people: "Holy Father, keep through Your name those whom You have given Me, that they may be one as We are. . . . I do not pray for these alone, but also for those who will believe in Me through their word; that they all may be one. . . . That the world may know that You have sent Me, and have loved them as You have loved Me."

Christ gave His chosen church into the Father's arms. For Him the last battle with Satan waited, and He went out to meet it.

# The Awesome Struggle in Gethsemane*

The Savior made His way to the Garden of Gethsemane with His disciples. The Passover moon shone from a cloudless sky. As He neared Gethsemane, He became strangely silent. Throughout His life on earth He had walked in the light of God's presence. But now He was numbered with the transgressors. He must bear the guilt of fallen humanity. Its weight was so great that He was tempted to fear that it would shut Him out forever from His Father's love. He exclaimed, "My soul is exceedingly sorrowful, even to death."

Never before had the disciples seen their Master so utterly sad. His body swayed as if He were about to fall. On reaching the garden, the disciples looked anxiously for His usual place of seclusion, so that their Master could rest. Twice His companions supported Him, or He would have fallen.

Near the entrance, Jesus left all but three of the disciples, asking them to pray for themselves and for Him. With Peter, James, and John, He entered the garden's inner areas. In His great struggle, Christ wanted their presence near Him. Often they had passed the night with Him in this retreat. After a

season of prayer, they would sleep undisturbed until He awoke them in the morning to go out again to work. Now He wanted them to spend the night with Him in prayer, yet He could not bear for even them to witness the agony He was about to endure.

"Stay here," Jesus said, "and watch with Me." He went a little distance—not so far that they could not see and hear Him—and fell facedown on the ground. He felt that He was being separated from His Father by sin. The gulf was so broad, so black, so deep, that His spirit shuddered as He faced it. He must not exert His divine power to escape this agony. As a man He must suffer the consequences of human sin. As a man He must endure God's anger against transgression.

## The Terrible Temptation

Christ was now standing in a different relationship to God from that in which He had always stood before. As our Substitute, Christ was suffering under divine justice. Before this He had been an intercessor for others; now He longed to have an intercessor for Himself.

* This chapter is based on Matthew 26:36–56; Mark 14:32–50; Luke 22:39–53; John 18:1–12.

As Christ felt His unity with the Father being broken up, He feared that in His human nature He would not be able to endure the conflict. The tempter had come for the last fearful struggle; if he failed here, the kingdom of the world would finally become Christ's and he himself would be over-thrown. But if he could overcome Christ, the earth would become Satan's kingdom, and the human race would be in his power forever.

Satan told Christ that if He became the Substitute for a sinful world, He would be identified with Satan's kingdom and would never again be one with God. And what would He gain by this sacrifice? Satan pressed the situation on the Redeemer: The people who claim to be above all others in spiritual advantages are seeking to destroy You. One of Your own disciples will betray You. One of Your most zealous followers will deny You. All will forsake You. It pierced Christ's heart to think that those whom He loved so much would unite in the plots of Satan. The conflict was terrible. The sins of humanity weighed heavily on Christ, and the sense of God's anger against sin was crushing out His life.

In His agony, He clung to the cold ground, as if to prevent Himself from being drawn farther from God. From His pale lips came the bitter cry, "O My Father, if it is possible, let this cup pass from Me." Yet even now He added, "Nevertheless, not as I will, but as You will."

## Jesus Hungered for Human Sympathy

The human heart longs for sympa-thy in suffering. Christ felt this longing to the very depths of His being. He came to His disciples yearning to hear some words of comfort. He longed to know that they were praying for Him and for themselves. How dark seemed the evil of sin! Terrible was the temptation to let the human race bear its own guilt, while He stood innocent before God. If He could only know that His disciples appreciated this, it would strengthen Him.

But He "found them sleeping." If He had found them seeking refuge in God so that satanic agencies would not be victorious over them, He would have been comforted. But they had not heeded His warning, "Watch and pray." They had not intended to forsake their Lord, but they seemed paralyzed by a stupor that they could have shaken off if they had continued pleading with God. When the Savior needed their prayers the most, they were asleep.

The disciples woke up when Jesus spoke to them, but they hardly knew Him, His face was so changed by anguish. Addressing Peter, Jesus said, "Simon, are you sleeping? Could you not watch one hour? Watch and pray, lest you enter into temptation. The spirit indeed is willing, but the flesh is weak." Jesus feared that they would not be able to endure the test of His betrayal and death.

Again the Son of God came under superhuman agony, and fainting and exhausted, He staggered back to the place of His former struggle. His suffering was even greater than before. "His sweat became like great drops of blood falling down to the ground."

The cypress and palm trees were the silent witnesses of His anguish. From their leafy branches heavy dew dropped on His stricken form, as if nature wept over its Author wrestling alone with the powers of darkness.

A short time before, Jesus had stood like a mighty cedar, withstanding the storm of opposition that exhausted its fury on Him. Now He was like a reed beaten and bent by the angry storm. Like Someone who was already glorified, He had claimed to be one with God. Now His voice rose on the still evening air, and it was full of human anguish, "O My Father, if this cup cannot pass away from Me unless I drink it, Your will be done."

Again Jesus felt a longing for some words from His disciples that would break the spell of darkness that nearly overpowered Him. But their eyes were heavy, "and they did not know what to answer Him." They saw His face marked with the bloody sweat of agony, but they could not understand His anguish of mind. "His visage was marred more than any man, and His form more than the sons of men." Isaiah 52:14.

### When the World's Fate Trembled in the Balance

Turning away, Jesus went again to His place of seclusion and fell facedown. The humanity of the Son of God trembled in that trying hour. The awful moment to decide the destiny of the world had come. The fate of humanity trembled in the balance. Christ could even now refuse to drink the cup allotted for guilty humanity. He could wipe the bloody sweat from His brow and leave us to perish in our iniquity. He could say, "Let the transgressor receive the penalty of his sin, and I will go back to My Father. Will the innocent suffer the consequences of the curse of sin, to save the guilty?" "O My Father, if this cup cannot pass away from Me unless I drink it, Your will be done."

Three times He drew back from the last, crowning sacrifice. But now He sees that the human race is helpless. He sees the power of sin. The woes of a doomed world rise before Him. He sees its impending fate, and He makes His decision. He will save humanity at any cost to Himself. He has left the halls of heaven to save the one world that has fallen by transgression. And He will not turn from His mission.

Having made the decision, He fell dying to the ground. Where now were His disciples, to place their hands beneath the head of their fainting Master? The Savior trod the winepress alone, and from the people there was none with Him. See Isaiah 63:3.

But God suffered with His Son. Angels witnessed the Savior's agony. There was silence in heaven. No harp was touched. In silent grief, the angelic host watched the Father separating His beams of light, love, and glory from His beloved Son.

Satan and his allies in evil watched intently. What answer would come to Christ's prayer, repeated three times? In this awful crisis, when the mysterious cup trembled in the hand of the Sufferer, the mighty angel who stands in God's presence came to Christ's side. The angel did not come to take the cup from Christ's hand, but to strengthen Him with the assurance of His Father's love. He assured Him that His death would result in the complete defeat of Satan, and that the kingdom of this world would be given to the saints of the Most High. He told Him that He would see a great number of the human race saved, eternally saved.

## How Christ's Prayer Was Answered

Christ's agony did not end, but His depression and discouragement left Him. The storm had not lessened, but He was strengthened to meet its fury. A heavenly peace rested on His blood-stained face. He had borne what no human being could ever bear, for He had tasted the sufferings of death for everyone.

The sleeping disciples, suddenly awakened, saw the angel. They heard his voice speaking words of comfort and hope to the Savior. Now they had no further fear for their Master; He was under the care of God. Again the disciples yielded to the strange stupor that overpowered them, and again Jesus found them sleeping.

Looking sorrowfully at them Jesus said, "Are you still sleeping and resting? Behold, the hour is at hand, and the Son of Man is being betrayed into the hands of sinners." Even as He spoke, He heard the footsteps of the mob in search of Him, and said, "Rise, let us be going. See, My betrayer is at hand."

No traces of His recent agony were visible as Jesus stepped forward to meet His betrayer. "Whom are you seeking?"

They answered, "Jesus of Nazareth."

Jesus replied, "I am He." As He spoke these words, the angel who had ministered to Jesus moved between Him and the mob. A divine light illuminated the Savior's face. In the presence of this divine glory, the murderous crowd staggered back. Even Judas fell to the ground.

The angel withdrew, and the light faded away. Jesus had opportunity to escape, but He remained in the midst of that hardened rabble, now on the ground and helpless at His feet.

But quickly the scene changed. The Roman soldiers, the priests, and Judas gathered around Christ, fearful that He would escape. They had had evidence that He who stood before them was the Son of God, but they would not be convinced. To the question, "Whom are you seeking?" they answered again, "Jesus of Nazareth." The Savior then said, "I have told you that I am He. Therefore, if you seek Me, let these go their way"—pointing to the disciples. He was ready to sacrifice Himself for them.

Judas the betrayer did not forget the part he was to act. He had given a sign to Jesus' pursuers, saying, "Whomever I kiss, He is the One; seize Him." Now, coming close to Jesus, he took His hand as a familiar friend. With the words, "Greetings, Rabbi," he kissed Him repeatedly, and he appeared to weep as if in sympathy with Jesus in His danger.

Jesus said, "Friend, why have you come?" His voice trembling with sorrow, He added, "Judas, are you betraying the Son of Man with a kiss?" This appeal should have awakened the betrayer's conscience, but honor and human tenderness had left him.

He had given himself up to Satan and had no power to resist him. Jesus did not refuse the traitor's kiss.

The mob now laid hold of Jesus and set about to bind those hands that had always been employed in doing good.

The disciples were disappointed and indignant as they saw the cords brought forward to bind the hands of the One they loved. In anger Peter drew his sword and cut off an ear of the high priest's servant. When Jesus saw what had happened, He released His hands, though held firmly by the Roman soldiers, and saying, "Permit even this," He touched the wounded ear, and it was made whole instantly.

Then He said to Peter, "Put your sword in its place, for all who take the sword will perish by the sword. Or do you think that I cannot now pray to My Father, and He will provide Me with more than twelve legions of angels?"—a legion in place of each disciple. "Oh, why," the disciples thought, "does He not save Himself and us?" Answering their unspoken thought, He added, "How then could the Scriptures be fulfilled, that it must happen thus?" "Shall I not drink the cup which My Father has given Me?"

The scheming priests and elders had joined the temple police and rabble in following Judas to Gethsemane. What a company for those dignitaries to unite with—a mob armed with all kinds of implements, as if in pursuit of a wild beast!

Turning to the priests and elders, Christ spoke words they would never forget: "You come out against Me with swords and clubs as you would against a thief or a robber. Day by day I sat teaching in the temple. You had every opportunity to lay hands on Me, and you did nothing. The night is better suited to your work. 'This is your hour, and the power of darkness.' "

The disciples were terrified as they saw Jesus permit Himself to be taken and bound. They were offended that He would allow this humiliation to Himself and them. They could not understand His conduct, and they blamed Him for submitting. In their indignation and fear, Peter proposed that they save themselves. Following this suggestion, "they all forsook Him and fled."

# The Illegal Trial of Jesus *

Through the hushed streets of the sleeping city they hurried Jesus. It was past midnight. Bound and closely guarded, the Savior moved painfully to the palace of Annas, the ex-high priest. Annas was the head of the officiating priestly family, and in deference to his age the people recognized him as high priest. The leaders regarded his counsel as the voice of God. He must be present at the examination of the prisoner, for fear that the less-experienced Caiaphas might fail to secure the result for which they were working. They must use Annas's cunning and subtlety, for they had to obtain Christ's condemnation.

Christ was to be tried formally before the Sanhedrin, but before Annas in a preliminary trial. Under Roman rule, the Sanhedrin could only examine a prisoner and pass judgment, to be ratified by the Roman authorities. It was therefore necessary to bring charges against Christ that both the Romans and also the Jews would regard as criminal. Christ's teaching had brought conviction to more than a few priests and rulers. Joseph of Arimathea and Nicodemus were not called to this trial, but others might dare to speak in favor of justice. The trial must unite the Sanhedrin against Christ. The priests wanted to establish two charges. If they could prove that Jesus was a blasphemer, the Jews would condemn Him. If they could convict Him of undermining Rome's rule, it would secure His condemnation by the Romans.

The second charge was what Annas tried to establish first. He questioned Jesus, hoping the Prisoner would say something to prove that He was seeking to establish a secret society with the purpose of setting up a new kingdom. Then the priests could deliver Him to the Romans as a creator of revolt.

As if reading the inmost soul of His questioner, Christ denied that He gathered His followers secretly and in the darkness to conceal His plans. "I spoke openly to the world," He answered. "I always taught in synagogues and in the temple, where the Jews always meet, and in secret I have said nothing."

The Savior contrasted His manner of work with the methods of His ac-

---

* This chapter is based on Matthew 26:57–75; 27:1; Mark 14:53–72; 15:1; Luke 22:54–71; John 18:13–27.

cusers. They had hunted Him to bring Him before a secret tribunal, where they might use perjury to obtain what it was impossible to gain by fair means. The midnight arrest by a mob, the mockery and abuse before He was even accused—this was their manner of work, not His. Their action was in violation of the law. Their own rules declared that everyone should be treated as innocent until proved guilty.

Turning upon His questioner, Jesus said, "Why do you ask Me?" Had not spies been present at every gathering of the people and carried information to the priests about all His sayings and doings? "Ask those who have heard Me what I said to them. Indeed they know what I said."

Annas was silenced. One of his officers, filled with anger, struck Jesus on the face, saying, "Do You answer the high priest like that?" Christ calmly replied, "If I have spoken evil, bear witness of the evil; but if well, why do you strike Me?" His calm answer came from a heart sinless, patient, and gentle, that would not be provoked.

Christ received every indignity from the hands of the beings for whom He was making an infinite sacrifice. And He suffered in proportion to His holiness and hatred of sin. His trial by men who acted as demons was a perpetual sacrifice for Him. To be surrounded by human beings under the control of Satan was revolting. And He knew that by flashing out His divine power, He could lay His cruel tormentors in the dust. This made the trial harder to bear.

The Jews expected a Messiah to change the current of people's thoughts by one flash of overmastering will and force them to acknowledge His supremacy. So when Christ was treated with contempt, a strong temptation came to Him to show His divine character, to make His persecutors confess that He was Lord above kings and rulers, priests and temple. It was difficult to keep the position He had chosen as one with humanity.

## Angels Would Gladly Have Delivered Christ

The angels of heaven longed to deliver Christ. Watching the shameful scene, how easily could they have consumed the adversaries of God! But God commanded them not to. It was part of Jesus' mission to bear in His humanity all the abuse that human beings could heap on Him.

Christ had said nothing that could give His accusers an advantage, yet He was bound, to signify that He was condemned. There must, however, be the form of a legal trial. This the authorities were determined to accomplish quickly. They knew the high regard the people had for Jesus, and they feared a rescue attempt. Again, if the execution did not happen right away, there would be a week's delay because of the Passover. This might defeat their plans. During a week's delay, a reaction would likely set in. The better part of the people would come forward with testimony to vindicate Him, bringing to light the mighty works He had done. The Sanhedrin's proceedings would be condemned, and Jesus would be set free. So the priests and rulers determined that before their intentions could become known, Jesus must be delivered into the hands of the Romans.

But first, they had to find an accusation. They had gained nothing so far. Annas ordered Jesus to be taken to Caiaphas. Though lacking in force of character, Caiaphas was fully as heartless and as willing to use any means necessary as was Annas. It was now early morning and dark. By torches and lanterns, the armed band with their Prisoner proceeded to the high priest's palace. While the Sanhedrin were coming together, Annas and Caiaphas again questioned Jesus, but without success.

In the judgment hall, Caiaphas took his seat as presiding officer. On either side were the judges and those specially interested in the trial. Roman soldiers were on the platform below the throne. At the foot of the throne stood Jesus. The excitement was intense. Of all the crowd, He alone was calm and serene.

Caiaphas had thought of Jesus as his rival. The people were eager to hear the Savior, and this prompted the bitter jealousy of the high priest. But now, as Caiaphas looked at the prisoner, he was struck with admiration for His noble, dignified bearing. A conviction came over him that this man was like God. The next instant he banished the thought and, in haughty tones, demanded that Jesus work one of His mighty miracles. But the Savior acted as though He had not even heard the words. The question arose in the minds of that hardened crowd, Should this man of godlike presence be condemned as a criminal?

The enemies of Jesus were perplexed. They did not know how to bring about His condemnation. Caiaphas wanted to avoid stirring up conflict. There were plenty of witnesses to prove that Christ had called the priests and scribes hypocrites and murderers, but this was not useful to bring out. Such testimony would have no weight with the Romans. There was much evidence that Jesus had spoken irreverently of many of the Jews' regulations. This evidence also would have no weight with the Romans. Christ's enemies did not dare to accuse Him of Sabbath breaking, since an examination would bring to light His miracles of healing.

The leaders had bribed false witnesses to accuse Jesus of trying to establish a separate government. But their testimony turned out to be vague and contradictory. Under examination they falsified their own statements.

Early in His ministry Christ had said, "Destroy this temple, and in three days I will raise it up." In this way He had foretold His own death and resurrection. "He was speaking of the temple of His body." John 2:19, 21. Of all that Christ had said, the priests could find nothing to use against Him except this. The Romans had engaged in rebuilding and beautifying the temple, and they took great pride in it. If anyone showed contempt for it, they would be offended. Here Romans and Jews had common ground, for all regarded the temple with great respect.

One witness who had been bribed to accuse Jesus declared, "This fellow said, 'I am able to destroy the temple of God and to build it in three days.'" If the witness had reported Christ's words exactly as He spoke them, they would not have brought about His condemnation even by the Sanhedrin. His declaration would only have indicated an unreasonable, boastful spirit, but not blasphemy. Even as the false witnesses misrepresented His words, they contained nothing the Romans regarded as a crime worthy of death.

At last Jesus' accusers were entangled, confused, and angry. It seemed that their plottings were going to fail. Caiaphas was desperate. He had only one last resort—to force Christ to condemn Himself. The high priest stood up suddenly from the judgment seat, his face contorted with passion. "Do You answer nothing?" he exclaimed. "What is it these men testify against You?" Jesus remained silent.

He was oppressed and He was afflicted,
Yet He opened not His mouth;
He was led as a lamb to the slaughter,
And as a sheep before its shearers is
    silent,
So He opened not His mouth.

Isaiah 53:7

Finally, Caiaphas addressed Jesus in the form of a solemn oath: "I put You under oath by the living God: Tell us if You are the Christ, the Son of God!"

To this appeal Christ could not remain silent. He knew that to answer now would make His death certain. But the appeal came from the highest acknowledged authority of the nation and in the name of the Most High. He must plainly declare His character and mission. Jesus had said to His disciples, "Whoever confesses Me before men, him I will also confess before My Father who is in heaven." Matthew 10:32. Now by His own example He repeated the lesson.

Every eye was focused on Jesus' face as He answered, "It is as you said." A heavenly light seemed to illuminate His pale features as He added, "Nevertheless, I say to you, hereafter you will see the Son of Man sitting at the right hand of the Power, and coming on the clouds of heaven." For a moment the high priest trembled before the penetrating eyes of the Savior. Never from then on did he forget that searching glance of the persecuted Son of God.

### Caiaphas Almost Convinced

The thought that all would stand at the judgment bar of God, to be rewarded according to their works, terrified Caiaphas. The scenes of the final judgment rushed into his mind. For a moment he saw the graves giving up their dead, with the secrets he had hoped were forever hidden. He felt as if the eternal Judge was reading his heart, bringing to view mysteries supposed to be hidden with the dead.

Caiaphas had denied the resurrection, the judgment, and a future life. Now a satanic fury maddened him. Tearing his robe, he demanded that the counsel condemn the Prisoner for blasphemy. "What further need do we have of witnesses?" he said. "Look, now you have heard His blasphemy! What do you think?" And they all condemned Him.

Caiaphas was furious with himself for believing Christ's words, and instead of having his heart broken and confessing that Jesus was the Messiah, he tore his priestly robes in determined resistance. This act was deeply significant. He did it to secure Christ's condemnation, but in doing so, the high priest had condemned himself. By the law of God, he was disqualified for the priesthood. He had pronounced on himself the death sentence.

A high priest was not to tear his garments. By the Levitical law, under no circumstances was the priest to tear his robe. Christ had expressly commanded Moses concerning this. See Leviticus 10:6. Finite man might rend his own heart by showing a contrite and humble spirit. But no one must tear the priestly robes, for this would mar the representation of heavenly things. The high priest who dared to engage in the service of the sanctuary with a torn robe was considered to have cut himself off from God. Caiaphas's action showed human passion, human imperfection.

By tearing his garments, Caiaphas made the law of God of no effect and followed human traditions. A man-made law provided that in case of blasphemy a priest might tear his garments in horror at the sin and not be guilty. In this way the law of God was set aside by human laws. But in this act, Caiaphas himself was committing blasphemy.

When Caiaphas tore his garment, his act signified the place the Jewish nation would occupy toward God after this. The Jewish people had rejected Him who was the fulfillment of all their symbols, the substance of all their shadows. Israel was divorced from God. Well might the high priest tear his robes in horror for himself and for the nation.

## The Injustice of Christ's Trial

The Sanhedrin had pronounced Jesus worthy of death, but it was contrary to Jewish law to try a prisoner by night. In legal condemnation nothing could be done except in the light of day and in a full session of the council. Despite this, the Savior was now treated as a condemned criminal, to be abused by the lowest of humankind. Through the open courtyard, Jesus was taken to the guardroom, surrounded by people mocking His claim to be the Son of God. They jeeringly repeated His words, "Coming on the clouds of heaven." While in the guardroom awaiting His legal trial, Jesus was not protected, and the ignorant rabble took the opportunity to reveal all the satanic elements of their nature. Christ's godlike bearing filled them with an insane rage. Mercy and justice were trampled upon. Never was a criminal treated in so inhuman a manner as was the Son of God.

But no enemy's hand could have dealt the blow that gave Jesus the deepest pain. While He was undergoing the examination before Caiaphas, one of Christ's own disciples had denied Him.

Peter and John had dared to follow—at a distance—the mob that had Jesus in their custody. The priests recognized John and let him into the hall, hoping that as he witnessed his Leader's humiliation, he would scorn the idea that such a one could be the Son of God. John spoke in favor of Peter and gained an entrance for him also.

In the courtyard a fire had been kindled, for it was cold, being just before dawn. People gathered around the fire, and Peter presumptuously joined them. By mingling with the crowd, he hoped to be taken for one of those who had brought Jesus to the judgment hall.

## Peter Fails

But the woman doorkeeper looked carefully at him. She noticed the dejection on his face and thought he might be a disciple of Jesus. Curious to know, she asked, "You are not also one of His disciples, are you?" Peter was startled and confused; he pretended not to understand. But she persisted. Peter felt compelled to answer, and he said angrily, "Woman, I do not know Him." This was the first denial, and immediately the rooster crowed. In pretending to have no involvement with Jesus, Peter had become an easy prey to temptation.

Someone else called attention to him the second time, claiming he was a follower of Jesus. Peter now declared with an oath, "I do not know the Man!" Another hour passed, when a close relative of the man whose ear Peter had cut off asked him, "Did I not see you in the garden with Him?" "Surely you are one of them; for you are a Galilean." At this Peter flew into a rage. In order fully to deceive his questioners and justify his pretended identity, Peter now denied his Master with cursing and swearing. Again the rooster crowed. Peter heard it and remembered the words of Jesus, "Before the rooster crows twice, you will deny Me three times." Mark 14:30.

While the degrading oaths were fresh on Peter's lips and the shrill crowing of the rooster was ringing in his ears, the Savior turned and looked directly at His poor disciple. At the same time, Peter's eyes were drawn to his Master. In that gentle expression he read deep pity and sorrow, but no anger.

The sight of that suffering face, those quivering lips, pierced his heart like an arrow. Peter remembered his promise of a few short hours before, when the Savior told him he would deny his Lord three times that very night. Peter now realized how accurately his Lord had read his the falseness of heart, which he had not known himself.

A tide of memories rushed over him. The Savior's long-suffering, His patience—he remembered it all. He reflected with horror on his own falsehood, his perjury. Once more he saw an ungodly hand raised to strike his Master in the face. Unable to endure the scene any longer, he rushed, heartbroken, from the hall.

He hurried on in solitude and darkness, not knowing or caring where. At last he found himself in Gethsemane. He remembered with bitter remorse that Jesus had agonized in prayer alone. He remembered His solemn instruction, "Watch and pray, lest you enter into temptation." Matthew 26:41. It was torture to his bleeding heart to know that he had added the heaviest burden to the Savior's humiliation and grief. Peter fell on his face and wished that he would die.

If he had spent those hours in the garden in watching and prayer, Peter would not have been left to depend on his own feeble strength. He would not have denied his Lord. If the disciples had watched with Christ in His agony, they would have been prepared to witness His suffering on the cross. Amid the gloom of the most trying hour, hope would have lighted up the darkness and sustained their faith.

## Determined Efforts to Condemn Jesus

As soon as it was day, the Sanhedrin assembled again, and once more Jesus was brought into the council room. He had declared Himself to be the Son of God, but they could not condemn Him on this, for many had not been there at the night session and had not heard His words. And they knew that the Roman official would find nothing worthy of death in those words. But if they could all hear from His own lips His claim to be the Messiah, they might twist this into a treasonous political claim.

"If You are the Christ," they said, "tell us." But Christ remained silent. They continued to press Him with questions. At last He answered, "If I tell you, you will by no means believe. And if I also ask you, you will by no means answer Me or let Me go." But He added the solemn warning, "Hereafter the Son of Man will sit on the right hand of the power of God."

"Are You then the Son of God?" they asked. He said to them, "You rightly say that I am." They cried out, "What further testimony do we need? For we have heard it ourselves from His own mouth."

And Jesus was to die. All that was necessary now was for the Romans to ratify this condemnation.

Then came the third scene of abuse, worse even than what the ignorant rabble had done. It took place in the very presence of the priests and rulers, with their approval. When the judges pronounced Jesus' condemnation, a satanic fury took possession of the people. The crowd made a rush toward Jesus. If it had not been for the Roman soldiers, He would not have lived to be nailed to the cross of Calvary. He would have been torn in pieces. Roman authority intervened and restrained the violence of the mob by force of arms.

Heathen men were angry at the brutal treatment of One against whom nothing had been proved. The Roman officers declared that it was against Jewish law to condemn a man to death on his own testimony. This brought a momentary lull in the proceedings; but the Jewish leaders were dead both to pity and to shame.

Priests and rulers forgot the dignity of their office and abused the Son of God with foul names. They taunted Him about His parentage. They declared that His proclaiming Himself the Messiah made Him deserving of the most shameful death. Someone threw an old garment over His head, and His persecutors struck Him in the face, saying, "Prophesy to us, Christ! Who is the one who struck You?" One poor wretch spat in His face.

Angels faithfully recorded every insulting look, word, and act against their beloved Commander. One day the evil men who scorned the calm, pale face of Christ will look upon it in its glory, shining brighter than the sun.

# How Judas Lost His Soul

The history of Judas presents the sad ending of a life that could have been honored by God. If Judas had died before his last journey to Jerusalem, he would have been thought of as worthy of a place among the Twelve, one who would be greatly missed. The abhorrence that has followed him through the centuries would not have existed. But his character was revealed to the world as a warning to all who would betray sacred trusts.

Since the feast at the house of Simon, Judas had had opportunity to reflect on the deed he had agreed to perform, but his decision was unchanged. He sold the Lord of glory for the price of a slave.

By his nature Judas had a strong love for money, but he had not always been corrupt enough to do something like this. He had nurtured the spirit of greed until it had become stronger than his love for Christ. Through one vice he gave himself to Satan, who would drive him to any lengths in sin.

Judas had joined the disciples when the crowds were following Christ. He witnessed the Savior's mighty works in healing the sick, casting out devils, and raising the dead. He recognized the teaching of Jesus as superior to everything that he had ever heard. He felt a desire to be changed in character, and he hoped to experience this through connecting himself with Jesus.

The Savior did not reject Judas. He gave him a place among the Twelve and granted him power to heal the sick and cast out devils. But Judas did not surrender himself fully to Christ. He did not give up his worldly ambition or his love of money. He did not allow God to shape his life, but cultivated a frame of mind to criticize and accuse.

Judas had great influence over the disciples. He had a high opinion of his own qualifications, and he considered his fellow disciples as greatly inferior to himself. Judas told himself, with satisfaction, that the church would often come into embarrassment if it were not for his ability as a manager. In his own estimation he was an honor to the cause, and this is how he always presented himself.

Christ placed him where he would have opportunity to see and correct his weakness of character, but Judas indulged his desire for money. The small amounts that came into his hands were a continual temptation. When he did some small service for Christ, he paid himself out of this meager fund. In his own eyes these false reasons excused his action, but in God's sight he was a thief.

Judas had marked out a course of action that he expected Christ to follow. He had planned that Jesus would deliver John the Baptist from prison. But John remained there and was beheaded. And Jesus, instead of avenging John's death, went away into a country location. Judas wanted more aggressive warfare. He thought that if only Jesus would not prevent the disciples from carrying out their schemes, the work would be more successful. He saw Jesus leave the Jewish leaders' challenge unanswered when they demanded that He show them a sign from heaven. Judas's heart was open to disbelief, and the enemy provided thoughts of rebellion. Why did Jesus predict trial and persecution for Himself and His disciples? Were Judas's hopes for a high place in the kingdom to be disappointed?

## Working Against Christ

Judas was always advancing the idea that Christ would reign as king in Jerusalem. At the miracle of the loaves, it was Judas who started up the project to take Christ by force and make Him king. His hopes were high, his disappointment bitter.

Christ's message concerning the Bread of Life was the turning point. Judas saw Christ offering spiritual rather than worldly good. He thought he could see that Jesus would have no honor and could grant no high position to His followers. He determined not to unite himself so closely to Christ that he could not draw away. He would

watch. And he did watch.

From that time he expressed doubts that confused the disciples. He introduced controversies and texts of Scripture that had no connection with the truths Christ was presenting. These texts, separated from their context, perplexed the disciples and increased the discouragement pressing in on them. Yet Judas appeared honorable and upright. So in a very religious and apparently wise way, he was attaching a meaning to Jesus' words that He had not conveyed. Judas's suggestions were constantly stirring up ambitious desire for higher positions and honors. The argument over who should be greatest was generally started by Judas.

When Jesus presented the condition of discipleship to the rich young ruler, Judas thought that He had made a mistake. Such men as this ruler would help finance Christ's cause. Judas thought that he personally could suggest many plans to benefit the little church. In these things, he thought he was wiser than Christ.

## Judas's Last Opportunity to Repent

In everything that Christ said to His disciples, there was something with which Judas, in his heart, disagreed. Under his influence, the leaven of discord was doing its work. Jesus saw that Satan was opening up a channel through which to influence the other disciples. Yet Judas made no outward complaint until the feast in Simon's house. When Mary anointed the Savior's feet, Judas showed his covetous attitude. When Jesus reproved him, wounded pride and desire for revenge broke down the barriers. This will be the experience of everyone who persists in tampering with sin.

But Judas was not yet completely hardened. Even after he had twice committed himself to betray the Savior, he had opportunity to repent. At the Passover supper, Jesus tenderly included Judas when He ministered to the disciples. But Judas did not respond to love's last appeal. The feet that Jesus had washed went out to do the betrayer's work.

Judas reasoned that if Jesus was supposed to be crucified, the event must happen. His act would not change the result. If Jesus was not supposed to die, Judas's betrayal would only force Him to deliver Himself. He decided that he had made a sharp bargain in betraying his Lord.

Judas did not, however, believe that Christ would permit Himself to be arrested. In betraying Him, Judas intended to teach Him a lesson. He wanted to make the Savior careful to treat him with due respect from then on. Often when the scribes and Pharisees had picked up stones to throw at Him, He had made His escape. Since He had escaped so many traps, He certainly would not now allow Himself to be taken.

Judas decided to put the matter to the test. If Jesus really was the Messiah, the people would proclaim Him king. Judas would have the credit for having placed the king on David's throne, and this would secure the first position for him, next to Christ, in the new kingdom.

In the Garden, Judas said to the leaders of the mob, "Hold him fast [securely]." Matthew 26:48, KJV. He fully believed that Christ would escape. Then if they blamed him, he could say, "Did I not tell you to hold Him fast?"

In amazement Judas saw the Savior allow Himself to be led away. At every movement he looked for Him to surprise His enemies by appearing before them as the Son of God. But as hour after hour went by, a terrible fear came to the traitor that he had sold his Master to His death.

As the trial came to a close, Judas could no longer endure his guilty conscience. Suddenly a hoarse voice rang through the hall: "He is innocent! Spare Him, O Caiaphas!" The tall form of Judas pressed through the startled crowd. His face was pale, and sweat stood on his forehead. Rushing to the judgment throne, he threw down in front of the high priest the pieces of silver that had been the price of his Lord's betrayal. Grasping Caiaphas's robe, he begged him to release Jesus. Caiaphas angrily shook him off, but he did not know what to say. The treachery of the priests was plain to everyone. They had bribed the disciple to betray his Master.

"I have sinned by betraying innocent blood." But the high priest, regaining his composure, answered, "What is that to us? You see to it!" Matthew 27:4. The priests had been willing to make Judas their tool, but they despised his low character.

## Judas's Agony of Remorse

Judas now threw himself at Jesus' feet, acknowledging Him to be the

Son of God and begging Him to deliver Himself. The Savior knew that Judas felt no deep, heartbreaking grief that he had betrayed the spotless Son of God. Yet He spoke no word of condemnation. He looked at Judas with pity and said, "For this hour I came into the world."

With amazement the assembly saw the patience of Christ toward His betrayer. This Man was more than mortal! But why did He not free Himself and defeat His accusers?

His pleadings in vain, Judas rushed from the hall exclaiming, "It is too late! It is too late!" He felt that he could not live to see Jesus crucified, and in despair he went out and hanged himself.

Later that day, the crowd that was leading Jesus to the place of crucifixion saw the body of Judas at the foot of a dead tree. His weight had broken the cord by which he had hanged himself. Dogs were now devouring his mangled body. Divine punishment seemed already to be coming on those who were guilty of the blood of Jesus.

# Christ's Trial Before the Roman Governor*

Christ stood bound as a prisoner in the judgment hall of Pilate, the Roman governor. Around Him was the guard of soldiers. The hall was quickly filling with spectators. Just outside were the judges of the Sanhedrin, priests, rulers, and the mob.

After condemning Jesus, the Sanhedrin had come to Pilate to have him confirm and execute the sentence. But these Jewish officials would not enter the Roman judgment hall. According to their ceremonial law, entering that place would defile them and prevent them from taking part in the Passover. They did not see that murderous hatred had defiled their hearts. They did not see that since they had rejected Christ, the real Passover Lamb, for them the great feast had lost its significance.

Pilate looked on the Savior with no friendly eyes. Called from his bedroom in haste, he determined to do his work as quickly as possible. Putting on his most severe expression, he turned to see what kind of Man he had to examine.

He gazed intently on Jesus. He had had to deal with all kinds of crimi-

nals, but never had a Man of such goodness and nobility been brought before him. On His face, he saw no sign of guilt, no fear, no boldness or defiance. He saw a man whose expression bore the signature of heaven.

Pilate's better nature was stirred. His wife had told him something of the wonderful deeds the Galilean Prophet had performed, curing the sick and raising the dead. He recalled rumors that he had heard from several sources. He demanded that the Jews state their charges against the Prisoner. "Who is this Man, and why have you brought Him?" They answered that He was a deceiver called Jesus of Nazareth.

Again Pilate asked, "What accusation do you bring against this Man?" The priests did not answer his question. In irritation, they said, "If He were not an evildoer, we would not have delivered Him up to you." When the Sanhedrin brings you a man it considers worthy of death, is there need to ask for an accusation against him? They hoped to lead Pilate to give in to their request without going through many preliminaries.

---

* This chapter is based on Matthew 27:2, 11–31; Mark 15:1–20; Luke 23:1–25; John 18:28–40; 19:1–16.

Before this, Pilate had hastily condemned to death men who did not deserve to die. In his opinion, whether a prisoner was innocent or guilty was of no special importance. The priests hoped that Pilate would inflict the death penalty this time on Jesus without giving Him a hearing.

But something about the Prisoner held Pilate back. He did not dare do it. He remembered how Jesus had raised Lazarus, a man who had been dead four days, and he made up his mind to know the charges against Him and whether they could be proved.

"If your judgment is sufficient," he said, "why bring the Prisoner to me?" "You take Him and judge Him according to your law." The priests said they had already passed sentence on Him, but they must have Pilate's sentence to make their condemnation valid. "What is your sentence?" Pilate asked. "Death," they answered. They asked Pilate to enforce their sentence; they would take the responsibility of the result. Weak though he was in moral power, Pilate refused to condemn Jesus until they had brought a charge against Him.

The priests were in a dilemma. They must not allow it to appear that they had arrested Christ on religious grounds, because this would have no weight with Pilate. They must make it appear that Jesus was a political offender. The Romans were constantly on the watch to repress everything that could lead to an outbreak.

In their desperation, the priests called false witnesses. "And they began to accuse Him, saying, 'We found this fellow perverting the nation, and forbidding to pay taxes to Caesar, saying that He Himself is Christ, a King.' " Three charges, each without foundation. The priests knew this but were willing to commit perjury.

## Pilate Convinced of a Plot

Pilate did not believe that the Prisoner had plotted against the government. He was convinced that a deep plot had been laid to destroy an innocent Man. Turning to Jesus, he asked, "Are You the King of the Jews?" The Savior answered, "It is as you say." And as He spoke, His face lighted up as if a sunbeam were shining on it.

When they heard His answer, Caiaphas called Pilate to witness that Jesus had admitted the crime with which He was charged. Pilate said, " 'Do You answer nothing? See how many things they testify against You!' But Jesus still answered nothing."

Standing behind Pilate, in view of all in the court, Christ heard the abuse, but to all the false charges He answered not a word. He stood unmoved by the fury of the waves that beat around Him. It was as if the heavy surges of anger, rising like the waves of the ocean, broke around Him but did not touch Him. His silence was like a light shining from the inner to the outer Man.

Pilate was astonished. Does this Man not care to save His life? As he looked at Jesus, he felt that He could not be as unrighteous as the priests, who were shouting angrily. To escape the turmoil of the crowd, Pilate took Jesus aside and again asked, "Are You the King of the Jews?"

Jesus did not answer directly. The

Holy Spirit was working on Pilate's heart, and He gave him opportunity to acknowledge his conviction. "Are you speaking for yourself about this," He asked, "or did others tell you this concerning Me?" Pilate understood Christ's meaning, but he would not acknowledge the conviction that pressed upon him. "Am I a Jew?" he said. "Your own nation and the chief priests have delivered You to me. What have You done?"

### Jesus Tries to Save Pilate

Jesus did not leave Pilate without further light. He made it clear to him that He was not seeking an earthly throne.

"My kingdom is not of this world," He said. " 'If My kingdom were of this world, My servants would fight, so that I should not be delivered to the Jews; but now My kingdom is not from here.' Pilate therefore said to Him, 'Are You a king then?' Jesus answered, 'You say rightly that I am a king. For this cause I was born, and for this cause I have come into the world, that I should bear witness to the truth. Everyone who is of the truth hears My voice.' " Christ wanted Pilate to understand that only by receiving and assimilating truth could his ruined nature be reconstructed.

Pilate's mind was confused. His heart stirred with a great longing to know what the truth really was and how he could obtain it. "What is truth?" he asked. But he did not wait for an answer. The priests were shouting for immediate action. Going out to the Jews, he declared emphatically, "I find no fault in Him at all."

As the priests and elders heard this from Pilate, their disappointment and rage knew no limits. As they saw that Pilate might release Jesus, they seemed ready to tear Him in pieces. They denounced Pilate loudly and threatened him with the disapproval of the Roman government. They accused him of refusing to condemn Jesus who, they claimed, had set Himself up against Caesar. Angry voices declared that Jesus' influence toward revolt was well known throughout the country. "He stirs up the people, teaching throughout all Judea, beginning from Galilee to this place."

At this time Pilate had no thought of condemning Jesus. He knew that the Jews had accused Him because of hatred and prejudice. Justice demanded that he should release Christ. But if he refused to give Jesus into the hands of the people, a riot would result, and this he feared to meet. When he heard that Christ was from Galilee, he decided to send Him to Herod, the ruler of that province, who was in Jerusalem then. In this way Pilate thought to shift the responsibility to Herod. He also thought this would be a good opportunity to heal an old quarrel between himself and Herod. And so it proved to be. The two magistrates made friends over the trial of the Savior.

Amid the insults of the mob, Jesus was hurried to Herod. "When Herod saw Jesus, he was exceedingly glad." He had "heard many things about Him, and he hoped to see some miracle done by Him." This Herod was the one whose hands were stained with the blood of John the Baptist. When

Herod first heard of Jesus, he was filled with terror and said, "This is John . . . raised from the dead!" Mark 6:16. Yet he wanted to see Jesus. Now he had an opportunity to save the life of this Prophet, and the king hoped to banish forever from his mind the memory of that bloody head brought to him on a platter. He also wanted to satisfy his curiosity and thought that if he offered Christ a prospect of release, He would do anything that was asked of Him.

When the Savior was brought in, the priests and elders excitedly urged their accusations against Him. But Herod commanded silence. He ordered that Jesus' chains be removed, at the same time charging His enemies with treating Him roughly. He as well as Pilate was satisfied that Christ had been accused through hatred and envy.

Herod questioned Christ in many words, but the Savior kept a profound silence. At the command of the king, the lame and maimed were then called in, and Herod ordered Christ to prove His claim by working a miracle. Jesus did not respond, and Herod continued to urge: "Show us a sign that You have the power that rumor has credited to You." But the Son of God had taken upon Himself human nature, and He must do as we must do in like circumstances. Therefore, He would not work a miracle to save Himself the pain and humiliation that we must endure in a similar situation.

Herod promised that if Christ would perform some miracle, He would be released. Fear came over Christ's accusers that He would now work a miracle. Such a manifestation would prove a deathblow to their plans and might even cost them their lives. Raising their voices, the priests and rulers declared, "He is a traitor, a blasphemer! He works His miracles through the powers of the prince of devils!"

Herod's conscience was now far less sensitive than when he had trembled with horror at Herodias's request for the head of John the Baptist. His moral perceptions had become more and more degraded by his self-indulgent, immoral life. He could even boast of the punishment he had inflicted on John for daring to rebuke him. And now he threatened Jesus, declaring that he had power to condemn Him. But Jesus gave no indication that He heard a word.

Herod was irritated by this silence. It seemed to show complete indifference to his authority. Again he angrily threatened Jesus, who still remained unmoved and silent.

Christ's mission was not to gratify idle curiosity. If He could have spoken any word to heal sin-sick souls, He would not have kept silent. But He had no words for those who trample truth under their unholy feet. Herod had rejected the truth spoken to him by the greatest of the prophets, and he was to receive no other message. The Majesty of heaven had not a word for him. Christ's lips were closed to the haughty king who felt no need of a Savior.

Herod's face grew dark with rage. He angrily denounced Jesus as an impostor. Then he said to Christ, "If You will give no evidence of Your claim, I will deliver You up to the soldiers and the people. If You are an impostor, death is what You deserve. If You are the Son of God, save Yourself by working a miracle."

No sooner had he spoken these words than, like wild beasts, the crowd rushed upon their prey. They dragged Jesus this way and that, and Herod joined the mob in trying to humiliate the Son of God. If the Roman soldiers had not intervened, the Savior would have been torn in pieces.

"Herod, with his men of war, treated Him with contempt and mocked Him, [and] arrayed Him in a gorgeous robe." The Roman soldiers joined in this abuse. All that these corrupt soldiers and the Jewish dignitaries could unleash was heaped upon the Savior. Yet His patience did not fail.

## Some Trembled Before Jesus

But there were some who trembled in Christ's presence. Some who came forward to mock Him turned back, afraid and silenced. Herod was convicted. The last rays of merciful light were shining on his sin-hardened heart. Divinity had flashed through humanity. Herod felt that he was looking at a God on His throne. Hardened as he was, he dared not ratify the condemnation of Christ. He sent Jesus back to the Roman judgment hall.

Pilate was disappointed when the Jews returned with their Prisoner. He reminded them that he had already examined Jesus and found no fault in Him. They had not been able to state a single charge. And Herod, one from their own nation, also had found in Him nothing worthy of death. "I will therefore chastise Him and release Him."

Here Pilate showed his weakness.

Jesus was innocent, yet he was willing to sacrifice justice in order to quiet His accusers. This placed him at a disadvantage. The crowd took advantage of his indecision. If Pilate had stood firm from the beginning, refusing to condemn a Man whom he found guiltless, he would have broken the fatal chain that was to bind him in remorse as long as he lived. Christ would have been put to death, but the guilt would not have rested on Pilate. But Pilate had taken step after step in violation of his conscience, and now he found himself almost helpless in the hands of the priests and rulers.

## Pilate's Last Chance

Even now Pilate was not left to act blindly. An angel had visited his wife and in a dream she had talked with the Savior. Pilate's wife was not a Jew, but as she looked at Jesus in her dream, she knew that He was the Prince of God. She saw Pilate give Jesus to the scourging after he had declared, "I find no fault in Him." She saw him give Christ up to His murderers. She saw the cross uplifted, the earth wrapped in darkness, and she heard the mysterious cry, "It is finished!"

Still another scene met her gaze. She saw Christ seated on the great white cloud and His murderers fleeing from His glorious presence. With a cry of horror, she awoke and immediately wrote words of warning to Pilate.

A messenger pushed through the crowd and handed him the letter from his wife, which read, "Have nothing to do with that just Man, for I have suffered many things today in a dream because of Him."

Pilate's face grew pale. He was confused by his own conflicting emotions. While he had been delaying to act, the priests and rulers were inflaming the minds of the people. He now thought of a custom that might serve to gain Christ's release. It was customary at this feast to release one prisoner whom the people might choose. There was not a shadow of justice in this custom, but the Jews greatly prized it. The Roman authorities at this time held a prisoner named Barabbas, who was under sentence of death. This man claimed authority to establish a different order of things. Whatever he could obtain by theft and robbery was his own. He had gained a following among the people and had stirred up revolt against the Roman government. Under cover of religious enthusiasm he was a hardened criminal, bent on rebellion and cruelty.

By giving the people a choice between this man and the innocent Savior, Pilate thought he might awaken a sense of justice in them.

"Whom do you want me to release to you? Barabbas, or Jesus who is called Christ?" Like the bellowing of wild beasts came the answer, "Release to us Barabbas." Thinking that the people had not understood his question, Pilate asked, "Do you want me to release to you the King of the Jews?" But they cried out again, "Away with this Man, and release to us Barabbas." "What then shall I do with Jesus who is called Christ?" Demons in human form were in the crowd, and what could be expected but the answer, "Let Him be crucified!"

## Pilate Did Not Foresee the Consequences

Pilate had not thought it would come to that. He shrank from delivering an innocent Man to the most cruel death that could be inflicted. "Why, what evil has He done?" But the case had gone too far for argument.

Still Pilate tried to save Christ. "He said to them the third time, 'Why, what evil has He done?' " But the very mention of His release stirred the people to frenzy. Louder and louder they cried, "Crucify Him, crucify Him!"

Faint and covered with wounds, Jesus was scourged. "Then the soldiers led Him away into the hall called Praetorium, and they called together the whole garrison. And they clothed Him with purple; and they twisted a crown of thorns, put it on His head, and began to salute Him, 'Hail, King of the Jews!' Then they . . . spat on Him; and bowing the knee, they worshiped Him. And . . . they . . . mocked Him." Occasionally some wicked hand struck the crown, forcing the thorns into His temples and sending the blood trickling down His face.

A maddened crowd surrounded the Savior of the world. Mocking and jeering mingled with oaths of blasphemy. Satan led the mob. It was his plan, if possible, to provoke the Savior to retaliate or to drive Him to perform a miracle to release Himself. One stain upon His human life, and the Lamb of God would have been an imperfect offering and the redemption of humanity a failure. But with perfect calmness He submitted to the coarsest insult and outrage.

Christ's enemies had demanded a miracle as evidence of His divinity.

They had evidence far greater than any they had asked for. His meekness and patience proved His relationship to God. The blood drops that flowed from His wounded temples were the pledge of His anointing with "the oil of gladness" as our great High Priest. See Hebrews 1:9. Satan's rage was great as he saw that the Savior had not departed in any detail from the will of His Father.

## Compromise Leads to Ruin

When Pilate gave Jesus up to be scourged, he hoped the crowd would decide that this was enough punishment. But with keen perception, the Jews saw the weakness of punishing a Man who had been declared innocent. They were determined not to let Jesus be released.

Pilate now sent for Barabbas to be brought into the court and presented the two prisoners side by side. Pointing to the Savior he said, "Behold the Man!" There stood the Son of God, stripped to the waist, His back showing the long stripes from which blood flowed freely. His face was bloodstained and bore the marks of pain, but never had it appeared more beautiful than now. Every feature expressed the tenderest pity for His cruel foes. In His manner there was the strength and dignity of long-suffering.

In striking contrast was the prisoner at His side. Every line of Barabbas's face proclaimed him a hardened criminal. The contrast spoke to every onlooker. As some gazed at Jesus they wept, their hearts full of sympathy. The priests and rulers were convicted that He was all that He claimed to be.

The Roman soldiers that surrounded Christ were not all hardened. They looked at the divine Sufferer with feelings of pity, His silent submission stamped on their minds. They would never forget that scene until they either acknowledged Him as the Christ or decided their own destiny by rejecting Him.

Pilate had no doubt that the sight of this Man in contrast with Barabbas would move the Jews to sympathy. But he did not understand the priests' fanatical hatred. Again priests, rulers, and people raised that awful cry, "Crucify Him, crucify Him!" Finally, losing all patience with their unreasoning cruelty, Pilate cried out despairingly, "You take Him and crucify Him, for I find no fault in Him."

The Roman governor, though familiar with cruel scenes, was moved with sympathy for the suffering Prisoner. But the priests declared, "We have a law, and according to our law He ought to die, because He made Himself the Son of God."

## Jesus' Kindness to Pilate

Pilate was startled—it might be a divine Being that stood before him! Again he said to Jesus, "Where are You from?" But Jesus gave no answer. The Savior had spoken freely to Pilate, explaining His mission. Pilate had disregarded the light. He had abused the high office of judge by yielding to the demands of the mob. Jesus had no further light for him. Irritated by His silence, Pilate said haughtily, "Are You not speaking to me? Do You not know that I have power to crucify You, and power to release You?"

Jesus answered, "You could have no power at all against Me unless it had been given you from above. Therefore the one who delivered Me to you has the greater sin." Christ meant Caiaphas, who represented the Jewish nation. They had light in the prophecies that testified of Christ and unmistakable evidence of the divinity of the One they condemned to death. The heaviest responsibility belonged to those who stood in the highest places in the nation. Pilate, Herod, and the Roman soldiers were comparatively ignorant of Jesus. They had not had the light that the Jewish nation had received so abundantly. If the light had been given to the soldiers, they would not have treated Christ as they did.

Again Pilate proposed to release the Savior. "But the Jews cried out, saying, 'If you let this Man go, you are not Caesar's friend.' " Of all the opponents of Roman rule, the Jews were most bitter. But to accomplish Christ's destruction, they would profess loyalty to the foreign rule that they hated.

"Whoever makes himself a king," they continued, "speaks against Caesar." Pilate was under suspicion by the Roman government and knew that such a report would ruin him. He knew the Jews would leave nothing undone to get their revenge.

Pilate again presented Jesus to the people, saying, "Behold your King!" Again the mad cry arose, "Away with Him! Crucify Him!" In a voice heard far and near, Pilate asked, "Shall I crucify your King?" But from profane, blasphemous lips came the words, "We have no king but Caesar!"

By choosing a heathen ruler, the Jewish nation rejected God as their king. From then on they had no king but Caesar. The priests and teachers had led the people to this. They were responsible for this, with all the fearful results that followed. A nation's sin and a nation's ruin were due to the religious leaders.

"When Pilate saw that he could not prevail at all, but rather that a tumult was rising, he took water and washed his hands before the multitude, saying, 'I am innocent of the blood of this just Person. You see to it.' " Pilate looked at the Savior and said in his heart, "He is a God." Turning to the multitude he declared, "I am clear of His blood. Crucify Him, but I pronounce Him a just Man. May the One whom He claims as His Father judge you and not me for this day's work." Then to Jesus he said, "Forgive me for this act; I cannot save You." And when he had scourged Jesus again, He delivered Him to be crucified.

Pilate longed to deliver Jesus, but he saw that he could not do this and still keep his own position. Rather than lose his worldly power, he chose to sacrifice an innocent life. How many similarly sacrifice principle! Conscience and duty point one way and self-interest another. The current goes in the wrong direction, and anyone who compromises with evil is swept away into the thick darkness of guilt.

But in spite of his precautions, the very thing Pilate dreaded happened to him. He was deposed from his high office and, stung by remorse and wounded pride, not long after the Crucifixion he ended his own life.

When Pilate declared himself innocent of the blood of Christ, Caiaphas answered defiantly, "His blood be on us and on our children." The mob echoed the awful words in an inhuman roar of voices. The whole crowd said, "His blood be on us and on our children."

The people of Israel had made their choice—Barabbas, the robber and murderer, the representative of Satan. Christ, the representative of God, they rejected. In making this choice they accepted the one who from the beginning was a liar and a murderer. Satan was their leader. His rule they must endure.

The Jews had shouted, "His blood be on us and on our children." That prayer was heard. The blood of the Son of God was on their children and their children's children. Terribly was the prayer fulfilled in the destruction of Jerusalem and in the condition of the Jewish nation for nearly two thousand years—a branch severed from the Vine, dead. From land to land throughout the world, from century to century, dead in trespasses and sins!

That prayer will be terribly fulfilled in the great Judgment Day. Christ will come in glory. Thousands and thousands of angels, the beautiful and triumphant sons of God, will escort Him on His way. All nations will be gathered before Him. In the place of thorns, He will wear a crown of glory. On His robe and on His thigh a name will be written, "KING OF KINGS AND LORD OF LORDS." Revelation 19:16.

The priests and rulers will again see the scene in the judgment hall. Every incident there will appear as if written in letters of fire. Then those who prayed, "His blood be on us and on our children," will receive the answer to their prayer. In awful agony and horror they will cry to the rocks and mountains, "Fall on us." See Revelation 6:16, 17.

# Jesus Dies on Calvary<sup>*</sup>

And when they had come to the place called Calvary, there they crucified Him."

The news of Christ's condemnation had spread, and people of all classes and ranks flocked toward the place of crucifixion. The priests and rulers had been bound by a promise not to trouble Christ's followers if He Himself were delivered to them, and the disciples and believers joined the crowd.

The cross that had been prepared for Barabbas was placed on Jesus' bleeding shoulders. Two companions of Barabbas were to die at the same time, and crosses were placed on them also. Since the Passover supper with His disciples, Jesus had taken neither food nor drink. He had endured the anguish of betrayal and had seen His disciples forsake Him. He had been taken to Annas, to Caiaphas, to Pilate, to Herod, then again to Pilate. All that night, there had been scene after scene to test a person to the utmost. Christ had not failed. He had borne Himself with dignity. But when after the second scourging the cross was laid on Him, human nature could bear

no more. He fell fainting beneath the burden.

The crowd showed no compassion. They taunted Him because He could not carry the heavy cross. Again the soldiers placed the burden on Him, and again He fell. His persecutors saw that it was impossible for Him to carry His burden further. Who would bear the humiliating load? The Jews could not, because the defilement would prevent them from keeping the Passover.

At this time a stranger, Simon from Cyrene, coming in from the country, met the crowd. He stopped in astonishment at the scene, and as he expressed compassion, they took hold of him and placed the cross on his shoulders.

Simon's sons were believers in the Savior, but he himself was not. Carrying the cross to Calvary was a blessing to Simon. It led him later to take the cross of Christ from choice and from then on cheerfully to stand beneath its burden.

Many women were in the crowd that followed the Uncondemned to His cruel death. Some had brought

---

<sup>*</sup> *This chapter is based on Matthew 27:31–53; Mark 15:20–38; Luke 23:26–46; John 19:16–30.*

Him their sick and suffering ones. Some had themselves been healed. They were amazed at the hatred of the crowd toward Him. And despite the angry words of priests and rulers, as Jesus fell beneath the cross these women broke out in wailing. This attracted Christ's attention. He knew that they were not mourning for Him as one sent from God, but He did not scorn their sympathy. It awakened in His heart a deeper sympathy for them. "Daughters of Jerusalem," He said, "do not weep for Me, but weep for yourselves and for your children." Christ looked ahead to the time of Jerusalem's destruction when many who were now weeping for Him would die with their children.

## A Wider Judgment

Jesus' thoughts turned from the fall of Jerusalem to a wider judgment. In the unrepentant city's destruction He saw a symbol of the final destruction to come on the world. " 'Then they will begin "to say to the mountains, 'Fall on us!' and to the hills, 'Cover us!' " For if they do these things in the green wood, what will be done in the dry?' " The green wood or tree represented Himself, the innocent Redeemer. God's wrath against transgression fell on His beloved Son. What suffering, then, would the sinner bear who continued in sin? The unrepentant would know a sorrow that language would fail to express.

Many in the crowd that followed the Savior to Calvary had accompanied Him with hosannas and palm branches as He rode triumphantly into Jerusalem. Many people who had then shouted His praise because it was popular, now swelled the cry, "Crucify Him!" When Christ rode into Jerusalem, the disciples pressed in close around Him, feeling that it was a high honor to be connected with Him. Now in His humiliation they followed Him at a distance.

## The Agony of Christ's Mother

At the place of execution, the two thieves wrestled in the hands of those who placed them on the cross, but Jesus did not resist. His mother, supported by John, had followed her Son's steps to Calvary. She had longed to place a supporting hand beneath His wounded head. But she was not permitted this sad privilege. She still cherished the hope that Jesus would deliver Himself from His enemies. Again her heart would sink as she recalled how He had foretold the very scenes then taking place.

As the thieves were bound to the cross, she looked on with agonizing suspense. Would He who had given life to the dead allow Himself to be crucified? Must she give up her faith that He was the Messiah? She saw His hands stretched on the cross. The soldiers brought the hammer and nails, and as they drove the spikes through the tender flesh, the disciples bore the fainting form of the mother of Jesus away from the cruel scene.

The Savior made no complaint, but great drops of sweat stood on His brow. There was no pitying hand to wipe the death dew from His face, no words of sympathy and loyalty to encourage His human heart. While the soldiers were doing their fearful work,

344                                HUMBLE HERO

Jesus prayed, "Father, forgive them, for they do not know what they do." His mind passed from His own suffering to the terrible retribution that would be theirs. He did not call down any curses on the soldiers who were handling Him so roughly. He invoked no vengeance on the priests and rulers. He breathed only a plea for their forgiveness—"they do not know what they do."

But their ignorance did not remove their guilt, for it was their privilege to know and accept Jesus as their Savior. Some would yet see their sin and would repent and be converted. Some by refusing to repent would make it impossible for the prayer of Christ to be answered for them. Yet just the same, God's purpose was reaching its fulfillment. Jesus was earning the right to become the One who pleads our case in the Father's presence.

That prayer of Christ for His enemies took in every sinner from the beginning of the world to the end of time. The guilt of crucifying the Son of God rests on us all. To all, Jesus freely offers forgiveness.

As soon as Jesus was nailed to the cross, strong men lifted it and thrust it violently into the place prepared for it. This caused intense agony. Pilate then wrote an inscription in Hebrew, Greek, and Latin and placed it on the cross above Jesus' head. It read, "JESUS OF NAZARETH, THE KING OF THE JEWS." This irritated the Jews. They had shouted, "We have no king but Caesar." They had declared that whoever should acknowledge any other king was a traitor. Pilate wrote what they had expressed. No offense was

mentioned, except that Jesus was the King of the Jews, a virtual acknowledgment of the allegiance of the Jews to Rome. It declared that whoever might claim to be the King of Israel they would judge as worthy of death. In order to destroy Christ, the priests had been ready to sacrifice even their national existence.

The priests asked Pilate to change the inscription. "Do not write, 'The King of the Jews,' but, 'He said, "I am the King of the Jews." ' " But Pilate, angry with himself, replied coldly, "What I have written, I have written."

In the outworking of God's plans, that inscription was to awaken investigation of the Scriptures. People from all lands were at Jerusalem then, and the inscription declaring Jesus the Messiah would come to their attention. God had guided its writing.

The sufferings of Christ on the cross fulfilled prophecy.

The congregation of the wicked has
    enclosed Me.
They pierced My hands and My feet. . . .
They divide My garments among
    them,
And for My clothing they cast lots.
                        Psalm 22:16–18

His clothing was given to the soldiers. His tunic was woven without seam, and they said, "Let us not tear it, but cast lots for it, whose it shall be."

In another prophecy the Savior declared,

I looked for someone to take pity, but
    there was none;
And for comforters, but I found none.

They also gave me gall for my food,
And for my thirst they gave me vinegar
   to drink.

                  Psalm 69:20, 21

To those who were put to death on the cross, it was permitted to give a stupefying drug to deaden the pain. But when Jesus had tasted it, He refused it. His faith must keep hold on God, His only strength. To cloud His senses would give Satan an advantage.

Priests, rulers, and scribes joined the mob in mocking the dying Savior. The Father's voice from heaven had earlier witnessed to Christ's divinity. Now it was silent. No testimony was heard in His favor. He suffered alone.

"If You are the Son of God," they said, "come down from the cross." "Let Him save Himself if He is the Christ, the chosen of God." Satan and his angels, in human form, were present at the cross, cooperating with the priests and rulers who were joined in a satanic frenzy.

Jesus heard the priests declare, "He saved others; Himself He cannot save. Let the Christ, the King of Israel, descend now from the cross, that we may see and believe." Christ could have come down from the cross. But because He refused to save Himself, the sinner has hope of pardon and favor with God.

### One Crucified Thief Believes

One gleam of comfort came to Jesus on the cross—the prayer of the repentant thief. Both men crucified with Jesus taunted Him at first, and one only became more desperate and defiant in his suffering. But his companion was not a hardened criminal; he was less guilty than many who stood beside the cross insulting the Savior. He had seen and heard Jesus but had been turned away from Him by the priests and rulers. In trying to stifle conviction, he had plunged into sin, until he was arrested and condemned.

On the cross he saw the great religious leaders ridicule Jesus. He heard his companion in guilt take up the abusive speech: "If You are the Christ, save Yourself and us." But among the passersby he heard many repeating Jesus' words and telling of His works. The conviction came back that this was the Christ. Turning to his fellow criminal, he said, "Do you not even fear God, seeing you are under the same condemnation?" The dying thieves no longer had anything to fear from human sources. But the conviction pressed in on one of them that there is a God to fear, a future to cause him to tremble. And now his life history was about to close. "And we indeed justly, for we receive the due reward of our deeds; but this Man has done nothing wrong."

When condemned for his crime, the thief had sunk into despair, but strange, tender thoughts now sprang up. The Holy Spirit illuminated his mind, and little by little the chain of evidence joined together. In Jesus, mocked and hanging on the cross, he saw the Lamb of God. Hope mingled with anguish in his voice as the dying man threw himself on a dying Savior. "Lord, remember me when You come into Your kingdom."

Quickly the answer came, the tone

soft and melodious, the words full of love and power: "Assuredly, I say to you today, you will be with Me in Paradise."* With longing heart Jesus had listened for some expression of faith from His disciples. He had heard only the mournful words, "We were hoping that it was He who was going to redeem Israel." Luke 24:21. How welcome then to the Savior was this statement of faith and love from the dying thief! While even the disciples doubted, the poor thief called Jesus "Lord." No one acknowledged Him on the cross except the repentant thief, saved at the last moment.

The tone of the repentant man caught the attention of bystanders. Those who had been quarreling over Christ's garments stopped to listen and waited for the response from Christ's dying lips.

As He spoke the words of promise, a living light pierced the dark cloud that seemed to enshroud the cross. Christ in His humiliation was glorified. He who in all other eyes appeared conquered, was Conqueror. He had been acknowledged as the Sin Bearer. They could strip His clothing from Him, but they could not rob Him of His power to forgive sins. It is His royal right to save all who come to God by Him!

"I say to you today, you will be with Me in Paradise." Christ did not promise that the thief would be with Him in Paradise that day. He Himself did not go to Paradise that day. He slept in the tomb, and on the morning of the resurrection He said, "I have not yet ascended to My Father." John 20:17. But Jesus gave the promise on the day of apparent defeat. "Today" while dying on the cross as a criminal, Christ assured the sinner, "you will be with Me in Paradise."

Christ's placement "in the center" between the thieves was done by direction of the priests and rulers to indicate that He was the greatest criminal of the three. But as Jesus was placed "in the center," so His cross was placed in the center of a dying world lying in sin. And the words of pardon that He spoke to the repentant thief kindled a light that will shine to earth's farthest limits. In His humiliation, Jesus as a Prophet had addressed the daughters of Jerusalem; as Priest and Advocate He had pleaded with the Father to forgive His murderers; as Savior He had forgiven the sins of the repentant thief.

At the foot of the cross stood His mother, supported by John. She could not endure to remain away from her Son, and John, knowing that the end was near, had brought her again. Looking into her grief-stricken face, He said to her, "Woman, behold your son!" then to John, "Behold your mother!" John understood and accepted the trust. From that hour onward he cared for Mary tenderly. The Savior had no money with which to provide for His mother, but He provided what she needed most—the tender sympathy of one who loved her because she loved Jesus. And John

---

* *The comma in Luke 23:43 is often misplaced in English translations. No comma existed in the Greek text.*

received a great blessing—she was a constant reminder of his beloved Master.

For nearly thirty years, by His daily labor Jesus had helped bear the burdens of the home. And now, even in His last agony, He provided for His sorrowing, widowed mother. Those who follow Christ will respect and provide for their parents. From the heart that cherishes His love, father and mother will never fail to receive thoughtful care and tender sympathy.

And now the Lord of glory was dying. All He could see was oppressive gloom. It was not the dread of death nor the pain of the cross that caused Christ's agony. His suffering came from a sense of the terrible evil of sin. Christ saw how few would be willing to break from its power. Without help from God, humanity must die, and He saw great numbers dying within reach of help.

## The Terrible Weight That Christ Bore

The iniquity of us all was laid on Christ as our Substitute and Security. The guilt of every descendant of Adam was pressing on His heart. All His life Christ had been proclaiming the good news of the Father's pardoning love, but now with the terrible weight of guilt upon Him He could not see the Father's forgiving face. This pierced His heart with a sorrow that no human can ever fully understand. This agony was so great that He hardly felt His physical pain.

Satan wrung the heart of Jesus with fierce temptations. Hope did not tell Him that He would come out from the grave a conqueror, nor did it tell

Him that the Father accepted His sacrifice. Christ felt the anguish the sinner will feel when mercy will no longer plead for the guilty race. It was the sense of sin, bringing the Father's wrath on Him as our Substitute, that broke the heart of the Son of God.

Angels hid their faces from the fearful sight. The sun refused to look on the awful scene. Its full, bright rays were illuminating the earth at midday, when suddenly it seemed to be blotted out. Complete darkness surrounded the cross. "Until the ninth hour there was darkness over all the land." There was no natural cause for this darkness, which was as deep as midnight without moon or stars. It was a miraculous God-given testimony that would confirm the faith of later generations.

In that thick darkness God hid His presence. God and holy angels were beside the cross. The Father was with His Son. Yet He did not reveal His presence. In that dreadful hour Christ was not to be comforted with the Father's presence.

In the thick darkness, God veiled the last human agony of His Son. All who had seen Christ in His suffering had been convicted that He was divine. Through long hours of agony He had been open to the view of the jeering multitude. Now He was mercifully hidden by the mantle of God.

A nameless terror held the crowd gathered around the cross. Cursing and insults stopped. Vivid lightning occasionally flashed from the cloud and revealed the crucified Redeemer. Priests, rulers, executioners, the mob, all thought their time to be punished had come. Some whispered that Jesus would now come down from the cross.

At the ninth hour, the darkness lifted from the people but still enclosed the Savior. No eye could penetrate the deep gloom that enshrouded Christ's suffering. Then "Jesus cried out with a loud voice, saying, 'Eloi, Eloi, lama sabachthani?' that is, 'My God, My God, why have You forsaken Me?' " Many voices exclaimed, "The vengeance of heaven is upon Him because He claimed to be the Son of God!" Many who believed on Him heard His cry of despair. Hope left them. If God had forsaken Jesus, in what could His followers trust?

### Last Chance to Show Human Pity

When the darkness lifted, Christ became aware again of His physical suffering and said, "I thirst!" One of the Roman soldiers, touched with pity, took a sponge, dipped it in vinegar, and offered it to Him. But the priests mocked His agony. His words, "Eloi, Eloi, lama sabachthani?" they misinterpreted. They said, "This Man is calling for Elijah!" They refused the last opportunity to relieve His sufferings. "Let Him alone," they said, "let us see if Elijah will come to save Him."

The spotless Son of God hung upon the cross, His flesh lacerated with stripes, His hands nailed to the wooden bars, His feet spiked to the tree, His royal head pierced by thorns. And all that He endured—the agony that racked His body, and the unutterable anguish that filled His soul at the hiding of His Father's face—speaks to each child of humanity, declaring, For

you the Son of God consents to bear this burden of guilt; for you He plunders the domain of death; for you He opens the gates of Paradise; for you He offers Himself as a sacrifice—from love to you.

### Christ Dies Triumphant

Suddenly the gloom lifted from the cross. In trumpetlike tones that seemed to echo throughout creation, Jesus cried, "It is finished!" "Father, 'into Your hands I commit My spirit.' " A light encircled the cross, and the face of the Savior was radiant with a glory like the sun. He then bowed His head and died.

Amid the awful darkness, Christ had drained the last drops in the cup of human woe. In those dreadful hours He had relied on the evidence of His Father's acceptance given Him earlier. He knew His Father's character, and by faith He rested in Him, the One He had always found joy in obeying. And as He committed Himself to God, the sense of having lost His Father's favor was withdrawn. By faith, Christ was victor.

Again darkness settled on the earth, and there was a violent earthquake. Wild confusion followed. In the surrounding mountains, rocks were torn apart and went crashing into the plains. Tombs broke open, and the dead were thrown out. Priests, soldiers, executioners, and people lay face down on the ground.

When the loud cry, "It is finished!" came from the lips of Christ, it was the hour of the evening sacrifice. The lamb representing Christ had been brought to be killed. The priest stood with the knife lifted, the people looking on. But the earth trembled, for the Lord Himself drew near. With a ripping noise the inner veil of the temple was torn from top to bottom by an unseen hand, throwing open to the gaze of the crowd a place once filled with the presence of God. The Most Holy Place of the earthly sanctuary was no longer sacred.

Terror and confusion were everywhere. The priest was about to sacrifice the victim, but the knife dropped from his unnerved hand, and the lamb escaped. Symbol had met fulfillment. The great sacrifice had been made. A new and living way was prepared for all. Afterward the Savior was to officiate as Priest and Advocate in the heaven of heavens. "He entered once for all into the Holy Place . . . with his own blood, thus obtaining eternal redemption." Hebrews 9:12, NRSV.

# How Christ's Death Defeated Satan

Christ had accomplished the work He came to do, and with His dying breath He exclaimed, "It is finished!" John 19:30. He had won the battle. All heaven triumphed in the Savior's victory. Satan knew his kingdom was lost. It was for the angels and unfallen worlds as well as for us that Jesus had accomplished the great work of redemption. Until the death of Christ, Satan had so thoroughly wrapped himself in deception that even holy beings had not understood his principles nor clearly seen the nature of his rebellion.

Lucifer had been the covering cherub, the highest of all created beings. He had been foremost in revealing God's plans to the universe. After he had sinned, his power to deceive was all the more deceptive, and unmasking his character was more difficult because of the exalted position he had held with the Father.

God could have destroyed Satan and his sympathizers, but He did not do this. Force, compelling power, is found only under Satan's government. The Lord's authority rests on goodness, mercy, and love, and He works by presenting these principles. God's government is moral, and truth and love are to be the power used in it.

In the councils of heaven, God decided that Satan must be given time to develop the principles of his government. He had claimed that these were superior to God's. So God gave time for Satan's principles to work and for the heavenly universe to see them. For four thousand years, Christ was working to lift up the human race, and Satan to ruin it. And the heavenly universe watched it all.

From the time when Jesus appeared as a baby in Bethlehem, Satan worked to destroy Him. He tried to prevent Him from developing a perfect childhood, a faultless manhood, a holy ministry, and an unblemished sacrifice. But he was defeated. He could not lead Jesus into sin. All the efforts of Satan to overcome Him only brought out His spotless character in a purer light.

With intense interest heaven and the unfallen worlds followed the closing scenes of the conflict. They heard His bitter cry, "Father, if it is possible, let this cup pass from Me." Matthew 26:39. They saw Him so greatly sorrowful that it exceeded what people experience in the last great struggle with death. The bloody sweat was forced from His pores, and three times the prayer for deliverance was wrung from His lips. Heaven could no longer endure the sight, and a messenger of comfort was sent to the Son of God.

## Earth the Stage, Heaven the Audience

Heaven witnessed the Victim betrayed and hurried with violence from one tribunal to another. It heard the sneers of His persecutors and the denial, with cursing, by one of His disciples. It saw the Savior dragged back and forth from palace to judgment hall, arraigned twice before the priests, twice before the Sanhedrin, twice before Pilate, and once before Herod, mocked, scourged, condemned, and led out to be crucified.

Heaven viewed with amazement Christ hanging on the cross, blood flowing from His wounded temples, His hands, His feet. The wounds gaped as the weight of His body dragged on His hands. He panted under the burden of the sins of the world. All heaven was filled with wonder when Christ prayed in the midst of His terrible suffering, "Father, forgive them, for they do not know what they do." Luke 23:34.

The powers of darkness around the cross cast the hellish shadow of unbelief into the hearts of the people gathered there. Satanic agencies led the people to believe that Christ was the chief of sinners and to make them detest Him. Those who mocked Christ were filled with the spirit of the first great rebel. He inspired their taunts. But Satan gained nothing from all this.

If Christ had yielded to Satan in one particular to escape the terrible torture, the enemy would have triumphed. Christ bowed His head and died, but He held tightly to His faith. "Then I heard a loud voice saying in heaven, 'Now salvation, and strength, and the kingdom of our God, and the power of His Christ have come, for the accuser of our brethren, who accused them before our God day and night, has been cast down.' " Revelation 12:10.

Satan saw that his disguise was torn away. He had revealed himself as a murderer. By shedding the blood of the Son of God, he had uprooted himself from the sympathies of the heavenly beings. From then on he could no longer wait for the angels as they came from the heavenly courts and in their hearing accuse Christ's followers of being clothed with the defilement of sin. The last link of sympathy between Satan and the heavenly world was broken.

Yet the angels did not even then understand all that was involved in the great controversy. The principles at stake were to be revealed more fully. Human beings as well as angels must see the contrast between the Prince of light and the prince of darkness. Each one must choose whom to serve.

In the opening of the great controversy, Satan had declared that no one could obey the law of God, that justice was inconsistent with mercy, and that, if the law were once broken, it would be impossible for the sinner to be pardoned. If God were to cancel the punishment for sin, Satan claimed, He would not be a God of justice. When our first parents broke the law of God, Satan declared that this proved that the law could not be obeyed; mankind could not be forgiven. Because he had been banished from heaven after his rebellion, Satan claimed that the human race must be shut out forever from God's favor. God could not be just, he argued, and yet show mercy to the sinner.

But mankind was in a different situation from that of Satan. Lucifer had sinned in the full light of God's glory. Understanding the character of God, Satan still chose to follow his own selfish will. There was no more that God could do to save him. But human beings were deceived, their minds darkened by Satan's subtle reasoning. They did not know the height and depth of the love of God. By beholding His character, they could be drawn back to God.

### How Justice Is Blended With Mercy

Through Jesus, God's mercy was exhibited to humanity, but mercy does not set aside justice. The law could not be changed, but God sacrificed Himself in Christ for our redemption. "God was in Christ reconciling the world to Himself." 2 Corinthians 5:19.

The law requires a righteous life, a perfect character, and this we do not have. But Christ, as a human being, lived a holy life and developed a perfect character. These He offers as a free gift to all who will receive Him. His life stands for their life. In this way they have forgiveness of sins that are past. More than this, Christ fills them with the attributes of God. He builds up the human character in the likeness of the divine character. And so "the righteous requirement of the law" is fulfilled in the believer in Christ. Romans 8:4. God can "be just and the justifier of the one who has faith in Jesus." Romans 3:26.

It had been Satan's aim to divorce mercy from truth and justice. But Christ showed that in God's plan they are joined together. The one cannot exist without the other. "Righteousness and peace have kissed." Psalm 85:10.

By His life and His death, Christ proved that God's justice did not destroy His mercy. He proved that sin could be forgiven and that the law is righteous and can be perfectly obeyed. Christ refuted Satan's charges.

Now Satan would bring forward another deception. He declared that the death of Christ abolished the Father's law. If it had been possible for the law to be changed or abolished, then Christ would not have needed to die. But to do away with the law would be to immortalize sin and place the world under Satan's control. Because the law was changeless, Jesus died on the cross. Yet the very means by which Christ established the law, Satan claimed had destroyed it. This will be the focus of the last conflict in the great controversy.

### Satan's "New Model" Lie

Satan now puts forward the claim that some portion of the law spoken by God's own voice has been set aside. He does not need to attack the whole law. If he can lead people to disregard one commandment, he achieves his purpose. For "whoever shall keep the whole law, and yet stumble in one point, he is guilty of all." James 2:10. By consenting to break one commandment, people come under Satan's power. Concerning the great apostate power, the representative of Satan, prophecy declares,

" 'He shall speak pompous words
    against the Most High,
Shall persecute the saints of the Most
    High,
And shall intend to change times and
    law.
Then the saints shall be given into his
    hand.' "

Daniel 7:25

Human beings will set up laws to work against the laws of God, and in their zeal to enforce these laws they will oppress their fellow men.

The warfare against God's law will continue until the end of time. Everyone will have to choose between God's law and human laws. There will be only two classes of people. Every character will be fully developed. All will show whether they have chosen the side of loyalty or that of rebellion.

Then the end will come. God will prove the justice of His law and will deliver His people. He will cut off Satan and all who join him in rebellion. Sin and sinners will die, root and branch. See Malachi 4:1.

This is not an arbitrary act on God's part. The rejecters of His mercy reap what they have sown. God is the Fountain of life, and when people choose sin, they cut themselves off from life. Christ says, "All those who hate Me love death." Proverbs 8:36.

God gives them existence for a time so that they can develop their characters and reveal their principles. When this is done, they receive the results of their own choice. Satan and all who unite with him place themselves so out of harmony with God that the very presence of Him who is love will destroy them.

At the beginning of the great controversy, the angels did not understand this. If Satan and his followers had died then, doubt about God's goodness would have remained in the angels' minds as evil seed, ready to produce its deadly fruit of sin.

But it will not be that way when the great controversy will come to an end. Then, with the plan of redemption having been completed, the character of God stands clearly revealed to all created intelligences. The principles of His law are seen to be perfect and unchangeable. Sin has revealed its nature, Satan his character. The extermination of sin will prove God's love and establish His honor before the universe.

In light of all this, the angels could well rejoice as they looked on the Savior's cross. Although they did not understand everything then, they knew that Satan's destruction was made certain, human redemption was assured, and the universe was made eternally secure.

Christ Himself looked forward to all these results of His sacrifice when on the cross He cried out, "It is finished!"

# Jesus Rests in Joseph's Tomb

At last the long day of shame and torture was over. As the setting sun ushered in the Sabbath, the Son of God rested in Joseph's tomb, His work completed.

In the beginning, the Father and the Son had rested on the Sabbath after their work of Creation. See Genesis 2:1. All heavenly beings rejoiced in looking at the glorious scene. Now Jesus rested from the work of redemption, and though there was grief among those who loved Him on earth, there was joy in heaven. God and angels saw a redeemed race that, having conquered sin, could never fall—this was the result to flow from Christ's completed work.

When there will be a "restoration of all things" (Acts 3:21), the creation Sabbath, the day on which Jesus lay at rest in Joseph's tomb, will still be a day of rest and rejoicing. "From one Sabbath to another" (Isaiah 66:23) the nations of the saved will bow in joyful worship to God and the Lamb.

The closing events of the Crucifixion day saw a new witness to Christ's divinity. When the Savior had uttered His dying cry, another voice spoke up, saying, "Truly this was the Son of God!" Matthew 27:54.

These words came in no whispered tones. Who had spoken? It was the centurion, the Roman soldier. The divine patience of the Savior, His sudden death, the cry of victory on His lips, had impressed this heathen. In the broken body hanging on the cross, the centurion recognized the Son of God. On the very day of the Redeemer's death, three men had declared their faith—the one who commanded the Roman guard, the one who carried Jesus' cross, and the one who died by His side.

As evening approached, an unearthly stillness hung over Calvary. Many had flocked to the crucifixion from curiosity, not from hatred toward Christ. Still, they looked on Christ as a criminal. Under unnatural excitement they had united in shouting abuse against Him. But when the earth was wrapped in blackness, they felt guilty of a great wrong. When the darkness lifted, they made their way home in solemn silence, convinced that the charges of the priests were false, that Jesus was no pretender. A few weeks later, when Peter preached on the day of Pentecost, they were among the thousands who became converts to Christ.

But the Jewish leaders were unchanged; their hatred had not subsided.

The darkness at the Crucifixion was not more dense than the darkness that still shrouded their minds. Inanimate nature had known Christ and borne witness to His divinity. But the priests and rulers of Israel did not recognize the Son of God. They had put Christ to death, but even in the hour of their apparent triumph, doubts troubled them. What would take place next? They had heard the cry, "It is finished!" John 19:30. They had felt the mighty earthquake, and they were uneasy. They dreaded the dead Christ far more than they had feared the living Christ. They dreaded any further attention to the events surrounding His crucifixion. They would not allow His body to remain on the cross during the Sabbath for any reason. It would violate the Sabbath's sanctity for the bodies to hang on the cross. So, using this as an excuse, leading Jews requested Pilate to speed up the death of the victims and to remove their bodies before the sun set.

Pilate agreed, and the soldiers broke the legs of the two thieves to hurry their death. But Jesus was already dead. The coarse soldiers, softened by what they had heard and seen of Christ, were restrained from breaking His legs. This fulfilled the law of the Passover, " 'They shall leave none of it until morning, nor break one of its bones.' " Numbers 9:12.

The priests and rulers were amazed to find that Christ was dead. It was unheard of for anyone to die within six hours of crucifixion. The priests wanted to make sure of Jesus' death, and at their suggestion a soldier thrust a spear into the Savior's side. From the wound flowed two distinct streams, one of blood, the other of water.

John states, "One of the soldiers pierced His side with a spear, and immediately blood and water came out. And he who has seen has testified, and his testimony is true. . . . These things were done that the Scripture should be fulfilled, 'Not one of His bones shall be broken.' And again another Scripture says, 'They shall look on Him whom they pierced.' " John 19:34–37.

After the Resurrection, the priests circulated the report that Christ did not die on the cross, that He merely fainted and later revived. The action of the Roman soldiers proves that He was already dead. If His life had not been already extinct, this wound would have caused instant death.

But it was not the spear thrust nor the pain of the cross that caused the death of Jesus. That cry, uttered "with a loud voice" (Matthew 27:50; Luke 23:46) at the moment of death, and the stream of blood and water declared that He died of a broken heart—broken by mental anguish, killed by the sin of the world.

### The Disciples Discouraged

With the death of Christ the hopes of His disciples also died. Until the last they had not believed that He would die; they could hardly believe that He was dead. They were overwhelmed with sorrow, and nothing that He had said gave them comfort now. Their faith in Jesus had died, but never had they loved their Lord as now, never had they felt their need of His presence so much.

Christ's disciples longed to give Him an honored burial, but they did not know how to accomplish this. People put to death for treason against the Roman government were assigned to a burial ground for criminals. John and the women from Galilee could not leave the body of their Lord to be handled by unfeeling soldiers and buried in a dishonored grave. Yet they could expect no favors from the Jewish authorities and had no influence with Pilate.

In this emergency, Joseph of Arimathea and Nicodemus came to the disciples' help. Both were members of the Sanhedrin, were wealthy and influential, and were acquainted with Pilate. They were determined to see that the body of Jesus received an honorable burial.

## Help From an Unexpected Place

Joseph went boldly to Pilate and asked him for the body of Jesus. For the first time, Pilate learned that Jesus was dead. The knowledge of Christ's death had been purposely kept from him. When he heard Joseph's request, he sent for the centurion who was in charge at the cross and got a report from him of the events at Calvary, confirming the testimony of Joseph.

Joseph returned with Pilate's order for the body of Christ, and Nicodemus came bringing an expensive mixture of myrrh and aloes, about a hundred pounds of it, to embalm Him. The most honored in all Jerusalem could not have been shown more respect in death. The disciples were astonished.

Neither Joseph nor Nicodemus had openly accepted the Savior while

He was living. Such a step would have excluded them from the Sanhedrin, and they had hoped to protect Him by their influence in its councils. But the wily priests had made their plans useless. Jesus had been condemned when Joseph and Nicodemus were absent. Now these two men no longer hid their attachment to Him. They came boldly to the aid of the poor disciples.

Gently and reverently, with their own hands they removed the body of Jesus from the cross. Tears of sympathy fell as they looked on His bruised and lacerated form. Joseph owned a new tomb, cut out of rock, reserved for himself. But it was near Calvary, and he now prepared it for Jesus. There, with John's help, they straightened the mangled arms and legs and folded the bruised hands on the pulseless chest. They rolled the heavy stone over the entrance to the tomb, and the Savior was left at rest.

While the evening shadows were gathering, Mary Magdalene and the other Marys lingered around their Lord's resting place, shedding tears of sorrow. "Then they returned and . . . rested on the Sabbath according to the commandment." Luke 23:56.

The disciples, the priests, rulers, scribes, and people would never forget that Sabbath. The Jews observed the Passover as they had done for centuries, while He to whom it pointed lay in Joseph's tomb. Worshipers filled the courts of the temple. The high priest was there, splendidly robed. Priests, full of activity, performed their duties.

But some who attended were restless as the blood of bulls and goats was offered for sin. They were not conscious that symbol had met fulfillment, that an infinite Sacrifice had been made for the sins of the world. But never before had they witnessed that service with such conflicting feelings. A sense of strangeness spread over everything. The Most Holy Place had always been sacredly guarded from intrusion, but now, with the heavy veil torn from top to bottom, it was open to all eyes—a place no longer recognized by the Lord. The uncovering of the Most Holy Place filled the priests with dread of coming disaster.

## Many Turn to Bible Study

Between the Crucifixion and the Resurrection, many sleepless eyes were searching the prophecies, some to find evidence that Jesus was not what He claimed to be, and others searching for proofs that He was the true Messiah. Though searching with different goals in view, all were convicted of the same truth—prophecy had been fulfilled; the Crucified One was the world's Redeemer. Many never again took part in the Passover rites. Many even among the priests searched the prophecies and after His resurrection acknowledged Jesus as the Son of God.

Nicodemus remembered Jesus' words spoken by night on the Mount of Olives: "As Moses lifted up the serpent in the wilderness, even so must the Son of Man be lifted up, that whoever believes in Him should not perish but have eternal life." John 3:14, 15. The words Jesus had spoken to him were no longer mysterious. He felt that he had lost much by not connecting himself with the Savior during His

life. Christ's prayer for His murderers and His answer to the dying thief spoke to the heart of the educated councilor. Again he heard that last cry, "It is finished!" spoken like the words of a Conqueror. His faith was forever established. The event that destroyed the hopes of the disciples convinced Joseph and Nicodemus of Jesus' divinity.

Never had Christ attracted so much attention from the crowds as He did now that He was in the tomb. People brought their sick to the temple courts. Everywhere they were calling out, "We want Christ the Healer!" The friendly hands of Jesus, that had never refused to touch the loathsome leper with healing, were folded on His chest. The lips that had answered the leper's request with, "I am willing; be cleansed" (Matthew 8:3), were now silent. Many were determined to have the living Christ among them again. With persistent earnestness they asked for Him. But the leaders drove them away from the temple courts, and soldiers were stationed to keep back the crowds with their sick and dying.

Sadness crushed the sufferers in their disappointment. The sick were dying for lack of Jesus' healing touch. No doctors could help. There was no skill like that of Him who lay in Joseph's tomb.

To thousands of minds came the conviction that a great Light had gone out of the world. Without Christ, the earth was darkness. Many whose voices had joined in the cry, "Crucify Him, crucify Him!" now realized the disaster that had fallen on them.

When the people learned that the

priests had put Jesus to death, they began to make inquiries. The details of His trial were kept as private as possible, but reports about the inhumanity of the priests and rulers circulated everywhere. People of intellect called on these priests and rulers to explain the prophecies concerning the Messiah. While trying to frame some falsehood in reply, they became like madmen. They could not explain the prophecies that pointed to Christ's sufferings and death.

The priests knew that they were meeting the strong criticism of the people. The ones they had influenced against Jesus were now horrified by their own shameful work. These priests trembled for fear that Christ Himself would rise from the dead and appear before them again. They remembered that He had said, "Destroy this temple, and in three days I will raise it up." John 2:19. Judas had told them the words Jesus spoke on the last journey to Jerusalem: "The Son of Man will be betrayed to the chief priests and to the scribes; and they will condemn Him to death, and deliver Him to the Gentiles . . . to crucify. And the third day He will rise again." Matthew 20:18, 19. They remembered that so far Christ's predictions had been fulfilled. Who could say that this also would not happen as predicted?

They longed to shut out these thoughts, but they could not. The image of Christ would intrude on their minds, serene and uncomplaining before His enemies, enduring their taunts and abuse without a complaint. An overpowering conviction came to them that He was the Son of God. At any time He might stand before them, the accused to become the accuser, the slain demanding justice in the death of His murderers.

Though they would not step over a Gentile's threshold for fear of defilement, on the Sabbath they held a council concerning the body of Christ. "The chief priests and Pharisees gathered together to Pilate, saying, 'Sir, we remember, while He was still alive, how that deceiver said, "After three days I will rise." Therefore command that the tomb be made secure until the third day, lest His disciples come by night and steal Him away, and say to the people, "He has risen from the dead." So the last deception will be worse than the first.' Pilate said to them, 'You have a guard; go your way, make it as secure as you know how.' " Matthew 27:62–65.

The priests gave directions for securing the tomb. A great stone had been placed over the opening. Across this stone they placed cords, sealing them with the Roman seal. Then they stationed a guard of one hundred soldiers around the tomb to prevent anyone from tampering with it. Jesus was sealed as securely in His tomb as if He were to remain there through all time.

But the efforts they made to prevent Christ's resurrection are the most convincing arguments in its proof. The greater the number of soldiers placed around the tomb, the stronger would be the testimony that He had risen. Roman might was powerless to confine the Lord of life within the tomb. The hour of His release was near.

# "The Lord Is Risen"*

The night of the first day of the week had worn slowly away. Christ was still a prisoner in His tomb. The Roman seal was unbroken; the Roman guards were keeping their watch. If it had been possible, the prince of darkness would have kept the tomb that held the Son of God sealed forever. But heavenly angels who excel in strength were waiting to welcome the Prince of life.

"And behold, there was a great earthquake; for an angel of the Lord descended from heaven." The bright beams of God's glory illuminated his pathway. "His countenance was like lightning, and his clothing as white as snow. And the guards shook for fear of him, and became like dead men."

This messenger was the angel who fills the position that Satan lost. As he rolled away the stone, heaven seemed to come down to earth. The soldiers saw him removing the stone as if it were a pebble, and they heard him cry, "Son of God, come out; Your Father is calling You." They saw Jesus come out from the grave and heard Him proclaim over the open tomb, "I am the resurrection and the life." As He came out in majesty and glory, the multitude of angels welcomed Him with songs of praise.

At sight of the angels and the glorified Savior, the Roman guard had fainted and become like dead men. When the heavenly procession was no longer visible, they got up and, staggering like drunken men, hurried to the city, telling those whom they met the wonderful news. They were making their way to Pilate, but the priests and rulers sent for them to come first to meet with them. Trembling with fear, their faces colorless, the soldiers told all, just as they had seen it. They said, "It was the Son of God who was crucified; we have heard an angel proclaiming Him as the Majesty of heaven, the King of glory!"

## Caiaphas Urges Deceit

Caiaphas tried to speak. His lips moved, but they uttered no sound. The soldiers were about to leave when Caiaphas at last found speech. "Wait, wait," he said. "Tell no one the things you have seen."

"Tell them," said the priests, "His disciples came at night and stole Him away while we slept." Here the priests overdid their story. If the soldiers were

---

* This chapter is based on Matthew 28:2–4; 11–15.

asleep, how could they know? And if the disciples had been proved guilty of stealing Christ's body, would not the priests have been first to condemn them? Or if the sentinels had slept, would not the priests have been the leaders in accusing them to Pilate?

The soldiers were horrified. Sleeping at their post was an offense punishable with death. Should they lie and place their own lives in danger? How could they stand the trial, even for the sake of money, if they perjured themselves?

The priests promised to secure the safety of the guard, saying that Pilate would not want to have such a report circulated any more than they did. The Roman soldiers sold their integrity for money. They came to the priests burdened with a startling message of truth. They went out with a burden of money and with a lying report on their tongues.

Meanwhile the report of Christ's resurrection had reached Pilate. Though he had condemned the Savior unwillingly, he had felt no real pangs of conscience until now. In terror he now shut himself inside his house, determined to see no one. But the priests made their way into his presence and urged him to overlook the sentinels' neglect of duty. He himself questioned the guard privately. They did not dare to conceal anything, and Pilate drew from them an account of all that had happened. He did not take any further legal action, but from then on there was no peace for him.

In putting Christ to death, the priests had made themselves the tools of Satan. Now they were entirely in his

power, entangled in a trap from which they saw no escape but to continue their warfare against Christ. The only hope for them was to prove Christ an impostor by denying that He had risen. They bribed the soldiers and arranged for Pilate's silence.

But there were witnesses whom they could not silence. Many had heard of the soldiers' testimony about Christ's resurrection. And certain ones of the dead who came from the tombs with Christ appeared to many and declared that He had risen. The priests and rulers were in continual dread that in walking the streets or within the privacy of their own homes they would come face to face with Christ. Bolts and bars were poor protection against the Son of God. By day and by night that awful scene was before them when they had cried, "His blood be on us and on our children." Matthew 27:25.

## The Guarantee of Our Resurrection

When the mighty angel spoke at Christ's tomb, saying, "Your Father is calling You," the Savior came out from the grave by the life that was in Himself. Christ had proclaimed in triumph, "I am the resurrection and the life." Only the Deity could speak these words. All created beings are dependent on God, receiving life from Him. Only He who is one with God could say, "I have power to lay down My life, and I have power to take it up again." See John 10:18.

Christ rose from the dead as the first fruits of those who slept, and His resurrection took place on the very day when the wave sheaf was to be presented before the Lord. For more than a thousand years when the people went up to Jerusalem to the Passover, the sheaf of first fruits, the first heads of ripened grain, was waved before the Lord as a thank offering. The grain harvest could not continue until this was presented. The sheaf dedicated to God represented the harvest. So Christ's resurrection is the representation and pledge of the resurrection of all the righteous dead. "For if we believe that Jesus died and rose again, even so God will bring with Him those who sleep in Jesus." 1 Thessalonians 4:14.

### Many Resurrected With Jesus

As Christ arose, He brought from the grave a multitude of captives. See Matthew 27:52. They were those who had borne their testimony to the truth at the cost of their lives. Now they were to be witnesses for Him who had raised them from the dead.

During His ministry, Jesus had raised the dead to life. But these resurrected ones were not clothed with immortality. They were still subject to death. But those who came from the grave at Christ's resurrection were raised to everlasting life. Later they ascended with Him as trophies of His victory over death and the grave. But now they went into the city and ap-

peared to many, declaring, "Christ has risen from the dead, and we are risen with Him." Risen redeemed ones bore witness to the truth of the words, "Your dead shall live; together with my dead body they shall arise." Isaiah 26:19.

In our Savior, the life that was lost through sin is restored. He is granted the right to give immortality. "I have come," He said, "that they may have life, and that they may have it more abundantly." John 10:10. "Whoever eats My flesh and drinks My blood has eternal life, and I will raise him up at the last day." John 6:54. To the Christian, death is only a sleep, a moment of silence and darkness. "When Christ who is our life appears, then you also will appear with Him in glory." Colossians 3:4.

The Voice that cried from the cross, "It is finished!" will penetrate the graves and unlock the tombs, and the dead in Christ will rise. At the Savior's resurrection a few graves were opened, but at His second coming all the precious dead will hear His voice and come forth to glorious immortal life. The same power that raised Christ from the dead will raise His church above all powers, not only in this world, but also in the world to come.

# "Woman, Why Are You Weeping?"*

On the first day of the week, very early, the women who had stood by the cross made their way to the tomb to anoint the Savior's body. They did not think about His rising from the dead. The sun of their hope had set. They did not remember His words, "I will see you again." John 16:22.

Not aware of what was even then taking place, they came near the garden, saying, "Who will roll away the stone from the door of the tomb for us?" And suddenly, the heavens were ablaze with glory. The earth trembled. The great stone was rolled away. The grave was empty!

Mary Magdalene was the first to reach the place, and seeing that the stone was removed, she hurried to tell the disciples. Meanwhile the other women came. A light was shining around the tomb, but the body of Jesus was not there.

As they lingered, suddenly they saw that they were not alone. A young man in shining clothing was sitting by the tomb. It was the angel who had rolled away the stone. He had taken the form of humanity so that he would not alarm these friends of Jesus. Yet the light of the heavenly glory was still shining around him, and the women were afraid. "Do not be afraid," the angel said, "for I know that you seek Jesus who was crucified. He is not here; for He is risen, as He said. Come, see the place where the Lord lay. And go quickly and tell His disciples that He is risen from the dead."

They looked into the tomb, and another angel in human form said, "Why do you seek the living among the dead? He is not here, but is risen! Remember how He spoke to you when He was still in Galilee, saying, 'The Son of Man must be delivered into the hands of sinful men, and be crucified, and the third day rise again.' "

The women remembered now—He said He would rise again! What a day this is! Quickly they left "with fear and great joy, and ran to bring His disciples word."

Mary had not heard the good news. She went to Peter and John with the sorrowful message, "They have taken away the Lord out of the tomb, and we do not know where they have laid Him." The disciples hurried to the tomb and saw the shroud and

---

* This chapter is based on Matthew 28:1, 5–8; Mark 16:1–8; Luke 24:1–12; John 20:1–18.

the napkin, but they did not find their Lord. Yet even here was evidence that He had risen. The graveclothes were not thrown carelessly aside, but carefully folded, each in a place by itself. John "saw and believed." He now remembered the Savior's words foretelling His resurrection.

Christ Himself placed those graveclothes with such care. As the mighty angel from heaven rolled away the stone, another entered the tomb and undid the wrappings from the body of Jesus. But it was the Savior's hand that folded each and laid it in its place. In the sight of Him who guides both the star and the atom, nothing is unimportant.

Mary had followed John and Peter to the tomb. When they returned to Jerusalem, she remained. Grief filled her heart. Looking into the empty tomb, she saw the two angels, one at the head and the other at the foot where Jesus had lain. "Woman, why are you weeping?" they asked her. "Because they have taken away my Lord," she answered, "and I do not know where they have laid Him."

Then she turned away, thinking that she must find someone who could tell her what had been done with the body. Another voice addressed her: "Woman, why are you weeping? Whom are you seeking?" Through tear-dimmed eyes, Mary saw a man, and thinking it was the gardener, said, "Sir, if You have carried Him away, tell me where You have laid Him, and I will take Him away." If this rich man's tomb was thought too honorable for Jesus, she herself would provide a place for Him. There was a grave that

Christ's own voice had made vacant, the grave where Lazarus had lain.

But now in His own familiar voice, Jesus said to her, "Mary." Turning, she saw in front of her the living Christ! Springing toward Him as if to embrace His feet, she said, "Rabboni!" [Teacher]. But Christ raised His hand, saying, Do not detain Me; "for I have not yet ascended to My Father; but go to My brethren and say to them, 'I am ascending to My Father and your Father, and to My God and your God.' " Mary went on her way with the joyful message.

Jesus refused the homage of His people until He ascended to the heavenly courts and heard the assurance from God Himself that His atonement for our sins had been ample, that through His blood all could have eternal life. The Father ratified the covenant made with Christ, that He would receive repentant and obedient men and women and would love them even as He loves His Son. All power in heaven and on earth was given to the Prince of life, and He returned to His followers in a world of sin, so that He could give to them of His power and glory.

While the Savior was in God's presence, receiving gifts for His church, the disciples mourned and wept. The day of rejoicing for all heaven was a day of confusion and perplexity to them. Their unbelief in the testimony of the women shows how low their faith had sunk. They could not believe the news. It was too good to be true, they thought. They had heard so much of the so-called scientific theories of the Sadducees that they scarcely knew what the resurrection from the dead could mean.

"Go," the angels had said to the women, "tell His disciples—and Peter—that He is going before you into Galilee; there you will see Him, as He said to you." The message of these angels to the disciples should have convinced them that it was true. Such words could have come only from the messengers of their risen Lord.

Since the death of Christ, Peter had been bowed down with remorse. His shameful denial of the Lord was always on his mind. Of all the disciples, he had suffered most bitterly. The angels' message gave him the assurance that his repentance was accepted. They had mentioned him by name.

When Mary Magdalene had told the disciples that she had seen the Lord, she repeated the call to meet Him in Galilee. And even a third time the message was sent to them. After He had ascended to the Father, Jesus appeared to the other women, saying, "Go and tell My brethren to go to Galilee, and there they will see Me."

Christ's first work after His resurrection was to convince His disciples of His undiminished love and tender regard for them. He wanted to draw the bonds of love still closer around them. "Go tell My brethren," He said, "that they are to meet Me in Galilee."

But even now the disciples could not throw off their doubt and perplexity. Even when the women declared that they had seen the Lord, the disciples thought they were under an illusion.

Trouble seemed to follow trouble quickly. They had seen their Master die; they found themselves deprived of His body; and they were accused of having stolen it for the sake of deceiving the people. They had little hope of ever correcting the false impressions that were gaining ground. They feared the hatred of the priests and the anger of the people. They longed for Jesus' presence.

They often repeated the words, "We were hoping that it was He who was going to redeem Israel." Luke 24:21. Lonely and sick at heart, they met together in the upper room. They closed and fastened the doors, knowing that at any time the fate of their beloved Teacher might be theirs.

And all the time they could have been rejoicing in the knowledge of a risen Savior! Many are still doing what these disciples did. The Savior is close beside them, but their tear-blinded eyes do not recognize Him. He speaks to them, but they do not understand.

"Go quickly and tell His disciples that He is risen." Look not to the empty tomb. From grateful hearts, from lips touched with holy fire, let the glad song ring out, Christ is risen! He lives to make intercession for us.

# The Walk to Emmaus*

Late in the afternoon on the day of the Resurrection, two disciples were on their way to Emmaus, a little town eight miles from Jerusalem. These disciples had come to keep the Passover and were greatly perplexed by the events that had taken place. They had heard the news about the removal of Christ's body and also the report of the women who had seen the angels and had met Jesus. Now returning home, they were talking over the scenes of the trial and Crucifixion. Never had they been so completely discouraged.

On their journey, they were joined by a Stranger, but they were so absorbed in their gloom that they did not observe him closely. They continued expressing the thoughts of their hearts, discussing the lessons Christ had given, which they seemed unable to comprehend. Jesus longed to comfort them. He understood the conflicting, perplexing ideas that brought to their minds the thought, Can this Man, who allowed Himself to be so humiliated, be the Christ? They wept. Jesus longed to wipe away their tears and fill them with joy and gladness. But He must first give them lessons they would never forget.

"He said to them, 'What kind of conversation is this that you have with one another as you walk and are sad?' Then the one whose name was Cleopas answered and said to Him, 'Are You the only stranger in Jerusalem, and have You not known the things which happened there in these days?' " They told Him of their disappointment in regard to their Master, "who was a Prophet mighty in deed and word before God and all the people," but "the chief priests and our rulers delivered Him to be condemned to death, and crucified Him." With quivering lips they added, "We were hoping that it was He who was going to redeem Israel. Indeed, besides all this, today is the third day since these things happened."

Strange that they did not remember Christ's words, that He had foretold that He would rise again the third day. The priests and rulers did not forget!

## Jesus, Unrecognized, Explains the Scriptures

"Then He said to them, 'O foolish ones, and slow of heart to believe in all that the prophets have spoken! Ought

---

* This chapter is based on Luke 24:13–33.

not the Christ to have suffered these things and to enter into His glory?' " Who could this be, to speak with such earnestness and sympathy? For the first time, they began to feel hopeful. Often they looked earnestly at their Companion and thought that His words were just the words that Christ would have spoken.

Beginning at Moses, the start of Bible history, Christ explained the things concerning Himself in all the Scriptures. If He had made Himself known to them first, they would have hungered for nothing more. But it was necessary for them to understand the symbols and prophecies of the Old Testament. Their faith must be established on these. Christ performed no miracle to convince them. It was His first work to explain the Scriptures. He showed from the prophets that His death was the strongest evidence for their faith.

Jesus showed the importance of the Old Testament as a witness to His mission. The Old Testament reveals the Savior as clearly as the New. Light from the prophetic past brings out the life of Christ and the teachings of the New Testament with clearness and beauty. Comparing the prophecies of the Old Testament with the history of the New gives even stronger proof than the miracles of Christ.

The disciples had expected a Messiah who would take His throne and kingly power in the manner that people wanted, but this had been misleading. His disciples must understand about the cup of suffering that had been given to Him. He showed them that the awful conflict was the fulfill-ment of the covenant made before the foundation of the world. Christ must die, as every transgressor of the law must die if he continues in sin. All this was to happen, but it would not end in defeat but in glorious victory. Jesus told them that they must make every effort to save the world from sin. His followers must live as He lived and work as He worked, with persistent ef-fort.

Christ talked in this way to His disciples to help them understand the Scriptures. As He told them of the overthrow of Jerusalem, they wept as they looked on the doomed city. But little did they suspect yet who their traveling Companion was, for Christ referred to Himself as though He were another person. He walked as carefully as they did over the rough stones, stopping with them now and then for a little rest.

### Their Hearts Were Drawn to the Stranger

During their journey, the sun had gone down and the laborers in the fields had left their work. As the disciples were about to enter their home, the stranger appeared as though He was going to continue His journey. But the disciples hungered to hear more from Him. "Abide with us," they urged. He did not accept the invitation immediately, but they pressed Him. "It is toward evening, and the day is far spent." Christ yielded to this request and "went in to stay with them."

If the disciples had failed to press their invitation, they would not have known that their traveling Companion was the risen Lord. Christ never forces His company on anyone. He will gladly enter the humblest home, but if its residents are too indifferent to ask Him to stay with them, He passes by.

The disciples had soon prepared the simple evening meal and placed it before the Guest, who had taken His seat at the head of the table. Now He stretched out His hands to bless the food in exactly the same way as their Master used to do. The disciples sat bolt upright in astonishment. They looked again and saw the print of nails in His hands. Both of them exclaimed, "It is the Lord Jesus!"

They got up to throw themselves at His feet, but He had vanished. They looked at the place occupied by One whose body had so recently lain in the grave, and they said to each other, "Did not our heart burn within us while He talked with us on the road, and while He opened the Scriptures to us?"

With this great news to communi- cate, their weariness and hunger were gone. They left their meal uneaten and hurried back on the same path by which they had come, to tell the disciples in the city. They climbed over steep places, slipping on smooth rocks, wanting to go faster than they dared. They lost the way but found it again. Sometimes running, sometimes stumbling, they hurried on, their unseen Companion beside them all the way.

The night was dark, but the Sun of Righteousness was shining upon them. They seemed to be in a new world. Christ is risen—over and over they repeated it. They must tell the sorrowing ones the wonderful story of the walk to Emmaus. They must tell who joined them along the way. They carried the greatest message ever given—glad news on which the hopes of the human family depend for time and eternity.

# The Resurrected Christ Appears*

On reaching Jerusalem the two disciples entered through the eastern gate, made their way along the narrow streets by the light of the rising moon, and went to the upper room where Jesus had spent the last evening before His death. They knew they would find the other disciples there. The door was securely barred. They knocked to be let in, but no answer came. All was quiet. Then they gave their names. The door was carefully unbarred, they entered, and Another, unseen, entered with them. Then the door was locked again, to keep out spies.

The travelers found all of their fellow disciples in surprised excitement. Various ones were saying, "The Lord is risen indeed, and has appeared to Simon!" Then the two, panting from their hurried journey, told how Jesus had appeared to them. Some were saying that they could not believe it, for it was too good to be true, when suddenly another Person stood before them. No stranger had knocked for entrance, and they had heard no footstep. The disciples were startled. Then they heard the voice of their Master, clear and distinct, "Peace to you."

"But they were terrified and frightened, and supposed they had seen a spirit. And He said to them, 'Why are you troubled? And why do doubts arise in your hearts? Behold My hands and My feet, that it is I Myself. Handle Me and see, for a spirit does not have flesh and bones as you see I have.' When He had said this, He showed them His hands and His feet.

"But while they still did not believe for joy, and marveled, He said to them, 'Have you any food here?' So they gave Him a piece of a broiled fish and some honeycomb. And He took it and ate in their presence." "Then the disciples were glad when they saw the Lord." Faith took the place of unbelief, and they acknowledged their risen Savior.

## We Will Recognize Our Loved Ones

The face of the risen Savior, His manner, His speech, were all familiar to His disciples. As Jesus rose from the dead, so those who sleep in Him will rise again. We will know our friends, as the disciples knew Jesus. In the glorified body their identity will be perfectly preserved. We will recognize those we love.

Jesus reminded His disciples of the

* This chapter is based on Luke 24:33–48; John 20:19–29.

words He had spoken before His death. "And He opened their understanding, that they might comprehend the Scriptures. Then He said to them, 'Thus it is written, and thus it was necessary for the Christ to suffer and to rise from the dead the third day, and that repentance and remission of sins should be preached in His name to all nations, beginning at Jerusalem. And you are witnesses of these things.' " Christ's life, His death and resurrection, the prophecies that pointed to these events, the sacredness of God's law, the mysteries of the plan of salvation, the power of Jesus to forgive sins—all these they were to make known to the world.

"And when He had said this, He breathed on them, and said to them, 'Receive the Holy Spirit. If you forgive the sins of any, they are forgiven them; if you retain the sins of any, they are retained.' " Christ would give His Holy Spirit to them more abundantly after His ascension. But He breathed His Spirit on them now to impress them with the fact that without the Holy Spirit they could not fulfill their official duties in connection with the church.

The gift of the Spirit is the gift of the life of Christ. It endows the receiver with the attributes of Christ. Only those who possess the inward working of the Spirit and in whose life the Christ-life is revealed are to minister in behalf of the church.

"If you forgive the sins of any," said Christ, "they are forgiven them; if you retain the sins of any, they are retained." Christ here gives no liberty for anyone to pass judgment on others. This right belongs to God. But He places a responsibility for the individual members on the organized church. The church has a duty to those who fall into sin to warn them, instruct them, and if possible to restore them. Deal faithfully with wrongdoing. Call sin by its right name. Declare what God has said about lying, Sabbath breaking, stealing, and every other evil. If they persist in sin, the judgment you have declared from God's Word is pronounced on them in heaven. The church must show that she does not approve of their deeds, or she herself dishonors her Lord. She must deal with sin as God directs, and heaven ratifies her action.

But there is a brighter side. "If you forgive the sins of any, they are forgiven." Let this thought be your focus. The shepherds should speak to the erring about the forgiving mercy of the Savior. Let them encourage the sinner to repent and believe in Him who can pardon. "If we confess our sins, He is faithful and just to forgive us our sins and to cleanse us from all unrighteousness." 1 John 1:9. Place the trembling hand of the repenting one in the loving hand of Jesus. Such a forgiveness is ratified in heaven.

## Only God Can Forgive

Only in this sense does the church have the power to free the sinner from the sin. We can obtain forgiveness of sins only through the merits of Christ. God gives no person or human organization the power to free anyone from guilt. The name of Jesus is the only "name under heaven given among men by which we must be saved." Acts 4:12.

When Jesus first met the disciples in the upper room, Thomas was not with them. He heard the reports of the others that Jesus had risen, but gloom and unbelief filled his heart. If Jesus had really risen, there could be no hope of a literal earthly kingdom. And it wounded his pride to think that his Master would reveal Himself to all except him. He was determined not to believe, and for a whole week he brooded over his misery.

He repeatedly declared, "Unless I see in His hands the print of the nails, and put my finger into the print of the nails, and put my hand into His side, I will not believe." He would not exercise faith that was dependent on the testimony of his fellow disciples. He loved his Lord, but he had allowed jealousy and unbelief to take possession of his heart.

One evening Thomas decided to meet with the others in the familiar upper room. He had a faint hope that the good news was true. While eating their evening meal, the disciples talked of the evidences Christ had given them in the prophecies. "Jesus came, the doors being shut, and stood in the midst, and said, 'Peace to you!' "

Turning to Thomas, He said, "Reach your finger here, and look at My hands; and reach your hand here, and put it into My side. Do not be unbelieving, but believing." The doubting disciple knew that none of his companions could have told the Master about his unbelief. He had no desire for further proof. His heart leaped for joy, and he threw himself at the feet of Jesus, exclaiming, "My Lord and my God!"

Jesus accepted his acknowledgment but gently reproved his unbelief: "Thomas, because you have seen Me, you have believed. Blessed are those who have not seen and yet have believed." If the world now followed the example of Thomas, no one would believe, for all who receive Christ must do so through the testimony of others. Many who, like Thomas, wait for all cause of doubt to be removed will never have that desire fulfilled. They gradually become confirmed in unbelief. They are sowing seeds of doubt, and they will have a harvest of doubt to reap. Then when faith and confidence are most essential, many will find themselves powerless to hope and believe.

Jesus' treatment of Thomas shows how we should treat those who make their doubts prominent. Thomas had been most unreasonable in dictating the conditions of his faith, but Jesus' generous dealings with him broke down all the barriers. We seldom overcome unbelief by controversy. But if we reveal Jesus, in His love and mercy, as the crucified Savior, many once-unwilling lips will speak Thomas's acknowledgment, "My Lord and my God!"

# By the Sea Once More*

Jesus had made an appointment to meet His disciples in Galilee. Their absence from Jerusalem during Passover week would have been interpreted as dissent and heresy. But when this was over, they gladly turned homeward to meet the Savior as He had directed.

Seven of the disciples were together. They were poor in worldly goods, but rich in the knowledge of the truth. For three years the greatest Educator the world has ever known had been their Teacher. They had become intelligent and refined, agents who could lead others to a knowledge of the truth.

The disciples gathered in a place where they were not likely to be disturbed. Within sight was the beach where more than ten thousand people had been fed from a few small loaves and fishes. Not far away was Capernaum, the scene of many miracles.

Peter, who still had much of his old love for boats and fishing, proposed that they go out on the lake and throw their nets. They were in need of food and clothing, and the proceeds from a successful night's fishing would supply these things. So they went out, but they worked all night without success.

Through the long hours they talked of their absent Lord. They puzzled over their own future and grew sad at the prospect before them.

Finally the morning dawned. The boat was only a little way from shore, and the disciples saw a Stranger standing on the beach who greeted them with the question, "Children, have you any food?" When they answered, "No," "He said to them, 'Cast the net on the right side of the boat, and you will find some.' So they cast, and now they were not able to draw it in because of the multitude of fish."

John recognized the Stranger and exclaimed to Peter, "It is the Lord!" Peter was so glad that he threw himself into the water and was soon standing by the side of his Master. The other disciples came in their boat, dragging the net with the fish. "As soon as they had come to land, they saw a fire of coals there, and fish laid on it, and bread."

"Jesus said to them, 'Bring some of the fish which you have just caught.' " Peter rushed for the net, which he had dropped, and helped drag it to shore. After the work was done, Jesus divided the food among them. All seven

---

* This chapter is based on John 21:1–22.

recognized Him and acknowledged who He was. But a mysterious awe was on them, and in silence they gazed at the risen Savior.

Vividly they recalled the scene beside the sea when Jesus had invited them to follow Him. He had called them to leave their fishing boats and had promised to make them fishers of men. To bring this scene to their minds and to deepen its impression, He had performed the miracle again as a renewal of the commission to the disciples. Their Master's death had not reduced their obligation to do the work He had assigned them. Though they would not have support from their former employment, the risen Savior would provide for their needs. If they labored in connection with Him, they could not fail to succeed.

### Peter Is Restored to Confidence

Christ had another lesson to give. Peter had denied his Lord in shameful contrast to his earlier professions of loyalty. He had dishonored Christ, and the other disciples thought he would not be allowed to take his former position among them. He himself felt that he had forfeited his calling to be a disciple. He must give evidence of his repentance in front of them all. Without this, his sin might destroy his influence as a minister of Christ. The Savior gave him opportunity to regain the confidence of the others and, as far as possible, to remove the discredit he had brought on the gospel.

Here is a lesson for all of Christ's followers. We should confess secret sins to God in secret, but open sin requires open confession. The disciple's sin causes Satan to triumph and wavering followers to stumble. By giving proof of repentance the disciple is to remove this disgrace.

While Christ and the disciples were eating together, the Savior said to Peter, "Simon, son of Jonah, do you love Me more than these?" referring to the other disciples. "Yes, Lord," he said, "You know that I love You." Jesus told him, "Feed My lambs." Peter made no vehement claim that his love was greater than that of the others.

Again Jesus applied the test: "Simon, son of Jonah, do you love Me?" The second response was like the first, free from extravagant claims: "Yes, Lord; You know that I love You." Jesus said to him, "Tend My sheep."

Once more the Savior asked the testing question: "Simon, son of Jonah, do you love Me?" Peter was grieved. He knew that his Lord had reason to distrust him, and with an aching heart he answered, "Lord, You know all things; You know that I love You." Again Jesus said, "Feed My sheep."

Three times Peter had openly denied his Lord, and three times Jesus pressed home that pointed question like a barbed arrow to his wounded heart. In front of the assembled disciples Jesus revealed the depth of Peter's repentance and showed how thoroughly humbled the once boasting disciple was.

Just before Peter's fall, Jesus had said to him, "I have prayed for you, that your faith should not fail; and when you have returned to Me, strengthen your brethren." Luke 22:32. The transformation in Peter was plain to see. Because of his humiliation and repentance, Peter was better prepared than before to act as shepherd to the flock.

The first work Christ entrusted to Peter was to feed the "lambs"—to minister to those who were young in the faith, to teach the ignorant, to open the Scriptures to them and educate them for usefulness in Christ's service. For this work his own suffering and repentance had prepared him.

Before his fall, Peter was always ready to correct others and to express his mind. But the converted Peter was very different. He retained his former energy, but the grace of Christ regulated his zeal. He could then feed the lambs of Christ's flock as well as the sheep.

The Savior's manner of dealing with Peter taught the disciples to meet the sinner with patience, sympathy, and forgiving love. Remembering his own weakness, Peter was to deal with his flock as tenderly as Christ had dealt with him.

## Christ Tells How Peter Will Die

Before His death, Jesus had said to Peter, "Where I am going you cannot follow Me now, but you shall follow Me afterward." To this Peter had replied, "Lord, why can I not follow You now? I will lay down my life for Your sake." John 13:36, 37. He failed when the test came, but again he was to have opportunity to prove his love for Christ. So that he could be strengthened for the final test of his faith, the Savior opened to him his future. After a life of usefulness, when

age was wearing out his strength, he would indeed follow his Lord. Jesus said, " 'When you were younger, you girded yourself and walked where you wished; but when you are old, you will stretch out your hands, and another will gird you and carry you where you do not wish.' This He spoke, signifying by what death he would glorify God."

In this way Jesus foretold that Peter's hands would be stretched out on the cross. Again He invited His disciple, "Follow Me." Peter was not discouraged by the revelation. He felt willing to accept any death for his Lord.

Up to now Peter had loved Christ as a man; he now loved Him as God. Now he was prepared to share in his Lord's mission of sacrifice. When at last Peter was brought to the cross, at his own request he was crucified with his head downward. He thought it was too great an honor to suffer in the same way as his Master did.

Before this Peter had tried to plan for the work of God instead of waiting to discover and follow God's plan. But Jesus told him, "Follow Me." Do not run ahead of Me. Let Me go before you, and then the enemy will not overcome you.

As Peter walked beside Jesus, he saw that John was following. A desire came over him to know his future, and he "said to Jesus, 'But Lord, what about this man?' Jesus said to him, 'If I will that he remain till I come, what is that to you? You follow Me.' " Peter should have considered that his Lord would reveal to him everything that it was best for him to know. In saying about John, "If I will that he remain till I come," Jesus gave no assurance that this disciple would live until the Lord's second coming. But even if He decided that this would happen, it would not affect Peter's work in any way. Obedience was the duty that Jesus required of each.

How many today are interested in the affairs of others, anxious to know their duty, while in danger of neglecting their own! It is our work to look to Christ and follow Him. Beholding Him, we will become transformed.

John lived to see the destruction of Jerusalem and the ruin of the temple—a symbol of the last ruin of the world. To his last days he closely followed his Lord. Jesus had restored Peter to his apostleship, but the honor Peter received from Christ had not given him supremacy over the others. Christ made this plain in answer to Peter's question, "What about this man?" He had said, "What is that to you? You follow Me." Peter was not honored as the head of the church. He had much influence in the church, but the lesson Christ taught him by the Sea of Galilee Peter carried with him throughout his life.

Writing to the churches, Peter said, "The elders who are among you I exhort, I who am a fellow elder and a witness of the sufferings of Christ, . . . Shepherd the flock of God . . . not as being lords over those entrusted to you, but being examples to the flock; and when the Chief Shepherd appears, you will receive the crown of glory that does not fade away." 1 Peter 5:1–4.

# "Go . . . Teach All Nations"*

Standing only a step from His heavenly throne, Christ gave the commission: "All authority has been given to Me in heaven and on earth. Go therefore and make disciples of all the nations." "Go into all the world and preach the gospel to every creature." Mark 16:15. Jesus repeated the words again and again so that the disciples would grasp their significance. The light of heaven was to shine on all the inhabitants of the earth in clear, strong rays.

Jesus had given the commission to the Twelve in the upper room, but now it was to go to a larger number. All the believers who could be called together were assembled for the meeting on a mountain in Galilee. The angel at the tomb reminded the disciples of Jesus' promise to meet them in Galilee. They repeated the promise to the believers at Jerusalem during Passover week, and through them it reached many who were mourning the death of their Lord. With intense interest, all looked forward to the meeting. They came from every direction with wondering hearts.

At the time appointed, about five hundred believers gathered in little knots on the mountainside, eager to learn all they could from those who had seen Christ since His resurrection. The disciples went from group to group, telling all that they had seen and heard of Jesus and reasoning from the Scriptures, as He had done with them.

Suddenly Jesus stood among them. No one could tell from where He had come or how. Many had never seen Him before, but in His hands and feet they saw the marks of the Crucifixion. When they saw Him, they worshiped Him.

But some doubted. It will always be this way. There are those who find it hard to exercise faith, and they place themselves on the doubting side. They lose much because of their unbelief.

This was the only interview that Jesus had with many of the believers after His resurrection. His words, coming from lips that had been closed in death, thrilled them. Now He declared that "all power" (KJV) was given to Him. This lifted the minds of His hearers to the highest understanding of His dignity and glory.

Christ's words were the announcement that His sacrifice in humanity's

---

* This chapter is based on Matthew 28:16–20.

behalf was full and complete. He had accomplished the work that He came to this world to do. He was on His way to the throne of God. He had started on His work as Mediator. Possessing limitless authority, He gave His commission: "Go therefore and make disciples of all the nations, baptizing them in the name of the Father and of the Son and of the Holy Spirit, teaching them to observe all things that I have commanded you; and lo, I am with you always, even to the end of the age." He commissioned His disciples to proclaim a faith that would have nothing of caste or country in it, a faith adapted to all peoples, nations, and social classes.

Christ plainly stated the nature of His kingdom. His purpose was to establish a spiritual kingdom, not to reign as an earthly king on David's throne. He said, "You see that all I revealed to you concerning My rejection as the Messiah has happened. All that I said about the humiliation I would endure and the death I would die has been verified. On the third day, I rose again. All these things have fulfilled the specifications of prophecy."

Christ commissioned His disciples to do the work He had left in their hands, beginning at Jerusalem. Jerusalem had been the scene of His amazing condescension for the human race. Few had recognized how near heaven came to earth when Jesus was among them. The work of the disciples must begin at Jerusalem.

The disciples could have pleaded for a more promising field, but they made no such appeal. Christ had scattered the seed of truth, and the seed would yield an abundant harvest. The first offers of mercy must go to the murderers of the Savior.

Many in Jerusalem had secretly believed on Jesus, and many had been deceived by the priests and rulers. The disciples must call them to repentance. While all Jerusalem was stirred by the thrilling events of the past few weeks, the preaching of the gospel would make the deepest impression.

But the work was not to stop here. It was to be extended to earth's farthest limits. To His disciples Christ said, "Although Israel has rejected Me as the Scriptures foretold, they will still have another opportunity to accept the Son of God. To you, My disciples, I commit this message of mercy. It is to go to Israel first, then to all nations, tongues, and peoples. You are to gather all who believe into one church."

## The Holy Spirit Makes Their Work Effective

Through the Holy Spirit, signs and wonders would confirm the disciples' testimony. Not only the apostles, but those who received their message would work miracles. "In My name they will cast out demons; they will speak with new tongues; they will take up serpents; and if they drink anything deadly, it will by no means hurt them; they will lay hands on the sick, and they will recover." Mark 16:17, 18.

At that time unprincipled people did not hesitate to poison those who stood in the way of their ambition. Jesus knew that many would think they were doing God a service to put His witnesses to death. For this reason, He promised them protection from this danger.

And He promised a new gift: the disciples were to preach among other nations, and they would receive power to speak other tongues. The apostles and their associates were unschooled men, yet through the outpouring of the Spirit on the Day of Pentecost their speech, whether in their own language or a foreign tongue, became pure and accurate, both in word and accent.

In this way Christ gave His disciples full provision to carry out the work, and He took on Himself the responsibility for its success. "Go to all nations," He instructed them. "Go to the farthest part of the habitable globe, but know that My presence will be there. Work in faith and confidence."

The Savior's commission includes all believers to the end of time. It is fatal to suppose that the work of saving others depends on the ordained minister alone. For this work the church was established, and all who take its vows pledge themselves to be co-workers with Christ. Whatever our calling in life, our first interest should be to win others for Christ. We may not be able to speak to congregations, but we can work for individuals. Near and far-off there are people weighed down by guilt. It is not hardship or poverty that degrades humanity. It is guilt, wrongdoing. Christ wants His servants to minister to sin-sick hearts.

### Where We Can Begin

Everyone is to begin where he is. In our own families there may be people starving for the bread of life. There are heathen at our very doors. If we perform the work with faith, it will reach to the uttermost parts of the earth. The humblest worker, moved by the Holy Spirit, will touch invisible chords, and their vibrations will ring to the ends of the earth and make melody through eternal ages.

God promises the gifts of the Spirit to meet every believer's need for the Lord's work. The promise is just as trustworthy now as in the days of the apostles.

Christ came to heal the sick, to proclaim deliverance to Satan's captives. He infused His life into the sick and the demon-possessed. He knew that those who asked Him for help had brought disease on themselves, yet He did not refuse to heal them. And many were healed of their spiritual disease as well as their physical illnesses. The gospel still possesses the same power. Christ feels the troubles of every sufferer. When fever is burning up the life forces, He feels the agony. He is just as willing to heal now as when He was personally on earth. He wants to exercise His power through His servants.

### Healthful Living a Part of the Gospel

In the Savior's method of healing there were lessons for His disciples. Only the power of the Great Healer could work the cure, but Christ made use of simple and natural remedies. He taught that disease is the result of violating God's laws, both natural and spiritual. The great misery in the world would not exist if people lived in harmony with the Creator's plan. He taught that health is the reward of obedience to the laws of God. The Great Physician had spoken to His people from the pillar of cloud: "If you diligently heed the voice of the Lord your God and do what is right in His sight, . . . I will put none of the diseases on you. . . . For I am the Lord who heals you." Exodus 15:26.

For the sick we should use the remedies that God has provided in nature and point them to Him who alone can restore. We should teach them to believe in the Great Healer, to take hold of His strength.

Only as we receive of Christ's love, through faith, can the life-giving energy flow from us to the people. There were places where the Savior Himself could not do many mighty works because of their unbelief. Today, as well, unbelief separates the church from her divine Helper. Her lack of faith disappoints God and robs Him of His glory. Where there is no active labor for others, love dies down and faith grows dim.

Angels marvel at our shallow appreciation of God's love. How would a mother and father feel if they knew that their child, lost in the cold and the snow, had been left to die by those who might have saved it? The sufferings of every person are the sufferings of God's child, and those who reach out no helping hand to their dying fellow beings stir up His righteous anger.

## How the Gospel Has Power

Christ gave His disciples their message. Teach the people, He said, "to observe all things that I have commanded you." The things He had spoken, not only in person but through all the Old Testament, are included here.

There is no place for tradition, human theories, or laws established by church authority. "The Law and the Prophets," with the record of His own words and deeds, are the treasure we are to give to the world.

We are to present the gospel not as a lifeless theory but as a living force to change the life. Those whose actions have been most offensive to Him He freely accepts. When they repent, He gives them His divine Spirit and sends them into the camp of the disloyal to proclaim His infinite mercy. Through His grace human beings may possess a Christlike character and rejoice in His great love.

He is not content simply to announce these blessings. He presents them in the most attractive way, to awaken a desire to possess them. This is also how His servants are to present the riches of the unspeakable Gift. The wonderful love of Christ will melt and subdue hearts when merely reciting doctrines would accomplish nothing. Words alone cannot tell it. Let it show in the life. Christ is posing for His portrait in every disciple. Every one of them is to reveal His longsuffering love, His mercy and truth, to the world.

The first disciples prepared themselves for their work. Before Pentecost, they met together and put away all differences. Unitedly they prayed in faith, feeling deeply the burden for others to be saved. Then it was that the Holy Spirit was poured out, and thousands were converted in a day.

It can be the same way now. Preach the Word of God. Let Christians put away their disagreements and give themselves to God for saving the lost. If they will ask in faith for the blessing, it will come. The outpouring in the apostles' days was the "former rain," and the result was glorious, but the "latter rain" will be more abundant. See Joel 2:23.

All who consecrate soul, body, and spirit to God will constantly receive new reserves of physical and mental power. When they cooperate with Christ, He enables them in their human weakness to do the deeds of the Almighty.

The Savior longs to reveal His grace and stamp His character on the whole world. He wants to make people free and pure and holy. Through the blood He shed for the world they may achieve triumphs that will bring glory to God and the Lamb. Christ "shall see the labor of His soul, and be satisfied." Isaiah 53:11.

# Christ's Triumphal Entry Into Heaven*

The time had come for Christ to ascend to His Father's throne as a divine Conqueror. After His resurrection, He remained on earth for a time so that His disciples could become familiar with Him in His glorified body. Now He was ready to leave them. His disciples no longer had to associate Him with the tomb. They could think of Him as glorified in the sight of the heavenly universe.

As the place for His ascension, Jesus chose the Mount of Olives—the spot so often made holy by His presence while He lived on earth. His prayers and tears had consecrated its groves and secluded valleys. At its foot in the garden of Gethsemane He had prayed and agonized alone. On its summit His feet will rest when He comes again as a glorious king, while Hebrew hallelujahs mingle with Gentile hosannas and a mighty gathering swells the shout, "Crown Him Lord of all!"

Now with the eleven disciples Jesus made His way toward the mountain. As they passed through the gate of Jerusalem, many people were amazed to see the little company, led by One whom the rulers had crucified a few weeks before. The disciples did not know that this was to be their last conversation with the Master. Jesus spent the time talking with them, repeating His former instruction. As they approached Gethsemane, He paused. He looked at the vine by which He had represented the union of His church with Himself and His Father. Again He repeated the truths He had unfolded then.

In the world for thirty-three years, Christ had endured scorn, insult, and mockery. He had been rejected and crucified. Now as He reviewed the ingratitude of the people He came to save, would He withdraw His sympathy and love from them? No; His promise is, "I am with you always, even to the end of the age." Matthew 28:20.

When they reached the Mount of Olives, Jesus led the way across the summit to the vicinity of Bethany. Here He paused, and the disciples gathered around Him. He looked at them lovingly. He did not criticize them for their faults and failures. Words of deep tenderness were the last they heard from their Lord. With hands outstretched in blessing, as if to

---

* This chapter is based on Luke 24:50–53; Acts 1:9–12.

assure them of His protecting care, He slowly ascended from among them, drawn toward heaven by a power stronger than any earthly pull. As He rose, the disciples strained to catch a last glimpse of their ascending Lord. A cloud of glory hid Him, and the words came back as the cloudy chariot of angels received Him, "I am with you always." At the same time the sweetest and most joyous music from the angel choir floated down to them.

## Received by Chariots of Angels

While the disciples were still looking upward, two angels in the form of men spoke. "Men of Galilee, why do you stand gazing up into heaven? This same Jesus, who was taken up from you into heaven, will so come in like manner as you saw Him go into heaven."

These angels, the most exalted among the angel ranks, were the two who had come to the tomb at Christ's resurrection. They longed to join the heavenly assembly that welcomed Jesus, but in sympathy for those whom He had left, they waited to give them comfort.

Christ had ascended in human form—the same Jesus who had broken bread with them and who that very day had climbed with them up the slope of the Mount of Olives. The angels assured them that the very One whom they had seen go into heaven would come again just as He had ascended. He will come "with clouds, and every eye will see Him." "The Lord himself, with a cry of command, with the archangel's call and with the sound of God's trumpet, will descend from heaven, and the dead in Christ will rise." "When the Son of Man comes in His glory, and all the holy angels with Him, then He will sit on the throne of His glory." Revelation 1:7; 1 Thessalonians 4:16, NRSV; Matthew 25:31.

This will fulfill the Lord's own promise to His disciples: "If I go and prepare a place for you, I will come again and receive you to Myself; that where I am, there you may be also." John 14:3.

After the trial and crucifixion, the disciples' enemies expected to see an expression of sorrow and defeat on their faces. Instead of this there was gladness and triumph. Their faces glowed with a happiness that did not originate on earth. With rejoicing they told the wonderful story of Christ's resurrection and ascension, and many people believed them.

## The Disciples' Fear Was Gone!

The disciples no longer had any distrust about the future. They knew that Jesus was in heaven and that His sympathies were still with them. They knew that they had a friend at the throne of God, and they were eager to present their requests in the name of Jesus. In awe they bowed in prayer, repeating the assurance, "Whatever you ask the Father in My name He will give you. . . . Ask, and you will receive, that your joy may be full." John 16:23, 24. And Pentecost brought them fullness of joy when the Comforter came to be with them, as Christ had promised.

All heaven was waiting to welcome the Savior. As He ascended, He led the way, and the multitude of captives set free at His resurrection followed. As they approached the city of God, the escorting angels gave the challenge—

Lift up your heads, O you gates!
And be lifted up, you everlasting
    doors!
And the King of glory shall come in.

Joyfully the angels waiting at the gates responded—

Who is this King of glory?

They said this, not because they did not know who He was, but because they wanted to hear the answer of exalted praise—

The Lord strong and mighty,
The Lord mighty in battle.
Lift up your heads, O you gates!
Lift up, you everlasting doors!
And the King of glory shall come in.
                    Psalm 24:7–9

Then the gates of the city of God were opened wide, and the angel throng swept through the gates in a burst of ecstatic music. The commanders of the angel hosts and the sons of God representing unfallen worlds were assembled to welcome the Redeemer and to celebrate His triumph.

But He waved them back—not yet. He entered into the presence of His Father. He pointed to His wounded head, His pierced side, His marred feet; He lifted His hands bearing the print of nails. He presented those raised with Him as representatives of that great number who will come from the grave at His second coming. Be-fore the earth was created, Father and Son had clasped hands in a solemn pledge that Christ would become the Redeemer for the human race. When Christ on the cross cried out, "It is finished," He addressed the Father. The agreement had been fully carried out. Now He declared, "Father, I have completed the work of redemption." "I desire that they also whom You gave Me may be with Me where I am." John 17:24.

The voice of God proclaimed that justice was satisfied, that Satan was vanquished. Christ's toiling, struggling ones on earth were "accepted in the Beloved." Ephesians 1:6. The Father's arms encircled His Son, and He gave the word, "Let all the angels of God worship him." Hebrews 1:6.

Heaven seemed to overflow with joy and praise. Love had conquered! The lost was found! Heaven rang with voices in lofty tones proclaiming,

"Blessing and honor and glory and
    power
Be to Him who sits on the throne,
And to the Lamb, forever and ever!"
                    Revelation 5:13

From that scene of heavenly joy, there comes back to us on earth the echo of Christ's words, "I am ascending to My Father and your Father, and to My God and your God." John 20:17. The family of heaven and the family of earth are one. For us our Lord ascended, and for us He lives! "Therefore He is also able to save to the uttermost those who come to God through Him, since He always lives to make intercession for them." Hebrews 7:25.